Lecture Notes in Artificial Intelligence   3413

Edited by J. G. Carbonell and J. Siekmann

Subseries of Lecture Notes in Computer Science

Klaus Fischer   Michael Florian
Thomas Malsch (Eds.)

Socionics

Scalability of Complex Social Systems

 Springer

Series Editors

Jaime G. Carbonell, Carnegie Mellon University, Pittsburgh, PA, USA
Jörg Siekmann, University of Saarland, Saarbrücken, Germany

Volume Editors

Klaus Fischer
German Research Center for Artificial Intelligence (DFKI) GmbH
Stuhlsatzenhausweg 3, 66123 Saarbrücken, Germany
E-mail: Klaus.Fischer@dfki.de

Michael Florian
Thomas Malsch
Hamburg University of Technology
Department of Technology Assessment
Schwarzenbergstr. 95, 21071 Hamburg, Germany
E-mail: {florian,malsch}@tuhh.de

Library of Congress Control Number: 2005937167

CR Subject Classification (1998): I.2.6, I.2.9, I.2, I.5.1, J.4, K.4.3

ISSN   0302-9743
ISBN-10   3-540-30707-9 Springer Berlin Heidelberg New York
ISBN-13   978-3-540-30707-5 Springer Berlin Heidelberg New York

Springer is a part of Springer Science+Business Media

springer.com

© Springer-Verlag Berlin Heidelberg 2005
Printed in Germany

Typesetting: Camera-ready by author, data conversion by Boller Mediendesign
Printed on acid-free paper   SPIN: 11594116   06/3142   5 4 3 2 1 0

Preface

This book is an outcome of the Socionics Research Framework.[1] The roots of Socionics lie in the 1980s when computer scientists in search of new methods and techniques of distributed and coordinated problem-solving first began to take an engineering interest in sociological concepts and theories. Just as biological phenomena are conceived of as a source of inspiration for new technologies in the new research field of bionics, computer scientists working in Distributed Artificial Intelligence (DAI) became interested in exploiting phenomena from the social world in order to construct Multiagent Systems (MAS) and, generally, to build open agent societies or complex artificial social systems.

Socionics is driven by the underlying assumption that there is an inherent parallel between the 'up-scaling' of MAS and the 'micro-macro link' in sociology. Accordingly, one of the fundamental challenges of Socionics is to build large-scale multiagent systems which are capable of managing 'societies of autonomous computational agents ... in large open information environments' ([9, p. 112]). As more sophisticated interactions become common in open MAS, the demand to design reliable mechanisms coordinating large-scale networks of intelligent agents grows. Suitable design mechanisms may enhance the developement of 'truly open and fully scalable multiagent systems, across domains, with agents capable of learning appropriate communications protocols upon entry to a system, and with protocols emerging and evolving through actual agent interactions' ([10, pp. 3]) which is considered as the ultimate goal in fulfilling the roadmap of agent technology. With the introduction of mobile agent platforms for e-commerce applications, the quest for reliable mechanisms coordinating large-scale networks of intelligent agent programs has been put on the agenda. To illustrate the practical need for large-scale architectures and techniques, one might mention the growing demand for agent-based applications such as electronic commerce, business process management, entertainment, medical care, tele-voting, tele-shopping, real-time sports brokering, etc. (for a detailed list of agent-based applications, cf. [10]).

In relation to the Internet and the World Wide Web, scalability turns out to be crucial for DAI systems. Since achieving run-time efficiency in small environments does not guarantee achieving run-time efficiency also in large environments, it is clear that designing large-scale applications for open societies with several thousand agents differs significantly from designing small-size applications with around a hundred agent programs. With regard to open agent platforms that will have to support a new generation of e-commerce applications on the Internet, scalability as a technological desideratum is still in its infancy. What we need is to address the problem of scalability in a new way by relating specific engineering demands to general dimensions of complexity (most obvious: number and heterogeneity of agents and inter-agent linkages; less obvious: robustness, flexibility).

---

[1] The Socionics Research Framework SPP 1077 is funded by the German national research foundation (DFG) from 1998 to 2005 and has published several books: [1], [2], [3], [4], [5], [6], [7], [8].

Having done that, we need to turn to sociological concepts, asking the following questions: How is coordination (by means of normative structures, power relations, and so on) achieved in human societies at different levels of aggregation (micro-interaction, meso-organisation, macro-society) and how can we translate these achievements into engineering methods and tools for social simulation? Of course, there is no such thing as the 'one best way' of posing or answering these questions, neither in sociology nor in DAI. Thus, the articles collected in this volume take different stances, exposing a wide array of sociological research approaches and a plurality of engineering perspectives, and leaving it to the reader to draw his or her own conclusions.

A book like this is the result of the successful cooperation of a significant number of people to whom the editors are now indebted. The minimum that we can do is to express our gratitude to all who were involved in making the book a realreality. First to be mentioned are the authors who actively contributed to the book with articles. However, most of the articles are results of fruitful discussion and cooperation in the context of the Socionics Research Framework funded by the DFG. We are therefore also grateful for the cooperation and support that we got from people working in this context. We further want to thank people at Springer supporting us in the publishing process of this volume. Last but not least, we would like to say thanks to the people that gave feedback to the authors by reviewing the articles and especially to Christian Hahn, who went through the trouble doing the finial editing of the master copy.

Saarbrücken, Hamburg
August 2005

Thomas Malsch
Michael Florian
Klaus Fischer

References

1. Malsch, T., ed.: Sozionik. Soziologische Ansichten ber künstliche Sozialität. Edition Sigma, Berlin (1998)
2. Kron, T., ed.: Luhmann modelliert. Sozionische Ansätze zur Simulation von Kommunikationssystemen. Leske + Budrich, Opladen (2002)
3. Rammert, W., Schulz-Schaeffer, I., eds.:   Können Maschinen handeln? Soziologische Beiträge zum Verständnis von Mensch und Technik. Campus, Frankfurt/Main et al. (2002)
4. Ebrecht, J., Hillebrandt, F., eds.: Bourdieus Theorie der Praxis. Erklärungskraft - Anwendung - Perspektiven. Westdeutscher Verlag, Opladen/Wiesbaden (2002)
5. Burkhard, H., Uthmann, T., Lindemann, G.: Proceedings des Workshops Modellierung und Simulation menschlichen Verhaltens. Technical Report 163, Humboldt-Universität zu Berlin, Institut für Informatik (2003)
6. v. Lüde, R., Moldt, D., Valk, R., eds.:   Sozionik - Modellierung soziologischer Theorie. Volume 2 of Wirtschaft - Arbeit - Technik. LIT Verlag, Münster (2003)
7. Florian, M., Hillebrandt, F., eds.: Adaption und Lernen in und von Organisationen - Beiträge aus der Sozionik. VS Verlag für Sozialwissenschaften, Wiesbaden (2004)
8. Lindemann, G., Moldt, D., Paolucci, M., eds.: Regulated Agent-Based Social Systems. First International Workshop, RASTA 2002. Bologna, Italy, July 2002. Revised Selected and Invited Papers. Lecture Notes in Artificial Intelligence. Springer, Berlin et al. (2004)
9. Huhns, M.N., Stephens, L.M.: Multiagent systems and societies of agents. In Weiss, G., ed.: Multiagent Systems. A Modern Approach to Distributed Artificial Intelligence. The MIT Press, Cambridge, Massachusetts (1999)
10. Luck, M., McBurney, P., Shehory, O., Willmott, S.: Agent Technology Roadmap Draft: A Roadmap for agent-based computing. AgentLink (2005) Electronically available, http://www.agentlink.org/roadmap/.

Table of Contents

Chapter IV   From an Agent-Centred to a Communication-Centred Perspective

Contribution of Socionics to the Scalability of Complex Social Systems: Introduction

Klaus Fischer[1] and Michael Florian[2]

[1] German Research Center for Artificial Intelligence (DFKI) GmbH,
Stuhlsatzenhausweg 3, 66123 Saarbrücken, Germany
Klaus.Fischer@dfki.de
[2] Hamburg University of Technology, Department of Technology Assessment,
Schwarzenbergstraße 95, 21071 Hamburg, Germany
florian@tu-harburg.de

Abstract. The aim of the introduction is to provide insight into the interdisciplinary research program of Socionics and to clarify fundamental concepts like micro-macro linkage and scalability from the two different perspectives of Sociology and DAI&MAS research. Far away from the intention to offer final answers, the article rather tries to provide a framework to understand the contributions of the book as well as to relate their content to each other. The introduction also informs the reader about the scientific context of the interdisciplinary field of Socionics and deals with basic concepts and comments from the point of view of both Sociology and DAI&MAS research.

1 Motivation

The interdisciplinary field of research we call *Socionics* originated from the recognition of a shared interest between sociologists and researchers on Distributed Artificial Intelligence (DAI) in the exploration of the emergence and dynamics of artificial social systems [1]. Combining Sociology and Informatics, Socionics aspires "to form a new research discipline with the aim of developing intelligent computer technologies by picking up paradigms of our social world" and, vice versa, "uses computer technology in order to verify and to develop sociological models of societies and organizations." [1]. Based on a close cooperation between sociologists and computer scientists, it was suggested that socionic research is mainly focused on the emergence and dynamics of artificial social systems as well as hybrid man-machine societies [1]. In this context, the problem of scaling multi-agent systems (MAS), which is generally associated with the challenge of realizing *open systems* (cf. [2], [3], and [4]), aligns socionic research to "adapting solutions for the sociological micro-macro problem" by investigating "the mutual correlation of conditions and enabling mechanisms with respect to individual behaviour and higher social structures at different levels of coordination" [1]. While we agree with the fruitfulness of this enterprise we, however, feel that the DAI problem of emergence and scalability has been equated too quickly with the question of micro-macro linkage in DAI as well as on the sociological side by [1]. Before stating similarities between concepts in both disciplines, more precise ideas about definitions and basic concepts used in Distributed AI and sociology need to be developed. When

K. Fischer, M. Florian, and T. Malsch (Eds.): Socionics, LNAI 3413, pp. 1–14, 2005.
© Springer-Verlag Berlin Heidelberg 2005

we try to come up with such definitions, the admonition by [1] has to be taken seriously that one-to-one transformations of sociological concepts to computer models obviously will not be feasible and as an approach would even be misleading. As ([5, 156]) puts it, the central issue is "whether and how Socionics will be capable of transforming sociological theories, and not just social metaphors or naive theories of sociality, into new technological potentials." Therefore, the challenge of Socionics is to provide appropriate state-of-the-art foundations for the problems under investigation within each discipline, which moreover serve the interdisciplinary work.

This introduction tries to clarify concepts like micro-macro linkage and scalability from the two different perspectives. The article does not try to offer final answers but rather to provide a framework that should help the reader in understanding the contributions of this book as well as relating their content to each other. With this goal in mind this introduction presents basic concepts and comments from the perspectives of both Sociology and DAI&MAS research. However, we also try to capture some of the scientific context which we consider relevant.

2   Some Remarks on History and Context

It is difficult to mark exactly the starting point of the novel research paradigm of Distributed Artificial Intelligence (DAI). In the early 1980ies, various computer scientists were looking for new ways to tackle the difficulties experienced with traditional AI models in designing problem-solving systems useful in practice [6]. [7], [8], and [9] summarise early results of DAI research. Social scientists already got interested in DAI research at an early stage (cf. [10], [5]). Particularly Castelfranchi, Conte, and Star made seminal contributions to DAI research as well as to the appreciation of this research in the social science community. Since protagonists of the DAI community in the U.S.A. (e.g., Gasser, Hewitt, and Bond) had been involved in a long-standing practical cooperation with social scientists (e.g., Star, Gerson, and Suchman) from an interactionist and pragmatist background (cf. [10], [5]), "interactionist concepts have deeply influenced DAI models" [10] from the very beginning. The discipline of traditional AI needed some time to pick-up the new research topics. It took till 1994 that IJCAI introduced a specialised session on DAI into its technical programme. At this time the separation of DAI into the two primary areas of research *Distributed Problem Solving* (DPS) and *Multiagent Systems* (MAS) [7] was widely accepted.

It is reported that Les Gasser opened the AAAI workshop on *Knowledge and Action at Social and Organizational Level* in 1991 with the question *Society or Individual: Which Comes First?* [11]. Gasser's claim, related to Hewitt's perspective on *open systems*, is that we need an adequate foundation for DAI and that we must begin to lay firm *social foundations* for it. In this perspective, DAI should have autonomous basis with respect to traditional AI: DAI foundation lies in sociology (Durkheim) and in social psychology (Mead), while AI traditionally refers to cognitive science and psychology. DAI constitutes a new paradigm for AI. It is based on a different philosophy of mind in which the mind is seen as a social (not individual, mental) phenomenon. Therefore, Gasser's answer to the original question is *society comes first*. This *social foundation* is opposed to the more *individualistic and psychological approach* of (D)AI. However,

Castelfranchi and Conte [11] object against both the dichotomy and this type of social foundation. There are also many sociologists and social psychologists who are precisely in search of the individualistic basis of social action and of the microfoundational explanation of macro-social phenomena (cf. e.g. [12], [13], [14] [15]).

No matter which of these two positions we would like to subscribe to, as a matter of fact we have acknowledge that to the end of the 1990's MAS in general and especially the term *agent* got more and more attention. Interesting enough IJCAI's session names changed from sessions on DAI to sessions on MAS. It seems like the research became again more and more interested in the concept of individual agents and with that back to more traditional AI topics. However, the agents were considered to be problem solvers that are embedded in some dynamic environment which was not necessarily assumed in more traditional AI research. For example [16] as a standard text book of traditional AI does not include any topics related to the interaction of multiple agents other than assuming that such agents might hide in an anonymous environment. The ATAL workshop which was established in 1994 [17] and possibly more prominently the Autonomous Agents conference [18] which was first held in 1997 mark significant corner stones in this development. It is important to keep this development in mind when looking at the interaction of DAI research with Social Science theories.

Although it is obvious that in present days terms like "agent"[1] and "MAS" seems to be much more en vogue than other concepts of DAI, we still want to use the label DAI in the remainder of this article when referring to the whole research area. The main reason for this is that it would be quite difficult and result in clumsy phrases if we would use MAS for both concrete systems and the overall research community. So we stick with DAI when referring to the research community and stress that this does not reflect the current trends.

3 The Micro-macro Linkage in Sociology and DAI

From a sociological point of view, macro phenomena are the primary focus of attention. Unfortunately, the concepts of micro and macro "have not been systematically analysed in sociology" ([19, 86]). Diverse meanings are disseminated in the sociological literature and "these meanings are not always consistent with one another" ([20, 357]). In the 1980s, the *micro-macro linkage* as well as the relationship between *agency* and *structure* emerged as the central problems in sociological theory (cf. [21], [22], [23], [24], [25]) and it continues to be of focal concern up to now. Kemeny (in [26]) already complained that the relationship between micro and macro as levels of analysis is one of *distinction* and *mutual neglect*: the micro sociological study of face-to-face interactions has generally ignored the necessity of a systematic framework to interpret micro social phenomena in the context of macro structures and, vice versa, the study of macro social phenomena has not taken empirical findings and research at the micro level into account. Consequently, the micro-macro problem in sociology primarily refers to analytical concepts, i.e. to the problem of integrating competing sociological theories and to the link between different levels of social analysis (cf. [21, 223ff.], [27]).

---

[1] It is interesting to know that it is reported that Carl Hewitt in his work avoided the term "agent" because of its overuse. So opinions on this seem to change over time.

Sociological concepts of macro-social level range from "the structure of different positions in a population and their constraints on social relations" ([28]) to collective social phenomena like norms, institutions, authority systems (hierarchy), and markets (cf. [29]) to the study of societal structures, whole societies and *world-systems* ([21, 493]).[2] Generally, the macro level refers to social structures that "constitute both opportunities and constraints on individual behavior and interactions" ([20, 357]). With regard to micro-social issues many sociologists will agree that the "equation of micro with individual is extremely misleading, as, indeed, is the attempt to find any specific size correlation with the micro/macro difference" ([27, 290]). Consequently, Alexander [27, 290] claims, that there can be no empirical referents for micro or macro as such: "They are analytical contrasts, suggesting emergent levels within empirical units, not antagonistic empirical units themselves."

The definition of macro issues in sociology clearly differs from the common meaning in DAI research. All kind of social phenomena[3] are located on what is called the *macro level*. In contrast to that, individual agents mark the *micro level*. The link between agent's actions and behaviors (including internal mental or cognitive aspects of agent's cognition) and external social forces and structures is usually referred to as micro-macro link in DAI research or sometimes as micro-macro gap because even today well-understood theories that would in general explain how micro and macro level are linked do not exist. Although the micro-macro gap plays such a central role in DAI research, it cannot be considered a standard term in the literature. [30] refers to the micro and macro level as agent and group level respectively and refers to sociology to introduce the problem of micro macro linkage. [31] defines the macro level more general as everything that happens between agents but neglects the link to sociological research.

The problem of how individual action and structural rules interact in a set of agents is a foundational issue for both DAI and sociology [32]. Hence, the understanding of the link between micro and macro would mean a substantial advance in designing agents for dynamic and large-scale agent-based social simulation as well as a deeper understanding of human societies. The micro-macro problem is perceived in DAI research as a central issue, because it directly refers to problems of agent coordination and it also affects the scalability of MAS. The definition of DAI as opposed to the parent discipline of artificial intelligence heavily depends on aspects that are only introduced by problems that occur when multiple actors face the results of each others' actions [30]. Furthermore, modelling the macro aspect in agent theories is considered to be essential for DAI research, as this concept substantially contributes to the distinction between AI and DAI. For this enterprise, a scientific cooperation with sociology is of great benefit to DAI. However, it is important to note that the definitions of micro and macro

---

[2] Note that in sociology society is studied as a macro-social phenomenon *sui generis* that basically differs from formal organizations (meso-level) and social interactions (micro-level) with regard to time (*long-term* duration of societies) and space (*large-scaled* spatial extension of societies).

[3] A sociologist might object against using the phrase "social phenomena" for the kind of interaction that is usually going on in a MAS at least to the degree that this has been done so far. The reason for this might become clearer from the discussion in the rest of this article

in sociology differ significantly from the definitions in MAS research. The micro level that is identified in sociology actually starts at the macro level of DAI research. Moreover, it is an open research question whether the sociological macro level of human society/societies can be identified or adequately represented formally in a MAS.

Because both Sociology and DAI use the terms "micro" and "macro" but actually with regard to quite different things, we propose to clearly distinguish the different levels in sociological and DAI research and propose the following definitions:

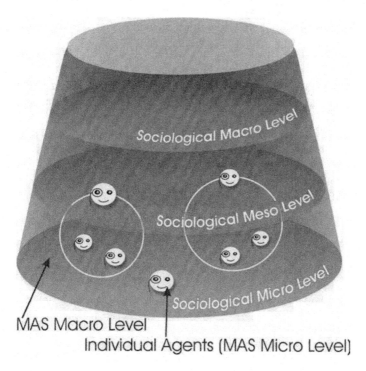

Fig. 1. Differences between Micro and Macro Level in MAS and Sociology

Agent Level (AL): Individual agents, their architecture as well as internal representations, and reasoning. This is what DAI literature usually refers to when talking
about the micro level. We might use the term "MAS micro level" as a synonym
when referring to this level of MAS design.

MAS Level (MASL): The interaction and communication between agents, the decomposition and distribution of tasks, coordination and cooperation, conflict resolution
via negotiation, etc. (see also [31]). This defines the macro level in DAI literature
and we therefore might refer to it with the term "MAS macro level" as a synonym
as well.

Sociological Micro Level (SMiL): Individual actors (including their thoughts, mental
preferences and actions [21, 643]), social (face-to-face) interactions, encounters

and communication among copresent individuals as well as "social processes that engender relations between persons" [28].

Sociological Meso Level (SMeL): A wide range of social phenomena intermediating between micro and the macro (e.g., social groups, collectivities or networks as well as formal organizations). Note that the characteristics of the meso level depend on the unit of analysis, i.e. the difference of micro, meso, and macro is not based on clear dividing lines separating real social units of different size but rather is motivated by useful *analytical* distinctions.

Sociological Macro Level (SMaL): The society as a whole, groups of societies, societal structures as well as collective social phenomena of a large extent within time and space (e.g., social institutions, culture, markets, etc.).

The most important differences to notice are that the AL itself is not a matter of interest in social science research. Furthermore, even agent interaction per se, i.e. the MASL, does not necessarily constitute what social scientists refer to as SMiL, like for example the purely mechanical interaction between two machines in a flexible manufacturing example is not of interest for social science research. It would be of course nice if socionic research could come-up with precisely defined discriminating properties that would draw clear boundaries between the different layers. However, up to now we can only say that we started to get some understanding of some properties that seem to make the differences for some of the specified levels.

4   Possible Misconceptions of Micro and Macro

The different points of view when referring to concepts like "micro" and "macro" can lead to misunderstandings in discussions as well as in articles of DAI and sociological research. In our work we found the following positions as instances of such misunderstandings [32].

Mechanism design is macro level design: In DAI, mechanism design is usually the coordination of actions of individuals to achieve some invariants of the behaviour of a group of individuals ([33]; etc.). However, unless there is structure or dynamics in the system that goes beyond the single interaction, there will be no manifestation of societal structures or institutions. In social psychology there is a collection of work inspired by game theory on penalty systems and their emergence in games (e.g. [34]). This could be viewed as advancing to the meso (group) level.

Macro level behaviour is emergent behaviour: According to Langton [35] emergence is a result that was not defined statically (i.e. before run-time). Such a not-predefined result is not necessarily a macro level result: see for instance SWARM-like simulations. Although they can produce patterns (of action) they do not lead to the emergence of higher-level institutions that shape and keep a society together. A similar argument holds for the reverse direction: macro level structures can be implemented in a simulation statically without the need to let them emerge.

Value aggregation is an analysis of macro phenomena: One way to distinguish attributes for modelling and reasoning, is to differentiate between dimensional (i.e. numerical attributes) and structural aspects (e.g. relationships on cause-effect, or acquaintance, trust, influence etc.). In this differentiation the sociological approach on the macro level (namely to look at structures) is extremely opposed to the one used in current DAI research. The macro perspective here means to aggregate values from the individual to the group layer and focus on dimensional parameters like score, speed, number of communication acts, voting results etc., where aggregation is straightforward. The structural interpretation that could lead to more sophisticated social reasoning, like it is done by [36] is rarely applied.

Populations of artificial agents are artificial societies: Especially for applied MAS (the representational approach) it holds that these agents are created with the intention of delegating actions (and in fact delegation is viewed as a central notion in DAI: e.g. by [37]). In this sense many assumptions about human behaviour and the user's goals and desires are represented by the agent acting in the MAS. Therefore observed phenomena in this population will not only be caused by artificial actors, but also by the intentions of the human user. As a consequence it would not be correct to speak of an artificial society, the nature of the intersection of intentions requires this to be termed a *hybrid* society [1] (cf. Schulz-Schaeffer and Meister et al. in this book). In addition, sociologists would require that this population exhibits macro aspects of the human society (see above) before it can be considered an artificial *or* hybrid society.

We do not claim that we can resolve all problems with the definition of the terms as we give them in this article. However, what we like to achieve is to rise the awareness that Sociology and DAI should be more careful with the use of these concepts when they approach each other.

5   The Meso Level: First Steps Towards a Common View on Scalability

We are confident that differences in defining micro or macro issues will not impede fruitful cooperation between DAI and sociology. Sociology's interest in DAI research is that systems investigated in DAI research by definition exhibit artefacts which can empirically be compared with phenomena social science theories investigate in human societies. From a DAI perspective the stability and flexibility of human societies and their ability to face change with respect to structural dynamics (cf. Schimank in this book) is most attractive. Especially robustness and adaptability towards disturbances appears to be a specific quality of many social systems in human societies that is extremely interesting for both DAI and sociology. Although robustness is always listed as an advantage of MAS system design, robustness is no automatic property of a MAS. Robustness requires a system to be able to dynamically adapt to changing requirements, to be resistant against conflicts and attacks, and to be scalable. With regard to scalability we can distinguish different dimensions. Scalability of MAS refers to the ability of the MAS to gracefully change performance under variation of different parameters. On the one hand, we can distinguish *quantitative* scalability which depends on quantitative changes in parameters like resources and number of agents. *Qualitative* scalability depends, on the other hand, on scaling the complexity of social relationships from simple interactions to creating organisations or even further to forming artificial societies with increasing agent complexity, i.e. improving the abilities of agents to deal with complex situations, as well as increasing problem complexity, i.e. the complexity of the overall objective the MAS was designed for (cf. [38]).

With this view to scalability in MAS it is important to note that neither the step from the MAS micro level to the MAS macro level nor the steps from micro to meso to macro in a sociological sense can directly be identified as dimensions of scalability. From a MAS perspective it is an open research question how macro phenomena in the sociological sense can be adequately represented in a MAS and even for phenomena on the sociological meso level only little research has been done [39,40]. The increase in number of participating agents, a quantitative parameter of an MAS, can of course bring about complex structures on the MAS macro level. However, the number of agents is per se not a distinguishing factor of different sociological levels.

Scalability of the complexity of social relationships is especially interesting for socionic research. From what has already been said about the MAS micro and macro level, it is obvious that this dimension of scalability in MAS is purely located on the MAS macro level. Unfortunately, there are hardly any general theories on explaining phenomena on the MAS macro level. Work on task allocation [41,42,43,44], auction mechanisms [33], and coalition formation [45,46] at least partially deal with the MAS macro level. In this work the mechanisms that produce the effects and phenomena that can be identified on the MAS macro level are exclusively represented in the individual agents, i.e. the MAS micro level. Only little work has been done investigating how MAS macro structures can be explicitly represented outside of individual agents, i.e. explicitly in the MAS macro level (cf. Nickles&Weiß) and how such structures perform with respect to scalability [47].

The orientation towards social organization in DAI meets a novel attention in social theory and sociology to social phenomena on the meso level of sociality. The emergence of the network approach (cf. [48]), the plea for meso- and multi-level approaches in organizational sociology (cf. [49]) and a promising analytical scope the search for "social mechanisms" (cf. HedstroemSwedberg1998; Schimank in this book) indicate a new sociological awareness of the middle-range level mediating between micro- and macro-sociological perspectives. Starting from this background, socionic research is well-advised to consider multi-level approaches to bridge the micro-macro gap in the study and modelling of complex social systems. Keeping the difference between micro-macro issues in DAI and sociology in mind, we are convinced that focussing on meso-level issues (e.g., organization and self-organization) will help DAI and sociology to match their different interests and perspectives on a common ground.

6   The Structure of the Book

What has been said so far should give enough evidence that the investigation of social structures and mechanisms which form the basis that produces specific phenomena on the sociological micro, meso, and macro level provides input to the understanding of micro-macro linkage in both disciplines and at the same time contributes to the improvement of current theories.

The overall objective of this book is to give an overview on what has been already achieved so far. It is separated into 5 chapters. The introduction deals with basic concepts and sets the scene for the individual contributions in the different chapters. These chapters have been organised according the following four major topics:

Multi-Layer Modelling:

From a sociological point of view, the scalability of actor constellations is examined by *Schimank*. The author distinguishes two principal directions of an up-scaling of sociological and "socionic" models: quantitative and qualitative up-scaling. He argues that in sociology problems of up-scaling result from the fact that sociological explanations of structural dynamics do not work with laws but with mechanisms. In contrast to scientific laws or simple correlations, a mechanism is a step-by-step analytical description of the social dynamics which bring about the respective structural effect. The author argues that although sociological and "socionic" models are always constructed for specific cases, with all implications of "dirtiness", "clean" mechanisms are not only helpful but indispensable: The "dirtier" our models become with up-scaling, the "cleaner" must be the mechanisms we use in modeling.

Based on the Habitus Field Theory of sociologist Pierre Bourdieu, *Hillebrandt* explores the holonic approach in MAS. From his sociological point of view, holons are autonomous and self-organising social entities that differ from simple forms of coordination single agents use to interact. Considering holons both as social fields and corporate agents, the author proposes a "matrix of delegation" to define organizational relationships in task assignment MAS as a new dimension of emergent system behaviour.

Köhler et al. discuss how the sociological problem of micro-macro linking can be combined with the computational problem of recursiveness. They introduce a scalable MAS model based on the recursive formalism of reference nets as an extension of Petri nets that allow understanding nets as tokens. They argue that MAS architecture *Mulan* serves as a description language for the sociological model, which is fundamental for their socionic MAS architecture (*Sonar*). The authors propose that an architecture based on Mulan and Sonar allows to cover the micro- as well as the macro-perspective in agent-oriented modelling as a basis for scalable agent systems.

Concepts for Organisation and Self-Organisation:

Rana et al. examine infrastructure requirements and computational costs of scalable virtual communities. With regard to Socionics, the main focus of the article is on the use of sociological foundations to support the construction of large-scale MAS and, particularly, on the exploration how social structures existing within human scientific communities may influence the selection of MAS roles and their interactions. The authors argue that if the number of participants or the resources they share increases, it will be useful to apply metrics to identify particular types of virtual communities as well as particular features of such communities that are likely to lead to successful collaborations.

Schillo&Spresny discuss two different ways of scaling. While qualitative scaling is concerned with increasing (social) complexity requiring new dimensions in perception and decision making, quantitative scalability tackles the problem how goals can be achieved under the constraints imposed by a growing population. They argue that organizations and inter-organisational networks are an important cornerstone for the analysis of qualitative scaling and demonstrate by empirical evaluation that an elaborate theoretical concept of such networks increases the quantitative scalability of multiagent systems.

Meister et al. introduce an integrated approach to the conceptualisation, implementation and evaluation of a MAS which is based on sociological concepts of practical roles and organisational coordination via negotiations. As the starting point for MAS design they propose a middle level of scale located between interaction and the overall organisational structure with formal and practical modes of coordination to be distinguished over all relevant levels of scale. The authors also discuss a methodology for the investigation of processes of hybridisation, which means the re-entering of artificial sociality in a real-world domain, and explore the resulting consequences for Socionics as an interdisciplinary approach.

Paetow et al. propose a system theoretical framework for analyzing scalability and scaling processes. They refer to the terminology of Niklas Luhmanns sociological system theory and general complexity science to clarify the vocabulary used in the debate on scalability issues in multiagent systems. To evaluate the heuristic strength of their analytical framework, the authors apply it to an exemplary socionic model of a scalable system. They argue that, from a sociological point of view, a scalable MAS has to be conceptualised as an organised system.

The Emergence of Social Structure:

Rovatsos&Paetow examine micro-scalability as a novel design objective for social reasoning architectures operating in open multiagent systems. Micro-scalability is based on the idea that social reasoning algorithms should be devised in a way that allows for social complexity reduction, and that this can be achieved by operationalising principles of interactionist sociology. The authors propose a formal model of InFFrA agents called m^2InFFrA that utilises two cornerstones of micro-scalability (principles of social abstraction and transient social optimality). They also demonstrate the usefulness of their concept by presenting experimental results with a novel opponent classification heuristic ADHOC that has been developed using the InFFrA social reasoning architecture.

Fley&Florian suggest a sociological multi-level concept of trust to provide suitable solutions to problems of large-scale open MAS. They analyse DAI concepts dealing with the notion of trust and examine effects of trust on the scalability of MAS. The authors argue that trust itself must be modelled as a social mechanism that allows the scaling up of agent coordination in open MAS. They introduce a multilevel approach to trust by referring to sociologist Pierre Bourdieu's concept of the economy of symbolic goods including basic social mechanisms in order to cope with the coordination of large numbers of heterogeneous agents.

With regard to the problem of social order and how it is generated, is stabilised, and changes itself, *Lasarczyk&Kron* analyse the emergence of order in its simplest variant, the coordination problem. The authors follow the model of "double contingency" as described by Sociologists Talcott Parsons and Niklas Luhmann to examine the relevance of certain scalings on the basis of simulation experiments. The main focus of the article is on large actor populations and their capability to produce order depending on different actors constellations. The authors show that systems with small-world constellations exhibit highest order on large populations which gently decreases on increasing population sizes.

Schulz-Schaeffer analyses the social coordination of self-governed entities in the absence of pre-established coordination structures. He argues that self-commitment is the basic mechanism to solve coordination problems and that such commitments have an inherent tendency to become more and more generalised and institutionalised. The author proposes a theoretical framework based on a reinterpretation of the sociological concept of generalised symbolic media. He suggests that this framework is applicable to coordination problems between human actors as well as to coordination problems between artificial agents in open multi-agent systems.

From an Agent-Centred to a Communication-Centred Perspective:

Nickles&Weiß analyse the "autonomy dilemma" of agent-based software engineering. They argue that agent autonomy on the one hand enables features of agent-based applications like flexibility, robustness and emergence of novel solutions, but on the other hand autonomy might be the reason for undesired or even chaotic agent behavior. As a solution for this dilemma, the authors introduce a novel architecture for open multiagent systems based on special middle agents, the so-called Mirror-Holons. Instead of restricting agent autonomy by means of normative constraints, Mirror- Holons allow for a uncoupling of agent interaction and functionality. Their main purpose is to derive and adopt social programs from the observation and compilation of agent communication and design objectives. These structures can either be executed by the Mirror-Holons themselves or communicated to the agents and the system designer in a holonic way, similar to mass media in human societies.

Nickles et al. examine communication systems (CS) as a unified model for socially intelligent systems. Their model is derived from sociological systems theory and combines the empirical analysis of communication in a social system with logical processing of social information to provide a general framework for computational components that exploit communication processes in multiagent systems. The authors present an elaborate formal model of CS that is based on an improved version of expectation networks and their processing by illustrating how the CS layer can be integrated with agent-level expectation-based methods. They also discuss the conversion between CS and interaction frames in the InFFrA architecture.

Internet communication as a major challenge for anyone claiming to design scalable multiagent systems is analysed by *Albrecht et al.*. They compare and discuss two different approaches to modeling and analyzing such large-scale networks of communication: Social Network Analysis (SNA) and Communication-oriented Modeling (COM). With respect to scalability, the authors demonstrate that COM offers striking advantages over SNA. Based on this comparison, they identify mechanisms that foster scalability in a broader sense, comprising issues of downscaling as well.

The individual contributions to this book might not give a complete understanding of the overall picture that we propose in this article (cf. Figure 1). There are open questions like for example a concise description of concepts that represent the Sociological Macro Level (SmaL) and a complete theory of how the concepts at the different levels relate and interact with each other. Our hope is that this book at least sheds some light on these basic research topics and that the contributions are possibly seminal for future research into this direction.

References

1. Müller, J., Malsch, T., Schulz-Schäffer, I.: Socionics. Introduction and potential. Journal of Artificial Societies and Social Simulation **1** (1998) http://www.soc.surrey.ac.uk/JASSS/1/3/5.html.
2. Hewitt, C.E.: Offices are open systems. ACM Transactions on Office Information Systems **4** (1986) 271–287
3. Hewitt, C.E.: Open information systems semantics for distributed artificial intelligence. Artificial Intelligence **47** (1991) 79–106
4. Gasser, L.: Social conceptions of knowledge and action. DAI foundations and open systems semantics. Artificial Intelligence **47** (1991) 107–138
5. Malsch, T.: Naming the unnamable. Socionics or the sociological turn of/to Distributed Artificial Intelligence. Autonomous Agents and Multi-Agent Systems **4** (2001) 155–186
6. Hayes-Roth, F.: Towards a framework for distributed AI. Sigart Newsletter **73** (1980) 51 pp.
7. Bond, A., Gasser, L., eds.: Readings in Distributed Artificial Intelligence. Morgan Kaufmann (1988)
8. Huhns, M.N., ed.: Distributed Artificial Intelligence. Pitman/Morgan Kaufmann, San Mateo, CA (1987)
9. Gasser, L., Huhns, M.N., eds.: Distributed Artificial Intelligence, Volume II. Research Notes in Artificial Intelligence. Morgan Kaufmann, San Mateo, CA (1989)
10. Strübing, J.: Bridging the gap. On the collaboration between symbolic interactionism and distributed artificial intelligence in the field of multi-agent systems research. Symbolic Interaction **21** (1998) 441–464
11. Castelfranchi, C., Conte, R.: Distributed artificial intelligence and social science: Critical issues. In P., O.G.M., Jennings, N.R., eds.: Foundations of Distributed Artificial Intelligence. John Wiley & Sons, Inc. (1996) 527–542
12. Hechter, M.: The Microfoundations of Macrosociology. Temple University Press, Philadelphia (1983)
13. Collins, R.: On the microfoundations of macrosociology. American Journal of Sociology **86** (1981) 984–1010
14. Coleman, J.: Microfoundations and macrosocial behavior. [22] 153–173
15. Coleman, J.: Foundations of Social Theory. The Belknap Press, Cambridge, Mass./London (1990)
16. Russel, S.J., Norvig, P.: Artificial Intelligence — A Modern Approach — Second Edition. Prentice Hall, Englewood Cliffs (2003)
17. Wooldridge, M.J., Jennings, N.R., eds.: Proceedings of the ECAI-94 Workshop on Agent Theories, Architectures and Languages: Intelligent Agents I. Volume 890 of LNAI., Springer (1995)
18. Johnson, W., Hayes-Roth, B.: Proceedings of the First International Conference on Autonomous Agents. ACM Press, Marina del Rey, CA USA (1997)
19. Gerstein, D.: To unpack micro and macro: Link small with large and part with whole. [22] 86–11
20. Münch, R., Smelser, N.J.: Relating the micro and macro. [22] 356–387
21. Ritzer, G.: Sociological Theory. Fourth edn. McGraw-Hill, New York etc. (1996)

22. Alexander, J., Giesen, B., Münch, R., Smelser, N., eds.: The Micro-Macro Link. University of California Press, Berkeley, Los Angeles, London (1987)
23. Huber, J., ed.: Macro-Micro Linkages in Sociology. Sage Publications, Newbury Park, London, New Delhi (1991)
24. Knorr-Cetina, K., Cicourel, eds.: Advances in Social Theory and Methodology. Methuen, New York (1981)
25. Wiley, N.: The micro-macro problem in social theory. Sociological Theory **6** (1988) 254–261
26. Kemeny, J.: Perspectives on the micro-macro distinction. Sociological Review **24** (1976) 731–752
27. Alexander, J.: Action and its environments. [22] 289–318
28. Blau, P.: Contrasting theoretical perspectives. [22] 71–85
29. Coleman, J.: Social theory, social research, and a theory of action. American Journal of Sociology **91** (1986) 1309–1335
30. Weiß, G., ed.: Multi-Agent Systems: A Modern Approach to Distributed Artificial Intelligence. MIT Press (1999)
31. Nwana, H.S.: Software agents: An overview. Knowledge Engineering Review (1996) 205–244
32. Schillo, M., Fischer, K., Klein, C.: The micro-macro link in DAI and sociology. [50]
33. Sandholm, T.: Distributed rational decision making. [30]
34. Yamagishi, T.: The provision of a sanctioning system as a public good. Journal of Personality and Social Psychology **51** (1986) 110–116
35. Langton, C.G., ed.: Artificial Life I (ALIFE-87): 1st Interdisciplinary Workshop on the Synthesis and Simulation of Living Systems, Los Alamos, NM, USA, Addison-Wesley (1989)
36. Sichman, J.S., Conte, R., Castelfranchi, C., Demazeau, Y.: A social reasoning mechanism based on dependence networks. In Cohn, A.G., ed.: Proc. of the 11th European Conf. on Artificial Intelligence (ECAI'94). (1994)
37. Castelfranchi, C., Falcone, R.: Principles of trust for MAS: Cognitive anatomy, social importance, and quantification. In Demazeau, Y., ed.: Proc. of the 3rd Int. Conf. on Multi-Agent Systems (ICMAS98). (1998)
38. Durfee, E.: Scaling up agent coordination strategies. IEEE Computer **34** (July 2001) 39–46
39. Fischer, K., Schillo, M., Siekmann, J.: Holonic multiagent systems: The foundation for the organization of multiagent systems. In: Proceedings of the First International Conference on Applications of Holonic and Multiagent Systems (HoloMAS'03). Volume 2744 of Lecture Notes in Artificial Intelligence., Springer (2003) 71–80
40. Schillo, M., Fischer, K., Siekmann, J.: The link between autonomy and organisation in multiagent systems. In: Proceedings of the First International Conference on Applications of Holonic and Multiagent Systems (HoloMAS'03). Number 2744 in LNAI, Springer-Verlag (2003) 81–90
41. Rosenschein, J.S., Zlotkin, G.: Rules of Encounter: Designing Conventions for Automated Negotiation among Computers. MIT - Press, Cambridge, Massachusetts - London, England (1994)
42. Fischer, K., Müller, J.P., Pischel, M.: A model for cooperative transportation scheduling. In: Proceedings of the 1st International Conference on Multiagent Systems (ICMAS'95), San Francisco (1995) 109–116
43. Schillo, M., Kray, C., Fischer, K.: The eager bidder problem: A fundamental problem of DAI and selected solutions. In: Proceedings of the First International Conference on Autonomous Agents and Multiagent Systems (AAMAS'02). (2002) 599–608
44. Lesser, V., Decker, K., Wagner, T., Carver, N.and Garvey, A., Horling, B., Neiman, D., Podorozhny, R., Nagendra Prasad, M., Raja, A., Vincent, R., Xuan, P., Zhang, X.Q.: Evolution of the GPGP/TAEMS domain-independent coordination framework. Autonomous Agents and Multi-Agent Systems **9** (2004) 87–143

45. Klusch, M.: Agent-mediated trading: Intelligent agents and e-business. In Hayzelden, A., Bourne, R., eds.: Agent Technology applied to Networked Systems. John Wiley & Sons (2000)
46. Klusch, M.: Information agent technology for the internet: A survey. In Fensel, D., ed.: Journal on Data and Knowledge Engineering, Special Issue on Intelligent Information Integration. Volume 36., Elsevier Science (2001)
47. Turner, P.J., Jennings, N.R.: Improving the scalability of multi-agent systems. In: Proc. 1st Int. Workshop on Infrastructure for Scalable Multi-Agent Systems, Barcelona, Spain (2000)
48. Wellman, B., Berkowitz, S., eds.: Social Structures: A Network Approach. Cambridge University Press (1988)
49. House, R., Rousseau, D., Thomas-Hunt, M.: The meso paradigm: A framework for the integration of micro and macro organizational behavior. Research in Organizational Behavior **17** (1995) 71–114
50. Moss, S., Davidsson, P., eds.: Multi-Agent Based Simulation: Second International Workshop on Multi-Agent Based Simulation. Volume 1979 of LNAI., Boston MA, USA, Springer (2000)

From "Clean" Mechanisms to "Dirty" Models: Methodological Perspectives of an Up-Scaling of Actor Constellations

Uwe Schimank

Institut für Soziologie
FernUniversität in Hagen
58084 Hagen, Germany
uwe.schimank@fernuni-hagen.de

Abstract. Quantitative and qualitative directions of an up-scaling of sociological and socionic models are discussed. In sociology, problems of up-scaling result from the fact that explanations of structural dynamics do not work with laws but with mechanisms. In contrast to scientific laws or simple correlations, a mechanism is a step-by-step analytical description of the social dynamics which bring about the respective structural effect. If models are up-scaled, the relations between their various independent and dependent variables become more and more "fuzzy" and a tension can be identified between "clean" mechanisms and "dirty" models. Although sociological and socionic models are always constructed for specific cases, with all implications of "dirtiness", it will be argued that "clean" mechanisms are not only helpful but indispensable: The "dirtier" the models become with up-scaling, the "cleaner" must be the mechanisms used in modelling to support scientific generalization.

1 Introduction

Some years ago, Paul Hirsch [1] in an article titled "'Dirty Hands' Versus 'Clean Models'" worried about the question, formulated in the sub-title: "Is Sociology in Danger of Being Seduced by Economics?" The "dirty hands" were meant as an honourable quality of sociologists. They deal with real-life, with social dynamics in all their complexity, whereas economists are liable to reduce this complexity up to the point where theoretical models can be formulated which are tractable with mathematical algorithms—but for the price of losing contact with reality.

However accurate this contrast of both disciplines may be, the tension pointed out is a very real one, as attempts to transform sociological ideas into formal models have shown again and again. The "socionic" venture is just one in a long series of efforts. The homo oeconomicus and the perfect market of neo-classic economics are comparatively easy stuff for computer simulations. The reason is that these concepts are very strong abstractions from real-life economic affairs. In contrast, sociological theorising about actors and their constellations is very hard to handle in this way because it is full

K. Fischer, M. Florian, and T. Malsch (Eds.): Socionics, LNAI 3413, pp. 15–35, 2005.

of diffuse, ambivalent, indecisive statements about variables and their causal relations. For sure, part of this vagueness could be corrected if sociologists would take more care to spell out their theoretical ideas as precisely as possible. But the other, probably even greater part, is a kind of indetermination which is essential to the sociological perspective on social life. This vagueness is an expression of those manifold facets of social action and interaction which make up its complexity. Insofar as sociology understands itself as that discipline of the social sciences which, more than other disciplines, looks after this complexity, instead of deliberately disregarding it, there is no hope that the indetermination of its ideas can be overcome. Indeed, to achieve this would not be a decisive success but the ultimate failure of sociology.

In other words, sociology's typical explanatory problems do not allow for such strong abstractions as the problems of economics do. It is obvious that this feature of sociology makes computer simulations of its theoretical ideas about social dynamics much more difficult. This difficulty increases even more when the social situations dealt with consist not just of two actors who both behave in a rather simple way but when more actors interact in more complicated ways. On the other hand, such an up-scaling of actor constellations is a very important challenge for "socionics". If it turns out to be unable to deal with up-scaled constellations, its relevance both for the improvement of sociological thinking and for the practical design of hybrid systems would be rather limited.

This assessment is the starting point of my reflections in this paper. I will proceed in three steps. First, I will distinguish two principal directions of an up-scaling of sociological and "socionic" models: quantitative and qualitative up-scaling. In the second step, I will turn to quantitative up-scaling and discuss the problems and possibilities of modelling. In the third step, I will make at least some brief remarks on qualitative up-scaling.

2   Two Directions of Up-Scaling

Problems of up-scaling result from the fact that sociological explanations of structural dynamics—the emergence, maintenance, change, or destruction of social structures—do not work with laws but with mechanisms [2, pp. 3–10]; [3, pp. 29–34]; [4]; [5]. A scientific law is a relation of very few independent and dependent variables—often only one of both types of variables—which states a causal effect in the form of a mathematical function, most of the time not a deterministic but only a probabilistic one. *How* this causality works is not spelled out in a law; it just declares *that*, for example, y increases if x increases. A *mechanism*, in contrast, is a step-by-step analytical description of the social dynamics which bring about the respective structural effect. This is exactly what sociologists are interested in. They are not satisfied with finding out a correlation, say, between the growing rate of employed women, on the one hand, and the growing rate of divorces, on the other. Instead, they want to know how this correlation results from the individual actions and interactions of millions of women and men, and furthermore, under which circumstances this result, and under which a different one occurs.

The reason why sociologists work with mechanisms rather than laws is that there is not one single law about structural dynamics which was not quickly empirically falsified [6]; [7, pp. 6–9]. That the rate of divorces grows with the rate of employed women may be formulated as a general law—but it is not always and everywhere the case. Instead of general laws, sociology identifies—as James Coleman [8, pp. 516-519] once called them—"sometimes true" propositions about structural dynamics. [1] But for these partial generalisations to be useful for sociological explanations, it is necessary to specify as precisely as possible the conditions under which they are valid. This task, in turn, can be best achieved by the analytical reconstruction of the causal "mechanics" which underlies the respective structural dynamics.

As Hartmut Esser [9, pp. 1-140] shows, this means that sociology has to study three "logics" and their interrelationship. To illustrate this, let me continue the example of increased divorce rates in a very simplified way. One may assume that women and not men make the decision to divorce, and that these women's "logic of selection" of their actions is guided by utility maximisation. Then, a sociological analysis has to pay attention to the "logic of situation" and ask: Which social structures shape these women's decisions to continue or end their marriage? As the empirically identified correlation already shows, one of these structures is the labour market. But others must be added to the picture: the educational system, or the division of labour within families, among others. Thus, one may find out: If a woman had a vocational training or even holds a university degree and is able to earn her living on her own, she has the opportunity to end a frustrating marriage; and when the division of labour within the family remains the traditional one so that the wife, although she has a full-time job, has to do most of the household work, this is a strong factor of frustration which motivates her with a certain probability to take the opportunity offered by her educational and financial resources. Thus having detected the crucial variables in the women's situation, one must finally turn to the "logic of aggregation". This concerns the interplay of all the single decisions made by millions of women to either continue or end their marriage from which results the rate of divorces. Here, there is firstly, just a simple adding-up of many decisions which were made independent from each other. But secondly, mutual observation among married women is at work. It results in many women's assessment that divorce is not only possible and individually rational but also actually done by many others in similar circumstances. This assessment strongly reinforces the individual liability to divorce.

Only an analysis of this kind—which of course would have to go into much more detail—leads to a satisfactory sociological explanation. But because sociology must refer to individual action and the interplay of individual actions to explain structural dynamics, it is decisive for sociological and "socionic" models how complex on the one, simplified on the other hand actors and actor constellations are analytically conceived. Up to now, most "socionic" modelling has been rather simple in this respect. Often, constellations modelled consist of just two actors. In addition, the "socionic" modelling

---

[1] It is true that for every general law, for instance in physics, there is a reservation which is at least implicitly kept in mind by the so-called ceteris-paribus assumptions. As long as these assumptions are true in the overwhelming number of cases there is no problem. What distinguishes sociology from physics, and probably economics as well, is the fact that these exceptions from the rule are much more frequent in sociological phenomena. This is a consequence of sociology's already mentioned openness to social complexity.

of actors simplifies them very much. They behave according to a one-dimensional utility function or are only striving for stable mutual expectations; accordingly, their range of perception is very limited as well as their memory; and they select their action according to a calculus of perfect rationality. Such dyads of very simple actors may be sufficient for an analytical understanding of elementary problems of the emergence and stability of social order.[2] But such an abstract level of reasoning belongs more to social philosophy than to sociology, understood here to be a basically "down to earth" discipline dealing with much more complex real-life phenomena.

It is probably true that a very simple sociological and "socionic" modelling must be the starting point for the construction of *"clean" mechanisms* in the sense of clear-cut analytical assumptions and rules of causal interplay which are easy to think through and produce unequivocal results. From a computer science point of view, a mechanism is a well-defined computational procedure. But as such, these mechanisms are far too abstract for a more than superficial sociological understanding of the respective structural dynamics. What has to be done is the construction of theoretical models which bridge the gap between these abstract mechanisms and concrete empirical phenomena. These will be *"dirty" models* because they cannot but come into touch with the "dirty hands" of those who do not ignore but scrutinise carefully the complexity of social life. That the models are "dirty" suggests, at this point of my argument, that they are vague in the sense explained earlier; in the next section I will explore more deeply various sources of "dirtiness". A "dirty" model, often consisting of a combination of several "clean" mechanisms, can no longer be formulated as an **exact** algorithm but only as a heuristics. Whereas the former guarantees a definite solution of the explanatory problem by following a clearly specified sequence of calculation, a heuristics only promises that it leads the reflection of the problem most of the time into the right direction.[3] No more, but no less is what sociology can hope to attain by a mechanism-based modelling of structural dynamics.

Such a step-by-step advance to the complexity of social reality can take two complementary directions of up-scaling sociological and "socionic" models:

- One direction is *quantitative up-scaling*. Here constellations are modelled which consist of more than two actors. Sometimes these may be two dozen, as in the study of a soccer game. But a model which tries to grasp the demographic dynamics of the world population has to come to terms with several billions of actors.
- The other direction is *qualitative up-scaling*. Here the actors are modelled as multi-faceted entities whose intentions go back to different kinds of motivational driving-forces, who are equipped with differentiated capacities of perception and memory, and who rely on a repertoire of strategies of bounded rationality. This rich inner world of the actors corresponds to their rich environment which consists, among other things, of an extensive institutional context or a widespread distribution of various sources of social influence.

---

[2] See especially discussions of the problem of double contingency [10];[11, pp. 148–190]. But compare [12,13,14] for "socionic" explorations which up-scale the problem of double contingency in various respects.

[3] See [15, pp. 153–172] for the distinction of algorithms and heuristics in decision theory.

Quantitative as well as qualitative up-scaling increases the "requisite variety" [16] of sociological and "socionic" models. Their own analytical complexity is levelled up to optimise the explanatory fit to the concrete complexity of the respective aspect of social reality. Optimisation does not mean maximisation. Models are supposed to reduce complexity instead of duplicating it. They are more complex than mechanisms, but remain far less complex than reality. The trade off between the reduction of concrete complexity by a model, on the one hand, and the explanatory adequacy of the model must always be paid attention to in modelling [17].

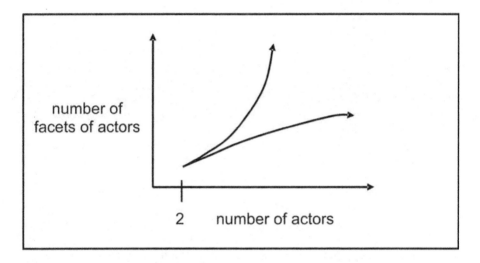

Fig. 1. Two Directions of Up-Scaling

Both directions of up-scaling are coordinates of the space within which the up-scaling of sociological and "socionic" models has to move (see Fig. 1). Progress of modelling—in the sense of a higher adequacy to reality—can be pursued, on the one hand by enlarging the number of actors that can be handled in a model. This may go hand in hand with equipping modelled actors with some more facets. However, in this respect the limits of analytical complexity which can be still dealt with are soon reached. On the other hand, when progress is pursued by modelling multi-faceted actors the number of actors can also be increased a little bit beyond two. But again, one has to stop at a comparatively small number.

These are the two pure directions of up-scaling. Each one focuses on one dimension of complexity—either quantity or quality of actors—and includes the other only insofar as it is possible within this focus. Perhaps one might also go into a mixed direction of up-scaling both quantity and quality to a medium level. This is an open question for further research. I will now turn to quantitative up-scaling.

3   Quantitative Up-Scaling: Large Constellations

My example for an exploration of quantitative up-scaling is the population of students and teaching staff of sociology at the German university of open distance teaching, the FernUniversität Hagen. About a dozen professors and teaching assistants are in charge of more than 3,000 students. In open distance teaching, there are few face-to-face contacts of students and teachers. In the middle of the '90s, the different kinds of communication had—according to a rough guess—the following share: 60% by letter, 35% by phone, and 5% face-to-face. Five years later this distribution has changed radically: 10% by letter, 25% by phone, 5% face-to-face—and 60% by email.

Thus, the structural dynamics to be modelled consist of a rapid and far-reaching shift of the preferred kinds of communication within a large constellation of actors. Simply put, emails have marginalised letters and to some extent substituted phone calls. This has happened without much use of social influence and without negotiations. Students have not been ordered to change to email by their teachers or the university administration; no financial or other kinds of incentives have been employed, and there have been no campaigns to persuade students of the advantages of email; and no formal contracts have been settled among representatives of students and the university about a mutual commitment to turn to email. Thus, the constellation has been no constellation of influence or negotiation but of mutual observation [18, pp. 207-246]. The structural dynamics has resulted from "mutual adjustment" [19].

In such a constellation, all actors involved "... respond to the status quo that has been created by the past moves of all the other players." [3, p. 109] It must be added that an actor selects his own actions not only in consideration of how others acted before but also in anticipation of how they will act in future—which he can try to foresee on the basis of their past actions. Therefore, each actor reacts with his actions to the given and probable future state of the constellation, which itself is a result of the interplay of all actors involved up to now. Everybody adapts to everybody—including himself. Under some circumstances, such a constellation dominated by mutual observation results in the maintenance of a given structure; in other cases, like the one studied here, mutual observation brings about structural change.

During the five years studied each actor—student or teacher—has been confronted again and again with the question whether to write a letter, make a phone call, or write an email. Students with closer contacts to teachers, for instance during their preparation for an examination, have been especially exposed to this choice; and for teachers, this has been almost a daily issue. Each of these more than 3,000 actors is a unique individual. No biography is identical with another, and everybody's actual situation is different. As a consequence, one actor's decision situation with respect to the kind of communication to be used is unlike another one's; and an actor's decision situation at a particular time is not the same as the respective situations before or after. But if everybody's "logic of situation" is significantly different from everybody else's, the "logic of aggregation" manifests an exploding complexity. Every actor has more or less others in view and chooses what he does on the basis of this—more or less correct—observation. Unique actors in unique situations react to a number of other unique actors in unique situations, and vice versa. Is not Niklas Luhmann's [20, p. 132] despair understandable who feared that an actor-theoretical explanation of structural dynamics overburdens sociological analysis with the need to take into consideration "billions of simultaneously acting actors"?[4]

Even if a constellation does not consist of billions or just some thousand actors, the problem of complexity remains a very substantial one. As Georg Simmel [21, pp. 32–100] showed, the explosion of contingency starts as soon as a third actor is added to a dyad. Among other things, several coalitions or "divide et impera" strategies become possible. In game theory, the same problem appears with respect to the identification of equilibria in n-person games. Fritz Scharpf [22, p. 5] states: "With only five players having to choose among three strategies each, that would already require comparison among $3^5 = 243$ different outcomes." It is no wonder that game theory still prefers to deal with 2 x 2 games in which only two actors can choose between just two alternatives. But a closer view reveals that even this most simple constellation is still very complex, as Thomas Schelling [23, pp. 221–223] reminds us: "... even the simplest of situations, involving two individuals with two alternatives a piece to choose from, cannot be exhaustively analysed and catalogued. Their possibilities are almost limitless." With two actors and three alternatives on each side there exist more than three and a half million different possible patterns of the constellation.

How can this be handled? Are there really any chances for a quantitative up-scaling of sociological and "socionic" models? I will now sketch two basic theoretical strategies to cope with large constellations. One of these strategies learns from how real-life actors come to terms with constellations like the one in my example. The other strategy, in contrast, takes a view on large constellations which the actors involved usually do not have. The keywords for the two strategies are: typifications and social networks.

Typification is a central feature of "games real actors play" [3]. It consists basically of a drastic reduction of attention to very few aspects of the concrete complexity of actors and constellations. Typifications are enormous simplifications which do justice neither to actors nor to constellations [24, pp. 277–290]. But the other side of this neglect is the orienting function of typifications. When an actor typifies others around him, himself as well, and the constellation of him and these others, this enables him to handle the situation—with superior indifference to almost everything of what the situation is made up. Thus, typifications have a fictitious character. When an actor uses them, he treats situations as if they were nothing but what the particular typifications highlight. However, as soon as typifications guide action, they become real. They transform the respective situations in the manner of self-fulfilling prophecies.[5] When many or all actors in a situation use the same or complementary typifications, they become institutionalised over time [26, pp. 65–109]. From then on, experienced actors automatically refer to the relevant typifications whenever they become involved in such a situation, and presuppose that other actors will do the same. Typifications can even become reified in the sense that they provide actors—as it appears to them—with the only possible way to handle the respective situation. No other views come into the actors' minds any longer.

---

[4] Incidentally, this overload of complexity is not reduced if one conceives social life not in actor-theoretical terms but as an autopoiesis of communication, as Luhmann proposes. In each societal sub-system occur daily billions of simultaneous operations of communication.

[5] See Schimank [25] for the case of the sub-systems of modern society.

Typifications are, first of all, an accomplishment of the actors involved in a situation. However, sociological observers can make use of these constructs. Sociologists can reconstruct institutionalised typifications in their theoretical models. Of course, in contrast to real-life actors sociologists should always be aware of the fact that typifications are never "naturally" given as they are, but could be quite different. In other words, sociologists must keep in mind the socially constructed character of typifications. Still, sociological and "socionic" modelling can adopt the real-life typifications. These drastic reductions of concrete complexity for the actors involved provide modelling with corresponding reductions of analytical complexity.

In my example, several kinds of typifications are at work. Looking first at individual persons and their actions, a number of typifications add up to reduce the complexity of unique biographies and situations. The persons are, first, typified as *role players*: students and teachers. These typifications consist of sets of expectations which refer to the interaction of students with other students, teachers with other teachers, and students with teachers. Secondly, the interplay of role players is typified by a number of *scripts* such as "negotiating the subject of a thesis" [27, pp. 199–235]. Scripts prescribe sequences of an ordered co-production of a particular event or performance by several actors. It is regulated who takes the initiative, how the others have to react to this, what happens then, and so on—up to the final step with which one of the actors finishes the script. Scripts do not exist for every action and interaction, and many scripts are not very detailed. They often allow more than one possibility to act at certain points. Still, they delimit possibilities sharply. Thirdly, role expectations and scripts can set the stage for an even more focused typification which gives the actor a *dichotomous alternative* to act by emphasising one specific possibility in front of the background of all other ones. For instance, for a student the script "negotiating the subject for a thesis" might at some point end up in the alternative: "write an email" vs. all other possible kinds of communication.

Whereas the typifications mentioned up to now restrict the search for action alternatives by highlighting only a few or sometimes just one of them, other typifications exist for the comparative evaluation of the different alternatives. Actors relying on these typifications spare themselves the time and mental energy which are the costs of difficult choices. Here, I think the analytical perspective of "actor-centred institutionalism" [28, p. 66] is most helpful. This perspectives states that in many situations sufficiently clear *norms* exist which are, moreover, subject to effective social control. Then it can be presupposed that an actor behaves as a norm-conforming homo sociologicus. Students, for instance, might conform with the norm of "respectful approach to teachers" and think that a letter is more appropriate than an email; or students might remember a formal stipulation that applications for the supervision of a thesis must be signed which is impossible in an email.

When there is no clear-cut prescription of a specific way to act by norms, considerations of *utility* can come into play within the scope of what the norms allow; and when there are no norms which regulate a situation, actors can orient themselves according to their own utility functions from the beginning. The subjective utility of some action alternative may be operationalised by manifold and sometimes very idiosyncratic goals and interests. But often actors pursue *"standard interests"* [28, p. 54] like maintenance or extension of their autonomy or their domain, growth of their resources or prestige, minimisation of effort and expenses, or preservation of stable expectations. These "standard interests" can frequently be inferred quite easily from the situation in which an actor is. For instance, a student's preference for email could be an expression of his interest to minimise his expenses. Furthermore, society institutionalises certain typifications of utility considerations as *rationality fictions*.[6] This means that particular goals and means are declared as rational so that an actor does not have to reflect upon what is rational in his specific situation. Probably by now, there exists a rationality fiction which proposes that email is the most efficient way to communicate in situations such as the one studied here.

Other driving-forces of action, such as emotions or identity maintenance, should be taken into account only if norms as well as considerations of utility cannot explain the respective actions. For example, it may be that there are a few students or teachers who want to present themselves above all as persons who adhere to traditional kinds of communication. But the sociological observer who wants to explain, first of all, how most actors act in the respective situation should postpone this typification of identity as an explanatory variable.

The typifications sketched so far could suffice to explain and model the result of the respective structural dynamics. One could start with the proposal that the choice of the kind of communication used in this situation is not much regulated by norms, but strongly guided by considerations of utility—more precisely, an interest in efficiency which is itself shaped by certain rationality fictions. In the case studied, rationality fictions originate mainly from "mimetic isomorphism" [30]. Accordingly, an actor supposes that a way to act which is chosen by many other actors to whom he ascribes an interest in efficiency is efficient, indeed. Here, mutual observation becomes important. In addition, for a number of actors this consideration of efficiency is underlined by a self-understanding as an "up-to-date" person associated with the latest communication techniques. But even actors who do not bother much about efficiency of this communication and who have no ambition to express their "up-to-dateness" will decide for email as soon as the second-order typification gains plausibility that "everybody" uses email. To do the same simply means that one does not have to justify a divergent way to act, and that there is some probability that one adopts a way to act which at least is not totally inefficient; in addition, the "standard interest" to maintain stable mutual expectations may be relevant for these actors. To sum up, with the help of these few typifications it is possible to explain why email is by now the predominant kind of communication among students and teachers at the FernUniversität.

Not yet explained is how the dynamics of change from letters and phone to email has proceeded. To simplify, I assume that teachers are able to use email, prefer to do that, and react to any communication by email from one of their students by email themselves; but teachers cannot initiate email communication with a student because they do not know his email address. In fact, they do not even know whether he has an email address at all. Thus, what must be explained is how students shift to email as their preferred kind of communication.

---

[6] This is a central topic of sociological neo-institutionalism which speaks about "myths" of rationality [29].

At this point, Mark Granovetter's [31] mechanism of varying *threshold levels* can be built into the modelling of the situation. In general, this mechanism states that each actor has a particular threshold level with respect to the rate of other actors within a population who act in a specific way. If the actual rate is below the threshold level, he will not join in doing the same; as soon as the rate reaches the threshold level, he joins. These threshold levels vary between actors which can be explained especially by different motivational driving-forces [32, pp. 202–214]. There are actors whose self-understanding commits them to be pioneers for each technical novelty; other actors' identity prescribes them to do what they think is the best thing to do, regardless of how many others do something different. Other actors follow primarily considerations of utility and change to a new pattern of action not before so many others have adopted it that the sometimes high costs which pioneers have to pay no longer come up whereas the benefits of the new pattern can be reaped. Considerations of utility also guide those actors whose maxim is "rational imitation" [33] and who adopt a new pattern of action only when a clear majority of others has already adopted it. Finally, there are actors with a very high threshold level. This may be motivated by a particular self-understanding—for example, not to do what "the mass" does. Or considerations of utility are the reason for not changing one's way to act. An example might be an elderly student who never worked with a personal computer and does not want to buy one because besides his study he sees no other uses.

What is decisive for the dynamics of change within the constellation is the distribution of threshold levels. A "band wagon" effect of a cumulative mobilisation of more and more students to adopt email occurs only if this distribution is appropriate. There must be enough students who act as pioneers; enough others must join them for considerations of utility, and enough others, in turn, must join those as "rational imitators". The other way round, the number of those with very high threshold levels must be small.

Partly, Granovetter's mechanism works if there is in fact an appropriate distribution of threshold levels within the respective population. Partly, however, it works on the basis of prevalent expectations about the distribution of threshold levels. Again, these are typifications—not about individual actors but about the population as a whole. Such typifications are important for "rational imitators" as well as for pioneers. In other cases, the homo sociologicus as well pays attention to the distribution of threshold levels. How firm somebody conforms with a norm often depends upon how many others actually conform, and how many others he expects to conform.

Based on all these typifications, the constellation and its dynamics can be modelled as a "nested game" [34]—more precisely, as two levels of 2 x 2 games (see Fig. 2). At one level, the two sub-populations of all teachers, on the one hand, and all students, on the other, are each modelled as a single composite actor. Here the interplay of teachers and students is analytically reconstructed, with identical dichotomous action alternatives on both sides: to use email or to use some other kind of communication. On a lower level, each of the two sub-populations is modelled from the point of view of one of its members. Here the interplay of one student's action—again with the dichotomous alternatives—with all other students' actions is reconstructed; and the same for teachers. At both levels of the game, the constellations are primarily based on mutual observation. Thus, each student as well as teacher looks in two directions to find orien-

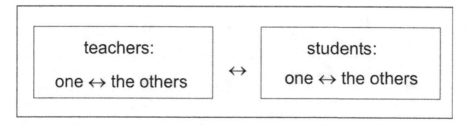

Fig. 2. Nested Game

tation for his own choice of action: What are others in his own sub-population doing, and what actors actors in the other sub-population doing?

I hope that this example demonstrates my main message that neither real-life actors nor their sociological observers have to find out an equilibrium for this constellation of several thousand actors. This would be impossible which means that no equilibrium would ever emerge. Instead, these "games real actors play" are radically simplified by various kinds of typifications so that real-life actors with limited capabilities can handle matters competently—and sociologists are able not only to describe but also to explain the resulting structural dynamics with "mechanism-based models" [5].

Further steps towards a parsimonious modelling of structural dynamics can be made with the help of social network analysis which has worked out an already plentiful repertoire of analytical tools to study *social networks* in which actors are positioned [35,36]. Network analysis highlights an aspect of social life which the mechanisms mentioned up to this point neglect. Thus far my proposal of modelling implicitly pre-supposes that there is a homogenous and tightly woven net of relations among all actors within the constellation. But this is a highly unrealistic assumption for most constellations, especially large ones. Instead, actors within a constellation differ strongly with respect to their network position. Some have many relations to others, others have only few. Some are sociometric "stars" whereas others are marginal. Moreover, turning to the constellation as a whole, some constellations exhibit a high density of relations among its actors, and in other constellations only very few relations exist. Existing relations are highly centralised in some constellations, rather decentralised in others. These kinds of differences between actors and constellations, which can be quite important for an explanation of structural dynamics, are the topic of social network analysis.

Turning to my example again, what must be explained is the diffusion of a new kind of communication within a population—more specifically, the speed and pattern of this process. It was exactly this kind of question which James Coleman et al. [37] posed in their classic empirical study of the diffusion dynamics of a new medicine among doctors within some regions of the United States. Another example is the mobilisation of individuals for social movements. Several studies show that the recruitment as well as the leaving of individuals is significantly determined by the shape of the social network to which they belong, and by their own position within it [38,5].

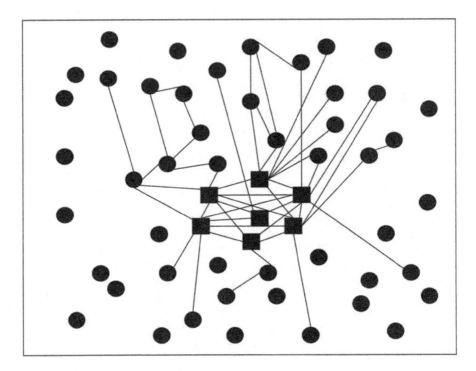

Fig. 3. Social network of teachers (■) and students (●)

For my example, the overall pattern of the network can be described like this (see Fig. 3): There is a small *core* of intense communication and high visibility which consists of the teaching staff. Within this core, everybody communicates with everybody else. This core is surrounded by a large *periphery* of about 3,000 students which is divided into two segments. The smaller segment of the periphery, about one third of the students, are those who have contacts to at least one teacher, sometimes to more than one, as well as to some other students—for example, on seminars or in learning groups. The other segment of the periphery, two thirds of it, are those students who have no or only very sporadic contacts to teachers or other students.

Even this rough picture shows several things which network analysis could describe precisely with its concepts. To begin with, the network has a very low *density*. Most actors are isolated. But there exist local areas of high density, some among students, and one among all teachers. The first segment of students is linked to teachers who have a very high *centrality* within the overall network. Some students are *linking pins* which indirectly connect other students to teachers. In addition to these formal characteristics, a more detailed analysis could distinguish different kinds of relations. Beyond information, social networks can also transport social influence or constitute affective bonds. Among other things, within the teaching staff the formal authority of professors over their assistants could be taken into account; however, assistants are often closer to students and get some information from them which professors can only get indirectly from their respective assistants. In terms of network analysis, these different dimensions of social relations could be conceptualised as different networks—an information network, a power network, a network of friendships, etc.—whose degree of similarity, measured as *multiplexity*, provides us with further insights.

Another feature of networks which has proven to be very important in many studies are *strong and weak ties* [39]. Strong ties are regular, intense relations among actors whereas weak ties are occasional, sometimes very rare contacts. Strong ties produce and reproduce shared knowledge, moral sentiments, and norms, including norms of reciprocity, among actors. Imitation, social control, and affective bonds rest on strong ties. Weak ties, in contrast, deliver new information and contacts. With respect to informal learning groups of students, it might be expected that, for example, a critical mass of traditionalists will stop those members who—by loose contacts to other students who regularly use email in their contacts with teachers—are willing to adopt this new kind of communication. However, if such a learning group has changed to email, it is not very probable that it will fall back again on letters because mutual reinforcement of the use of this new kind of communication is strong.

Without referring to additional concepts of network analysis, I hope to have shown that the shape of the social network within a population of actors is an important determinant of the structural dynamics of this constellation. Just think for a moment that your task is to bring about a quick adoption of email communication among students of the FernUniversität! You should ask yourself: Which actors have to be persuaded to use email at first? Who are the best actors to initiate a chain reaction within this constellation of mutual observation? I cannot dwell upon these questions here any longer. The important thing is that concepts of network analysis, just like social typifications, enable the sociological observer to characterise a constellation of many actors without having to go into detail with respect to each individual actor. Thus, network analysis, too, helps to cope with quantitative up-scaling.

I have discussed quantitative up-scaling here quite intentionally with close reference to a concrete example. It is not only that in this way the approach I propose becomes more vivid than by an enumeration of abstract methodological rules. The more basic point is that I am not sure whether such general rules for the kinds of sociological and "socionic" modelling discussed here exist at all. Perhaps on a general level we cannot state much more than the following suggestions:

– Sociology should equip itself with a *well-assorted tool box of precisely constructed theoretical mechanisms*. This is the best way to make sure that there are adequate analytical tools for each specific explanatory problem so that it is not necessary to use pincers to hit a nail into the wall.
– In my example, I used a mixture of analytical tools from a number of diverse sociological perspectives, as every sociologist will have noticed. From endless comparative debates, we know that, as general theoretical perspectives rational choice, role theory, social network analysis, phenomenology, and others exhibit a number of smaller and larger incompatibilities. But this must not hinder us from *combining specific mechanisms* from all these and other approaches to build more complex models.

– No mechanism and no combination of mechanisms can explain on its own any real-life phenomenon. Each mechanism has to be fed with empirical data about its independent variables. Thus, a sociological explanation implies a *description of the initial state of the model's parameters*.

To summarise, sociological and "socionic" modelling of actor constellations and their structural dynamics combine, with respect to the "logic of selection" and the "logic of aggregation", adequate mechanisms to a case-specific theoretical model; and this model is embedded in a description of the "logic of situation" which fits to the mechanisms. Supposed that the relevant mechanisms are "clean", that is precise and logically consistent accounts of the constellations and dynamics to which they refer, why and in what sense are the models built with these mechanisms "dirty"?

First of all, the "dirtiness" of models results from the case-specific combination of mechanisms. For this *"bricolage"* no general rules exist. There is no methodological meta-mechanism for the selection and combination of mechanisms. This central step of any explanation is nothing but "tinkering". Perhaps, over time, one gains some experience which may crystallise in heuristics which tell, for instance, when it is worthwhile to draw on the homo oeconomicus instead of the homo sociologicus for the explanation of some kind of action. "Tinkering" may work, or it may not work—there is no guarantee. This is one manifestation of the "dirtiness" inherent to any combination of mechanisms. The other aspect of "dirtiness" refers to the fact that diverse mechanisms seldom fit together as nicely as the many small wheels in a clockwork. Instead of smooth interfaces, there is usually considerable frictional loss. Nevertheless, it makes sense for certain explanatory purposes to build a model of "homo socio-oeconomicus" [40], for example, although as a general concept this would contain theoretically unacceptable incompatibilities.

Secondly, the "dirtiness" of sociological and "socionic" models is implied in the *finely grained descriptions* of the "logic of situation" which are often indispensable. This is different from most macro-economic models which rely on heroic simplifications of the respective situations. It is true that sociological modelling as well is not interested in a highly detailed historical account of a situation. Instead, which situational elements are included in the description, and on what level of preciseness, is strictly determined by the variables specified in the mechanisms used for explanation. Still, even such a theoretically disciplined description of the "logic of situation" most of the time ends up in a quite extensive list of facts. The number of descriptive aspects to be considered simply grows with the number of mechanisms combined within an explanatory model. As my example showed, it is not unusual that between half a dozen and a dozen mechanisms have to be used. Another reason which accounts for the amount of information to be needed to understand the "logic of situation" is the relative openness of many variables in sociological mechanisms. Sometimes this is a deficiency which can and should be corrected. But more often this openness is something sociologists have to live with. For example, which kinds of utility a homo oeconomicus pays attention to in a particular situation occasionally has to be detected with a great effort of painstaking observations and descriptions. These and other reasons make clear that there is no general checklist of situational elements for sociological modelling. One can never be sure not to have neglected some aspects important for the explanatory problem dealt with.

A third source of the "dirtiness" of sociological and "socionic" models is the ubiquity of *"Cournot effects"* [6, pp. 173–179]. "Cournot effects" are the results of coincidental interplays of two or more causal chains. For instance, if on a windy day a slate falls down the roof and hits a pedestrian who walks by the respective house, this event is a work of chance. Both causal chains—"wind tears off the slate" and "person walks by the house"—are not connected by any necessity. Such "Cournot effects" may be highly improbable, but they may also occur with considerable probability. If many pedestrians pass by the house each day, and if a storm rages for hours, and if the house is in a bad shape, one might even be tempted to say that such an accident was inevitable. But even for highly probable "Cournot effects" there is, again, no meta-mechanism which states that those mechanisms involved will jointly produce a certain result and nothing else. In my example of the FernUniversität, a "Cournot effect" which accelerates the structural dynamics studied could be the simultaneous appearance of several technical innovations which make possible email as a new kind of communication, on the one hand, and an increase of price for sending letters.

These three reasons for the "dirtiness" of sociological and "socionic" models are of a very fundamental nature. They do not occur only if a certain level of quantitative up-scaling has been reached. Still, it is plausible that there is some correlation between the level of up-scaling and the degree of "dirtiness" of models. The higher the concrete complexity to be captured within a theoretical model, the stronger these determinants of its "dirtiness" become. This is also true for qualitative up-scaling to which I will turn now.

4   Qualitative Up-Scaling: Many-Faceted Actors

I will not repeat here the principal methodological points which apply to both kinds of up-scaling, but focus on those aspects which are specific to qualitative up-scaling. My example are constellations of collective decision-making in German universities [41, pp. 222–258]. The structural dynamics that are to be explained in this case is not some kind of change but the absence of change: the impossibility to redistribute resources within as well as between faculties. More specifically, the faculty council and the dean on the faculty level, and the rectorate and the senate on the university level decide by majority vote about the allocation of certain resources. But this formal majority rule is de facto transformed into a rule of unanimity—which means that every professor and every faculty has a strong veto power against any decision which is to his or its disadvantage. Accordingly, everybody is able to maintain his relative status quo, which means that the whole faculty and, respectively, university is imprisoned in the status quo. This usual outcome of collective decision-making is strongly criticised by government which finances universities and demands for a long time a more efficient allocation of scarce resources. Moreover, many professors who are good performers and for whose teaching or research there is high demand could individually profit from redistributions of resources. Still, the logic of cooperativeness in university decision-making prevails.

What looks rather strange at first sight, on a closer view turns out to be a "logic of aggregation" which is the result of highly reasonable actions of individual professors. There are a number of good reasons for them to avoid taking or supporting initiatives of resource redistribution. The conflicts associated with challenging the established distribution of resources produce emotional stress, especially on the faculty level where one literally meets one's opponents every day. Such conflicts also destroy the collective solidarity and influence of the faculty or university against outside enemies. From this collective influence every professor profits. But most importantly, as risk-aversive actors, professors are well-advised to refrain from redistributive initiatives which might trigger future revenge. And even if no revenge is taken, establishing redistribution as a possibility of action always implies that one might be a victim of it oneself sooner or later. Central to this is an iterated prisoner's dilemma game: professors anticipate an ongoing mutual harm from redistribution; and this reflection brings about an "evolution of cooperation" [42].

This constellation consists of more than two actors; but there are much less actors than in my example of the last section. Here, a limited number of usually not more than two dozen actors are engaged in collective decision-making, with every one of them knowing each of the others comparatively well as individuals, and having frequent contacts with each other. Thus, the complexity of this constellation is not originating from a large number of actors but from the rich and idiosyncratic inner lives of the actors which, in turn, reflect the richness of their respective environments, especially their relations to others. Everybody can imagine, just for a moment, the faculty or organisational unit to which she or he belongs, and recollect some episodes of joint decision-making, or read one of the many campus novels with their graphic descriptions of university life [43]. Each of these real or fictional stories is unique in its constellation of highly idiosyncratic individuals, not to mention "Cournot effects". But all this is not the topic of sociological and "socionic" modelling. What it has to explain is why all these unique occurrences most often result in the same outcome: the factual unanimity in the preservation of the status quo. This is the constant "deep pattern" underneath the ever new surface of university decision-making.

But although sociological and "socionic" modelling does not want to reconstruct concrete individuals and circumstances in their uniqueness, it nevertheless has to equip actors and their relations with some more analytical facets. I will briefly mention six of them which are relevant in my example.

First, actors have to be modelled with a *social character* which includes, beyond conformity with norms and utility maximisation, *emotions* such as fear or envy and a personal *identity*—for instance, a professional self-understanding centred around the idea of autonomy of research and teaching—as significant driving forces of action [18, pp. 107-143]. The mixture of these components varies widely among actors and for the same actor over time. For example, an "academic entrepreneur" behaves very different from a traditional professor; and if a professor learns from experience that a too emotional self-presentation in the faculty is harmful to the pursuit of his interests, he will control himself better in the future. An analytically enriched social character could be built as a regulator with four sub-regulators for the homo oeconomicus, the homo sociologicus, the "emotional man", and the identity maintainer; for each of these sub-regulators it must be specified by which situational elements it is turned up or down; and the selection of action is the composite result of the interplay of all four sub-regulators [12].

Secondly, with respect to the homo oeconomicus one should be aware of the fact that not only one *"standard interest"* is prominent, or at most two of them are, but that three or more of them can simultaneously determine the selection of action. Modelling has to clarify which "standard interests" are activated, and with which priority each of them is, and how they manifest themselves concretely. In my example, one must consider an interest in the stability of mutual expectations, in the minimisation of effort, and in the maintenance of autonomy and one's own domain. It is also necessary that possible trade offs between these interests are paid attention to. For instance, maintenance of one's autonomy might conflict with minimisation of effort.

Thirdly, again concerning the homo oeconomicus, *bounded rationality* must be modelled. In my example, it would be misleading to assume a calculus of perfect rationality for the "logic of selection". Situations of collective decision-making within a faculty as a whole are much too complex to allow for more than bounded rationality.[7] Each actor has only limited information about issues and often cannot fully trust information from others, is subject to manifold social influences within sometimes far-reaching networks, must take into account all kinds of "Cournot effects" to happen, and has to make his decision within a limited amount of time. Under these circumstances, "satisficing" [45, pp. 140-141] might be an appropriate strategy of decision-making, according to which an actor selects the first alternative which comes into his mind and promises at least results which are sufficient on a certain level of aspiration. A modelling of "satisficing" requires that the dynamics of aspiration levels are taken into account. When a specific aspiration level is easily reached, perhaps after several attempts, actors tend to raise it whereas when it is several times missed they tend to lower it. Perhaps even more adequate might be Thomas Schelling's [46, pp. 15-17] "something better approach" which starts as "satisficing" but continues the search for a better alternative when there is some time left.

Fourthly, in my example from the last section only very few *institutionalised norms* were shaping action. For collective decision-making within universities, this is quite different. As a homo sociologicus, each actor is confronted with a number of formal and informal norms, some of which are in conflict with each other. The formal majority rule as well as the factual cooperativeness among professors are among the relevant norms in my example. Which norm has how much weight in the shaping of actions must be empirically explored to build it into the sociological and "socionic" model.

Fifthly, formal procedures of university and faculty self-government as well as informally practised routines of interplay among decision-makers can be modelled as *scripts* which are adhered to by actors. What is important in this respect—in contrast to the treatment of scripts in the last section—is to provide for more open scripts which branch at certain points without, however, allowing everything to happen.

Sixthly, my example in the last section demonstrated primarily a constellation of mutual observation. Collective decision-making within universities, on the other hand,

---

[7] Especially the conceptualisation of universities as "organisational anarchies" highlights many of the particular manifestations of complexity within this setting [44].

shows the two other basic modes of interaction: *social influence and negotiation*. Actors can mutually influence each other by threats, promises, information giving or withholding, or persuasion. In addition, actors have to negotiate to come to a binding agreement with each other. The interplay of these three modes—observation, influence, negotiation—must be modelled to explain the interaction of actors within universities and the resulting structural dynamics.

This is a long list, with each aspect mentioned being by itself a complicated task for modelling. It is even more complicated to put together these analytical components within one model which is still manageable. What makes qualitative up-scaling still more difficult is that there is almost no preparatory work for the modelling of any of these components.

I can give here at least a perspective for the modelling of institutionalised norms, following a suggestion by Reinhard Bachmann [47, pp. 230f—my translation]: "An institutional rule gets a stability value S according to its acceptance among agents. The more frequently agents do not deviate from this rule with their behaviour, the higher is this value." With respect to collective decision-making within universities, among other things the high acceptance of the norm of cooperativeness among professors must be modelled. To do this, one might adopt Robert Axelrod's [48] mechanism of the "norm game" which he himself has put into a "socionic" model. This game is a prisoner's dilemma in which iteration and reputation effects—both based on mutual observation—bring about conformity with a norm. Added to this is a second level game on which actors' conformity with the meta-norm to sanction observed deviance is stabilised. This extension of the initial simple "norm game" is analytically necessary because sanctioning is costly to the actor who does it; therefore, there is a liability among actors to avoid doing it; but widespread avoidance of sanctioning, in turn, would mean that actors' conformity with norms could not be established. Thus, only a two-level game is an adequate modelling of norm conformity[8].

If all the other analytical components mentioned—and additional ones as well, if they are needed for a particular model—could be also conceptualised as "clean" mechanisms, one would have come nearer to the goal of being able to build "mechanism-based models" for qualitative up-scaling. Of course, these models would also be "dirty" in the three senses discussed in the last section. There would be "bricolage" of mechanisms, fine-grained descriptions of situations, and "Cournot-effects" in qualitatively up-scaled models, just as in quantitatively up-scaled ones'. And the "dirtiness" of a model increases for qualitative up-scaling the more facets of actors are analytically included.

5   Conclusion

I have shown in which respects and why an up-scaling of sociological and "socionic" models leads to their increasing "dirtiness" so that the relations between their various independent and dependent variables become more and more "fuzzy". Both examples

---

[8] In principle, there is an infinite regress here which points to ever higher levels of meta-norms necessary to secure norm conformity. But in accordance with Scharpf's [3] maxim to model "games real actors play", it suffices for most analytical purposes to assume that adherence to the meta-norm is cost-free to the respective actor.

presented seem to me to be quite representative of the two directions of up-scaling. Therefore, I assume that the modelling approach illustrated by my examples—more elaborately with respect to the former—can be transferred to other cases of either quantitative or qualitative up-scaling. In this sense, methodological suggestions which can be demonstrated only with reference to particular cases nevertheless can be generalised.

I do hope that I also have properly emphasised the importance of "clean" mechanisms. When I started with a distancing of sociology from economics and the neglect of the complexities of social life in many of its models, I did not mean to say that the construction of precisely working mechanisms is unnecessary or even dangerous for the purposes of sociological explanations. Quite the contrary is true. Although sociological and "socionic" models are always constructed for specific cases, with all implications of "dirtiness" referred to, "clean" mechanisms are not only helpful but indispensable. Perhaps my basic proposition sounds less paradoxical now: *The "dirtier" our models become with up-scaling them, the "cleaner" must be the mechanisms we use in modelling.*[9]

References

1. Hirsch, P., Michaels, S., Friedman, R.: "dirty hands" versus "clean models": Is sociology in danger of being seduced by economics? American Sociological Review (1987) 317–336
2. Elster, J.: Nuts and Bolts for the Social Sciences. Cambridge University Press, Cambridge (1989)
3. Scharpf, F.W.: Games Real Actors Play. Actor-Centered Institutionalism in Policy Research. Westview, Boulder, CO (1997)
4. Hedström, P., Swedberg, R., eds.: Social Mechanisms: An Analytical Approach to Social Theory. Cambridge University Press, Cambridge (1998)
5. Hedström, P.: Mechanisms, Models, and the Micro-to-Macro Link. Working Papers on Social Mechanisms. Stockholm University, Department of Sociology (1999)
6. Boudon, R.: Theories of Social Change. A Critical Appraisal. Polity Press, Oxford (1986)
7. Esser, H.: Soziologie — Spezielle Grundlagen. Band 1: Situationslogik und Handeln. Campus, Frankfurt/M. (1999)
8. Coleman, J.: Introduction to Mathematical Sociology. Free Press, New York (1964)
9. Esser, H.: Soziologie — Allgemeine Grundlagen. Campus, Frankfurt/M. (1993)
10. Parsons, T.: The Structure of Social Action. Free Press, New York (1949)
11. Luhmann, N.: Soziale Systeme. Suhrkamp, Frankfurt/M. (1984)
12. Dittrich, P., Kron, T.: Complex Reflexive Agents as Models of Social Actors. In: Proceedings of the SICE Workshop on Artificial Society/Organization/Economy. Volume 25 of Meeting of Systems Engineering., Gkajutsu Sougou Center, Tokyo, Japan (2002) 79–88
13. Dittrich, P., Kron, T., Banzhaf, W.: On the Scalability of Social Order. Modelling the Problem of Double and Multi Contingency Following Luhmann. Journal of Artificial Societies and Social Simulation 6 (2003) http://jass.soc.surrey.ac.uk/6/1/3.html.

---

[9] It should also be clear that my strict distinction of models and mechanisms is a simplification made to deliver my argument with sufficient clarity. On closer view, mechanisms and models as I defined them here are poles of a continuum with numerous transitional points. Even the most "clean" mechanism is already somewhat "dirty" because it contains as variables situational elements which can never be defined totally unequivocally. The other way round, every model is much "cleaner" than social reality as it appears, to some degree, in historical studies. See Schimank [17] for a corresponding distinction of levels of abstraction of sociological models.

14. Kron, T., Lasarczyk, C., Schimank, U.: Doppelte Kontingenz und die Bedeutung von Netzwerken für Kommunkationssysteme. Ergebnisse einer Simulationsstudie. Zeitschrift für Soziologie (2003) 374–395
15. Kirsch, W.: Einführung in die Theorie der Entscheidungsprozesse. Gabler, Wiesbaden (1977)
16. Ashby, W.R.: Einführung in die Kybernetik. Suhrkamp, Frankfurt/M. (1956)
17. Schimank, U.: Theoretische Modelle sozialer Strukturdynamiken: Ein Gefüge von Generalisierungsniveaus. In Mayntz, R., ed.: Akteure, Mechanismen und Modelle. Campus, Frankfurt/M. (2002) 151–178
18. Schimank, U.: Handeln und Strukturen. Leske + Budrich, Opladen (2000)
19. Lindblom, C.E.: The Intelligence of Democracy. Decision Making Through Mutual Adjustment. Free Press, New York (1965)
20. Luhmann, N.:   Warum AGIL?   Kölner Zeitschrift für Soziologie und Sozialpsychologie (1988) 127–139
21. Simmel, G.: Soziologie. Duncker & Humblot, Berlin (1968)
22. Scharpf, F.W.: Games Real Actors Could Play: The Problem of Connectedness. Number 90/8 in MPIFG Discussion paper. Max-Planck-Institut für Gesellschaftsforschung, Köln (1990)
23. Schelling, T.:   What is Game Theory?   In: Choice and Consequence.   Harvard University Press, Cambridge, MA (1984) 213–242
24. Schütz, A., Luckmann, T.: Strukturen der Lebenswelt. Band 1. Volume 1. Suhrkamp, Frankfurt/M. (1977)
25. Schimank, U.:   Gesellschaftliche Teilsysteme als Akteurfiktionen.   Kölner Zeitschrift für Soziologie und Sozialpsychologie (1988) 619–639
26. Berger Peter, L., Luckmann, T.:   The Social Construction of Reality.   Penguin, Harmondsworth (1966)
27. Esser, H.: Soziologie — Spezielle Grundlagen. Band 5: Institutionen. Volume 5. Campus, Frankfurt/M. (2000)
28. Mayntz, R., Scharpf, F.W.: Der Ansatz des akteurzentrierten Institutionalismus. In Mayntz, R., Scharpf, F.W., eds.: Gesellschaftliche Selbstregelung und politische Steuerung. Campus, Frankfurt/M. (1995) 39–72
29. Powell, W., Maggio, P.d., eds.: The New Institutionalism in Organizational Analysis. University of Chicago Press, Chicago/London (1991)
30. DiMaggio, P.J., Powell, W.W.: The Iron Cage Revisited. American Sociological Review (1983) 147–160
31. Granovetter, M.: Threshold Models of Collective Behavior. American Journal of Sociology (1978) 1420–1443
32. Elster, J.: The Cement of Society: A Study of Social Order. Cambridge University Press, Cambridge (1989)
33. Hedström, P.: Rational Imitation. In Hedström, P., Swedberg, R., eds.: Social Mechanisms: An Analytical Approach to Social Theory. Cambridge University Press, Cambridge (1998) 306–327
34. Tsebelis, G.: Nested Games. Rational Choice in Comparative Politics. University of California Press, Berkeley (1990)
35. Wasserman, S., Faust, K.: Social Network Analysis. Cambridge University Press, Cambridge (1994)
36. Jansen, D.: Analyse sozialer Netzwerke. Leske + Budrich, Opladen (1999)
37. Coleman, J.S., Katz, E., Menzel, H.: Medical Innovation. Bobbs-Merrill, Indianapolis (1966)
38. Snow, D., Zurcher, L., Ekeland-Olsen, S.: Social Networks and Social Movements: A Microstructural Approach to Differential Recruitment. American Sociological Review (1980) 787–801
39. Granovetter, M.: The Strength of Weak Ties. American Journal of Sociology (1973) 1360–1380

40. Weise, P.: Homo oeconomicus und homo sociologicus. Die Schreckensmänner der Sozial-wissenschaften. Zeitschrift für Soziologie (1989) 148–161
41. Schimank, U.: Hochschulforschung im Schatten der Lehre. Campus, Frankfurt/M. (1995)
42. Axelrod, R.: The Evolution of Cooperation. Basic Books, New York (1984)
43. Kehm, B.M.: Universitätskrisen im Spiegel von Hochschulromanen. In Stölting, E., Schimank, U., eds.: Die Krise der Universität. Westdeutscher Verlag, Wiesbaden (2001) Leviathan Sonderheft 20/2001.
44. Cohen, M.D., March, J.G.: ˙Leadership and Ambiguity. The American College President. McGraw Hill, New York (1974)
45. March, J.G., Simon, H.: Organizations. Wiley, New York (1958)
46. Schelling, T.: Economic Reasoning and the Ethics of Policy. In: Choice and Consequence. Harvard University Press, Cambridge, MA (1984) 1–26
47. Bachmann, R.: Kooperation, Vertrauen und Macht in Systemen Verteilter Künstlicher Intel-ligenz. In Malsch, T., ed.: Sozionik — Soziologische Ansichten über künstliche Sozialität. Sigma, Berlin (1998) 197–234
48. Axelrod, R.: An Evolutionary Approach to Norms. American Potitical Science Review (1986) 1095–1111

Sociological Foundation of the Holonic Approach Using Habitus-Field-Theory to Improve Multiagent Systems*

Frank Hillebrandt

Arbeitsbereich Technikbewertung und Technikgestaltung
Technische Universität Hamburg-Harburg
Schwarzenbergstr. 95
21071 Hamburg, Germany
hillebrandt@tu-harburg.de

Abstract. In this paper, I discuss the most important aspects of a sociological foundation of holonic multiagent systems. Pierre Bourdieu's habitus-field-theory forms the sociological basis for my arguments. With this theory I would like to consider the special quality of holons as autonomous and self-organising social entities with clear distinction to the simple coordination of social interactions. Holons are viewed as organisational fields, which are both "autonomous social fields" and "corporate agents". To clarify the advantages of this approach, I introduce a matrix of mechanisms using delegation (task delegation and social delegation) as a central concept to define organisational relationships in task-assignment multiagent systems. Using the matrix of delegation as basic building block, I propose a new dimension of emergent system behaviour in a holonic multiagent system which allows new, qualitative forms of scalability in complex systems of distributed artificial intelligence.

1 Introduction

The task-management in multiagent systems (MAS) is a main topic of the research on Distributed Artificial Intelligence (DAI). In many application domains of MAS, tasks can be decomposed into particular subtasks performed by several agents, and often a domain allows hierarchical decomposition of tasks. This means that analysing a domain may show that a task requires the combination of activities of several agents. To model these combined activities, the concept *holonic agent* or *holon* was introduced (see [1], [2] and [3]) and since then has found increasing application (e.g. in holonic manufacturing systems [4], [5], [6]). The traditional concept of holons developed by Arthur Koestler [7] is based on the idea of recursive or self-similar structures in biological systems. Holons, if they are sub-holons, merge into a new holon the structures and

* This work is an outcome of the research-project "Modeling of Social Organisations using Habitus-Field Theory"—embedded in the German research-field of "socionics"—and was founded by Deutsche Forschungsgemeinschaft under contract FL 336/1-2. I am indebted to Michael Florian, Michael Schillo, Daniela Spresny, Bettina Fley, and Klaus Fischer for many fruitful discussions in our remarkable co-operation without which this article would not have been possible.

K. Fischer. M. Florian, and T. Malsch (Eds.): Socionics, LNAI 3413, pp. 36–50, 2005.

abilities which are similar to the sub-holons the new holon consists of. Any holon is part of a whole and contributes to achieve the goals of this superior whole. This model of recursivity or self-similarity is on the one hand useful to improve MAS architectures because it allows new concepts of scalability (see [8], [9]). Holonic agents are able to act together as a new holonic agent which is able to act as an agent itself. On the other hand, the rigidity of the concept allows poor flexibility of the architecture. Holons on a higher level act similar to holons on a lower level of aggregation. The qualities of the different levels of scale cannot be distinguished sharply.

Parts of DAI (see [3], [10] and [11]) adapted and improved Koestlers definition of holons. The term is used to develop conceptions of MAS which are more flexible and scalable. In this perspective, different forms of association are possible for a holon: Subagents can build a *loose federation*. They share a common goal for a defined period and separate after this period to regulate their own objectives. In this case the agents won't give up their autonomy in principle. In opposite to this scenario agents can fully *merge into a new agent* and give up all parts of their autonomy. In between this two scenarios any mix between both scenarios is possible. For instance, agents are able *to give up their autonomy for certain aspects while retaining it for others.*

This concept of holonic agents is a milestone on the way to develop flexible and different concepts of agent architectures to guide the modeling of scalable and robust MAS. Holons, described as body agents which in turn may be holonic agents them-selves, give up parts of their autonomy to a new holon. This new holonic agent may have capabilities that emerge from the composition of body agents, and it may have actions at its disposal that none of its body agents could perform alone. Furthermore, any holon can be represented by a distinguished head (head holon) which moderates the activities of the body agents and represents the holon to the outside.

This state of the art in modeling holonic MAS allows to specify the emergent sys-tem behaviour based on self-organisation. As we are able to construct various forms of holonic agents, we are able to improve the flexible decisions of agents. It depends on different conditions, either if body agents merge into a new holon by giving up their autonomy as a whole or if they decide to give up only parts of their autonomy to the new holon they participate in. This flexibility is a main condition for self-organisation in holonic MAS. Hence, the holonic approach in DAI allows a theory of self-organisation which can help to construct scalable MAS. Only self-organising MAS are able to reach higher levels of aggregation at runtime. To outline this argument, we have to con-sider that the literature of DAI treats self-organisation like an inherent feature of MAS. Nevertheless, there is no widely accepted definition of the term. Moreover, the term self-organisation is mostly used without any clear conception of what self-organisation could mean especially in the field of DAI. Thus, a few researchers in DAI adapted organisational concepts from social science for the design of self-organising MAS in which agents are not explicitly constructed to cooperatively achieve given goals, but act in a self-interested way and being part of a self-organising MAS (e.g. see [10]). In this view self-organisation is defined as "the process of generating social structure, which is the result of individual choices by a set of agents to engage in interaction in certain organisational patterns." [10]

This definition is related to the most important advantages for the coordination of task management in a distributed MAS.

1. Such self-organising systems will be robust systems because they are more flexible and reliable (see [12]).
2. The agents, a self-organizing MAS consists of, can find better ways to work around unforeseen problems. Thus in MAS the interrelationship between agents will be more dynamic (see e.g. [13], [14], [15]).
3. As distributed social systems, they offer these useful features and for this they are applicable in many domains which cannot be handled by centralised systems (see [16], [17]).

My thesis is that systems constructed in reference to sociological research will be able to work out this advantages in a better way. In this sense, a sociological concept of the study of self-organisation in holonic MAS is indicated. It is focused to improve performance and robustness in semi-open and scalable MAS. Therefore a concept of self-organisation in a strict sociological sense will be proposed in section two. The sociological point of view considers the special quality of self-organisation in autonomous social entities (holons) with a clear distinction to the simple coordination of social interactions. To show this, I will use the basic insights of the habitus-field-theory developed by Pierre Bourdieu. In section three I will connect this concept of self-organisation with a matrix of mechanisms using delegation (task delegation and social delegation) as a central concept to define organisational relationships in task-assignment MAS that we can create with a theory of flexible holons. This combination allows to build different forms of holons which can be described as different organisational forms[1]. With reference to this sociologically founded ideas, I conclude my discussion by describing holons both as self-organising social entities ("autonomous social fields") and "corporate agents" which are competing with other holons in the same domain (section four). In this context I avoid to give instructions for the implementation of the presented ideas. My aim is to create a sociological founded building block to solve some of the basic problems in the construction of highly complex and robust MAS.

2   Self-Organisation in Autonomous Fields

If it is appropriate that MAS, "as they involve multiple agents, are social in character" [19], sociological theory seems to be useful for the improvement of MAS.[2] To show this, I will outline a concept of flexible holons which is motivated by the argument

---

[1] I will not cover this aspect in detail. For further argumentation on organisational forms see the article by M. Schillo and D. Spresny in this volume and [18].

[2] "Much of traditional AI has been concerned with how an agent can be constructed to function intelligently, with a single locus of internal reasoning and control implemented in a Von Neumann architecture. But intelligent systems do not function in isolation—they are at the very least a part of an environment in which they operate, and the environment typically contains other such intelligent systems. Thus, it makes sense to view such systems in societal terms." ([16, p. 81])

that there is a close connection between robustness in terms of scalability and self-organisation in certain scenarios (for details see [20], [18]). The sociological reference for this concept is the habitus-field-theory developed by Pierre Bourdieu. This theory offers a new way to define self-organisation which is useful to develop robust, scalable, and dynamic MAS.

Bourdieu's theory is able to solve one of the major problems of self-organisation in MAS, how to get self-interested agents to arrange themselves to carry out a form of joint action (effectively), although they have distinct goals.[3] A major number of scholars in DAI adopted the idea of the invisible hand (Adam Smith) to overcome this problem. Self-organisation in this sense means that agents do not need to intend to cooperate or coordinate themselves. Social order rather emerges by self-organisation unintendedly from the self-interested interactions of the agents (see e.g. [13]). In the view of Bourdieu's social theory of practice, this concept of social order gives no explanation about the emergence, reproduction, and change of social order due to the actions of self-interested agents on all levels of social aggregation (groups, organisations, networks, society). Furthermore, Bourdieu points out that the self-interest of an agent cannot be reduced to a utility function lacking of content, but is socially structured within a social field (e.g. an organisation) and may change as the field changes. One basic insight of sociologist Bourdieu is: Even though agents are defined as the sources of practice (sociality), there are conditions of self-organisation which can not be related to agents' intentions and goals. Generally, sociality is, in the words of Bourdieu, "bounded not only because the available information is curtailed, and because the human mind is generically limited and does not have the means to fully figure out all situations, especially in the urgency of action, but also because the human mind is socially bounded, socially structured." ([24, p. 126]) In Bourdieu's habitus-field-theory, two forces shape every social context, in which practice is placed in. Firstly, the history of the social field is objectified in the social relationships between the available social positions of a field. Secondly, the individual histories of the agents (habitus) perceive their specific chances to act according to the objective possibilities available in the social field. Both phenomena are necessary conditions of practice. Practice itself influences both of its own conditions, so that field and habitus cannot remain static. They are in permanent change.

The term field within the theory of Bourdieu is an analytical category to describe the *structural* conditions of the practice of agents in general and in the matter of self-organisation. Structures and characteristics of social fields are necessary conditions of dynamic practice. To describe that we have to remark first that any field has its own logic, what makes it autonomous in comparison with other fields. For example, "business is business" (i.e., making profits) is the logic of the economic field. This logic excludes practices which are proceeding in another logic. [24] Furthermore, an analysis in terms of fields involves to map out the objective structure of the relations between the positions occupied by the agents' acting in the context of a specific field. Bourdieu defines a field as a historically developed structure of social forces which does

---

[3] For detailed discussion on this problem in the context of agent based modeling see, e.g., [21], [8], [22], [14], [15]. A discussion of this topic from a sociological point of view can be found in [23].

not consist of subjective links between individuals, but of objective relations between social positions. A position is defined by determinations it imposes upon agents, by the present and potential composition of all sorts of capital (economic, cultural, social, and symbolic capital), and by its relation to other positions. The agents need specific forms of cultural, economic, social, and symbolic capital to take a specific position related to other positions in the field. In these terms the agents' rationality depends on the forms of capital they possess and must be defined as practical sense for the game of the field (illusio).

In this sense, we can compare a field with a game which is not a product of a deliberate act of creation. The game of the field follows regularities that are not explicit and codified. Players (agents) agree to them by the mere fact of playing and not via contract. This collusion is the very basis of their competition. The game defines the worth of the specific forms of capital agents call their own. For this the game is the source of the structured relationship between the agents positions. In the game we have trump cards (capital) the worth of which varies depending on the game. "Just as the relative value of cards changes with each game, the hierarchy of the different species of capital (economic, social, cultural, symbolic) varies across the various fields. In other words, there are cards that are valid, efficacious in all fields—these are the fundamental species of capital—but their relative value as trump cards is determined by each field and even by the successive states of the same field." ([24, p. 98]) The structure of capital an agent holds determines about the access to the specific profits that are at stake in the field. These positions must not be conceived as roles which determine an agent. "It becomes activated and active only if the more or less institutionalised position... finds—like a garment, a tool, a book or a house—someone who sees in it enough of themselves to take it up and make it their own" [25]. In other words: Only if the agents are willing and able to act on the positions they have occupied, practice is possible. "Every field constitutes a potentially open space of play whose boundaries are dynamic borders which are the stake of struggles within the field itself." ([24, p. 104]) In this sense, every field of forces transforms itself into a field of struggle.

Moreover, Bourdieu assumes that agents take positions, because they are self-interested in a specific way. Their interests depend on their objective position in a field, i.e., their interests are socially shaped. Bourdieu assumes that agents act in the field like players in a game. They are taken by the play. Like in a game, agents are opposing one another, and they are interested in improving their relative positions in the field. To clarify this, we have to take into account that any field follows its own "rules". These are, in contrast to a game like it is defined by game-theory, neither explicit norms to be obeyed by individuals nor the product of an intentional act, but *regularities* of practice. As long as the agents in the field give credence to the game, to the profits that can be achieved as well as to the worthiness of the investment in the game, they are reproducing and changing the game, its regularities and structures. Thus, a field is a place "of endless change" [24]. According to Bourdieu, we view the agent as the force behind the development, change, and reproduction of social structure of any field. Therefore, the distribution of all species of capital, the regularities, and even the task structure of a social field can be objects of the agents' attempts to influence the structure of a field in favour of their socially structured interests. In other words: The objectified positions of the field impinge on their occupants, the agents, by their present and potential situations in the structure of the distribution of specific kinds of capital. The possession of social, cultural, and economic capital facilitates access to the specific profits, that are at stake in the field, as well as the objectified relations of the agent's field-position to other positions of the field (see [24, p. 97]). This central argument of the habitus-field-theory does not imply that individuals do not exist. In Bourdieu's view they exist as *agents* "who are socially constituted as active and acting in the field under consideration by the fact that they possess the necessary properties to be effective, to produce effects, in this field" ([24, p. 107]). The basis of this argument is the term *habitus*.

The concept of habitus illustrates that human action in general, and especially in the context of a specific field, is not an instantaneous reaction to immediate stimuli. Note that social reality not only exists in social fields but also exists in the habitus of agents. Bourdieu's theory exhibits the role of the habitus as a necessary intermediate between the social structure of forces and the social action in social fields. "The relation which exists between habitus and the field to which it is objectively adjusted... is a sort of ontological complicity, a subconscious and pre-reflexive fit." ([26, p. 107f.]) This gets clearer as the term field can not be thought independently from the term habitus and vice versa. The habitus of an agent is defined as a set of dispositions to specific ways to percept, think, and perform actions. These dispositions are bounded to the position of the agent within the social structure of a social field. They depend on the history of the individual agent in a field and what it experienced in the past. Dispositions may be incorporated or imitated, i.e., learned by observation and acquired by advice. An agent is only capable to take a position because these dispositions acquired in a specific field enables it to perceive its specific chances and to act according to the objective possibilities available in the social field (for more details see [27], [18], [20]).

This relationship between habitus and field manifests itself in a special sense of the game or feel for the game which emerges from the structures of the field. Only if this happens, the reproduction of practice is possible. Note that this is the meaning of self-organisation in the view of Bourdieu: *Practice cannot be thought as a mechanistic process. It is always a dynamic process which emerges out of the correspondence between habitus and field, based on conditions of practice produced before.*

In a nutshell, fields are self-organising, emergent social entities, because a field is a field of social forces. It shows an objective structure of relations between social positions, a game-like character, and regularities. Without these structures of the field, agents are unable to act. On the other hand, only if agents with habitus are willing and able to act on the positions they have occupied, practice is possible (for more details see [27], [25]). Agents are autonomous as far, as the structures and regularities of a field are getting changed by agents attempting to improve their position within the logic of the field. Fields are self-organising, not least, because the boundaries of a field are getting dynamically determined within the field itself. The limits of a field "are always at stake in the field itself" [28], because participants in a field work to reduce competition by imposing criteria of competency or membership.

MAS are able to profit from this sociological concept of sociality as self-organised practice, if it is possible to model different agents with the ability to reflect and handle the social structures of the society and the social field they act in. MAS with reference to habitus-field-theory not only need agents with a "practical sense" (Bourdieu) for the game they act in. In addition, they need well-modeled constraints representing the highly differentiated social structures of the field the game continues in. In different fields (e.g., organisations) we can identify different forms of rationality according to the socially structured interests of agents placed on different positions within the social field. Thus, it is not intended to conceptualise a model of MAS among cognitive models of social entities, like Panzarasa and Jennings [29] among many others do, as Carley and Gasser pointed out [30]. Instead, a concept is needed which uses the terms habitus and field to transform and implement social structures into the dispositions of agents. For this concept we have to take into account the following aspects:

- From a sociological point of view, self-organisation of sociality (practice) is not a mechanistic but dynamic process. It emerges from the correspondence between (1) the dispositions of an agent to perceive, think, and act (habitus) and (2) a social structure (field). The term field includes at least an objective structure of social positions in a field, specific regularities of practice, and a specific logic of the field.
- Thus, if we consider the agent as the force behind the generation, change, and reproduction of any social entity (field), we have to take into account that agents act in a self-interested way within a field as they try to improve their social positions.
- The self-interest of an agent cannot be represented by a utility function which remains identical in all situations. According to Bourdieu, the rationality of an agent is socially bounded, i.e. it depends on its social position within a field in relation to the positions of other agents, the regularities, the logic of a field, and it depends on the situation.
- The emergence of social fields throughout the interactions of single agents is a very important example for self-organising processes. Therefore, the outlined concept of social entities as autonomous fields is an example for self-organising MAS.
- Because the basic characteristic of a social field is that it is a formally structured social entity to carry out joint actions, it has to be considered as an autonomous field and a corporate agent.

If we describe holons as social fields, and if we consider furthermore the genesis of holons through the interactions between agents in a MAS as one of the most important advancements in the development of holonic MAS architectures, we can figure out the conditions for different decisions of agents in provision for the listed topics. Therefore, as the next step, we need to construct a clear concept of operations - in sociological terms: forms of practices - which are possible in a holonic MAS and which for this reason constrain and enable the self-organisation of a MAS like social structures do in the real social world.

3   Operation Mechanisms to Create Flexible Holons

If we take into account the outlined basic insights of sociologist Bourdieu, we are able to develop a more precise theory to clarify the basic operations of task orientated MAS. Research on MAS that solve a task-assignment problem has for a long time dealt with models of delegation which were restricted to two kinds of settings: settings where agents are benevolent, i.e., they are all designed to share common goals, or settings where agents simulate authority relationships (as in distributed problem solving). Recent work on delegation (see e.g. [28] for an extensive treatment), has shown that delegation is a complex concept highly relevant in MAS, especially in semi-open systems. But neither the benevolence assumption nor the reliance on pre-defined authority relations apply in semi-open MAS, where new agents may join the system because these agents may be self-interested and for which the designer may not have predetermined an organisational role to constrain them in their actions.

As argued above, to solve the task-assignment problem, the ability of agents to co-ordinate and organise themselves is needed.[4] Therefore, I introduce a matrix of mechanisms which allows both, decentralised coordination of assigning tasks as well as the generation of cooperative interrelationships between agents, which I will describe as holonic agents, to carry out tasks jointly. Finally, such a matrix can be used as a basic building block to define a spectrum of holonic organisational forms the agents can choose at run-time to arrange themselves in organisational patterns. Such a matrix can use delegation as a central concept. Following the sociological concept of social delegation, two types of delegation can be distinguished: task delegation and social delegation. Task delegation is the delegation of (autistic, non-social) goals to be achieved and social delegation does not consist of creating a solution or a product but comprises the representation of a group or an organisation. Both types of delegation are for two reasons essential for self-organisation: Firstly, they rely on becoming independent from particular individuals. Secondly, they make it possible to describe and explain the phenomena of our interests at a level of social practice, in particular: the organisation, building of structures, and power relations in the field of organisation.

Task delegation, well-known in DAI, is mainly based on an *economic logic*. Nevertheless, representing groups or teams is also an essential mechanism even in economic situations which have to deal with social processes of organisation, coordination, and social structures. For instance, the procedure of appointing an agent as representative for a group of agents is not exactly defined with the term task delegation. This form of social practice can be called *social* delegation. The task of social delegation is in many respects different from the tasks mentioned previously. It involves a long-termed dependency between delegated agent and represented agent, and the fact that another agent speaks for the represented agent may incur commitments in the future that are not under control to the represented agent. Implicitly, an authority structure is constituted by social delegation. Therefore, social delegation refers to trust and power, whereas task delegation is mainly based on economic principles. Social delegation is a type of operation, which allows much more flexibility and robustness in semi-open MAS. In holonic terms, *social delegation* is a task of the head which, in addition, can also be distributed according to a set of tasks to different agents. This makes social delegation a principle action in the context of flexible holons and provides the basic functionality for self-organisation in the sense of the emergence of social fields throughout the actions of agents.

Given the two types of delegation, it remains to explain how the action of delegation is performed. There are four distinct mechanisms for delegation (see Figure 1). Theo-

---

[4] For the following description see also [18].

retically, every combination of a mode and a mechanism is possible in task-orientated MAS.

- *Economic exchange* is a standard mechanism of markets: the delegate is being paid for doing the delegated task or representation. In economic exchange, a good or task is exchanged for money, while the involved parties assume that the value of both is of appropriate similarity (market price). This mechanism allows decentralised coordination. In order to achieve a global but unintended and uncalculated equilibrium, the price is the necessary and sufficient information the agent has to know to decide.
- *Authority* as a well known social mechanism represents the method of organisation used in distributed problem solving. It implies a non-cyclic set of power relationships between agents along which delegation is performed by order.
- *Gift exchange*, an important mechanism within the theory of Bourdieu, denotes the mutually deliberate deviation from the economic exchange in a market situation. The motivation for the gift exchange is the expectation of either reciprocation or refusal of reciprocation. Both are indications to the involved parties about the state of their relationship in the organisational field regarded, precisely the distribution of power and resources. This kind of exchange entails risk, trust, and the possibility of conflicts (continually no reciprocation) and the need for an explicit management of relationships in the agent. The aim of this mechanism is to accumulate strength in a relationship that may pay-off in the future.
- Another well-known mechanism is *voting*, whereby a group of equals determines one of them to be the delegate by some voting mechanism (majority, two thirds, etc.). As a distinguishing property, we observe that this is the only mechanism that performs a "many to one" delegation, while all other mechanism are used between a delegating agent and a delegate. The description of the mandate (permissions and obligations) and the particular circumstances of the voting mechanism (registering of candidates, quorum) are integral parts of the operational description of this mechanism and must be accessible to all participants.

Social Mechanism	Task Delegation	Social Delegation
Economic Exchange	X	X
Gift Exchange	X	X
Authority	X	X
Voting	X	X

Figure 1: The delegation matrix showing two modes of delegation and four mechanisms for performing each mode.

As is suggested by Figure 1, these four mechanisms work for both types of operation: for example, economic exchange can be used for social delegation as well as for task delegation. Possibly this set of mechanisms is not complete, however, many mechanisms which facilitate self-organisation in human societies, and that do not seem to be covered here, are combinations of the described mechanisms.

In comparison with deterministic models of delegation, task delegation and the choice of the delegate is the result of a reasoning process in this model. This means that agents decide on a case by case basis whether they delegate a task and to whom. The mechanism of delegation makes it possible to pass on tasks (e.g., creating a plan for a certain goal, extracting information) to other individuals and, furthermore, allows specialisation of these individuals for certain tasks (division of labour, task relevant differentiation). Especially the operation of social delegation and the mechanisms of voting and gift exchange support scalability in MAS in that they structure groups of agents. For instance, social delegation initiates in mixture with gift exchange co-operations between agents which in special cases merge into permanent interrelationships, e.g., into organisational forms (for more details see [18] and the article by Schillo and Spresny in this volume). If we combine this insight with the theory of flexible holons, we will see quickly the following: The emergence of groups, teams, or organisations in the real world is in the context of DAI the creation of a holon: „A holonic agent of a well-defined software architecture may join several other holonic agents to form a super-holon; this group of agents now acts as if it were a single holonic agent with the same software architecture." ([3, p. 7]) In reference to the matrix and the basic insights of the habitus-field-theory, we are able to figure out the characteristics of these "super-holons" more clearly. For that, I propose to describe holonic agents as social fields and corporate agents.

4   Holons as Social Fields and Corporate Agents

With Bourdieu's theory, as briefly outlined in section two, such holons can be compared with social fields which have to be characterised by "a structure of objective relations between positions of force" ([31, p. 101]; see also [25], [23]). Anyway, it is not adequate to reduce social fields, and that kind of holon consists of different bodies would be a electronic social field in my view, only to their formal structure (programs, statutes, written rules, etc.) that regulates aims of the social field, membership, communication, division of labour, competencies of members, etc. Bourdieu contradicts this thesis because it is a shortcoming of social theory to consider social fields as static and formal apparatuses only oriented towards a common function in which members adopt the aim of the field they act in mechanically as their own goal [25]. According to Bourdieu, agents are interested in improving their relative positions in the field. They act in a self-interested way. This might appear as an argument against using Bourdieu's theory for modeling MAS because in DAI-literature it is seen as an advantage that formal structures constrain self-interested agents to prevent opportunism. Nevertheless, this is one of the major advantages of considering holons as social fields concerning the problem of self-organisation as mentioned above. With respect to Bourdieu, agents cannot maximise an abstract utility function regardless of the objective structure of positions they occupy within the field as well as of the logic and regularities of a field.

The social structure of a social field in general is a cultural as well as a political construction of dominant and dominated agents. Some agents are dominating according to their property and practical use of powerful resources like economic, cultural, social, and symbolic capital. Therefore, the social structures of any field are formed by relations of power, whereby dominant agents like incumbents aim to reproduce their preeminent position over challengers and dominated agents which themselves try to conquer higher positions in the field-distribution of power and authority [25]. To improve their position in the field, the agents need to play the game according to its own logic. As long as the agents believe in the worthiness of playing the game they build, reproduce, and change the field in a self-interested way to improve their positions in the field using bounded social rationality [27]. The resulting structures and regularities may not be an optimal allocation of the interests or "utility" of every agent, but they enable joint action where decentralised mechanisms fail. Within the logic of special fields, members need to conceive means to carry out decisions and actions in the name of the whole to perform joint actions or tasks. Formal structures can be viewed as such means. In this context, formal structures might be i) an object some agents want to change in favour of their interests, ii) a kind of capital or resources some agents use in favour of their interests, or iii) constraints to which agents may act in a conform way because conformity is beneficial to them.

In principle, a social field of positioned agents is not only a field of forces, it can also be defined as a corporate agent able to act analog to an individual agent (see [23] for a concept of organisations as social fields and corporate agents). This means that these corporate agents, e.g., organisations, are competing with other corporate agents embedded in meta-fields, trying to improve their objective position. Thus holonic agents, e.g., organisations, are not only social fields that appear, get reproduced, and changed by the actions of a quantity of self-interested agents generating, reproducing, and changing formal structures. In addition to this, they are corporate agents: For the foundation of an organisation, member agents need to empower at least one individual agent to act for the whole. Bourdieu figures out, that it is necessary for the formation of a group or an organisation to delegate a representative which is empowered to speak for the other parts of the whole. Only this makes a social entity like an organisation visible to the social environment. Officially, the task of the delegate is to represent the interests of the organisation or group and of it's members. Nevertheless, the delegate has his own socially structured interests due to the position he has in the organisation or the group. These interests may deviate from those of the member agents [31]. This might seem to be a disadvantage for modeling MAS, because the delegate may abuse his position and his power in an opportunistic manner to improve or hold his own position within the organisation or group. In the context of a theory of flexible holons, this is an advantage because if all member agents of a holon would act according to their preferences, the holon as a whole might be unable to act and carry out joint action, it would be nothing more than a crowd of individuals. In this sense, social delegation constitutes a hierarchy between a quantity of agents and is a mechanism that enables coordination by authority. Therefore, this mechanism is necessary for agents to be able to found different flexible holons and to enable self-organisation in MAS. In short, the types of operation and mechanisms of the matrix, described in figure 1, are necessary conditions to model flexible holons as dynamic social fields and corporate agents.

Thus, the allegation that a „holonic multi-agent paradigm is proposed, where agents give up parts of their autonomy and merge into a ‚super-agent' (a holon), that acts – when seen from the outside – just as a single agent again" ([2, p. 1]), can be turned into a sociological paradigm to create flexible holons: If we use the topics of the habitus-field-theory to define the conditions for the cooperation and interrelationships of self-interested agents, we can figure out structural possibilities for the self-organised creation of different holons. Furthermore with this instrument we are able to describe the structures of social delegation in a differentiated way. Thus, we get a guideline to construct the boundary condition for the emergence of holon-heads. The social delegation of head-holons which represent a holon as a whole is the most important social structure to make a holon able to act as an agent. If we take into account that a "super-holon"—a corporate agent—acts differently from an individual agent, we can figure out the problem of scalability in MAS in a new way. Now it is possible to complete the quantitative scalability with a qualitative **dimension**. We are able to distinguish between different scales of social aggregation qualitatively. This opens a way to construct MAS with the ability to reach higher levels of social aggregation through self-organisation, like sociologists define it. The advantages of such scalable systems can be find in the reduction of the quantity of communication acts between different agents even though the agent population scales [18], [10]. Thus, the qualitative scalability of a MAS on higher levels of social aggregation via sociological improved holonic architectures allows a differentiated and flexible way to coordinate the system-operations. This is a basic condition for the robustness of high scalable MAS. Hence, the presented sociologically inspired argumentation creates a building block to overcome some basic problems in modeling and constructing high scaled task-orientated MAS. The construction and implementation of different organisational forms, as presented in the article by Spresny and Schillo in this volume, is a promising work to turn a theory of flexible holons into a treatable MAS (see also [18] for a detailed discussion of this topic).

5   Conclusion

In contrast to a biological foundation of the holonic approach (see, e.g., [6]), a sociological foundation offers a new way to model autonomy and self-organisation in task-assignment domains. It figures out the most important *social* conditions to conceptualise holons as *flexible social fields* and *corporate agents* which are different from individual agents. In short, the most important characteristics and advantages of the outlined theory of flexible holons can be summarised as follows:

1. Self-interested agents must be able to decide between different forms of operations as described in the matrix of delegation (figure 1).
2. These agents have to be provided with different resources that can be, according to Bourdieus habitus-field-theory, defined as economic, cultural, social, and symbolic capital. The process of decision making has to be a result of the combination of this different forms of capital an agent owns.
3. This conditions allow to model MAS that generate social structures at runtime. In holonic architectures these are different forms of flexible holons such as co-operations, groups of agents, networks, organisations, etc.
4. Especially the operation of gift exchange is one of the most important condition for the emergence of different holonic agents. It allows enduring interrelationships between single agents which possibly merge into a flexible holonic agent.

5. In the context of delegation, such flexible holonic agents can be viewed as corporate agents itself because they are able to find a representative out of the agents they consist of. Thus, social delegation is at least one of the most important operations that allows the self-organisation of corporate agents in a holonic MAS.

6. The scalability and robustness of such holonic MAS is based on the topic that it is possible to find a qualitative solution of the problem of scalability in MAS. The emergence of flexible holons, with abilities to act as agents, allows the aggregations of different, qualitative distinguishable levels of sociality in MAS. Thus, the theory of flexible holons is a promising way to define scalability in a sociological founded way.

7. Last but not least, the theory of flexible holons, based on the habitus-field-theory, allows a higher level of variability in the agent based modeling of MAS. This is the basic condition for experiments on social simulation which are able to improve basic assumptions of sociological theory.

The advantages of the outlined sociological concept—to organise a higher level of social aggregation via flexible holons—for the robustness of MAS are already discussed in other articles (see especially [10], [18] and the **contribution of** Schillo and Spresny as well as Fley and Florian, in this volume). This discussion shows that the new kind of social mechanism for social exchange (gift exchange) and a new model of social delegation enable MAS to reduce the quantity of communication acts without reducing the complexity of self-organisation as it is defined at the very beginning of this article. Future work will show that it is possible to iterate the already developed prototype of an flexible MAS, based on the presented main ideas of flexible holons, with the help of a sociological theory of social institutions. In principle, it is possible to improve the outlined concept of flexible holons step by step into more flexibility and for that reason on a higher level of robustness.

References

1. Gerber, C.: Self-Adaptation and Scalability in Multiagent Societies. PhD thesis, Computer Science Department, Universität Saarbrücken (1999)
2. Gerber, C., Siekmann, J., Vierke, G.: Holonic Multi-Agent Systems. Technical Report RR-99-03, German Research Center for Artificial Intelligence (DFKI), Saarbrücken, Germany (1999)
3. Gerber, C., Siekmann, J., Vierke, G.: Flexible Autonomy in Holonic Multiagent Systems. In: AAAI Spring Symposium on Agents with Adjustable Autonomy. (1999)
4. Fischer, K.: Agent-Based Design of Holonic Manufacturing Systems. Journal of Robotics and Autonomous Systems **27** (1999) 3–13
5. Ulieru, M., Walker, S., Brennan, B.: Holonic Enterprise as a Collaborative Information Ecosystem. In: Proceedings of the Workshop on Holons: Autonomous and Cooperating Agents for Industry, Autonomous Agents 2001. (2001)
6. Ulieru, M.: Emergence of Holonic Enterprises from Multi-Agent Systems: A Fuzzy Evolutionary Approach. In: Soft Computing Agents. IOS Press, Amsterdam (2002)
7. Koestler, A.: The Ghost in the Machine. Hutchinson & Co, London (1967)
8. Jennings, N.: Agent-based Computing: Promise and Perils. In: Proceedings of the 16th International Joint Conference on Artificial Intelligence (IJCAI-99). (1999) 1429–1436

9. Weiß, G.: Prolog. In: Multiagent Systems: A Modern Approach to Distributed Artificial Intelligence. MIT Press (1999) 1–23

10. Schillo, M.: Self-Organization and Adjustable Autonomy: Two Sides of the Same Medal? In Hexmoor, H., Falcone, R., eds.: Proceedings of the AAAI2002 Workshop on Autonomy, Delegation, and Control: From Inter-agent to Groups. (2002)

11. Schillo, M., Zinnikus, I., Fischer, K.: Towards a Theory of Flexible Holons: Modelling Institutions for Making Multiagent Systems Robust. In: 2nd Workshop on Norms and Institutions in MAS. (2001)

12. O'Hare, G.M.P., Jennings, N.R.: Foundations of Distributed Artificial Intelligence. John Wiley and Sons (1996)

13. Castelfranchi, C.: Engineering Social Order. In Omicini, A., Tolksdorf, R., Zambonelli, F., eds.: Engineering Societies in the Agent World, 1st International Workshop (ESAW 2000) in ECAI 2000. Lecture Notes in Computer Science, vol. 1972, Berlin et al., Springer-Verlag (2000) 1–18

14. Macy, M.W., Willer, R.: From Factors to Actors: Computational Sociology and Agent-Based Modeling. Annual Reviews of Sociology 28 (2002) 143–166

15. Sawyer, R.K.: Artificial Societies: Multiagent Systems and Micro-Macro Link in Sociological Theory. Sociological Methods and Research 31 (2003) 325–363

16. Huhns, M.N., Stephens, L.M.: Multiagent Systems and Societies of Agents. In: Multiagent Systems: A Modern Approach to Distributed Artificial Intelligence. MIT Press, Boston, MA (1999) 79 ff.

17. Weiß, G.: Adaptation and Learning in Multi-agent Systems: Some Remarks and a Bibliography. In: Adaptation and Learning in Multi-agent Systems. Springer (1996)

18. Schillo, M., Fischer, K., Fley, B., Florian, M., Hillebrandt, F., Spresny, D.: FORM - A Sociologically Founded Framework for Designing Self-Organization of Multiagent Systems. Lecture Notes in Computer Science, vol. 2934. In: Proceedings of the International Workshop on Regulated Agent-Based Social Systems: Theories and Applications, Lecture Notes in Artificial Intelligence. Springer-Verlag, Berlin et al. (2004) 156–175

19. Gasser, L.: Social Conceptions of Knowledge and Action: DAI Foundations and Open Systems Semantics. In: Readings in Agents. Morgan Kaufmann, San Francisco., Cal. (1997) 389–404

20. Schillo, M., Bürckert, H.J., Fischer, K., Klusch, M.: Towards a Definition of Robustness for Market-Style Open Multi-Agent Systems. In: Proceedings of the Fifth International Conference on Autonomous Agents (AA'01), New York, ACM Press (2001) 75–76

21. Carley, K.M., Prietula, M.J., Lin, Z.: Design Versus Cognition: The interaction of agent cognition and organizational design on organizational performance. Journal of Artificial Societies and Social Simulation 1 (1998)

22. Lesser, V.R.: Cooperative Multiagent Systems. A Personal View of the State of the Art. IEEE Transactions on Knowledge and Data Engeneering 11 (1999)

23. Dederichs, A.M., Florian, M.: Organisationen und Akteure – eine organisationssoziologische Skizze. In: Bourdieus Theorie der Praxis. Erklärungskraft - Anwendung – Perspektiven, Opladen, Wiesbaden. (2002) 69–96

24. Bourdieu, P., Wacquant, L.: An Invitation to Reflexive Sociology. Polity Press, Chicago (1992)

25. Bourdieu, P.: Pascalian Meditations. Polity Press, Cambridge (2000)

26. Bourdieu, P.: In Other Words. Essays Towards a Reflexive Sociology. Polity Press, Cambridge (1990)

27. Schillo, M., Fischer, K., Hillebrandt, F., Florian, M., Dederichs, A.: Bounded Social Rationality: Modelling self-organization and adaptation using habitus-field theory. In Jonker, C., Lindemann, G., Leita, I., Uthmann, T., eds.: Proceedings of the Workshop on Modelling Artificial Societies and Hybrid Organizations (MASHO) at ECAI 2000. (2000) 112–122

28. Castelfranchi, C., Falcone, R.: Towards a theory of delegation for agent-based systems. Robotics and Autonomous Systems **24** (1998) 141–157
29. Panzarasa, P., Jennings, N.R.: The Organisation of Sociality: A Manifesto for a New Science of Multi-agent Systems. In: Proceedings of the 10th Workshop on Mulit-agent systems. (MAAMAW '01). (2001)
30. Carley, K.M., Gasser, L.: Computational Organization Theory. In: Multiagent Systems: A Modern Approach to Distributed Artificial Intelligence. MIT Press, Cambridge, MA (1999) 299–330
31. Bourdieu, P.: Delegation and Political Fetishism. Thesis Eleven **10/11** (1984/1985) 56–70

Linking Micro and Macro Description of Scalable Social Systems Using Reference Nets

Michael Köhler, Daniel Moldt, Heiko Rölke, and Rüdiger Valk

University of Hamburg, Department of Computer Science
Vogt-Kölln-Str. 30, D-22527 Hamburg
{koehler,moldt,roelke,valk}@informatik.uni-hamburg.de

Abstract. Socionics attempts to release the architecture of multi-agent systems from the restrictive micro perspective viewpoint by the integration of the macro perspective in order to arrive at innovative agent systems. This paper shows how central research topics of sociology and computer science can be combined, in order to arrive at innovative agent systems. In the context of sociology the duality of micro and macro elements is relevant, while recursiveness of models appears in the perspective of computer science. These two elements are unified in our work to the socionic multi-agent architecture SONAR.

The formal model, on which the representation bases, is the recursive formalism of reference nets—an extension of Petri nets that permits to understand nets again as tokens. With the help of these nets first of all a compact implementation of the multi-agent architecture MULAN is designed, secondly it serves as a description language for the sociological model, which is the fundament of SONAR. The main result here is to present an architecture based on MULAN and SONAR allowing to cover the micro as well as the macro perspective in agent-oriented modelling. Doing so, we introduce a scalable model based on agent systems.

1 Introduction

Multi-agent systems (MAS) permit social behaviour by their structure, since they are conceived as a system, where agents furnish services in a co-operative way (for an introduction to this topic see [1]). Current research shows that the restriction to actor-centred aspects, which is taken by agent orientation, does not include relevant social aspects—as for example social norms (see [2]).

This lack of sociological founding is one of the challenges of the socionic approach. Programmatically, Malsch poses the question: "How can technology learn from sociology?" [3, p. 9].[1] We should not forget, however, that sociology does not supply final answers, but theories which have to be transformed into the form of models suitable for

---

[1] "Modern society offers a rich reservoir of archetypes for the modelling of multi-agent systems with their social roles and cultural values, norms and conventions, movements and institutions, power and governance conditions. By this, computer science may take profits in learning adaptiveness, robustness, scalability, and reflexivity of social systems and convert their building principles into efficient technologies." [4, own translation]

K. Fischer, M. Florian, and T. Malsch (Eds.): Socionics, LNAI 3413, pp. 51–67, 2005.
© Springer-Verlag Berlin Heidelberg 2005

computer science. Only such a modelling makes it possible to use the sociological concepts profitably for the foundation of MAS. Similarly, sociology profits from computer science, by receiving an instrument to validate their theories.[2]

For the research of the ASKO[3] project the question arose how to relate the core abilities of two entirely different scientific disciplines in such a way, that synergetic effects will appear. One of the main problems is to (re)present central theoretical elements present in each discipline such that both project partners can work on. This paper reflects the way computer and social scientists exchange their views in our project.

Within the scope of the ASKO project the MULAN-Architecture has been developed (see [5]). Duvigneau et al. [6] presented the FIPA (Foundation for Intelligent Physical Agents) compliant extension CAPA[4]. With ACE[5] it has been shown how to integrate CAPA and applications build on top of it into the *agentcities* network. All three tool sets have been implemented on the basis of the tool RENEW[6] [7] and on Java. Within our overall framework, interfaces for the connection to any Java accessible tool is provided. This allows for the inclusion of Prolog or any other language for the internal treatment of an agent if this seems to be appropriate.

Within this contribution we present a proposal for a sociological layer on top of this framework: SONAR. This is necessary since CAPA or ACE do not provide any support for the inclusion of social patterns. During the ASKO project and the associated ongoing research undertaken by our group the modelling of social theories was a permanent challenge. It became obvious that a technical framework with some special pattern and architecture support for sociological models is needed.

Therefore, we present the conceptual sociological patterns in this contribution derived from an intensive modelling process with sociologists. The general results in the area of modelling sociological theories, socionics, has been demonstrated: following the main ideas of C.A. Petri causal dependencies have been modelled (cf. [8]). One important sociological outcome of the project is the work of Langer [9] who provided, in parallel to our work in computer science, a thorough integration of sociological theories for the sociological community.

It is most noticeable that in the main concepts we came to very similar results. These are reflected in a three level schema, which illustrates a specific view on social systems. It allows relating actors and social structures via social processes. It is assumed that these are the main basic entities, which can be found in a social system. Furthermore, predisposed structures can be identified within these entities which characterise the relations to other entities and therefore make direct interaction superfluous. Taking an engineering viewpoint on our systems the MULAN-agents are some kind of basic actors, which are embedded in a proto-social reality. The models about the other agents and

---

[2] "Sociology may profit from computer science, by using the multi-agent technology as a simulation tool for the examination and elaboration of its own terms, models, and theories. Here new possibilities open to reproduce and experimentally test dynamic reciprocal effects between micro phenomena (social acting) and macro phenomena (social structure)." [4, own translation]

[3] Acting in social contexts (German: Agieren in sozialen Kontexten).

[4] Concurrent Agent Platform Architecture

[5] Agent Cities Environment

[6] Reference Net Workshop

itself *within* a MULAN-agent represent the incorporated social models for that particular agent. Since it is a mental model, which does not need to reflect any physical reality, this model can be incomplete, inconsistent etc. This leads to the entity model which is the key concept for the SONAR-architecture. Actors, processes, and structures can be considered to be first order objects within the *mind* of an agent.

Our main result is that we can provide an architecture for the integration of social models into our agents minds. The basis for the conceptual modelling are *reference nets* [10]. These nets provide the expressibility and flexibility that is required for such an elaborated architecture. The specific implementation within the actual practical framework uses reference nets again to obtain a first prototype, which illustrates the principle behaviour. For more elaborated implementation, our framework allows for the inclusion of any other programming language.

We can provide agents that have their own mind-models within which any kind of social model can be supported. It should be noted that the *micro-macro link* model allows to cope not only with the influence of norms on the behaviours of actors but also with the emergence of macro structures due to actions of actors. This adaption of the micro-macro duality into our MAS architecture contributes to the flexibility of the system, since on the one hand, it allows to control itself and on the other hand it allows to cope with unforeseen external disturbances by the emergence of (social) structures.

In particular our research investigates how the sociological treatment of the micro-macro duality contributes to scalable MAS architectures in computer science. On the other hand it is to observe that the research on recursive (or reflexive) systems leads to a valuable contribution to theory construction in sociology. The combination of both research questions connects in a two-fold way to the *scalation problem*: First of all a *qualitative* scaling on the level of concepts, since the actors perspective is not only to be regarded, but also the structure side, as well as the mutual influence of both. Thus, more expressive metaphors for MAS architectures are obtained. Secondly, recursive modelling results in scaling with respect to a more *quantitative* point of view, since it allows to reduce systems complexity by recursion.

Both, the technical representation of our MAS, and the conceptional transformation of the sociological theory are based on a recursive structure, so that a common base formalism seems to be convenient.

This contribution is organised as follows: Section 2 gives a short introduction towards the model of Petri nets and describes its specific extensions to reference nets. In Section 3, we discuss the basic concepts of multi-agent systems. We show how they are implemented in the reference net based MULAN architecture. The sociological part of the work begins in Section 4, with a representation of the micro-macro link and its connection to MAS. In Section 5 we will discuss the central connecting link between the micro and the macro level: It concerns the predisposition of actors, processes, and structures. The unification of the elements "actors", "processes", and "structure" with their mutual effects are investigated in Section 6. As a result the *entity model* is obtained. This model forms the background for the definition of socionic agents within the SONAR architecture, which is presented in Section 7. The final section summarises the main ideas.

2 Petri Nets and Reference Nets

A Petri net is a (bipartite) directed graph with two different kinds of nodes: *places* (passive elements) and *transitions* (active elements). Places represent resources that can be available or not, or conditions that may be fulfilled. Places are depicted in diagrams as circles or ellipses. Transitions are denoted as rectangles or squares. A transition that fires (or: occurs) removes resources or conditions (for short: tokens) from places and inserts them into other places. This is determined by arcs that are directed from places to transitions and from transitions to places (see also [11]). Petri nets are a well established means for the description of concurrent systems. Petri nets allow for an intuitive representation of the notions of causality, alternatives, parallelism, non-determinism, resource, action, and others. An example for the dynamics of Petri nets is given in Figure 1. The transition act *may* occur ("fire"), because the places p_1, p_2, and p_3 (the preconditions of transition act) are marked, but it does not have to fire. If the action is carried out, the marking of the net changes: now the places p_4 and p_5 (the postconditions) will be marked.

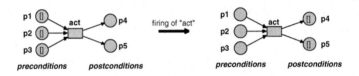

Fig. 1. A possible action and the outcome of the action.

Coloured Petri nets [12,13] allow to combine parts of a Petri net with the same structure by a *folding* operation. Arcs are inscribed with variables that are *bound* to available (coloured) tokens. So one transition may describe a multitude of possible actions dependent of its binding—each of these bindings is equivalent to a single transition in the unfolded ordinary (non-coloured) Petri net. Tokens are removed and created in accordance to the binding of the firing transition.

The paradigm of "nets-within-nets" introduced by Valk [14,15] formalises the aspect that tokens of a Petri net can also be nets (see Figure 2). Such *net tokens* are a conceptual advancement (from simple Petri nets to coloured Petri nets to nets-within-nets), because they introduce recursivity to the Petri net theory (see also [16,17]). Taking this as a view point it is possible to model hierarchical structures in an elegant way. Reference nets by Kummer [10] are a variant of this paradigm where net tokens are references to nets. The same net may be referenced several times. Reference nets are implemented in the Petri net simulator RENEW [7].

A net that contains nets as tokens is called a *system net*. The net tokens are *object nets*. Nested hierarchies with more than two levels are possible, even more, any reference structure including cyclic and hence reflective ones are allowed. In Figure 2 place p_1 of the system net contains an object net as a token. The inscription on:channel(42) of the transition t in the system net is a so called *downlink* to the object net. The cor-

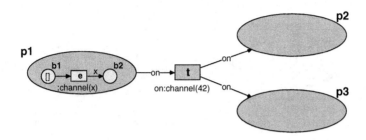

Fig. 2. A Petri net as a token.

responding *uplink* :channel(x) in the object net is inscribed to transition *e*. Uplink and downlink constitute a *synchronous channel*, a communication means in reference nets. Both transitions that form the parts of the synchronous channel may only fire synchronously. When firing, it is possible to exchange information from one transition to another (bi-directional). In the example, *t* and *e* may only fire together and if they do so, the value 42 is passed to the variable *x*. In more complex nets several downlinks and uplinks may match. They are bound at runtime as a part of the token-to-variable binding search of the Petri net simulator.

3   The Multi-agent System *MULAN*

Today, agents and multi-agent systems (MAS) are one of the most important structuring concepts for complex software systems (see for example [18]). By including attributes like autonomy, cooperation, adaptability, and mobility agents go well beyond the concept of objects and object-oriented software development.

The multi-agent system architecture MULAN [5] is based on the "nets-within-nets" paradigm, which is used to describe the natural hierarchies in an agent system. MU-LAN is implemented in RENEW, the integrated development environment (IDE) and simulator for reference nets. MULAN has the general structure as depicted in Figure 3: each box describes one level of abstraction in terms of a system net. Each system net contains object nets, which structures are made visible by the ZOOM lines.[7] The figure shows a simplified version of MULAN, since for example several inscriptions and all synchronous channels are omitted. Nevertheless this is an executable model.

The net in the upper left of Figure 3 describes an agent system, which places contain agent platforms as tokens. The transitions describe communication or mobility channels, which build up the infrastructure.[8]

By zooming into the platform token on place p1, the structure of a platform becomes visible, shown in the upper right box. The central place agents hosts all agents, which are currently on this platform. Each platform offers services to the agents, some of

---

[7] This zooming into net tokens should not to be confused with place refining.

[8] The multi-agent system net shown in the figure is just an illustrating example, the number of places and transitions or the interconnections have no further meaning.

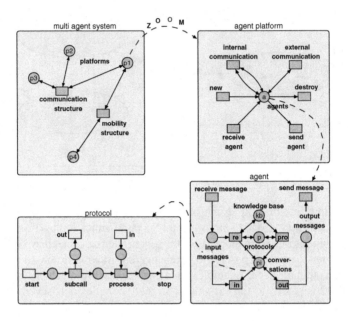

Fig. 3. Agent systems as nets-within-nets.

which are indicated in the figure.[9] Agents can be created (transition new) or destroyed (transition destroy). Agents can communicate by message exchange. Two agents of the same platform can communicate by the transition internal communication, which binds two agents, the sender and the receiver, to pass one message over a synchronous channel.[10] External communication (external communication) only binds one agent, since the other agent is bound on a second platform somewhere else in the agent system. Also mobility facilities are provided on a platform: agents can leave the platform via the transition send agent or enter the platform via the transition receive agent.

The figure abstracts quite some details of the platform for the reason of simplicity. An important feature that cannot be seen is that a platform may itself act like an agent. By this means, arbitrary hierarchies of agents and platforms are possible, in particular a platform is able to encapsulate its agents from the outside world.

An agent is a message processing entity. It must be able to receive messages, possibly process them and generate messages of its own. Each agent consists of exactly one *agent net* that is its interface to the outside world (in the lower right corner of the figure) and an arbitrary number of *protocols* (lower left corner) modeling its behaviour. The agent may exchange messages with other agents via the platform. This is done using the transitions receive message and send message. These two transitions are

---

[9] Note that only mandatory services are mentioned here. A typical platform will offer more and specialised services, for example implemented by special service agents.

[10] This is just a technical point, since via synchronous channels provided by RENEW asynchronous message exchange can be implemented.

the only interconnection of the agent to the rest of the (multi-)agent system, so the agent is a strongly encapsulated entity.

The central point of activity of a such an agent is the selection of protocols and therewith the commencement of conversations [19]. The protocol selection can basically be performed pro-actively (the agent itself starts a conversation) or reactively (protocol selection based on a conversation activated by another agent).[11] This distinction corresponds to the bilateral access to the place holding the protocols (**protocols**). The only difference in enabling and occurrence of the transitions **re** (reactive) and **pro** (pro-active) is the arc from the place **input messages** to the transition **re**. So the latter transition has an additional input place: the incoming messages buffer. It may only be enabled by incoming messages. Both the reaction to arriving messages and the kick-off of a (new) conversation is influenced by the knowledge of an agent. In the case of the pro-active protocol selection, the place **knowledge base** is the only proper enabling condition, the protocols are a side condition. In simple cases the knowledge base can be implemented for example as a subnet, advanced implementations as the connection to an inference engine are also possible (and have been put into practise).

The activities of an agent are modelled as protocol Petri nets (or short: protocols)—an example is given in the lower left corner of the figure. The variety of protocols ranges from simple linear step-by-step plans to complex dynamic workflows. Petri nets are well suited for the modelling of procedures or process flows what can be by their wide-spread use in the area of (business) process modelling [21]. A selected and activated protocol[12] is also called a conversation because it usually includes the exchange of messages with other agents. A conversation can, however, also run internally, therefore without message traffic. A freshly invoked conversation holds an unambiguous identification that is not visible in the figure. All messages belonging to a conversation carry this identification as a parameter to assign them properly. If an agent receives a message carrying such a reference to an existing conversation, transition **in** is enabled instead of transition **re**. The net inscriptions that guarantee this enabling are not represented in the figure for reasons of simplicity. The transition **in** passes incoming messages to the corresponding conversation protocol in execution.

4   The Micro-macro Link

Two major views exist within sociology: the micro-perspective and the macro-perspective. While the micro-perspective is actor-oriented—and hence usually related with MAS—the macro-perspective is structure-oriented, which usually applies categories like norms, values and roles to describe social phenomena. At the same time it is most noticeable that sociology does not separate both perspectives, even more, they are considered as being mutually relevant for each other. Examples are: Bourdieu [22,23] with the consideration of dialectic conception of Habitus and Field (German: Habitus-Feld), Elias [24] with the consideration of group norms and superego (German: Über-Ich)

---

[11] The fundamental difference between pro-active and reactive actions is of great importance when dealing with agents. For an introduction cf. [20].

[12] Following the object-oriented nomenclature one speaks of an instantiated net or protocol (that is represented in form of a net).

and Schimank [25] with the consideration of actors and structural dynamics (German: Strukturdynamik). In the same way Giddens [26] proposes to overcome the separation of the perspectives by the duality of structures: social actors reproduce by their actions those conditions (structures) that made their actions possible. Structures are medium and result of social actions at the same time. Esser [27] introduces the notions of *logic of the situation*, *selection*, and *aggregation*.

Socionics considers the micro-macro link (MML) to be especially important (see e.g. [4,28]). The reason is that the MML can be seen as the key concept for the construction of scalable MAS as their flexibility relies on the dual (re-)production of both. Since the MML is also a central issue of the ASKO project our work has led to a general model (see [29]). It shows the three basic elements *structure*, *process*, and *actor* with their mutual dependencies to illustrate that micro and macro levels are not refined or abstracted versions, but on the contrary can be integrated at the same modelling level.[13] The result was possible due to a vertical structuration of the model according to the underlying social theory. Figure 4 shows how the nets-within-nets Paradigm is used for modelling, based on the techniques of reference nets.

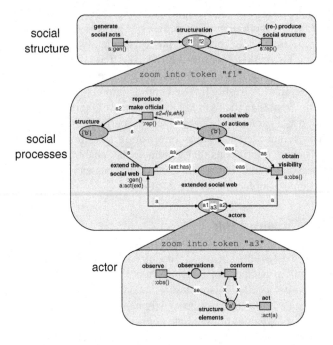

Fig. 4. Mutual relation of structure, process, and actor.

---

[13] The model does not *force* to consider neither the pre-determined micro structure as a result of macro structures as in [30] nor the other way around as in [31]. Therefore, the model should not overemphasise the structural or the interaction perspective. For a detailed discussion cf. Köhler and Rölke [8, Chapter 11 and 12].

The basic description level (the Petri net on the top of Figure 4) shows the dialectics of structure and action with their mutual influence and conditionality. Acting entities or actors, who can be found at the bottom of Figure 4, base their actions on the structuration elements which reflect their internal logic. Examples of such are the actor models of *homo sociologicus* and *homo oeconomicus* (see [25]).

The reciprocity of both, structure and actor, is analysed under the notion of processes: actions and structures reproduce each other mutually, often even identically (see the middle part of Figure 4). The processing entities are located at the actors' side and at the society's side. Between both sides (micro and macro) a process of exchange takes place, covering both directions. An example for a process with the direction of action from the macro level to the micro level is the adoption of actors with respect to normative expectations. For the other direction, creation of new institutions as the result of the common interaction of actors is an example. Typical processes are: power struggle (German: Machtkampf) [32], social distance or demarcation of groups (German: Abgrenzung) against outsiders [33], or war of capital (German: Kapitalkampf) [22].

5   Predisposed Structures

Analysis of the micro-macro-relations within social theories has shown consistently that existing social structures are built on some predisposition of social structures and actors. In the case of such predispositions social processes reproduce the status quo. Systems incorporating actors with predispositions are more difficult to irritate[14] since the structures are internalised, causing the actors to try to keep the actual state.

Elias describes predispositions as the adjustments of superego and social norms (see also Chapter 3 in [8]). His assumption with respect to actors is, that they fear to loose the love of others or their reputation. This fear causes the adoption to social supervision. It means that external obligations (German: Fremdzwänge) have been internalised by self obligations (German: Selbstzwänge). The internalisation is modelled as the superego, implying a separation from the *Ego* (German: Ich). This self control results in a behaviour which is in conformance with the norms. Fear of the actor gets reduced by the confirmation from the group. On the actor side norms and self control have a reciprocal relationship.

Bourdieu also introduced the idea of predisposition, however, he used the *Habitus* and *Field* concepts (see Chapter 5 in [8]). Habitus is the universal recognition, thought, and action schema of an actor that has been incorporated. This incorporated Habitus has been set by the Field that generates exactly those actions which caused its creation. In this way also the preconditions are reproduced which have led to the construction of the Field.

Something similar is described by Popitz on the basis of behaviour regularities (see Chapter 10 in [8]). Actors make their behaviour to be predictable by making it regular. With each of their innumerable ordinary small conform actions, the actors proceed to construct the order of relationships into which they get tied more and more. Since they invest into this order they want to keep it.

---

[14] Note, that this inertance might be positive or negative depending on the current state of the system.

The modelling of the micro-macro-link within the social theories on the basis of predisposed structures shows that it is not necessary to consider both perspectives *directly*, since they are indirectly reflected within the other one. To rephrase it: each actor incorporates the social structure, even if his view may be incomplete or blurred, and each structure appears as the normalised image of the underlying logic of the actions.

This mirroring in form of predisposed structures relieves computer science of a dilemma: on the one hand, it is not necessary to consider actors as equal model elements as processes and social structures, so that models can go conceptually beyond pure actor approaches. On the other hand, agents remain the key concept within agent systems. So the problem of representing both micro and macro elements is resolved since the agent does not look at its environment in terms of an agent system but as a system that consists of the three basic entities "social structure", "process", and "actor".

SONAR-agents incorporate these basic elements. Similar to the Habitus of Bourdieu or the superego of Elias, social entities are not a conscious form like e.g. *knowledge*. An appropriate implementation must follow on a level that is *below* the rational one, since the central impetus of the actors are concepts like the superego or the Habitus, which are not rational but incorporated and influenced by fears and emotions. For this reason every approach to extend the rational agent to a social-rational one (as in [34]) is not suitable. Norms are not followed due to rational planning processes, but they are incorporated, i.e. sub-rational. Norms can be seen as the summary of all behaviour rules of an agent. These rules are often of a symbolic nature. Even if they are represented explicitly this is no contradiction to our claim that norms should be represented implicitly: it is possible for the agent to conclude from the rules to its norms and to make them explicit by this, however, this process is also possible for humans. This act of self-reflection is usually very tedious and only happens in extreme situations. Therefore, this is not relevant for social acting in standard situations.

6   The Entity-Model

Recapitulating, an extended reflection of actor *and* structure *and* their processes results in a *scalability on a conceptual level*. There is no *single* dominating perspective and the reciprocal interaction comes to the fore. The metaphorical conception of our socionic MAS is based on the elements "structure", "process", and "actor". So, the system view is broadened, which leads to a conceptual improvement for our model, since not only actor-to-actor interactions are considered, but also process-like and structural effects.

For this extension, the scalation-problem reappears in different disguise. The questions now is: how can the interrelationship of structure, process, and actor be captured, such that emergent phenomena are possible. This theoretical question can be tackled by realising that the base elements (structure, process, and actor) are occurrences of the *same* element. These abstract elements are called *social entities* in the following. An entity is characterised by a more abstract structure and functionality, which subsumes the more concrete ones (cf. [9]).

From an analytical perspective all social entities are basically equal. Differences are only due to the observers perspective, i.e. the interpretation of an entity as a structure (or as a process or an actor) depends on the observing entity, which emphasises certain aspects of the entity, while disregarding others. So, the observer—an entity itself—treats other entities as a structure (process or actor) and thus creates social reality of the actual considered facet of this entity.

From a theoretical point of view this abstraction from the trinity of "structure", "process", and "actor" towards the base element "social entity" has great impact of the induced social model. The hierarchical model of Figure 4 is replaced by a *recursive* one: entities are related to entities, but also the relationship is an entity, which itself can interact with other entities and so on. It is easy to see, that the recursive structure is a necessary prerequisite for emergence, since it allows the emergent creation of new system qualities *without* the need for additional base elements in the model.[15]

The set of possible relationships between entities extends the dominant actor-actor relationship. For example, the relationship of structure and actor is the influence of norms and roles restricting the actor; the relationship of process and structure can be interpreted as the reproduction of social structure or the accreditation of common social patterns represented by the process.

On the abstract level of entities the interaction-mechanism can be based on three central concepts: acceptance, competence and symbols (cf. Chapter 12 in [8]). *Acceptance* is the basic mechanism for entities, which classifies a certain constellation of phenomena as socially relevant. So, one entity can be accepted by some entities and ignored by others. *Competence* is an attribute, which is appointed when other entities belief in the potential of the attributed entity. The ownership of competence discharges entities from demonstrating continually their abilities. Competence is usually exposed by symbols, e.g. titles. *Symbols* are needed to communicate the social structure. They are used constantly to negotiate "the right way" of doing.

7 The *SONAR*-Architecture

In the following we describe how a system of social entities can be put into practice using reference nets. Reference nets are the obvious choice for the implementation formalism since the recursive nature of entities is also inherent to reference nets (since nets are tokens of nets again).

To give an example consider the mental model $E(s_1)$ of the agent s_1 depicted in Figure 5. The entities (the boxed elements) are related by their social relationships (indicated by arrows). The entity system of Figure 5 has the actor-like entities s_1, s_4, and s_6—representing some students—and p_2 and p_4—representing professors. The individuals are connected to their roles, described by the structure-entities "students" and "professors". Also, an process-entity is present: "improvement of lectures" denotes the discussion process of students and professors about the quality of lectures.[16]

---

[15] If emergent system qualities need a new base element, an infinite regress starts, since emergent qualities based on emergent qualities need new base elements again.

[16] The close relationship to the recursive concept of holons is remarkable: similar to entities a holon is either an agent or is an aggregation of holons itself—analogously for entities. The basic relationship in holonic systems is delegation. This is different for entities, since structural effects—like social control, roles, or norms—cannot be subsumed by this metaphor. So,

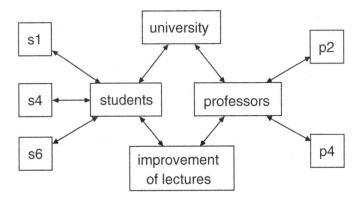

Fig. 5. An agent's mental model based on entities.

The concrete implementation of an entity as a reference net is shown in Figure 6. Social entities generate a web of relationships constructed by the mechanism of acceptance corresponding to the transition accept. The channel :an(x) is used to denote the accepted entity x. The emergent generation of social objects is modelled by the creation of new reference nets, implemented by the inscription e: new entity of the transition symbolise, which generates a new entity e. The assignment of competence creates new relationships, which is expressed by generating new references on the place references to other entities by the transition assign competence. The channel x:an(y) connects the firing of transition assign competence dynamically with transition accept. In the resulting state (the system's marking) the entity y is accepted in the entity net x.

The dynamics of a system of entity nets, i.e. the transition firing sequences and the nets being created, can be illustrated best by an example. In the following the system dynamics evolving from the state given in Figure 5 is considered. The representation of the entity system as a reference net system is shown in Figure 7. Each boxed net shows one instance of the entity net from Figure 6. The nets-within-nets references implementing the entity-to-entity relation are depicted as dashed arrows. One "owner" of the entity-system (e.g. s_1) might recognise for himself that the entity p_4 is heavily involved in the process "improvement of lectures". This recognised involvement can be made explicit by the transition symbolise resulting in a fresh entity-net. This entity is represented internally by the net's identity. For easier presentation the entity is called "concerned-about-lectures" in the following. Then, the relationship of p_4 and "concerned-about-lectures" as well as "improvement of lectures" and "concerned-about-lectures" is created by the firing of transition assign competence, which expresses that p_4 is concerned about lectures and this concern is embedded in the process of the improvement of lectures.

Assume furthermore that almost all actors have created the new entity "concerned-about-lectures" inside their mental models. The communication about the new entity

---

holonic models can be seen as a special case of the unity-model, where all entities are actor-like entities.

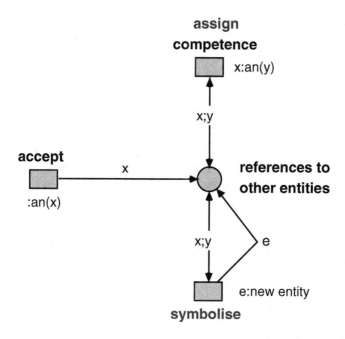

Fig. 6. Reference net model of a social entity.

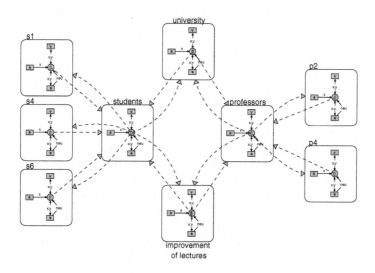

Fig. 7. System of entities implemented by reference nets.

then may lead to the creation of a structure-entity: the entity "concerned-about-lectures" is institutionalised resulting in the new entity "assistant dean for lecture quality". This entity is official, since it is connected with the entity "university".

The recursive structure of the entity model is the foundation of the social model of SONAR-agents. The dynamics of a concrete entity system can be constructed using the existing MULAN-architecture. Each entity can be implemented as a special agent: the entity-agent. So, the entity system is a special multi-agent system. As shown in Figure 8, MULAN-agents are located on platforms. This embedding—presented in Section 3—is recursive, since it is possible to use a MULAN-agent as a platform again. The recursive structure of MULAN is exploited to integrate the entity model into the SONAR-architecture: a SONAR-agent is the platform for the multi-agent system of entity-agents, i.e. the agent s_1 is the platform for his entity system $E(s_1)$ of Figure 5, analogously for s_4, s_6 etc. Thus, the SONAR-architecture induces a structure like the one of Figure 9.

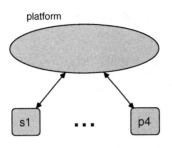

Fig. 8. MULAN-agents

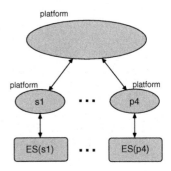

Fig. 9. SONAR—agents as a platform for a system of entity-agents

8 Summary

Requirements of today's systems demand for increasingly flexible architectures. To meet these requirements, powerful concepts suitable for modelling social theories must be used, whereby both the technical and the conceptual side should be sufficiently respected. Reference nets fulfil the modelling challenges of dynamic systems, since appropriate structures can be represented using Petri nets. This model is realised in a technical view via the MULAN architecture, in sociological and/or conceptual aspect in form of SONAR agents.

Tying up to the modelling of micro-macro phenomena, worked out by Langer [9] and to the predispositions of actors, proposed by Köhler et al. [29], an entity model is presented, whose central concepts—social structure, process, and actor—constitute fundamental units for social systems. These are understood as *social entities*, permitting to build the basis of a reflexive and recursive entity model.

Following fundamental ideas of important sociologists, entities can be understood as a most complex structure within agents. Such entity models are completely integrated within the SONAR agents, while the respective agents are modelled within the MULAN-architecture. This results in the modelling of arbitrary recursive structures, which represent sociologically adequate concepts intuitively and directly.

The problem of limited expressivity, which restricted past approaches straight on rational planning, can be overcome in such a way. Communication as a subject of communication becomes possible and structural couplings of arbitrary complexity is now representable. In this work examples of different mutual relations were given. Depending upon their interrelations, social entities become effective as *social structure, process,* or *actor.* Produced entities can reach the same abstraction levels depending upon their specific developments.

The fundamental mechanisms of recognising, ability and the symbolic representation are implemented in the SONAR architecture, directly apart from its MULAN counterpart. The strongly abstracting example in Section 7 clarifies the procedure in principle: within an agent, its internal recursive structure of social entities is extended by the production of a new social entity. Apparently, these are strong abstractions of reality—however their correspondence are found in fundamental sociological theories, which describe appropriate procedures over the mechanisms, indicated above.

Summarising, in this work an architecture is presented, permitting the construction of scalable multi-agent systems on the basis of reference nets and an agent-oriented design, respecting social mechanisms. All units can be provided on the basis of MULAN, since single MULAN-agents can be used as a platform for a whole system of entity-agents—resulting in the more complex SONAR-agent.

Scaling of the system becomes possible by the fact that the necessary predispositions take place within the individual agents. These predispositions permit stable and efficient acting well-known from social systems, without explicit co-ordination of all actions and decisions of the agents.

In this paper, we propose, how structuring has impact on the actors and their internal behaviour with the help of a basal formalism. By the embedding into our elaborated technical infrastructure, which permits again an embedding into current open multi-agent system (e.g. in the context of agent cities), the conceptional representation of the social leads to a complex, but appropriate modelling.

As a next step we will investigate how the mental models within the SONAR-layer can be further differentiated for the matter of agent engineering based development processes. One possibility is to build virtual realities that contain on a certain level "real" objects and agents. The question then is, when do "emergent" objects and agents "materialise".

References

1. Weiß, G., ed.: Multiagent systems: A modern approach to Distributed Artificial Intelligence. MIT Press (1999)
2. Castelfranchi, C.: Engineering social order. In Omicini, A., Tolksdorf, R., Zambonelli, F., eds.: Engineering Societies in the Agents World. First International Workshop, ESAW 2000, Berlin, Germany. Volume 1972 of LNAI., Springer-Verlag (2000) 1–18

3. Malsch, T.: Expeditionen ins Grenzgebiet zwischen Soziologie und Künstlicher Intelligenz. In Malsch, T., ed.: Sozionik: soziologische Ansichten über Künstliche Intelligenz. Edition Sigma (1996) 9–24

4. SPP Sozionik: Sozionik: Erforschung und Modellierung künstlicher Sozialität. http://www.tu-harburg.de/tbg/SPP/spp-antrag.html   (1998)   Antragstext   zum   DFG-Schwerpunktprogramm *Sozionik*.

5. Köhler, M., Moldt, D., Rölke, H.: Modeling the behaviour of Petri net agents. In Colom, J.M., Koutny, M., eds.: International Conference on Application and Theory of Petri Nets. Volume 2075 of Lecture Notes in Computer Science., Springer-Verlag (2001) 224–241

6. Duvigneau, M., Moldt, D., Rölke, H.: Concurrent architecture for a multi-agent platform. In: Proceedings of the 2002 Workshop on Agent Oriented Software Engineering (AOSE'02). Volume 2585 of Lecture Notes in Computer Science., Springer-Verlag (2003) 59–72

7. Kummer, O., Wienberg, F., Duvigneau, M., Schumacher, J., Köhler, M., Moldt, D., Rölke, H., Valk, R.: An extensible editor and simulation engine for Petri nets: Renew. In Cortadella, J., Reisig, W., eds.: International Conference on Application and Theory of Petri Nets 2004. Volume 3099 of Lecture Notes in Computer Science., Springer-Verlag (2004) 484 – 493

8. v. Lüde, R., Moldt, D., Valk, R.: Sozionik: Modellierung soziologischer Theorie. Wirtschaft – Arbeit – Technik. Lit-Verlag, Münster (2003)

9. Langer, R.:   Anerkennen und Vermögen: Verborgene Ordnungen und Selbstorgansiation-sprozesse in Schule, Universität und Gesellschaft. Dissertation, Universität Hamburg (2004)

10. Kummer, O.: Referenznetze. Logos Verlag (2002)

11. Girault, C., Valk, R.: Petri Nets for System Engineering – A Guide to Modeling, Verification, and Applications. Springer-Verlag (2003)

12. Reisig, W.: Petri nets and algebraic specifications. Theoretical Computer Science **80** (1991) 1–34

13. Jensen, K.: Coloured Petri nets, Basic Methods, Analysis Methods and Practical Use. Volume 1 of EATCS monographs on theoretical computer science. Springer-Verlag (1992)

14. Valk, R.: Petri nets as token objects: An introduction to elementary object nets. In Desel, J., Silva, M., eds.: Application and Theory of Petri Nets. Volume 1420 of Lecture Notes in Computer Science. (1998) 1–25

15. Valk, R.: Object Petri nets: using the nets-within-nets paradigm. In Desel, J., Reisig, W., Rozenberg, G., eds.: Advanced Course on Petri Nets 2003. Volume 3098 of Lecture Notes in Computer Science., Springer-Verlag (2003) 819–848

16. Köhler, M., Rölke, H.: Concurrency for mobile object-net systems. Fundamenta Informaticae **54** (2003)

17. Köhler, M., Rölke, H.:   Properties of object Petri nets. In Cortadella, J., Reisig, W., eds.: International Conference on Application and Theory of Petri Nets 2004. Volume 3099 of Lecture Notes in Computer Science., Springer-Verlag (2004) 278–297

18. Jennings, N.R.: On agent-based software engineering. Artificial Intelligence **117** (2000) 277–296

19. Cost, R.S., Chen, Y., Finin, T., Labrou, Y., Peng, Y.: Modeling agent conversation with colored Petri nets. In: Working notes on the workshop on specifying and implementing conversation policies (Autonomous agents '99), Springer-Verlag (1999) 565–579

20. Wooldridge, M.: Intelligent agents. [1] chapter 1

21. Aalst, W.v.d.: The application of Petri nets to workflow management. Journal of Circuits, Systems and Computers **8** (1998) 21–66

22. Bourdieu, P.: Sozialer Sinn. Suhrkamp (1993)

23. Bourdieu, P.: Praktische Vernunft. Suhrkamp (1998)

24. Elias, N.: Der Prozess der Zivilisation. Suhrkamp, Frankfurt (1976) (1939), zwei Bde.

25. Schimank, U.: Handeln und Strukturen. Einführung in die akteurstheoretische Soziologie. Weinheim (2000)

26. Giddens, A.: The Constitution of Society. Polity Press, Cambridge (1984)
27. Esser, H.: Soziologie. Allgemeine Grundlagen. Campus, Frankfurt (1993)
28. Schillo, M., Fischer, K., Klein, C.: The micro-macro link in DAI and sociology. In Moss, S., Davidsson, P., eds.: Second International Workshop on Multi-Agent Based Simulation. Volume 1979 of Lecture Notes in Computer Science., Springer-Verlag (2000) 133–148
29. Köhler, M., Rölke, H.: Modelling the micro-macro-link: Towards a sociologically grounded design of multi-agent systems. In Jonker, C., Lindemann, G., Panzarasa, P., eds.: Proceedings of the Workshop Modelling Artificial Societies and Hybrid Organization (MASHO'02), at the 25th German Conference on Artificial Intelligence (KI'2002). (2002)
30. Shoham, Y., Tennenholtz, M.: On social laws for artificial agent societies: off-line design. Artificial Intelligence **72** (1994) 231–252
31. Walker, A., Wooldridge, M.J.: Understanding the emergence of conventions in multi-agent systems. In: Proceedings of the 1st International Conference on Multiagent Systems (IC-MAS'95), San Francisco, CA (1995)
32. Popitz, H.: Prozesse der Machtbildung. Mohr, Tübingen (1976)
33. Elias, N., Scotson, J.L.: Etablierte und Außenseiter. Suhrkamp, Frankfurt (1990)
34. Castelfranchi, C., Dignum, F., Jonker, C., Treur, J.: Deliberate normative agents: Principles and architecture. In: Proceedings of the Sixth International Workshop on Agent Theories, Architectures, and Languages (ATAL 99). (1999)

Building Scalable Virtual Communities — Infrastructure Requirements and Computational Costs

Omer F. Rana[1], Asif Akram[1], and Steven J. Lynden[2]

[1] School of Computer Science,
Cardiff University, UK
[2] School of Computer Science
University of Newcastle, UK

Abstract. The concept of a "community" is often an essential feature of many existing scientific collaborations. Collaboration networks generally involve bringing together participants who wish to achieve some common outcome. Scientists often work in informal collaborations to solve complex problems that require multiple types of skills. Increasingly, scientific collaborations are becoming interdisciplinary—requiring participants who posses different skills to come together. Such communities may be generally composed of participants with complimentary or similar skills—who may decide to collaborate to more efficiently solve a single large problem. If such a community **wishes** to utilise computational resources to undertake their work, it is useful to identify metrics that may be used to characterise their collaboration. Such metrics are useful to identify particular types of communities, or more importantly, particular features of communities that are likely to lead to successful collaborations as the number of participants (or the resources they are sharing) increases.

1 Introduction and Motivation

The formation of collaboration networks is an important latent effect in many computational science undertakings. Various analysis of the formation of such networks already exist, in various disciplines, such as the formation of a business community [19], a school [8], ethnic communities [1] and even scientific collaborations [21]. Such networks are generally constructed through interview or questionnaire based techniques, and often involve a subjective assessment of the data. Work by Newman [20,21] involved an alternative automated approach, whereby a network was constructed based on co-authorship of participants. Such an "affiliation" network was established by evaluating co-authorship between groups of scientists—an approach which has also been used to construct connections between members in groups of other kinds, such as a network of movie actors compiled from the Internet Movie Database, etc.

Many such networks have been shown to possess scale-free topologies—whereby some nodes are selected to act as hubs through which a large number of other nodes integrate their functions and community structures. Such network structures are based on the observation that in a collaboration not all participants act in the same manner with respect to their interactions with others. Some prefer to establish a large number

K. Fischer, M. Florian, and T. Malsch (Eds.): Socionics, LNAI 3413, pp. 68–83, 2005.

of interactions, whilst others maintain a limited number of them. Similarly, some participants are likely to have a large connectivity with small data exchanges, whilst others may have a small connectivity with large data exchanges. Both of these interactions make such networks more resistant to random node failures, and consequently more adaptive to changes in the operating environment. The benefit of team and coalition formation in multi-agent systems (MAS) research has also demonstrated the benefit of creating interacting sub-systems as communities, operating within larger systems. The use of a hierarchy to structure such a system of communities is also often employed, to either limit interaction to a restricted set of participants, or to constrain interactions based on some other criteria of interest. Practically, such a hierarchy is useful to manage the system, and allow decision making (policy) to be restricted depending on the level of a hierarchy at which a particular member of the community is placed. The use of a hierarchy is also beneficial for improving resource management—as highly used resources can be placed at higher levels of the hierarchy to enable sharing between participants. According to this approach, resources may be more usefully divided based on interaction patterns within each community, such as in the Berkeley Service Discovery System [6]. In such a system, messages generated for the discovery of a service are always restricted first to a localised community (representing the lower levels of a hierarchy). If a service cannot be discovered at this lower level, only then the discovery request is propagated to higher layers—where it can reach a much larger number of participants (as illustrated in Figure 1). In this way, by selectively propagating messages across different levels in the hierarchy, a discovery request may be localised to a given set of community members (initially), and if not successful, automatically propagated to other members. Hence, the use of message propagation between community members arranged in a hierarchy allows traffic flows between members to be regulated in some way.

Mechanisms for structuring interaction between participants in a community are discussed in this chapter, along with ways in which utility could be assigned to such participants based on their community role. The key theme is to identify metrics that may be associated with such interactions—and relate these to implementation criteria that will be used to ultimately realise a community as a multi-agent system. Such metrics may be used to structure communities (such as the hierarchical scheme illustrated in Figure 1).

1.1   Relation to Socionics

According to Malsch [18], socionics research has three different aspects: (1) computer models to support sociological theorising, (2) use of sociological foundations to support the construction of (large-scale) MAS, and (3) analysis of hybrid societies of humans and software agents. The primary focus of this work is on criterion (2), in trying to explore how social structures which exist within the human scientific community, in particular, may influence the selection of MAS roles and their interactions. Based on such roles, one can perceive the establishment of a community, whereby participants can interact with a higher level of trust and reliance on each other. A reason for the formation of such communities may be to reduce the subsequent cost of interaction once

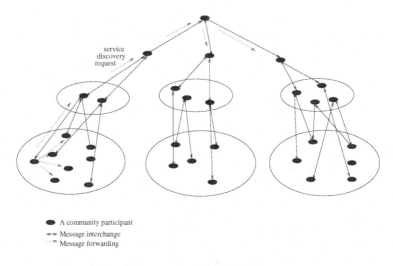

A community participant
Message interchange
Message forwarding

Fig. 1. *Hierarchical Service Discovery*

the community has been established. An agent may therefore decide to incur an initial cost to determine which community it should participate in, what actions it should undertake within the community (its role), which other participants it should communicate with (its interactions), and when to finally depart from the community. Based on such an analysis, an agent would have to pay an initial cost to make some of these decisions. Subsequently, the agent will only incur an "operational" cost—much lower than that for making some of these initial decisions. Quantifying these costs and using these as a basis for deciding whether a particular community should be joined (and whether the agent should remain within that community) therefore become important. These costs may also be viewed as: (i) those actually incurred by the agent, and (ii) perceived costs that are estimated by the agent prior to **perform** the action of joining or leaving a community. Identifying the expected or perceived costs, and providing an agent the capability to verify their validity, will play an important role in identifying how communities are established and sustained over long time periods.

Studies such as those of Newman [21] and Iamnitchi et al. [11] indicate the particular importance of "small world" interactions within the scientific domain. Such interactions can be deduced by exploring publication indices of scientists (especially in the natural sciences where a large number of authors collaborate) or the data and file sharing behaviour observed in large, collaborative projects [11], such as the D0 collaboration [7] involving hundreds of physicists from 18 countries. It is envisioned that many future scientific efforts will require a multi-disciplinary team of participants—often bringing a different perspective to the same scientific problem. Understanding how such dynamic scientific communities may be formed and sustained, and more importantly, how resources are shared and exchanged within the community becomes important—to ensure that the scientific objective being undertaken is successful. Analysing resource sharing behaviour between participants within such scientific experiments can also provide a useful guide to identify participants who are likely to work more effectively together. Therefore, the sharing of resources within such collaborative undertaking illustrates two particular characteristics:

1. Group Locality: whereby users tend to work in groups (not geographically co-located necessarily), and utilise the same set of resources (such as data files). For instance, a group of scientists may utilise newly generated data to undertake analysis and simulations—leading to new results that may be of interest to scientists within another group. Such formation of a community is generally focused also on specialist skills that a physicist or a group may have.
2. Time Locality: the same resources (files) may be requested multiple times within a short period. Such a characteristic may be influenced by the actual or perceived cost of storage of a file locally compared to downloading it from a remote repository.

Such a locality behaviour within a particular scientific experiment may be due to the perceived benefits and particular skills that physicists posses, or may be due to the limitations that current computational infrastructure imposes on collaboration. Analysing such interactions is particularly useful to identify how resources are consumed by such human agents over a network—and more importantly, how resource utilisation and availability could be improved to support such collaborative working. A particular example is the need to provide data replicas closer to the point of access for such scientific users, to prevent large downloads over public networks. A number of existing projects, such as OceanStore [15] and Giggle [4] address these issues.

Schillo, Fischer and Siekmann [24] outline different types of "organisational forms" that may be defined, based on whether the participants act in a cooperative, competitive or an authoritarian manner. They explore these concepts from the perspective of business organisations—however the basic classifications they provide can be applied more generally. The formation of a scientific community, as described above, is equivalent to establishing a "Virtual Enterprise"—essentially a collection of resources that are grouped together to be used for a single experiment. From the outside world, therefore, these resources appear as if they are owned by a single community undertaking the experiment. Such resources could range from computational hardware (such as parallel machines), data repositories, or specialist instruments— and are often under the control of different systems administrators. Such resources may be provided by different members of a community—and the criterion for membership of a community may be the requirement to provide access to such resources for use by other participants. Unlike business organisations, there are no formal contracts defining usage of these resources within the community. Recently, there have been efforts to apply economic models of resource sharing within the scientific community [3], and to explore different incentive structures to improve the utilisation of shared resources.

2   Communities

Communities that exist within a MAS can be of different types, and considerable research has already been undertaken within this area. The work in Holonic MAS shares many similarities with the formation of communities [9], and involves the establishment of a community as a *self-similar* structure that can be repeated multiple times. Other descriptions of communities are based on the types of activities undertaken by the agents. When participants within a community are cooperative, the community can be a "congregation", a "coalition", or a "team". A congregation generally consists of a meeting place, and the agents that assemble there (taken from the analogy of a club, a marketplace, a university department etc. in the context of human societies). Generally, members of such a congregation have expended some initial effort to organise and describe themselves so that they are considered to be useful partners with whom others can interact. Hence, within a community of this kind, agents somewhat know about the capabilities of others, and take 'for granted' some of the attributes that the other agents may possess. Brooks and Durfee [2] outline how such congregations may form, and various other infrastructure services that need to be made available (such as a MatchMaking service, the location of a congregation meeting place etc). The usefulness of a congregation-based community is the limited effort each agent within such a community needs to expend once it has established itself into a congregation. Such communities are therefore likely to involve repeated interactions and may generally exist over long time frames—as the whole point of developing such congregations is to allow an agent to have a greater level of trust in other participants (and therefore devote less resources to finding suitable partners for interaction). Panzarasa, Jennings and Norman [22] explore a formal model for specifying collaborative decision making, in which agents coordinate their mental models to achieve a common group objective. They indicate that such a decision making will be impacted by the social nature of agents, which also motivates their particular behaviour. The formation of such a community involves agents which provide some commitment to the group in which they belong.

In the analysis to follow, the particular focus is on implementing agent communities utilising existing software systems (such as FIPA-OS or JADE). The description of particular costs incurred is therefore closely related to the particular message transport and coordination schemes that these libraries support. However, based on some understanding of a particular type of community—say a scientific community—one may be able to establish interaction patterns that more closely reflect the information exchange within that community—achieved by the provision of a set of shared services. It is important to undertake such an analysis independent of the particular technologies that are subsequently used—as constraints imposed by a particular technology may be too restrictive. It is nevertheless important to also understand the implications of using particular implementation technologies in subsequent phases. Many existing MAS efforts that aim to establish application-specific communities are subsequently constrained by the implementation technologies they use. Therefore, getting a better appreciation of the impacts a particular implementation technology is likely to have on communication between participants within a community, or on the number of participants that can be accommodated on a particular machine, for instance, is useful to estimate the structure of the community that is likely to occur in reality. Identifying the roles that participants would undertake within such an environment would be a useful starting point to identify possible interactions. When identifying the nature of these roles, it would also be useful to better understand the resource implications such roles are likely to impose.

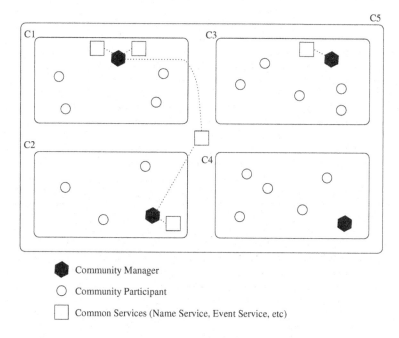

Fig. 2. *Hierarchical Communities*

For the work presented here, a community may be defined as a "collection of agents working towards some common objectives, or sharing some set of common beliefs". An agent may simultaneously belong to one or more communities, and must make a commitment to remain within a community for a particular duration. Each community may therefore be governed by a set of policy rules that all participants within the community must adhere to. A policy may be presented to the agent during the community formation phase, and must be accepted prior to the agent being allowed to operate within the community. To manage the policy, a community manager agent is provided—which must also register each agent that exists within a particular community. The community manager may mediate interaction between agents within a community, and may support a number of common services (such as an "Event Service", a "Name Service" etc). Groups may be defined, as illustrated in Figure 2—the C5 community includes C1–C4. Similarly, a community manager may share common services from a community at higher levels of the hierarchy (for C1,C2 for instance). In such a hierarchy, the community managers also act as gateways between multiple communities, and may facilitate inter-group query forwarding. Community managers at a higher layer can interact and delegate activities to community managers at lower layers, and also register the address of lower layer community managers. Service and participant information is not replicated at higher layer community managers—simply the names of community managers who may then be able to provide additional details about participants within a community. The structure of such a community is significant, as it impacts the search time for locating particular services and agents. It is assumed that once an agent has agreed to participate within a community by agreeing to a policy, the agent is given a higher level of trust by other agents, and the community manager. However, enforcement of policy rules is not considered here—and therefore the case where agents are malicious and violate policy rules is not considered.

2.1   Types of Communities

We consider four types of communities in which agents can participate. It is assumed that each agent has expertise and interests in particular resources owned by the community. We also assume the existence of a "Community Manager" (as illustrated in Figure 2). These interests govern how agents stay in or leave communities. The four types of communities are:

1. *Competing Communities*: In such communities agents provide the same set of services—although some service attributes may vary. When a service request is received by such a community, agents must compete with each other to respond to the request. The membership of a Competing community may consist of a predefined set of participants, or may be dynamic (with new participants entering and leaving the community). The community manager is responsible for selecting an agent to respond to the external request. Competing communities are analogous to commercial market places, where multiple providers offer the same service, and must therefore compete for incoming requests from users.

2. *Cooperative Communities*: In such communities agents provide different services. Either these services are complimentary, i.e. each agent provides a limited set of services which may not be utilised individually, but along with services being provided by other agents. Similar to a Competing community, a Cooperative community may also consist of a static or a dynamic membership. The community manager is responsible for coordinating the execution of the complete service, and for forwarding the eventual response. The multi-disciplinary scientific community is a useful example of a cooperative community, as scientists within a particular collaboration need the expertise of other scientists. Problem solving in such communities often requires different kinds of expertise, and such expertise is often not possessed by an individual.

3. *Goal-oriented Communities*: A variation on the Cooperative Communities idea is a "Goal-oriented" or "Domain-oriented" community, whereby a community is dynamically formed by a community manager inviting agents which offer a particular type of service. Membership in such a community is aimed at accomplishing a particular pre-assigned task. On meeting the desired goal, membership of the participants is terminated. Goal-oriented communities may also be important in self-organising systems, where interaction between member peers is not pre-defined. The Virtual Enterprise provides a useful example of such communities.

4. *Ad Hoc Communities*: In such communities, agents may belong to different communities regardless of the nature of those communities—but still work together to solve a particular task. In such communities, agents may interact with each other without intervention of their respective community managers.

Each of these different kinds of communities lead to different costs of communication and coordination. These costs are generally independent of the time to execute a particular service managed by an agent.

2.2   Communication Costs

Communication costs are incurred by participants of a community through message passing delays, and are based on the particular communication protocol supported by the agents. Generally, these can be divided into: (i) time per message, and (ii) the total number of messages exchanged over a given time period. As communities are established, it is possible that groups of agents are not topologically close to one another, and there is therefore a need to create a communication structure for message exchanges. Such a structure could utilise 'overlay networks' to minimise the average distance between communicating group members, or multicast based approaches to minimise message exchanges within a group. A particular coordination strategy may also be used between agents which minimises communication costs—assuming homogeneous agents. Identifying the costs for communication utilising regular graphs is outlined by Shehory [26]. Communication costs may be divided into the following factors:

– M_N: The number of messages sent between two agents
– M_t: The type of message sent from agent A to B (unicast, multicast or broadcast)
– T_d: The time taken to deliver a message from agent A to B
– T_p: The time taken to propagate a message from agent A to B (if message delivery involves a multi-hop transfer)
– M_s: The size of the message transferred between agents A and B

T_p is significant when there is no direct connectivity between interacting agents—and is dependent on the structure of the graph connecting the agents. In the limiting case, this graph will be dependent on the topology of the underlying network (however, it is also possible to define this metric in terms of some 'overlay' network). Each of the four types of communities defined in Section 2.1 may be characterised in terms of these communication costs—and is influenced by the types of collaboration occurring between different agents within a community.

2.3   Coordination Costs

Coordination costs are related to the type of community being formed, and may generally be incurred in two phases: (i) community 'formation' phase, and (ii) community 'operation' phase. The community formation phase involves agents trying to discover other agents of interest, and may involve a series of discovery operations to find other participants of interest. Matchmaking and registry services could be used to support such discovery operations, if a particular query format has been agreed upon. An agent wishing to join a particular community must also, during this phase, negotiate the terms of joining (the policy). Either the agent could accept the policy and agree to adhere by it, or the agent may negotiate terms of the policy. We assume here that such negotiation is only undertaken once—during the community formation phase. The formation phase may also involve co-locating an agent to a particular meeting point, or the ability to determine the particular services offered by an agent. The operation of a community would involve message exchanges between agents, over a particular time period, to achieve some goals. Such an operation phase would assume a particular functionality within other agents. Coordination costs may be divided into the following variables:

- T_a: time to discover other agents of interest
- T_a: time to propagate capability advertisement from the community manager to other agents
- T_n: time to reach convergence on a particular objective. Agents may employ a variety of techniques to agree on some common objectives—and the agreement may be reached in a one-shot or multi-shot negotiation.

The type of community (see Section 2.1) will influence the values of these parameters.

2.4   Metrics

Both communication and coordination costs are incurred during the formation and the operation phase of a community. However, Coordination costs are higher during the community formation phase, as agents interrogate community managers to determine the nature of the community, and the particular policy that an agent must accept to be part of the community. Interactions between community managers may be multi-shot—as they try to determine the types of services that are supported within other communities. As outlined in [23], infrastructure for multi-agent systems may be divided into four (broad) categories:

1. Implementation: which outlines the types of technologies used to build and develop agents, and multi-agent systems. The use of currently available toolkits, such as FIPA-OS, JADE, AgentBuilder, JACK etc, indicate that there is already a convergence towards particular implementation techniques (such as the use of Java) and tools.
2. Co-ordination and communication: which indicates how agents interact with each other. Co-ordination techniques may be explicitly defined—such as "Contract Net" or "Auction" based approaches, or may be implicit, such as the use of self-organisation and emergent interactions in an agent community (also dictated via a utility or objective function).
3. Multi-agent behaviour: which indicates how the behaviour of each agent is defined—such as use of logic based approaches, or machine learning approaches. Each agent is likely to be supported with a scheduler, a planner, and a knowledge base.
4. Organisation: to support interaction structures that define the roles of particular agents within a community. Such structures may be based on social systems or fabricated organisational structures in a particular application domain.

In order to assess the cost of building a multi-agent system utilising these four categories of infrastructure, we propose two types of metrics: (1) those related to system parameters (such as communication related parameters), (2) those related to coordination/organisational mechanisms. System metrics are generally associated with agent management on a particular host, the operations performed by an agent, and the transfer of agents or messages between hosts. The parameter being measured is generally wall-clock time as the number of agents are increased. The computational cost for achieving a working MAS may be evaluated from a number of perspectives, such as the performance of an individual element, the workload of a particular element, communication costs between elements, and persistence support for elements. Parameters that may be measured are the times to:

- Start an agent, which would involve loading-in and running a class file (in Java or C++, for instance). This will also include setup times to listen on a port for incoming messages from other agents. Subsequently, the execution of an agent may be measured by metrics such as inferences-per-second, rules executed per-second, or connection updates per-second. Such metrics may be used to compare the complexity of each agent, provided all agents are utilising similar description schemes for their behaviour.
- De-activate/activate an agent from disk, where persistence mechanisms are supported. This would involve check-pointing an agent and storing its current state. Such an operation is particularly important for building communities, as it may not be possible to keep a large number of agents in memory as the size of a community grows. It is also unlikely for all participants within a community to be active simultaneously—enabling such inactive participants to be stored on disk.
- Scheduling agent activities on a host: these can be handled in the same way as process and thread management on a host, or an application specific scheduling scheme may be implemented.
- Receiving and buffering incoming agents (especially relevant for mobile agents), and registering these with local stationary agents. With limited buffer sizes, a policy to determine when buffer sizes are exceeded is also needed—with an associated cost of buffer management.

These costs may be aggregated over all operating agents to provide a single value for comparing agent startup times. Performance values may also be weighted, based on some domain or system dependent constraint—such as the availability of specialist hardware or support for a particular scheduling library on a particular host. Costs for accessing common services, such as "Naming" and "Event Handling", must also be included when constructing an agent community. The emergence of Web Services as agent infrastructure—such as the provision of a services registry via UDDI [29], and the description of agent properties in WSDL [29] requires each service providing/using agent to communicate using an XML-based encoding. Message transfers utilising this approach now incur additional overheads in parsing in-coming messages, and generating XML for outgoing messages. It is therefore useful to obtain estimates for using a particular implementation technology—and basing the estimates for the communication and coordination costs (outlined in Section 2.1) on such estimates.

Event handling in multi-agent systems should support deferred synchronous messaging and provide mechanisms to overcome deadlock, event queues and polling. The latter are needed to prevent a large number of agents at a host to be simultaneously enabled, on the detection of a desired event—thereby increasing the computational cost of activating a large number of agents within a short time period. A coordination mechanism can be pre-defined, by a "Conversation Policy" [10] or by a global utility measure. The objective being to pre-determine the number of message transfers between agents, or to minimise conflicts between agents to facilitate convergence. Both scenarios will facilitate an increase in agent density, with better reinforcement algorithms contributing towards a better performance [28]. Metrics may be the total number of messages transfered between agents, wall-clock time to reach an agreement (converge on a solution), total number of agents involved, the maximal distance between agents involved and the number of agent sub-groups involved. Metrics may also be related to conversation policies, such as the total number of simultaneous conversations supported and the response time between conversations. Woodside [33] provides the 'Productivity' metric to measure scalability—as a factor based on improving the productivity of a particular undertaking, defining this as:

$$Productivity\ P(x)\ =\ \frac{Throughput(x) \times Value/response\ at\ given\ QoS(x)}{Cost(x)} \tag{1}$$

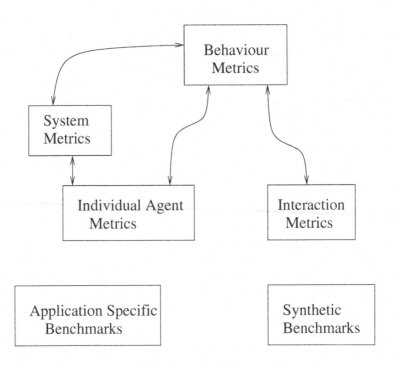

Fig. 3. *Metric Space*

where the improvement in productivity from an initial level 'k1' to a new level 'k2' is then the ratio $\frac{P(k2)}{P(k1)}$. In this instance, 'k1' and 'k2' are some user perceived metrics for measuring improvements in undertaking a particular task or the quality of service received from a particular community. According to this metric, the productivity of an application can be specified in terms of the improvement in quality as perceived by the user, and may involving adjusting parameters such as network loads, user response times etc, to obtain a given value of productivity in economic terms. This metric is subsequently used to evaluate tour length in a mobile agent, and the size of an agent required to reach a particular value of productivity. Utilising this property, a multi-agent systems developer is able to determine how many agents are necessary to reach a particular productivity criterion—or how many nodes a particular agent (or groups of agents) should visit to achieve a given QoS. Figure 3 outlines the various metrics that have been discussed, and how they relate to each other.

Each of the metric specified in Figure 3 may be defined in terms of parameters outlined in Section 2.1. Metrics related to particular applications (Application Benchmarks) or those related to particular functionality in agent systems—such as planning or scheduling, etc. Synthetic Benchmarks play an important role in comparing different kinds of agent communities attempting to solve the same problem. Defining interactions between participants is then reduced to specifying the parameters associated with these metrics for comparing computational costs of establishing communities.

3   LEAF Toolkit

The LEarning Agent FIPA toolkit (LEAF) allows the development of multi-agent communities that are based on the FIPA standard. The aim of the toolkit is to allow developers to construct MAS via an Application Programming Interface (API), and to support the coordination of agents via utility assignment. FIPA compliance is achieved by extending FIPA-Open Source from Emorphia Ltd.

LEAF agents use local machine learning techniques (e.g. reinforcement learning) and are coordinated using utility function assignment, based on COIN [32]. The essential concept in LEAF is that agents learn to maximise their local utility functions, which are assigned to agents with the aim of engineering a system in which improvements made to local utility are beneficial to the system globally. The mechanisms involved in such utility optimisation is independent of the task that an agent undertakes within a particular application. Although COIN generally configures local utility functions based on the specification of global utility, LEAF leaves the design of local and global utility functions up to the developer as application specific decisions. Hence, agents are required to undertake local optimisations based on the reward they receive for actions performed, where reward is either immediate (based on the increase in local utility following an action performed by an agent), or averaged over a finite time horizon. An agent may therefore adopt a strategy whereby it aims to lose out in the short term, but gain utility over a longer time period. Such a decision may be community specific (for instance, an agent may work on the assumption that the community will exist over a long time frame), or may be determined by the specific strategy employed by an agent. An agent may therefore use one of the following learning models (each of the these models assume that utility calculation is undertaken at discrete time intervals):

- Finite Horizon: the agent aims to optimise the *expected* reward for the next h state updates. U^t represents the utility at time t. In this instance, the agent is therefore calculating its utility from the current time to h intervals in the future—summing up the expected utility at each time interval until h. It is useful to note that U^t may also be negative:

$$\sum_{t=0}^{h} E(U^t)$$

- Infinite Horizon: the agent calculates the long term reward expected by the agent. In this case the agent may not achieve a high utility value in the short term, but expects to improve utility over a given time period. γ^t represents the discounting rate for future states. The factor γ is chosen by the agent developer, and if $(0 < \gamma < 1)$, then a reward at a point much further in time is considered to be less important than rewards in the near future. The value of γ is again based on an expectation a user has of how rewards are likely to change in the future. In the case where $\gamma > 1$, then rewards much further in the future are considered to be more important. The longer term rewards may be considered more important if the agent developer expects the community in which the agent operates to 'stabilise' in the longer term. It may also be possible to specify γ as some more complex function representing the agents perception of the future:

$$\sum_{t=0}^{\infty} E(\gamma^t U^t)$$

- Averaged Finite Horizon (gain optimal policy)

$$\frac{1}{h} \sum_{t=0}^{h} E(U^t)$$

this is midway between the Infinite Horizon and Finite Horizon schemes—whereby the further away the reward, the less important it is to an agent. Based on this approach an agent may be able to optimise its utility over the "medium" term. In this instance, the reward obtained by the agent is weighted by the number of time steps in the future at which it is received.

Hence, the kind of update mechanism in place is influenced by the rate of change of the environment (community) in which the agent exists. The following entities participate in a LEAF system:

- A set of LEAF communities, each of which is represented by an Environment Service Node (ESN). The ESN essentially acts as a community manager. Each agent within a community must trust the ESN managing the community, and must, by obligation, execute demands made on it by an ESN. Usually, these demands consist of utility function assignments, assigned by the ESN in order to coordinate agents toward the objectives of the community.
- A set of agents, each of which is of a specific LEAF agent type. An agent type defines certain application specific behaviour constraints that allow other agents and ESNs to make assumptions about the behaviour of agents based on their agent types.

– FIPA platform agents: the directory facilitator agent (DF) and agent management service (AMS).

3.1 Communities with LEAF

Establishing communities with LEAF requires a user to specify the operations to be supported by the ESN. It is assumed that there is one ESN per community—specialising in a particular application domain, and the ESN is responsible for allocating utility to agents within the community. The ESN is therefore also responsible for accepting new members into a community—depending on the types of operations they support. Once a community is deployed, agents may join the community and are subsequently assigned local utility functions. LEAF has been used to coordinate communities of market based buyer agents [16] and communities of computational resource agents [17].

4 Conclusion

The need and importance of establishing communities in scientific collaborations is first outlined, followed by various metrics that can be used to measure and monitor the community. These metrics are divided into (1) communication/system metrics, and (2) coordination metrics. How these relate to the general idea of community formation is discussed. The LEAF toolkit is subsequently described, which makes use these metrics to allocate "utility" to participants within a community, and as a result to coordinate activities within the community.

References

1. H. R. Bernard, P. D. Kilworth, M. J. Evans, C. McCarthy, and G. A. Selley, "Studying social relations cross-culturally", Ethnology 2, pp 155–179, 1988
2. C. H. Brooks and E. H. Durfee, "Congregation Formation in Multi-agent Systems", Journal of Autonomous Agents and Multi-Agent Systems, Volume 7, Issue 1-2 (Special Issue), 2003
3. R. Buyya, "Economic-based Distributed Resource Management and Scheduling for Grid Computing", PhD Thesis, Monash University, Australia, 2002. Available at: http://www.cs.mu.oz.au/ raj/thesis/
4. A. Chervenak, E. Deelman, I. Foster, L. Guy, W. Hoschek, A. Iamnitchi, C. Kesselman, P. Kunst, M. Ripeanu, B, Schwartzkopf, H, Stockinger, K. Stockinger, B. Tierney, "Giggle: A Framework for Constructing Scalable Replica Location Services", Proceedings of ACM/IEEE Supercomputing 2002 (SC2002), November 2002
5. F. Comellas, Javier Ozón and Joseph G. Peters, "Deterministic Small-World Communication Networks", Information Processing Letters, Vol.76, No.1–2, pp 83–90, 2000. Available at: http://citeseer.nj.nec.com/comellas00deterministic.html
6. S. E. Czerwinski, B. Y. Zhao, T. D. Hodes, A. D. Joseph, and R. H. Katz, "An Architecture for a Secure Service Discovery Service," in Proceedings of Mobile Computing and Networking, pp 24–35, 1999
7. The DZero Experiment, Fermi National Accelerator Laboratory, Chicago, US. See Web site at: http://www-d0.fnal.gov/
8. T. J. Fararo and M. Sunshine, "A study of a biased Friendship Network", Syracuse University Press, Syracuse, New York, 1964

9. K. Fischer, M. Schillo, and J. Siekmann, "Holonic Multiagent Systems: The Foundation for the Organisation of Multiagent Systems", Proceedings of the First International Conference on Applications of Holonic and Multiagent Systems (HoloMAS '03), 2003

10. M. Greaves, H. Holback, and J. Bradshaw. "What Is a Conversation Policy?", Proceedings of workshop on Specifying and Implementing Conversation Policies, at third annual conference on Autonomous Agents, May 1999.

11. A. Iamnitchi, M. Ripeanu, and I. Foster, "Locating Data in (Small-World?) Peer-to-Peer Scientific Collaborations", . Workshop on Peer-to-Peer Systems, Cambridge, Massachusetts, March, 2002.

12. R. Kasturirangan, "Multiple Scales in Small-World Networks", AIM-1663, 1999

13. S. Ketchpel, "Forming Coalitions in the Face of Uncertain Rewards", Proceedings of National Conference on AI, Seattle, WA, pp 414-419, 1994

14. J. Kleinberg, "Small-World Phenomena and the Dynamics of Information", Proceedings of Neural Information Processing Systems, 2001

15. J. Kubiatowicz, D. Bindel, Y. Chen, P. Eaton, D. Geels, R. Gummadi, S. Rhea, H. Weatherspoon, W. Weimer, C. Wells and B. Zhao, "OceanStore: An Architecture for Global-scale Persistent Storage", Proceedings of ACM ASPLOS, November 2000.

16. S. J. Lynden, "Coordination of FIPA compliant software agents using utility function assignment", PhD Thesis, Department of Computer Science, Cardiff University, 2003

17. S. J. Lynden, O. F. Rana, "Coordinated Learning to support Resource Management in Computational Grids", 2nd IEEE International Conference on Peer-2-Peer Computing, September 2002, Linkoping, Sweden. IEEE Computer Society Press

18. T. Malsch, "Naming the Unnameable: Socionics or the Sociological Turn of/to Distributed Artificial Intelligence", Journal of Autonomous Agents and Multi-Agent Systems, 4, pp 155–186, 2001

19. P. Mariolis, "Interlocking directorates and control of corporations: The theory of bank control", Social Sciences Quarterly **56**, pp 425–439, 1975

20. M. E. J. Newman, "Who is the Best Connected Scientist? A Study of Scientific Co-authorship Networks", Phys. Rev. E 64, 2001

21. M. E. J. Newman, "The structure of scientific collaboration networks", Proc. National. Academy of Sciences, USA, pp 404–409, 2001.

22. P. Panzarasa, N. R. Jennings, and T. J. Norman, "Formalizing Collaborative Decision-making and Practical Reasoning in Multi-agent Systems", Journal of Logic and Computation, Vol. 11, No. 6, pp 1–63, 2001

23. O. F. Rana, T. Wagner, M. S. Greenberg, and M. K. Purvis. "Infrastructure Issues and Themes for Scalable Multi-Agent Systems", Infrastructure for Scalable Multi-Agent Systems, LNAI 1887, Springer Verlag, 2001.

24. M. Schillo, K. Fischer, and J. Siekmann, "The Link between Autonomy and Organisation in Multiagent Systems", Proceedings of the First International Conference on Applications of Holonic and Multiagent Systems (HoloMAS'03)

25. U. Schimank, "From 'Clean' Mechanisms to 'Dirty' Models: Methodological Perspectives of the Scalability of Actor Constellations", in book 'Socionics: Contributions to the Scalability of Complex Social Systems' (Ed: Klaus Fischer and Michael Florian), Springer Verlag

26. O. Shehory, "A Scalable Agent Location Mechanism", Proceedings of Agent Theories, Architectures, and Languages (ATAL) conference, 1999

27. O. Shehory and S. Kraus, "Methods for Task Allocation via Agent Coalition Formation", Artificial Intelligence 101, pp 165–200, 1998

28. R. Sun and T. Peterson. "Multi-agent reinforcement learning: weighting and partitioning", Neural Networks (Elsevier Science), 12:727–753, 1999.

29. Universal Description, Discovery and Integration (UDDI). See Web site at: `http://www.uddi.org/`. See details on UDDI and WSDL at: `http://www.webservices.org/`.
30. D. Watts and S. Strogatz, "Collective dynamics of small-world networks", Nature, 393:440–442, 1998
31. D. Wolpert and K. Tumer. "An Introduction to Collective Intelligence", In J. M. Bradshaw, editor, Handbook of Agent Technology. AAAI Press/MIT Press, 1999.
32. D. Wolpert, K. Wheeler, and K. Tumer. "General Principles of Learning-Based Multi-Agent Systems", Proceedings of third annual conference on Autonomous Agents, May 1999.
33. M. Woodside. "Scalability Metrics and Analysis of Mobile Agent Systems", Proceedings of Workshop on Infrastructure for Scalable Multi-Agent Systems, at 4th Annual Conference on Autonomous Agents, June 2000.

Organization: The Central Concept for Qualitative and Quantitative Scalability*

Michael Schillo[1] and Daniela Spresny[2]

[1] German Research Center for Artificial Intelligence (DFKI),
Stuhlsatzenhausweg 3, 66123 Saarbrücken, Germany
schillo@virtosphere.de
[2] Department of Technology Assessment, Technical University of Hamburg-Harburg,
Schwarzenbergstr. 95, 21071 Hamburg, Germany
daniela.spresny@tu-harburg.de

Abstract. In sociology and distributed artificial intelligence, researchers are investigating two different ways of scaling. On the one hand, there is qualitative scaling, meaning that (social) complexity is increased, introducing regular practices of action, institutions, new fields of social action and requiring new dimensions in perception and decision making. On the other hand, researchers are interested in investigating quantitative scalability, i.e. how goals can be achieved under the constraints imposed by a growing population.
Our argument is structured as follows: firstly, we want to establish that organizations and interorganizational networks are an important cornerstone for the analysis of qualitative scaling. Secondly, we show by empirical evaluation that an elaborate theoretical concept of such networks increases the quantitative scalability of multiagent systems.

1 Introduction

In this chapter, we want to introduce selected results from our interdisciplinary research and illustrate how they advance the research field socionics as well as the participating disciplines, sociology and distributed artificial intelligence. For this purpose, we chose the subject area of social organizations, which is of relevance to both disciplines. Social organizations are on the one hand a well-elaborated research field in sociology as the organization theory is a broad field, gathering many heterogeneous approaches which are dealing with very diversified interests, aspects, perspectives and methodologies regarding organizations (for an overview see [11]). On the other hand, organizations are still an underexposed concept concerning establishing and strengthening the meso-level of social life, which is in our point of view an important analytical category between the micro- and macro-level of sociality (more details about the micro-, meso- and macro-level of sociality and their linkage are pointed out in Section 2.1).

As a contribution to sociological theory building, it is our aim for this chapter to (a) give reasons for strengthening and founding of the meso-level and (b) suggest a concept for social organizations on the basis of a sociological theory, which is popular for

---

* This work was funded by the Deutsche Forschungsgemeinschaft (DFG) in the priority programme *Socionics* under contracts Si 372/9-2 and FL 336/1-2.

K. Fischer, M. Florian, and T. Malsch (Eds.): Socionics, LNAI 3413, pp. 84–103, 2005.
© Springer-Verlag Berlin Heidelberg 2005

linking the social micro- and macro-level but actually not for an elaborated concept of organizations: the Habitus-Field-Theory of Pierre Bourdieu. We intend to give an encouragement for a theoretical advancement of this theory towards an enhanced concept of social organizations (this is the content of Section 2.2.)

We believe that organization will help us to better understand the concept of scalability, which we classify into the subtopics quantitative and qualitative scalability. In a nutshell, they are characterised as follows:

qualitative scalability: This is about (i) actors or agents with a more complex and richer inner life, i.e. with manifold interests and motives, abilities and features and advanced possibilities to build relationships to other actors or agents, or (ii) institutionalised behaviour patterns and regularities on different levels of sociality independent from special persons and interactions (like in organizations).

quantitative scalability: This form refers to the size of the constellation under research (whether it is composed of human actors in a social context or artificial agents in a multiagent system). Hence, the focus is on mechanisms that help increasing population sizes to reproduce sociality, and social order.

Scalability, as the main theme of this book, is a central concept, since it allows us to take differentiated perspectives on both the micro- and the macro-level of sociality and is a desired feature for multiagent systems. Hence, it is of importance to both sociology and distributed artificial intelligence. This common interest is best expressed by the topic of this chapter, namely to achieve multiagent system scalability by utilising a differentiated and sociologically well-founded concept of organizational networks. Therefore, we will present multiagent system compatible theory of organizational networks (Section 3) and show the effect in two empirical investigations on quantitative scalability using this theory (Section 4).

2 Organizations as the Meso-level of Social Action

2.1 The Micro-macro-Problem in Sociology

The subject of sociology can be boiled down to the explanation of social action and social structuration of the social world, assuming that both aspects are influencing each other reciprocally (see for example [18, p. 17]). In more detail, this reciprocal influence means on the one hand that social action produces, reproduces and transforms social structures (for example consumer habits, which are determining the market for a special product), and on the other hand socially structured life has effects on social actions, by making them possible or constraining them (for example institutionalized norms that regulate the actions of most people in a society). With the relation between action and structure a topic is addressed, which is not only of central importance for sociology, but also an issue that has often been cited and studied, but not resolved up to now.

Social actions[1] (which are executed by individual actors, who are referring their actions to the actions and expectations of other actors) are ascribed to the micro-level

---

[1] Depending on the theoretical orientation, one can also speak about behaviour, interaction or communication (for an overview, see for example [6, pp. 590] or [20]). One of the first foundations of social action refers to Weber [22].

Micro-level	Meso-level	Macro-level
– Individuals or small groups and their actions or behaviour – The interplay and the social relations between few directly interacting agents	– Organizations and interorganizational relations – Social networks and groups in a defined and easily observable scale (for example lobbies or professional associations)	– The society or societal structures – Spanning institutions and institutional arrangements as they occur in economy (here: markets) politics, science, justice – Large-scaled social groups and movements – Social classes and stratification

Table 1. Research perspective and objects of all three levels of sociality.

of sociality. Their counterpart are social structures[2], which constitute the macro-level of the social world. The social structure is a widespread, but not very clear-cut term in sociology. Also, the way how social structures are emerging and changing does not belong to the well-elaborated and widely agreed insights in the sociological community. What we want to refer to as social structures, are regular recurring courses of action and behaviour, no matter if they are codified in a formal manner (like laws which are regulating and controlling many aspects of life and actions) or if they are consolidated by an informal, but commonly shared and accepted way (like forms of action established in enduring relations). This is why the relation between social action and structure is also conceived as the micro-macro-problem in sociological theory.

Whether one chooses the micro- or the macro-perspective has extensive effects for the explanation of the social world. To confront the two perspectives, allow us a generalisation. While the micro-sociological view understands the social world based on individuals and their actions and tries to explain the rest through it, the macro-sociological view proceeds the opposite way: it starts to explain the social structuring of the world or the considered subject, and then concludes the actions and the behaviour from it. We do not want to conceal that there are several efforts to combine these two perspectives. Among others, Giddens [8], Bourdieu [1], Esser [6], and Schimank [18], who propose a theory-integrating approach for the relation between social action and social structure.

While most of the theorists discuss the two levels of sociality (micro and macro), together with a few other researchers we want to argue in this article, that it is a reasonable and profitable way to extend the sociological micro-macro-problem by the con-

---

[2] Other theoretical approaches prefer to talk about social order as the main subject of the macrolevel, for example the *rational choice theory*.

Micro-level	Meso-level	Macro-level
– Sporadic and tempo-rary meetings of actors, which are not regulated in a formal way but de-pendent on the particu-lar situation – Face-to-face interaction also with symbolic elements	– Formal and infor-mal structuring and processes – Relatively stable so-cial formations and relations – Differentiation of tasks and positions – Regulated memberships	– Broad spheres of the society spanning struc-tures with far-reaching effects like continuous models of social re-lations, positions and constellations

Table 2. Central characteristics of all three levels of sociality.

sideration of a third level: the meso-level of sociality.[3] The meso-level needs to be classified as an intermediate level between the micro- and the macro-level and consti-tutes the missing link for our multi-level-modeling approach (for more details of our multi-level-modeling approach see Dederichs and Florian (2002)).

As Tables 1 and 2 show[4], micro-social founded approaches deal with spatially and temporally limited actions and direct interactions with rather short-termed effects. Macro-sociology is engaged in spatially and temporally stable social forms and systems with long-termed effects. The problem is that under macro-sociology highly diversified social phenomena are summarised (the whole society as well as institutions), so that it is difficult to develop an unitary concept of them and to explain their functionality and the interdependencies between their single components. Whereas the micro-sociology deals with actions and interactions, but disregards phenomena, which are lying beyond the directly observable face-to-face interaction. Thus, there does not exist any well-elaborated notion of the society and its structure.

The meso-sociology refers to a level lying in-between and deals with constellations of cooperative and coordinated actions for a certain purpose (for which organizations are an important example). By this means we, are able to focus on many relevant social phenomena and mechanisms, which otherwise would remain unattended.

Micro, meso, and macro are just varying perspectives of analysis on sociality. The corresponding theories can be differentiated, since they are each working with different theoretical approaches, which are each focusing on other spheres of social phenomena to observe, interpret and explain. But this does not mean that there are three fully sepa-rated and independent spheres addressed. Rather, there are several connections between the three levels, because they determine each other reciprocally. The micro-level is em-

---

[3] Theorists who are dealing with the meso-level are for instance Luhmann [13] with his differen-tiation in interaction, organization and society, or Weymann [23], who formulates the require-ment of the meso-level as a qualitative different social form from the micro- and macro-level.

[4] Obviously, it is not possible to represent the whole theoretical research spectrum of sociology in two tables, rather they try to give a quick overview. For more detailed discussions of this topic see for example [6,8,18,23]).

bedded in the meso level, and the meso level is again embedded in the macro level of sociality.

One of the levels does not make sense without the others. For example, if we want to consider the interaction between two actors, a micro-social phenomenon, we have to take into account the meso- and macro-social context it takes place in as well. If the actors are occupying a certain position in different organizations and want to negotiate about a cooperation, the interaction is framed as well by the branch they belong to and the situation of the competition (meso-level) as the situation of the market and the economy in general (macro-level). One might say that sociality always takes place on the three levels at the same time.

2.2   Implications of Bourdieu's Habitus-Field-Theory on the Concept of Organization

Now we want to outline one sociological theory, which is well-known for a useful contribution to the micro-macro-problem in sociology: the Habitus-Field-Theory of Pierre Bourdieu. We will first have a look at three central concepts of the theory. These concepts are: Habitus, social field, and social practice. Figure 1 offers an illustration of the relation of the three concepts.

Habitus. The habitus is composed of stable and transferable dispositions of the individuals, or, in the words of Bourdieu habitus is a "socialised subjectivity" [3, p. 126]. Due to their habitus, individuals are equipped with patterns of thinking, perception, judgement, and action. It provides them with a specific sense and feel for the game of the social field, which is called *illusio*. The habitus is being developed through internalising processes during the life of the individuals, but this happens in dependence on the structures of the social field they are moving and acting in. It generates social practice.

Social Field. The concept of the social field is characterised by a structuring which is represented by the field positions and their objectified relations. In this sense, the field is a field of forces. The structuring of the field is a result of the distribution of different forms of capital (economic, social, cultural, and symbolic capital), which are relevant to the field and its game. The structuring of the social field varies from field to field, so that every field has a different logic and different interests are active. This is why a social field makes some actions more likely and promising than others and the actors are unable to act without the structured field.

Social Practice. Social practice is the concept where habitus and social field come together, because both, the habitus and the social field are necessary conditions for social practice. Due to the mutual interrelationship between habitus and field, Bourdieu defines practice as a dynamic process: it is enabled by habitus and field but influences them by itself. This means that there are changes possible for all of the three concepts in dependence of each other (for more details on the Habitus-Field-Theory see also for example [1,3,17]).

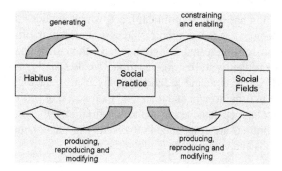

Fig. 1. The three basic concepts of Bourdieu's Habitus-Field-Theory in relation to each other.

Even though the Habitus-Field-Theory of Bourdieu is one of the most elaborated sociological theories with a fundamental contribution to the micro-macro-problem. On the one hand, on the other hand it does not provide an elaborated concept of the meso-level of sociality, i.e. for organizations. This does not mean that Bourdieu has no concepts or ideas for organizational issues, but he does not extend them to an integrative theoretical concept. All the more it is remarkable that some organization theorists already discovered the Habitus-Field-Theory as an inspiring approach for organization theory (for example [15, pp. 26]).

In fact, in a reanalysis of Bourdieu's theory we discovered, that there are many theoretical concepts and descriptions of the social world existing, which can be transformed to organizations in a sensible way. In the following, we want to argue the connection of the Habitus-Field-Theory with a theoretical conceptualisation of organizations. Prefixing, it is worthwhile to have a short look at the ideas and concepts of organizations as they are dominating organizational theory. For a long time in relevant literature, organizations were classified as solely goal-oriented, rational planned systems with a stable objectified and factual structure [21, p. 23] [14]. But during the last decades, a change on the perspective to organizations can be stated in many schools for organization research. According to Türk [21] there are four new perspectives on organizations to summarise and we will see that each of them corresponds to concepts of the Habitus-Field-Theory:

– The view of rational and deterministic social actions and processes in organizations is replaced by a view shaped by actions and processes, following an intrinsic logic depending on the special context, prevailing conditions, and activated structural relationships.
– The dynamic processes in organizations are accented, which take into account that organizations are permanent in motion and not fixed entities.
– There is a cultural and agile side of organizations, which means that organizations are composed of human beings, who are socialised in a way, who have special dispositions and interests, who cultivate certain rituals and ceremonies, and so on. These human characteristics are recovered as an important constitutional factor for organizations.

- Every organization has a micro-political facet, which includes that organizational effects and outcomes are not as predictable as assumed in traditional views on organizations. The self-interested individuals have their own goals, which are not necessarily concordant with the organizational goals. The organization has to be seen as a field, where strategic individuals play games, have fights and conflicts with each other in order to win and to extend their scope of action and their power. But this does not happen detached from the constitution of the organization because the fights and conflicts are embedded in the history of the organization and have to tie up to decisions and experiences made in the past.

All of the four aspects are covered by Bourdieus Habitus-Field-Theory. Especially, there are to stress and commemorate:

- the social field as a field of forces and a field of action,
- the dynamic relation between habitus, field and practice,
- the endowment and distribution of the capital forms, equipping actors with power and the chance to improve their position in the field, and last but not least
- the habitus of the actors, which provides them with a sense for the logic of the game in the field and helps them to develop strategies in order to follow their interests.

As a consequence of the portrayed changes of the perspective on organizations a large number of enhanced and novel approaches appeared on the organization research scene. This was accompanied and pushed by (partly extremely) fast and radical changes of the research objects, i.e. the organizations themselves. This is the result of modified market conditions, globalisation, new methods of production and management, partly aggravated competition relations, and economic crisis. To accentuate one very important example is the building of organizational relations and networks, which became an increasing significant form during the last three decades.

Even though inter-organizational networks are characterised by the collaboration of several single organizations, both, single organizations and inter-organizational network forms are assigned to the meso-level of sociality and can be described with the same analytical categories. This is based on the insight that single organizations and organizational networks process the same operations and mechanisms. Only the occurrence of the operation types and the mechanisms differ from organizational form to organizational form and have to be stressed more or less. In the end, every organizational form exhibits its own rationality and logic, which can be explored only through empirical research. For exploring organizational forms (whether they are single or networks of organizations), it is of central relevance to analyse the relations between the components and actors in it. It is useful to ask the following questions: Are they sporadically and fragile or stable and enduring? Are they in a permanent change or reproduced regularly through routines? Are they questioned and even ignored or widely accepted? And: are they based on case-by-case bargaining or are they highly standardised and regulated?

Answering these questions will give basic insights into the structuring and institutionalisation of the organizational forms (in the following: organizations) and the actions taking place. Bourdieus Habitus-Field-Theory offers the appropriate concepts to analyse the main organizational operations and mechanisms mentioned above. They will be made explicit as the matrix of delegation in Section 3.1. Furthermore, the theory makes it possible to discover the logic of the considered organizations. For this purpose, we will consider organizations as social fields and corporate actors. The term *social field* within the theory of Bourdieu is an appropriate analytical category to describe the structural conditions, the social practice of agents with respect to the dynamic processes taking place in an organization. Organizations as social fields can be described by four characteristics:

Firstly, any field shows an objective structure of the relations between the social positions occupied by the agents acting in the organization. A position is defined by restrictions and possibilities it imposes upon agents, by the present and potential composition of all sorts of resources an agent possesses (in terms of Bourdieu: economic, cultural, social and symbolic capital), and by its relation to other positions. The agents take a specific position related to other positions in the field depending on their capital-configuration.

Secondly, as any field can be compared to a game, also organizations follow its own "rules" and the agents are the players in this game. These are neither explicit norms to be obeyed by individuals nor the product of an intentional act, but regularities of social practice.

Thirdly, any organization as a social field has its own logic, that makes it autonomous in comparison to other fields. This logic excludes practices which are proceeding in another logic, e.g. practices in politics that focuses on obtaining power.

Fourthly, any organization is at the same time a field of struggles, where agents are opposing one another. In this sense, they are self-interested but in a specific way. The agent's rationality depends on the forms of capital it possesses and must be defined as a practical sense for the game of the field ("illusio"). Thus, their interests are socially shaped. As agents try to improve their relative positions, the distribution of all species of capital, the regularities, and even the task structure of a social field can be object of the agents' attempts to influence the organization structure in favour of their socially structured interests. Therefore, we view the agent as the force behind the development, change and reproduction of social structure of organizations as social fields.

Regarding these basic assumptions of Bourdieu's theory, the structures of organizations have to be considered as cultural and political constructions of dominant and dominated agents. Some agents are dominating according to their property and practical use of powerful resources. Therefore, social structures are formed by relations of power, whereby dominant agents aim to reproduce their pre-eminent position over challengers and dominated agents, which themselves try to conquer higher positions in the organizational distribution of power and authority [2].

The other analytical perspective is to consider organizations as *corporate agents*. As corporate agents organizations are seen as embedded into macro-fields (e.g. the economic field) of the society. This means that these organizational agents—as the organization as a whole—are competing with other corporate agents, trying to improve their objective position. As macro-social fields are sources of practice they constrain agents: organizations need to cope with the regularities of the field and to act according to its logic as they would not be able to act without the structures of the macro-field (e.g. economic organizations need to make profits, accept the institution of market, or cope with legal regulations). An organization, as a corporate agent, tries to improve its position in the macro-field. This is again depending on the interests and the capital equipment of the organization. The agents are developing specific "strategies" [3] how to reach a better position for the organization within the macro-field.

3 FORM — A Model for Realising Organization in MAS

As already mentioned, we hypothesise that this theoretical treatment can be turned into performance gains for multiagent systems, very much like they contribute to the pursuit of interests by human actors in social fields. In order to validate this hypothesis, we will now use the abstract sociological description of the mechanisms in the social field to elaborate the mechanisms at work in organizational networks and show how they can be used to structure the collaboration of multiple agents.

3.1 The Matrix of Delegation — A Grammar for MAS Organization

Recent work on delegation (see e.g. [5] for an extensive treatment), has shown that delegation is a complex concept highly relevant in multiagent systems. The mechanism of delegation makes it possible to pass on tasks (e.g. creating a plan for a certain goal, extracting information) to other individuals and furthermore, allows specialisation of these individuals for certain tasks (functional differentiation and role performance). We will refer to this interpretation as *task delegation*. Representing groups or teams is also an essential mechanism in situations which are dealing with social processes of organization, coordination and structuring. We distinguish two types of delegation: task delegation and social delegation. We call the procedure of appointing an agent as representative for a group of agents *social delegation*. Both types of delegation are essential for organizations, as they rely on becoming independent from particular individuals through task and social delegation.

Given the two types of delegation, it remains to explain how the action of delegation is performed. We observe four distinct mechanisms for delegation:

Economic exchange is a standard mode in markets: the delegate is being paid for doing the delegated task or representation. In economic exchange, a good or task is exchanged for money, while the involved parties assume that the value of both is of appropriate similarity.

Gift exchange, as an important sociological mechanism [2], denotes the mutually deliberate deviation from the economic exchange in a market situation. The motivation for the gift exchange is the expectation of either reciprocation or the refusal of reciprocation. Both are indications to the involved parties about the state of their relationship. This kind of exchange entails risk, trust, and the possibility of conflicts (continually no reciprocation) and the need for an explicit management of relationships in the agent. The aim of this mechanism is to accumulate strength in a relationship that may pay off in the future.

Authority is a well known mechanism, it represents the method of organization used in distributed problem solving. It implies a non-cyclic set of power relationships between agents, along which delegation is performed. However, in our framework authority relationships are not determined during design time, but the result of an agent deciding during runtime to give up autonomy and allow another agent to exert power.

Voting: is established as a mechanism whereby a number of equals determines one of them to be the delegate by some voting mechanism (majority, two thirds, etc.). Description of the mandate (permissions and obligations) and the particular circumstances of the voting mechanism (registering of candidates, quorum) are integral parts of the operational description of this mechanism and must be accessible to all participants.

As can easily be seen, all four mechanisms work for both types of delegation: for example, economic exchange can be used for social delegation as well as for task delegation. Possibly this set of mechanisms is not complete, however, many mechanisms occurring in human organizations that seem not be covered here, are combinations of the described mechanisms.

3.2 The Spectrum of Organizational Forms

In general, we allow agents to be members in several organizations at the same time. In order to tell which of their organizations is responsible for an incoming order, this general rule is limited to the case that all organizations were created for producing different types of jobs. Membership in organizations created for the same type of order are not allowed, so it is always clear how to process an order. We will now describe (building on the matrix of delegation from the previous section) seven different types of organization and non-organization for MAS in the order of increasing coupling between agents along a spectrum. The names for the different forms are derived from the types of firms that are observed by organizational sociology.

In our presentation we will proceed from the most autonomous form of coordination along organizational types where agents partially give up autonomy up to a stage where they even surrender identity and merge into a single new agent[5] and focus on the differences in order to avoid redundancy where forms exhibit similarities. The agents may shift from market interaction to an organizational type where they give up only little autonomy to a form where they give up more autonomy and vice versa during runtime. The criterion for giving up autonomy is the volume of tasks they delegate among themselves in order to execute a complex task. The concluding summary of this section will then give a synopsis of all organizational types.

For modelling each of the types of organization we specify regularities, formal structures and the logic of these fields, stating what the organization's member agents are allowed to do, what they are obliged to do, and what they are forbidden to do. The delegation matrix provides the concepts for describing the interaction between agents.

---

[5] A discussion of the relation of this work to the concept of adjustable autonomy can be found in [16].

Autonomous Agents: This form of coordination is not of practical relevance but rather the theoretical starting point, with fully uncoupled agents. All agents that provide services do not interact with each other to accomplish their tasks, the only interaction taking place is between providers and customers.

Market: In the market-style interaction, agents directly exchange jobs and some kind of payoff (here represented as money). This does not imply that agents build up relationships or an organization in the strict sense. Interaction is short-termed, based solely on a case by case basis (micro-level). The provider agent that re-delegates parts of a job acts as the representative for this specific job. As the basis for task-assignment, we apply the *Contract Net with Confirmation Protocol (CNCP)*. The CNCP uses the standards of the *Foundation for Intelligent Physical Agents (FIPA)* as a reference (cf. [7]). It extends Smith's contract-net protocol (CNET) [19] and avoids the problem of committing too early, which often leads to sub-optimal outcomes in the CNET, and can be applied in a cascading manner (for more detailed discussions see [12,16]). In the best case, the CNCP requires six messages between a contractor and a contractee to assign a job. The HNCP is used for inter-organizational communication, market interaction, and intra-organizational communication in the organizational forms *virtual enterprise* and *alliance*.

Virtual Enterprise: The virtual enterprise is a temporary network of legally independent companies to share skills, costs and access to each other's market. Virtual enterprises promise to offer the best of both worlds, flexibility and economy of scale. They are networks of legally and economically independent enterprises, each concentrating on its core competencies and out-sourcing the rest, modelled on the best-of-breed organization. The virtual enterprise appears and acts like a single enterprise to the outside [4]. Moreover, there is no physical institutionalization of central management functions. The contracts defining the relationships between the participating enterprises are deliberately left loose, in order to facilitate quick formation and greater flexibility in re-organization. In our model, a virtual enterprise consists of provider agents with equal rights, there is no single designated representative. A virtual enterprise is product-specific. Each member agent may accept jobs, but must start a new internal auction for each of its subtypes among its partners. This member agent becomes the representative of the virtual enterprise for this specific job, other members may be representatives of the organization for other jobs. There is no specific profit distribution other than the normal negotiation in the course of the internal auctions.

Alliance: An alliance as an organizational type is different to the virtual enterprise in that it is manifested by a long term contract among the participants and involves closer cooperation [9]. The relationships between the companies are formalised by contract, which is the result of negotiation between the different involved companies. Alliances are only to a degree economically and legally integrated. Therefore, the profit distribution is regulated for all internal transactions in advance. Alliances are founded to create at least one new product. As the companies are only partially integrated they are usually supplying other products apart from the alliance as well. Thus, they are generally allowed to join other organizational types apart from those which produce the same product as the alliance. As alliances are in some way legally integrated they need to appoint at least one CEO (representative). According to legal requirements, this is done by voting. The representation of the alliance incurs valuable reputation and contact to customer agents implies (economic) power. Quitting of one of the agents with many customer contacts may cause loss to the organization, as customers may prefer to interact with the provider agent they already are acquainted with, no matter in which organization it is in. We model the alliance so that only representatives can accept orders from outside. To decrease the incentive to join the alliance solely for this purpose and for the stability of the organization, and a focal participant, who is, due to his already powerful position, not reliant on this increase in reputation, is appointed by *social delegation* through *voting* to represent the alliance. The profit is distributed among the representative and all other agents necessary for performing the task by using *economic exchange* and *gift exchange*. However, on creation of the alliance, agents agree on a ratio (which is in our case fixed by the designer) that describes how profit is split between the representative agent and the other agents that are involved in performing the task.

Strategic Network: Strategic networks differ from virtual enterprises in that they use stronger legal contracts, and feature a *hub firm* that sets up the network, and takes proactively care of it [10]. The hub firm in a strategic network is usually significantly larger than the other members of the network. It coordinates activities in the strategic network, but the members retain their legal independence and autonomy. This network arrangement allows a participating firm to specialise in those activities of the value chain that are essential to its competitive advantage, reaping all the benefits of specialisation, focus, and, possibly, size. The time frame and financial volume are usually larger than in the case of virtual enterprises, but firms have still the right to leave the network.

Representatives know about the other agents' schedules and resources, and can instruct them to do a job at a given time. Strategic networks are product-specific, so multiple memberships are allowed. Since multiple memberships can result in a representative not being up-to-date about an agent's resource allocation, the underlying protocol (Direction with confirmation protocol, DCP, cf. [16]) contains a confirmation step for the case that the subordinate agent has accepted an order from outside the strategic network and his resource allocation has changed since he last informed the representative about it. In the best case of successful task-assignment the protocol uses four messages. Agents have to inform their representatives about changes in resource allocation as soon as possible. The profit distribution occurs according to a fixed ratio.

Group: Groups are formed from enterprises that retain their legal independence, but are bound by contract to the authority of the central firm. Here, we mean group as the organizational type of a firm as in "Bertelsmann group", not in the socio-psychological meaning "team". In contrast to the strategic network, no multiple memberships are allowed, and there usually is no exit option for subordinate firms. All economic activities are focused on the group and subject to directions from the superior enterprise. The interdependency between the firms is found in an authoritative hierarchy, whereas in strategic networks, it is based on economic relationships.

In our model, an agent who is a member of a group is not allowed to be a member of any other organization. Any incoming order has to be processed as group. Superior agents have to bounce incoming orders. Representatives may order other agents to do a specific job. This inclusion of all economic activity in the group results in the representative agent always being up-to-date about its body agents' resource allocations. The underlying group direction protocol (Direction protocol, DP; cf. [16]) does therefore not require a confirmation phase and is shorter than the strategic network protocol. A protocol instance consists only of two messages. The representative retains all the profit for orders completed by the group. Each round, it pays a fixed amount of money to each body agent.

Corporation: The corporation is the result of the complete inclusion of all legal and economic aspects of the original companies into a new entity. This organizational form is at the hierarchical end of the spectrum between market and hierarchy. Companies merging into a corporation give up all of their autonomy. The process is usually not reversible; once inside a corporation, the former status cannot be regained. In the business world, the process of merging usually happens when a large company assimilates a much smaller one. We model corporations by letting the head assimilate the resources of its body agents. After the assimilation, the body agents are removed from the simulation. The head then acts like a normal single agent, except that it does not form new organizations.

We chose to describe the models of multiagent organization starting with the most autonomous form and proceeded to the one with least autonomy. The model gives a framework for the agents decision during runtime, which depends on the current situation of all participating agents. In theory, each individual agent can be enabled to choose, depending on the situation in the multiagent system, whether it is in its interest to change its current status. As each organizational type has advantages and disadvantages, it may well be that a transition is not beneficial in the light of the current market situation.

4   Evaluation of the Performance Benefits of Organizations

The central setting for this evaluation is a market of two kinds of agents: customer agents that have jobs they need to be done, and provider agents that have resources to perform jobs. The jobs may require more types of resources than a single agent can provide, hence providers need to collaborate. The customers try to find providers who can complete the jobs by an auction mechanism. They are allowed to ask a limited number of agents for bids in each auction, as we assume that in practice it will not be feasible for every agent to communicate to every other agent. All agents are self-interested entities that do not necessarily have a common goal; we allow them to be designed and owned by different parties, which limits the possibilities of global control of the task assignment scenario. Another important condition is that the market is not totally predictable; the provider agents do not know what the future orders of the customers will be. In order to find out how efficient this market works and to measure the changes in performance that result from application of the proposed organizational forms, we investigate the number of messages sent in the system, the agent income, and the rate of performed jobs. A system that uses few messages exchanged between agents for assigning the same number of jobs is considered to be more efficient than one that uses many messages. Similarly, a system is considered more efficient if it succeeds in assigning a larger number of tasks.

If the system contains many agents or the jobs to be assigned require the collaboration of many providers, assigning the jobs with auctions becomes increasingly complex and methods to improve the performance of the system become more important. If the same type of job needs to be assigned several times or some parts of changing jobs are constant, the system might be more efficient if this repeating structure on the demand side were reflected by a repeating structure on the provider side, that is, if providers who are successful at completing a job together form relationships that facilitate long-term teamwork.

4.1 Self-Organization

The central issue for self-organization in our work is that we cannot predict what the best system organization will be to fulfil the customers' requirements. In such scenarios, the option we pursue is to let the providers organize themselves during runtime and let them decide what organizational structure is most profitable for them. One reasonable criterion for the selection of partners is the experience the agent had with them. If the agent has delegated many tasks to the other agent or received many task delegations from it, part of the preconditions of an efficient organization containing these agents are met. For this decision, we allow each agent to keep a record of the trade history with the other agents. Each agent has an agent model for each other agent containing the order volume of tasks it delegated to it and received from it. The decision process of whether to build a new organization and with whom rides on the normal auction process: whenever a customer has found a set of agents that together can complete its task, this set of agents checks whether it is in their interest to form an organization.

If agents decide to build an organization as described above, they form a virtual enterprise, the organizational form with the least commitment necessary. This organizational form can be upgraded to a form with more commitment if the collaboration in the organization has shown to be profitable for the agents, or it can be resolved if it turns out that the organization is inefficient and the agents are better off working as market agents again. The progression of organizational forms is along the spectrum of decreasing autonomy, that is, new organizations start out as virtual enterprises, which can be upgraded to alliances and to strategic networks. Strategic networks can be upgraded to groups, and those to corporations. All organizational forms except the corporation can be resolved. Agents who are part of a group that decides to form a corporation merge into a single agent and remain so for the rest of the simulation. Organizations that turn out to be inefficient do not downgrade one step down the spectrum, rather they resolve completely. The reasoning behind this is that the organization is likely to have become inefficient because the order situation has changed, so that a complete regrouping might be more reasonable than just lowering the commitments of existing organizations.

4.2 Test Environment

Time is modelled as discrete rounds. Each round, customers have the option to announce a job that can consist of several tasks and a deadline that can be the current or a future round. Elementary tasks, are termed by single letters: A, B, etc. They can be combined to form composed jobs, termed by strings whose letters specify the tasks they are composed of. For example, a job ABC can be performed by completing (independently) tasks A, B, and C. Each job has a deadline that specifies the maximum number of rounds the completion of the job may take.

Each new round, the customers announce their jobs to the providers by initiating a new auction for each job. An auction is started by sending orders to a number of provider agents asking for completion of the job. The round ends when all auctions have terminated. How providers react to calls for proposals sent to them depends on whether they have formed an organization with other providers or not and on the form of this organization. For example, a representative of a *strategic network* which receives an order ABC might ask two of its subordinate agents whether they can complete orders B and C, respectively. When starting new auctions, not all providers may be sent a call for proposals. We define a message limit that limits the number of providers that may be asked per auction (which remains constant across all configurations). Unlimited auctions are not realistic, especially if the number of agents becomes very large. This message limit is an independent variable **which** is set to two percent of the population (adapted when the population increases). Since not all providers can be asked, agents starting an auction evaluate all other agents taking the trade history into account. The trade history has also an effect when choosing peer agents to form an organization.

Agents that process an order in market fashion and not as members of an organization check how much of the order they can do by themselves. If they do not have the resources for all of the types in the order, they start a new auction asking other providers to complete the parts of the job they cannot do by themselves. They start only one auction (with several participants) for each order, that is, if the agent received an order ABC and can only do A, it will start an auction asking for BC. It will also take into account whether it is member of an organization (if member of an organization for AB, it will only start an auction for C). Agents receiving calls for an auction also consider their memberships (if an order for ABC comes in, and they are a member of various organizations they will make a bid for a type fulfilling as much as possible for the original bid.

4.3   Analysis of Scaling of Population

In our first scenario, we start the simulation with one hundred agents, which are divided into four groups of twenty agents that can each perform one of the task types A, B, C, and D and twenty customer agents. Every customer brings in one job of type ABCD per round. Every ten rounds, another one hundred agents with the same division in four by twenty agents per task type plus customers enter the simulation up to round ninety, from which on the population remains constant with one thousand agents scheduling two hundred jobs requiring four collaborators each in each round. Here, the number of jobs, i.e. the number of customers increases in constant relation to the provider agents. After each entry of new agents into the population, the population remains constant for ten rounds, before a new set of agents enters. After round one hundred, we let the simulation continue to run for twenty rounds to observe the effect of a longer period allowing for adaptation to a constant job demand. We ran this scenario with two configurations. First,

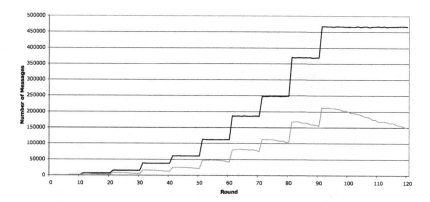

Fig. 2. The number of messages per round required to solve a task assignment problem (black line represents pure market scenario, grey line represents performance of the self organising agents). Fewer messages are considered to increase performance and hence, scalability.

only with agents in a market relationship and second, with agents that are enabled to engage in organizational structures, and can self-organize according to the effect of the organizational structure to the current customer demand. Both conditions are repeated ten times, the data presented is the average over all runs. For analysis, the results we receive are divided into three different performance measures.

Number of Messages. Regarding the number of messages needed for task fulfilment (cf. Figure 2), we observe a noticeable difference between market and organized agents. Although both configurations have in common that the number of exchanged messages increases every time new agents appear in the system (i.e. in round 11, 21, 31, 41 and so on), the number of messages between the market agents increases faster, while the organized agents seem to compensate the messages they exchange with the added agents in the subsequent rounds. The rising of the message numbers processes to a considerably lower degree.

Number of Completed Tasks. The number of completed tasks (not depicted) is almost identical for market and organized agents. This is remarkable as it is possible that the self organising agents specialise on types of tasks (e.g. ABC and BCD) that make it difficult to combine to the overall job required by the customer (e.g. ABCD). This result allows to directly compare the other parameters.

Income. Figure 3 shows for every form of institution which portion of the total income of each round it produces. It is easy to see that revenue is not distributed evenly. Until the first organizational forms come into existence, only the market relationship generates revenue. The large share for this institution is strengthened whenever new agents without organizational links enter the population (every ten rounds, illustrated by the peaks in each graph every ten rounds). After five rounds, the thresholds for building organizational networks are surpassed and virtual enterprises come into existence

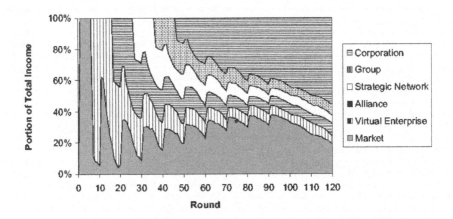

Fig. 3. Proportions of the total income for each type of organizational network per round.

and claim revenue. Ten rounds later, the first upgrades from the virtual enterprises are made, alliances generate revenue. The absolute number of virtual enterprises is not decreasing, because other single agents that entered the population in round ten, create virtual enterprises and add to the revenue of this form. The corporation shows a more continuous increase of income than the single agents who increase their income only as a result of new agents entering the system. Note that both, the corporation and the single agent share the attribute to be one inseparable agent, but there exists one crucial difference between them: the single agent has the resource to fulfil one task type (A, B, C, or D) and needs to find collaborators for each job, whereas the corporations have the resources to execute tasks with type ABCD. The revenue of agents interacting in market style increases up to round ninety but decreases when no further agents enter the system. From this point, all agents have time to adapt to the constant customer demand and upgrade their organizational networks without further perturbation. This suggests that the rate at which we enter agents into the system exceeds the system's ability to absorb new agents.

4.4 Scaling of Population — Change of Type of Job Stream

In this scenario, we start the simulation with fifty customer agents that request one job of type AB each round. Also, fifty provider agents with resource of type A, and fifty agents with resource B are present. As in the scenario before, this is chosen to allow each requested job to be done. We scale the population every twenty rounds up by fifty agents. However, this time the customer agents change their requested product. From round 21 on, they request jobs of type ABC, from round 41 on type ABCD and so on. Correspondingly, agents entering the simulation bring in a new type of resource. In round 21, fifty agents with resource of type C enter the system, in round 41 fifty

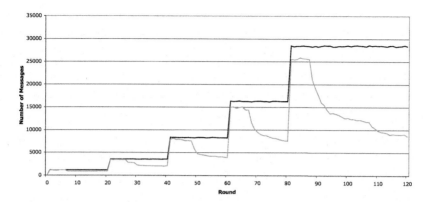

Fig. 4. Number of messages for the second investigation that changes the customer demand over time and only agents of a given resource type enter the population (black line represents pure market scenario, grey line represents performance of the self organising agents). Fewer messages are considered increased performance and hence, scalability.

agents with resource of type D join the others, etc. So the population starts with one hundred provider agents and is scaled up until round 81 from which on the population remains constant with three hundred agents scheduling the fifty jobs requiring two to six collaborators. Here, the number of jobs is constant, but each customer requires more and more agents to collaborate. As before, we let the simulation continue to run for twenty rounds at the end to observe the effect of a longer period allowing for adaptation to a constant job demand. Again, we ran this scenario with two configurations: with and without self-organization, for both, the presented data is averaged over ten runs each. This time, however, the task for new agents is not to find other agents to create networks for solving the jobs for (also new) customer agents, but to integrate with the already existing networks in the population.

The number of messages required in this scenario are shown in Figure 4. This data shows that, as in the previous investigation, self-organization allows for a considerable reduction of messages required for solving the task-assignment. Again, the arrival of new agents that are not integrated results in peaks that are decline after the process of self-organization can reduce the number of messages as integration of the agents proceeds.

From a sociological point of view, the results encourage the assumption that agents integrated in organizational networks have some advantages compared to interacting market agents. First of all, there is to mention the lower number of messages that have to be exchanged to manage the planned tasks. This is traced back to the in sociological and organizational theory popular fact of the stable social relations, which is developed as consequence of recurrent contacts and cooperative actions of agents. The agents become acquainted with each other and develop reciprocal expectations concerning the actions of the other agents (see for expectation structures [18, 176 pp.]. Moreover, the agents cultivate preferences for other agents of whom they know that they have the abilities and capacities to complete the task (e.g. of type C) fast, reliable, and in a qualitative good way. Therefore, the successful cooperation leads to further cooperation in future tasks, if they are of the same type and the same abilities are needed, and finally meet in building an organizational network. The agents, integrated in the same network, continue to intensify their relations, so they become more stable and reliable. An additional aspect is that in organizational networks the structuring of relations deepens (forced by authority, division of labour, social delegation, communication rules) so that one important result of network building is the reduction of messages, that have to be exchanged for task assignment. Referring to the introduced Habitus-Field-Theory of Bourdieu, the view of organizations as social fields and corporate agents is picked up here.

5   Conclusion

The central contribution of this paper is to show that achieving an explanational link between the level of interaction (micro-level) and the level of society (macro-level) assists the understanding of how social systems achieve quantitative scalability. In order to establish this link, we presented a framework, in which multiagent systems can form types of collaboration inspired by organizational networks in a natural fashion. This framework lays out different organizational forms relative to the parameters: mechanisms for task and social delegation, membership, profit distribution, number of representatives and protocol for task-assignment. This theory of how agents of different capabilities can be tied together is built on a sociological description of inter-organizational networks and creates a meso level of sociality inside the system.

We strengthened our argument by empircally investigating two settings, involving population sizes between one hundred and one thousand complex agents (quantitative scalability), each with differentiated behaviour creating a micro- and meso-level of sociality (qualitative scalability). These investigations showed considerable advantages of the qualitative scaling for quantitative scalability. In future work we want to naturally extend the model and our implementation to the macro-level, including other social fields that interact with the already demonstrated economic field. Particular interest lies in fields that regulate this economic field (like politics, law, jurisdiction) and again receive feedback from it. Our expectation is that further enriching our model in this fashion will provide new methods for increasing performance and ensuring quality of solutions, e.g when facing malicious agents.

6   Acknowledgements

We are indebted to sociologists Dr. Michael Florian, Dr. Frank Hillebrandt and Bettina Fley, and to Dr. Klaus Fischer and the Multiagent Systems Group at DFKI for many inspiring discussions. Tore Knabe provided great support in implementing the simulation testbed and conducting basic experiments.

References

1. P. Bourdieu. *In Other Words. Essays Towards a Reflexive Sociology.* University Press & Cambridge/UK: Polity Press, Stanford/Cal., 1990.
2. P. Bourdieu. *Pascalian Meditations.* Polity Press, Cambridge, Eng., Oxford, Eng., 2000.
3. P. Bourdieu and L. Wacquant. *An Invitation to Reflexive Sociology.* Polity Press, Chicago, 1992.
4. L.M. Camarinha-Matos, H. Afsarmanesh, C. Garita, and C. Lima. Towards an architecture for virtual enterprises. *Journal of Intelligent Manufacturing*, 9(2):189–199, 1998.
5. C. Castelfranchi and R. Falcone. Towards a theory of delegation for agent-based systems. *Robotics and Autonomous Systems*, 24:141–157, 1998.
6. H. Esser. *Soziologie - Allgemeine Grundlagen.* Campus Verlag, Frankfurt am Main, 1999.
7. FIPA. Foundation for Intelligent Agents http://www.fipa.org/repository/ips.html, 2002.
8. A. Giddens. *The Constitution of Society.* Polity Press, Cambridge, 1984.
9. R. Gulati and Martin Garguilo. Where do interorganizational networks come from? *American Journal of Sociology*, 104:1439–1493, 1999.
10. J. Carlos Jarillo. On strategic networks. *Strategic Management Journal*, 9:31–41, 1988.
11. A. Kieser. *Organisationstheorien.* Kohlhammer, Stuttgart, 2001.
12. T. Knabe, M. Schillo, and K. Fischer. Improvements to the FIPA contract net protocol for performance increase and cascading applications. In *International Workshop for Multi-Agent Interoperability at the German Conference on AI (KI-2002)*, 2002.
13. N. Luhmann. *Soziologische Aufklärung 2.* Westdeutscher Verlag, Opladen, 1975.
14. R. Mayntz and R. Ziegler. Soziologie der Organsiation. In Renate Mayntz, K. Roghmann, and Rolf Ziegler, editors, *Organisation - Militär, Handbuch der empirischen Sozialforschung*, pages 1–141. DTV, 1977.
15. W. Powell and P. DiMaggio. *The New Institutionalism in Organizational Analysis.* University of Chicago Press, London, 1991.
16. M. Schillo. Self-organization and adjustable autonomy: Two sides of the same medal? *Connection Science*, 14(4):345–359, 2003.
17. M. Schillo, K. Fischer, F. Hillebrandt, M. Florian, and A. Dederichs. Bounded social rationality: Modelling self-organization and adaptation using habitus-field theory. In *Proceedings of the Workshop on Modelling Artificial Societies and Hybrid Organizations (MASHO) at ECAI 2000*, 2000.
18. U. Schimank. *Handeln und Strukturen. Einführung in die akteurtheoretische Soziologie.* Juventa Verlag, Weinheim und München, 2000.
19. R. G. Smith. The contract net: A formalism for the control of distributed problem solving. In *Proceedings of the Fifth International Joint Conference on Artificial Intelligence (IJCAI-77)*, page 472, 1977.
20. A. Treibel. *Einführung in die soziologischen Theorien der Gegenwart.* Leske + Budrich, Opladen, 2000b.
21. K. Türk. *Neuere Entwicklungen in der Organisationsforschung. Ein Trendreport.* F. Enke, Stuttgart, 1989.
22. M. Weber. *Wirtschaft und Gesellschaft.* Mohr, Tübingen, 1922.
23. A. Weymann. Interaktion, Sozialstruktur und Gesellschaft. In Hans Joas, editor, *Lehrbuch der Soziologie*, pages 93–121. Campus Verlag, 2001.

Agents Enacting Social Roles.
Balancing Formal Structure and Practical Rationality in MAS Design

Martin Meister[1], Diemo Urbig[2], Kay Schröter[2], and Renate Gerstl[1]

[1] Technical University Berlin
Institute for Sociology
Technology Studies
{meister, gerstl}@ztg.tu-berlin.de
[2] Humboldt-Universität zu Berlin
Department of Computer Science
Artificial Intelligence Group
{urbig, kschroet}@informatik.hu-berlin.de

Abstract. We introduce an integrated approach to the conceptualisation, implementation and evaluation of a MAS (multi-agent system) which is based on sociological concepts of practical roles and organisational coordination via negotiations. We propose a middle level of scale, located between interaction and the overall organisational structure, as the starting point for MAS design, with formal and practical modes of coordination to be distinguished over all relevant levels of scale. In our contribution, we present the modelling principles of our MAS, the agent architecture and the implementation. In the next step the approach is extended to a methodology for the investigation of processes of hybridisation, which means the re-entering of artificial sociality in a real-world domain. The integrated approach is intended to contribute to a generalised understanding of the Socionics program, which in our view should be seen as the enrolment of independent, but subsequent steps in an overall interdisciplinary approach.

1 Introduction

Sociologist Pierre Bourdieu pointed to the subtle and often ignored difference between theoretical rationality and the "logic of practice" [10]. This difference, we will argue, has to be taken into account when trying to capture the robustness and flexibility of human organisations, and is especially important for any effort to model information systems on mechanisms of organisational coordination. In the INKA-Project[1], part of the German Socionics program, we took this insight as our very starting point. Computational agents that "act" and coordinate themselves in a way that, at least in principle,

---

[1] The acronym INKA stands for "INtegration of Cooperating Agents in complex organisations" and is carried out by the Artificial Intelligence Group (Prof. H.-D. Burkhard) of the Department of Computer Science at Humboldt-Universität zu Berlin, and the Institute for Sociology, Technology Studies (Prof. W. Rammert) at Technical University Berlin; see cf. [12]. The results reported here are based on the project's state as of end of 2003.

K. Fischer, M. Florian, and T. Malsch (Eds.): Socionics, LNAI 3413, pp. 104–131, 2005.

mimics human actors in organisational environments have to cope with the tension between the formal descriptions given by the organisation at large and the patterned expectations that derive from their daily interactions on the shop-floor level. In sociology, one way of coping with this tension is role theory, focussing on the different forms of enactment of formal role descriptions and practical roles. Furthermore, from organisational theory and empirical investigations we know that in the "real world" daily negotiations by the employees themselves are one way of working around the incoherencies of formal prescriptions, job descriptions and work schedules. Based on these considerations the INKA-project is oriented by two main objectives: to model and implement a technical system, in which the agents are capable of coordinating themselves via negotiating on the basis of practical roles, and to develop an approach for the investigation of hybrid sociality which emerges if those agents are re-entered into human organisations. Our application scenario are negotiations on shift exchanges in a hospital (for details see [34,23]).

Our contribution begins with a brief discussion of the conceptual problems that occur if computer programs are to be modelled on practical relations or on sociological concepts of practical modes of interaction; this leads us to the formulation of three general challenges (2.) within the Socionics program. In order to address these challenges, we propose an integrated approach (3.) that correlates all activities in Socionic systems development as four subsequent steps. In this contribution, we focus especially on the modelling step and on the hybridisation step. In the next sections we introduce in some detail (4.) our sociologically grounded modelling of practical roles and negotiating agents and (5.) our framework for a corresponding MAS-architecture. Afterwards (6.), we describe shortly the implementation of our system. As the last step of the cycle we present a methodological instrument (7.) for an investigation of hybridisation. We conclude with a brief discussion of the scalability issue (8.) for an approach that is, like the one presented, focussing on a middle-level of scale.

2   Practical Rationality: A Threefold Challenge Within the Socionics Program

Human organisations offer an effective way of coordinating individual behaviour while at the same time remaining capable of flexible adaptation to changing environments (cf. [2]). Concepts and theories from the sociology of organisations are thus perceived as a promising blueprint for the design of innovative information systems, especially in the realm of MAS research, where the overall functionality of the system is derived from the coordination of autonomous software entities. Moreover, human organisations, unlike many other social entities, tend to work out an explicit description of their own coordination principles—rules for membership, planning schedules, job descriptions adjusted to the internal division of labour, hierarchical chains of prescription and control, and so forth. These descriptions, often provided by management units, typically present a formally coherent and encompassing picture of the organisation's functioning. Sociological conceptualisations of organisational coordination, too, have elaborated this formal, explicit and hierarchical body of regulations as the basis for functionality, rational decision making (cf. [33]), or the type of sociality dominant in (Western) modernity. So, at a first glance it might seem to be quite easy to model information systems on principles of organisational coordination.

Revisiting the iron cage, however, weakened this notion of a consistent body of formal rules and regulations, and even contested the notion of any formal rationality[2] within organisations. The findings of empirical investigations in the "real life" of organisations pointed to a picture of "organised anarchies" (Cohen, March and Olsen [15]) because formalised descriptions turned out to be inconsistent and often conflicting with one another, thus creating individual frustration and large-scale inflexibility. Sociologists have drawn different conclusions from these findings for an adequate conceptualisation of organisational coordination, which lead to different consequences for the design of information systems, respectively. One way of dealing with inconsistencies in organisations is to uncover misleading or conflicting regulations and especially "concurrencies" (ibid.), and instructing a corresponding re-design of formal structure; most of today's business support software can roughly be located in the line of this approach. But more recent directions of sociological research claim that the picture of the iron cage does not describe any organisational reality at all, but rather serves as a resource for legitimacy (DiMaggio and Powell [18]). Even more, formal structures in this view "dramatically reflect the myths of their institutionalised environments instead of the demands of their work activities" (Meyer and Rowan [36], pp. 431), leading to the consequence of "decreased internal coordination and control ... Structures are decoupled from each other and from ongoing activities. In place of coordination, inspection, and evaluation, a logic of confidence and good faith is employed" (ibid.: 430). Following this description it is obvious that formal structures by no means can serve as a guiding line for computational support systems or the design of MAS.

Sociological approaches that exile formal rationality to the realm of "ceremony" (ibid.) can be seen as corresponding to another body of research, which focuses on the specific (and always messy) realities on the micro-level of an organisation— the daily work practices at the shop floor-level, or speaking more generally: on "situated action" (Suchman [52]). Most research in Groupware and especially in CSCW (cf. [13]; [42]) follows this micro-level approach, stating that successful computer support and the design of any software system has to begin with the particular circumstances of every single case. But leaving aside every formal description of organisational coordination comes at a prize: Declaring all of the organisational structures on higher levels of scale (including the organisation at large) to be irrelevant, leads directly to a strong scepticism about the very sense of modelling (cf. [7]).

This brief discussion of current directions in the sociology of organisations seems to end up in a paradoxical situation, at least if they are regarded as a promising 'blueprint' for the design of MAS: While on the one hand all these approaches point to the importance of practical modes of coordination which emerge bottom-up, on the other hand

---

[2] We use the term 'formal rationality' to point at the correspondence between the self-descriptions of real organisations and those theoretical descriptions from the sociology of organisations which, besides all differences in scope, state that formal rules and regulation are 'rational' because they are the prerequisite of the functioning of the organisation as a viable social unit. An overview for the context of the Socionics program is given in [50].

all these approaches seem to discourage every attempt to model information systems on principles of organisational coordination.

In the discussions about an adequate theoretical background for MAS design, there seem to be two possible alternatives to overcome this paradoxical situation.

The first alternative draws on sociological concepts of the duality of social structures over different levels of scale. In this line of argument in his talk at 2000 Seeon Socionics conference, Les Gasser recommended concepts of mutual constitution of large-scale structures and situated interactions (Giddens and Weick) as the very starting point in DAI and in Socionics (see cf. [39]; [49]: 226ff). Fley and Florian (in this volume) present an analogical approach to model the dialectics of the micro- and macro-level, based on Bourdieus habitus-field-theory.

In a recent contribution, Castelfranchi pointed to a second alternative [14]. In discussing a "formalising of the informal" as the guideline for computer supported interaction and MAS design, he distinguishes three types of social order: formal (orchestrated) social control, spontaneous social order ("deliberate action" and the "invisible hand"), and informal patterns of social control which reside somewhat in between the first two types. He then continues to state that "what is needed is some attempt to 'incorporate' part of these layers and issues in the technology itself ... [The agents] should be able to manage—and thus partially understand—for example permissions, obligations, power, roles, commitments, trust". Drawing on these considerations we focus on the practical (in Castelfranchi's terms: the "informal") side of coordination by "incorporating" practical roles in the architecture of our agents, which enables them to create emergent patterns of interaction as if they would have been socialised in a bottom-up manner.[3]

Compared to full-fledged concepts of mutual structuration, this is a less ambitious approach, but it allows a quite straightforward (nonetheless a sociologically "dirty", to quote Schimank in this volume) modelling of a MAS. Furthermore, we hope that this approach is expandable up to the point where structures at a middle-level of scale are in fact produced by the agents interactions, and not only "incorporated" into the agents by the designers. Crucial for such an approach is that it deploys the micro-macro-dimension on both the formal and the practical side of coordination, giving both modes of coordination their own right. This results in a balance of formal and practical rationality in order to create and maintain a robust and flexible coordination within organisations.

Before proceeding, we want to sketch the consequences of these considerations for Socionics as a "triangular research program" (Malsch [32]). In our view, focussing on practical modes of interaction leads to a threefold Socionics challenge. With respect to the "computational reference", our approach plays out the ambiguous meaning of

---

[3] Castelfranchi is not very clear in his definition of "spontaneous", "self-organising" or "decentralised" social order. We assume that this is resulting from a purely enumerative conception of "interpersonal normative relationships": In sociology, terms like "the informal, implicit, spontaneous, bottom-up forms of social control" denote highly different concepts and phenomena, and we at least tried to be as explicit as possible with terms like the ones mentioned when developing our conception of practical roles. We also differ from Castelfranchi's approach by focussing on the modelling and creation of practical patterns, while he is focussing on a "convention to violate" the formal, as he calls it: "designed" patterns of interaction.

the word "formal". Specifying our approach means to mathematically formalise those practical patterns of interaction which lie beyond the explicit formal descriptions of organisations. As described above, Castelfranchi coined the slogan "formalising the informal" for this challenge, and this is in our view, a promising way to overcome the paradoxes mentioned above, thus contributing to a more balanced blueprint for sociologically grounded MAS.[4]

The other way round, modelling and computer simulation of practical rationality should also serve as instruments for sociology. In our experience, this "sociological reference" of Socionics is especially manifest when it comes to modelling because of the necessity of explicit specification. Modelling situated, practical patterns of interaction brings a sociological challenge to the forth because these patterns are often seen as lying beyond any possibility of generalisation. Thus, a tapered concept of practical rationality in the context of organisation studies can help to enhance sociological concept-building. Furthermore, simulations can throw light on those practice-based patterns in organisational life that are hard to tackle by usual methods of empirical investigation. An example is the smooth fit of practical roles within organisational units (see Sections 4.4 and 7.3).

The third goal of the Socionics program is to explore the consequences that are likely to occur if a sociologically grounded MAS is re-entered into human contexts. In the INKA-project, this means to explore those hybrid settings in which practice-based computer agents and skilled human actors have to cooperate. In sociology as well as in computer science, there are no approaches that can avoid the pitfalls of purely theoretical considerations and implementation studies likewise. So the socionic challenge here is to develop methodological instruments that enable an investigation of these hybrid constellations.

3   An Integrated Approach for System Development in Socionics

The three challenges outlined in the last section can be arranged as consecutive working steps in an overall path to a hybrid system. This path—supplemented by the necessary implementation—follows the socionic development cycle as it is shown in Figure 1, and consists of four stages. While targeting all of the aspects mentioned in the "Socionics' triangle" [32], we arrange these aspects as distinct activities with distinct goals that build subsequently on one another. What follows is that, on the one hand, every step should not only address its own logic, but should also be seen in the light of the following steps. On the other hand from every step the developer might be forced to rephrase the model.[5] The cycle begins with the modelling phase where the principles of agent coordination are derived from sociological theories (see Section 4) or, as in the case of our project, from additional empirical investigation in a specific domain. Either way, model-building can be seen as the basic activity in Socionics. As in other

---

[4] In the long run this can also be seen as a contribution to the development of more successful tools for computer support.

[5] In our view it is one important gain of an integrated approach that all stages of development are to be processed by a joint team of computer scientists and sociologists. Our experience is that this can put the "going concern" of Socionics [51] on a more structured basis.

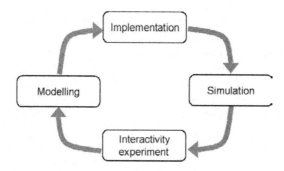

Fig. 1. The socionic development cycle.

fields of interdisciplinary research, models in Socionics serve as key "mediators" [37] between the disciplines involved, enabling a continuous dialogue between computer science and sociology; the prize for mediation is idealisation. Furthermore, the cycle itself produces requirements for the modelling process. It is of special importance that all models should be made complete, not only for reasons of internal theoretical consistence, but mainly because they are the starting point for any specification of the technical system.[6] For these two reasons, the basic model might seem "dirty" in an isolated view (to quote again Schimank in this volume), but at the end of the day we can see our agents to negotiate enacting practical roles.

In MAS design the sociological model has to be transformed in an explicit agent architecture. This is the computer scientists' part of the modelling. In our approach, the focus is on the formalisation of the negotiation process in the three-layered C-IPS framework with social roles being an architectural feature of the agents themselves (see Section 5). With respect to the intended usage of the system for interactivity experiments in hybrid settings, we require a distributed system that enables life-like negotiations between agents, between humans, as well as between agents and humans. Hence, it is necessary that the agents' negotiation behaviours are reasonable for humans. To ensure equitable interactions between humans and agents, humans interact with the system by "taking over" an agent. This requires agents with at least two degrees of autonomy: agents that act fully autonomous on behalf of humans and agents that are (partially) controlled by humans.

The next step in the cycle is the software engineering according to this agent architecture. In the case of our project, the model was implemented in a Java using the multi-agent platform JADE (see Section 6). The layered architecture of our agents enabled an incremental implementation, which made it possible to test every single layer in functional simulations in order to verify that the layers work properly.[7]

---

[6] In our project, the translation of the agent-based model into the formalised specifications of the technical MAS has led to a series of model revisions.

[7] The layered approach offered the opportunity to observe the behaviour of agents with an increasing autonomy: in a first run, the issue and partner of the negotiation were given, in a second run only the issue was given, and in a last run the agents' behaviour was unconstrained

Simulations, in the picture of the development cycle, can serve three different purposes: as mentioned, they first can be used as a check of the basic functionality of the technical system, and second they can serve as a check of the basic assumptions of the model. But in Socionics, simulations are mainly used as a special kind of methodology for sociological investigation: an artificial check of sociological hypotheses or an artificial 'expedition' into the foundations of social entities. In the case of our project these 'expeditions' are especially suited because they lead into the realms of practical coordination. This part of the social fabric is hard to tackle by conventional sociological methods because they remain mostly implicit in daily work practices and are hidden from the actors' perspectives as well as from the organisation's perspective.[8] All three purposes of simulation call for evaluation criteria. Because in MAS, especially if the agents are complex, the sheer number of relevant parameters is high, and random processes are likely to occur in the long run statistical methods to check the significance of simulation results should be developed and applied.

The last step of the Socionics' development cycle is the introduction of human actors into the simulation or the introduction of the MAS into a human social system which constitutes a hybrid sociality (see Section 7). Because an examination of the mixing of humans and agents, is in the Socionics program neither a question of software engineering nor a question of technology assessment, but in the first place a question of basic research, the challenge here is to develop a sound methodological approach.

In the following sections, we describe the steps of modelling, implementation (esp. the agent architecture) and interactivity experiments for the examination of hybridisation in some detail.

4   An Approach to Model Practical Roles

The first step in the design of a sociologically grounded MAS is to build a model of human social reality with respect to sociological concepts. As we argued in Section 2, this turns out to be a major challenge in the case of any modelling of organisational coordination, mainly because of the dichotomy between the purely formal and a purely practical conceptualisations. Furthermore, we generally argued for an approach which "incorporates" social mechanisms into the single agents and thus starts on a middle level of scale. In this section, we want to motivate in some detail why we choose social roles as the focus for modelling, and how this, in the overall picture, relates to negotiations. Based on this sketch of the 'backbone' of our modelling approach we outline the concrete modelling decisions that guide the basic principles of our agent architecture.

---

besides the allowance to negotiate. Again, these results sometimes made revisions of the model necessary.

[8] By running simulations, we especially want to gain insights in those mixing ratios of practical roles that enable or hinder a productive atmosphere, in which problems can be solved smoothly. In the case of our domain, this means that negotiations are often successful and do not take much time. For lack of space, we do not address this topic here.

4.1   Negotiations and Practical Roles in the Organisational Context

From sociological investigations in organisational coordination we know that one way of counteracting formal regulations and especially its incoherencies are negotiations by which the organisations' members themselves create a flow of problem solutions for their daily work practices. Negotiations can be defined as a situated mechanism for problem solving for those situations where actors (and our agents) have a high degree of autonomy and at the same time a high degree of mutual dependency. This view of negotiations at a first glace seems to be restricted for the interaction level of scale, but relating to sociological concepts (cf. [48]) we extend this insight to the organisational level of scale: Negotiations can also be conceptualised as a mechanism that constitutes a "negotiation system" within the organisation (cf. [25],[26],pp. 77-83), which is necessary for the achievement of an overall flexibility within the organisation.

But problem solving via negotiation clearly bears a danger: Permanent negotiations would be very time consuming and frustrating for the organisation's members, and it would be dysfunctional from the point of view of the organisation at large, simply because the members would be kept from getting their job done. So focussing on negotiations directly leads to the subsequent question: How can the dangers of permanent negotiations be avoided without destroying its advantages? In social life, there exists a solution for this problem: Every aspect of the negotiation process[9] can be based on patterned expectations about the future behaviour of the others. Drawing on these expectations can drastically reduce the expenses of negotiating. This is the point where social roles enter the picture because they are defined as patterned expectations.

4.2   From Role Theory to Modelling Principles

We argued that the concept of social roles is suitable and sufficiently concrete for our modelling purposes. But there is no smooth, or self-evident, way to transform role theory into a model for Socionics because in sociology there are two different and even competing conceptualisations of social roles.

The first conceptualisation is functionalist in nature. It states that all individuals are forced to play the roles assigned to them by institutions, and especially by formalised regulations of the division of labour. Force is defined as a (more or less rigid) normative pressure, or the "fear of sanctions" as in Dahrendorfs well known account on the "homo sociologicus" [17]. In consequence, focus has been on deviation from the roles ascribed to individuals, and on role conflicts within one individual. This first conceptualisation of roles has been strongly criticised, mainly because of its poor definition of the scope of social action, and because it has only a very narrow, if any, range of explanatory power (a summary of these arguments is given by Esser [20], pp. 82ff).

These critiques are crucial for the second conceptualisation of social roles, which mainly has been developed within the tradition of symbolic interactionism. In this tradition any assumption of "conformity" in human behaviour is rejected. Instead, focus is on the ongoing processes of interactively building (and re-building) social order. With

---

[9] In Section 5.2, we identify three important aspects: the selection of a promising issue, partner and next negotiation step.

respect to roles this is especially important for the role-taking process, which in this tradition is defined as follows: "Grouping behavior into 'consistent' units which correspond to generalizable types of actors" (Turner [53]: 32). In the organisational context, this means that the "formalized role prescriptions and the more flexible operation of the role-taking process" (ibid.) are different, and do have different consequences with respect to organisational coordination.

Our conceptualisation of practical roles draws strongly on the interactionist stance, with two major exceptions. Firstly, the interactionist tradition concentrates on the "sociology of the person", which relates to the various aspects of the role-taking process; role-making as a practical process of its own right is not addressed (we relate to this problem in Section 4.4). Secondly, all the aspects of formal prescriptions (and prerequisites) of coordination are marginalised or even deemed to be irrelevant.[10] See, for instance, the following quote: "The formal role itself, considered apart from the effective incorporation of the informal role, is merely a skeleton consisting of rules which are intended to invoke the appropriate informal roles. The formalized roles are to the full roles as detonators to explosives—merely devices to set them in motion" (ibid.: 28). As opposed to this view, we model formal roles and practical roles as two different processes, the first constraining the interaction possibilities, the latter to be emerging from this interaction (see Figure 2). The overall picture, then, does not show a merging process within one person (see, again, the quote from Turner above), but a balanced process within the organisation, with a clear emphasis on the practical side. In this picture, the concept of roles serves as a mediating level of scale between the daily negotiations and the structures of the organisation at large.[11]

4.3   Modelling Decisions

Within the picture given, some more detailed specifications had to be made explicit. Modelling, as opposed to considerations in texts, requires these kinds of decisions.

Formal Roles as Constraints. Organisations assign formal positions to their members in order to manage and control the internal division of labour. Here we made two modelling decisions. Firstly, formal roles are modelled as constraints for the agents'

---

[10] The duality between formal and practical descriptions within organisation science, which we outlined in Section 1, is repeated at this point.

[11] The details of the modelling and the concrete data are drawn from our empirical investigation in a specific domain, personal employment planning in hospitals. This domain shows all the characteristics of complex organisations mentioned above: The overlapping of different professions, hierarchies, and local styles (cf. [46]) leads to a high degree of incoherence in the official prescriptions and plans. Especially the official shift plans are conflicting with an adequate consideration of the individual leisure-time interests. Therefore, the employees negotiate and trade single work shifts aside of the official shift plan, thus making use of the scope the management intentionally leaves blank. These shift negotiations are a daily requirement under rigid time restrictions. Our theoretical assumption is that this works because the negotiations are carried out on the basis of a limited set of practical roles, an assumption that is backed by empirical evidence (for details see [34]).

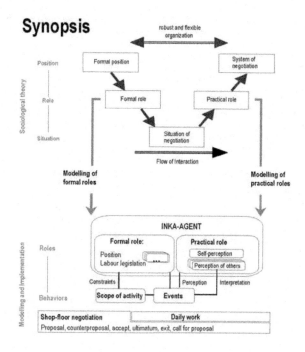

Fig. 2. The overall picture of the modelling approach

behaviour. Because in every developed organisation these formal prescriptions are multidimensional in itself, we distinguish three necessary aspects of the internal division of labour (this draws on a distinction introduced by Geller [22]): the professional division in the "functional circles" of physicians, nursing staff and administration; the hierarchical chains of commanding authority and duties; and the spatial division. We modelled all three aspects as constraints for the internal reasoning processes of the agents, thus limiting the scope of possible individual action in every situation. Additionally, we included external prescriptions like, e.g., labour time legislation and the salary stages regulated by labour agreement. The second modelling decision is that the agents are equipped with some amount of capital with respect to their formal position.

Multiple Capital Interests. Agents decide by considering their interests. This can be described mathematically as an expected increase in capital. This capital stock originates from the formal positions. Organisations, as depicted above, have to equip their members with some capital in order to fulfil their positions. Even on the formal side of organisational coordination a purely economic measure of interest would be Platonic (see Schimank this volume). Therefore, we modelled interest drawing on Bourdieu's capital sort theory [8,9] and distinguished economic, social, cultural and organisational capital, the latter transformed into symbolic capital on the practical side of coordination (for details of the computing see [34]).[12] These different types of capital are also important for the valuation of the single shifts that are the object of our agents' negotiations (see Section 5).

Practical Roles. The practical roles are modelled as emerging from the ongoing flow of situated interaction on the shop-floor level, thus filling the scope which the formal prescriptions—whether intentionally or not—leave blank. In human organisations, the process of roles emerging can be depicted as follows: Situations that are perceived as similar will increase patterned ascriptions, thus generating a relatively stable positioning of types of actors on the practical side of coordination (see Figure 2). In other words, some kind of resistance against disappointment of these expectations gets established and remains relatively stable after a while. In our MAS, these practical roles are "incorporated" in the agents.[13] We modelled these pattered perceptions of the interaction partners according to the concept of "group figures" [41], which can be observed among lasting informal groups (e.g., juvenile gangs) and also within organisational units (e.g., a bureau or a station in a hospital). Because the term "figure" captures ascriptions which can be assumed to differ only slightly between different social entities, we termed these patterned expectations "social types"[14]. These are described by two classes of parameters: the interest is computed as a type-specific weight in the four capital interests. The type-specific negotiation behaviour is computed as additional type characteristics (like willingness for compromise and sharing of information, or general willingness to negotiate at all).[15]

4.4 Role-Making and the Benefits of Diversity

In our modelling approach the practical side of organisational coordination is decoupled from the formal side. This calls for an explanation of the concept of practical roles on the organisational level of scale. Merton's well known concept of "role sets" [35] does not address this question because it focusses on different (and even conflicting) role ascriptions to one individual. The same holds true, as mentioned above, for interactionist

---

[12] Drawing on the distinction of different capital sorts does not mean that we in any way try to 'apply' or formalise Bourdieu's theory in all of its aspects. Especially his notion of an overarching "logic of practice" is, at least in the context depicted here, not suitable because it neglects the relevance of every formal prescription (see the discussion in Section 1). On the other hand, his proposals for a positioning in the "field of practice" can, in our view, be applied to organisational theory—but this is not an issue here.

[13] This means that at the present stage of system development it is not possible (and not intended) that the practical roles themselves emerge. Nonetheless, this capability can be achieved with an extension of the approach. As an intermediate step, we plan to introduce the automatic detection of the social types which are present at the given situation.

[14] See [3] for a summary of sociological conceptualisations of social types and the relation to the concept of social roles.

[15] At the moment, we are working with a set of nine social types. The profiles (and the names) of the types and their initial capital interests were constructed on the basis of empirical evidence from our domain.

conceptualisations. Nonetheless, these conceptualisations offer a starting point by highlighting that the consistency of roles is an achievement from "the process of organizing behavior vis-a-vis relevant others" ([53, pp. 32]). The differentiation of roles (ibid., p. 28), then, is a result of a mutual stabilisation of interpretations as part of the interaction process. This means that in practice there can be a fit of roles which makes collaboration (or negotiation) easy or complicated—as members of organisations we all refer to this with the folk concept of a "social chemistry". Because this fit of practical roles, within the overall picture of organisational coordination, works against the one-dimensionality of formal role prescriptions (and 'repairs' its incoherences), it can be assumed that a high degree of diversity is the prerequisite for this kind of practical coordination. What follows is the question: Are there mixing ratios of social types which do work better than others (or even optimal)? We address this topic in Section 7.3 in some detail.

5   An Architecture for Role Based Negotiating Agents

The computer scientists' part of the modelling is the conceptualisation of an agent architecture that hardwires the sociological model. As we pointed out above, our guideline was to "incorporate" the essential features of social roles directly into the agent architecture, thus tackling the challenge of "formalising the informal". In the last section, we outlined the most important features: formal and practical roles, social types, and capital interests. Now we want to describe how these approaches can be applied to our multiagent system.

As mentioned before, our application scenario is the exchange of shifts in a hospital, and some of the features of our system will be described in terms of this domain. But our approach does not only intend to cover this concrete example; it is a generalised approach to agent negotiations.

5.1   Formalising the Negotiation Process

Based on empirical studies, we identified three important facets that define the proceeding in human negotiations: the application of social types, the influence of experiences, and the utilisation of strategic behaviour. All three facets relate to the practical role of our agents.

Social types define typical preferences and characteristic behavioural parameters for classes of agents. They are used in two ways. First, they serve as a guideline for the agent's own behaviour (self-image). Second, they provide an estimation of the partners' attitudes (partner-images).

We enable our agents to collect experiences, so that the agents can develop a tendency to prefer certain agents as negotiation partners. As our agents only interact by negotiations, these experiences can only be related to negotiations. Additionally, agents might tend to be more cooperative towards partners they have good experiences with. The experiences are collected regarding a certain agent (personal experiences) as well as regarding social types (typified experiences). The latter allow the application of experiences even if the agent is not well known yet. These generalised experiences as well

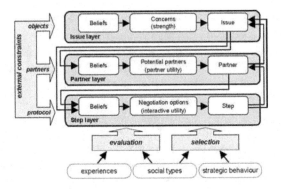

Fig. 3. The C-IPS framework.

as the overall concept of social types simplify the handling of large numbers of agents, i.e., it increases the scalability (see Section 8).

Observing humans negotiating, it can furthermore be seen that the currently best option is not always chosen. Often, this deviation from the optimum is caused by anticipation of middle-term or long-term effects. Introducing this concept as strategic behaviour of our agents, we can foster the realism of their negotiations and give them more autonomy in selecting a negotiation step.

Usually, classical approaches conceptualise agent negotiations by distinguishing the negotiation object, the negotiation protocol, and the internal reasoning process [6,27]. These approaches do not address the negotiation partner explicitly, and the reasoning process itself is not structured at all. But both are necessary for us. We require agents that are fully autonomous in all decisions regarding the negotiation, and we need a clearly structured decision process to localise where the social aspects have to be integrated. Hence, we extended and restructured the classic approach to negotiation modelling and developed the C-IPS framework [54].

5.2   The C-IPS as a General BDI-based Architecture

It can be assumed that in our domain, as well as in every other negotiation, agents have to make decisions about three important aspects: They have to choose the negotiation issue, the negotiation partner, and the next negotiation step. The latter is the communicative act to be issued next in the negotiation process. While these three aspects are interrelated, the corresponding decision processes can usually be separated. This clear separation enables an explicit definition of various interdependencies. Therefore, we follow a three-layered approach to agent architecture (see Figure 3), where each layer represents one of the three decision processes mentioned above ((I)ssue, (P)artner, and (S)tep). Initially, we defined a simple sequential dependency between the layers, which implies that decisions are taken and withdrawn step-by-step, starting at the issue layer or the at step layer, respectively. All decision processes are restricted by external (C)onstraints.

The decision process at each of the three layers is structured according to the BDI approach [45,38].[16] Beliefs represent the layer-specific part of the agent's knowledge about the world. During the evaluation process, the agent builds desires based on the beliefs and according to its individual preferences. These desires represent preferable choices for the decision process. In our three-layered approach, desires are concerns the agent wants to negotiate on, they are potential partners, or they are useful negotiation options (exchanges) respectively. At each layer, the desires are ranked according to a numeric function, i.e., strength for concerns at the issue layer, partner utility for promising partners at the partner layer, and interactive utility for negotiation options at the step layer. Some desires may turn out to be impossible due to decisions made on other layers or due to the flow of negotiation. These desires are marked as temporally impossible. The marking is revised after a certain period of time. From all possible desires at each layer the agent finally selects a specific intention, which actually determines the agent's behaviour. Thus, the agent's enacted intention is a specific negotiation step aiming at a particular issue in a negotiation with a particular partner. A more detailed and formalised description of the C-IPS framework and its application to the shift negotiation domain can be found in [54].

5.3 External Constraints

External constraints avoid unnecessary, useless or undesired negotiations. This allows keeping the reasoning somewhat simple. There are two sources of external constraints: domain dependent formal restrictions and restrictions set by the system designer. The compliance of the agents' behaviour with these restrictions ensures the fulfillment of the formal role.

Our agents only negotiate on shift exchanges. Exchanges between different professions or qualifications (e.g., physician and nurse) are not allowed. For a certain issue, an agent can only select partners that are able to take the shift of the issue, i.e., they are not already scheduled for that shift. The negotiation object is the shift the partner has to take in return. The shift of the initiating agent is fixed. Agents only offer shifts they are scheduled for. Furthermore, in the first version of our system the agents can only negotiate with one agent at the same time.

A very important constraint that influences the step layer is the negotiation protocol. As mentioned before, we require a protocol that enables life-like negotiations. Our protocol structures the negotiation into three phases: the pre-negotiation phase, the main negotiation phase and the post-negotiation phase. During the pre-negotiation phase, the protocol requires that the initiator of a negotiation—we distinguish between the initiator and the responder—asks the selected partner whether a negotiation is useful, i.e., whether there has been new information since the last negotiation on the same topic, and whether the other agent is not 'busy', i.e. is currently not engaged in another negotiation. If these conditions hold, the initiator starts the main negotiation phase by

---

[16] The possibility of a combination of layered architectures and BDI approaches has already been described by [11,21,56]. These authors frequently used layered architectures to represent different levels of complexity and abstraction. We, contrarily, use the layers to represent different interdependent parts of the complete negotiation process.

doing the first negotiation step. Following speech act theory, we define each step as a performative act where motivation is combined with content (e.g., a specific exchange). The performatives for the first step can be a call-for-proposal (CFP), a proposal, or an ultimatum. With the exception of the terminating performatives agree and cancel, every single negotiation step will be answered by the partner. Every proposal can be followed by an agree, a cancel, a CFP, an ultimatum or a counter-proposal. An ultimatum is a very restrictive performative because it forces a cancel or an agree. If a cancel or agree is uttered, the post-negotiation phase starts. The agents' experiences are adjusted based on the result of the negotiation. If there is an agreement, the initiator asks the administration for confirmation and then forwards the administration's answer to the responder.

These external constraints are clearly distinguished from the agent's internal reasoning model, which is structured by IPS. Furthermore, an initiator conducts a different or at least more complicated reasoning process than the responder. If the responder is 'not busy', he always accepts a negotiation request. When it comes to the beginning of a negotiation, the responder simply sets the negotiation issue and partner to the corresponding values.

5.4   Issue Selection

At the issue layer, the agent selects a shift as a negotiation object. This is a shift that is assigned to the agent according to the shift plan and that is in conflict with the agents' leisure time interests.

All shifts assigned to the agent are considered as concerns. The agent assigns a strength value to each concern. The strength is inversely related to the utility of a shift, i.e., the bigger the utility the less is the agent's interest to exchange that shift and vice versa. The utility of a shift depends on the worth of the shift and on the leisure time interest for that particular shift. The worth of a shift is calculated by comparing the agent's capital stock (composed of the four capital sorts) with and without that particular shift. The capital stock itself is evaluated according to the capital interests, which are set in the social type. As the capital accumulations that can be achieved by future shift exchanges cannot be known in advance, we use shift type specific estimations instead. These estimations result from different characteristics of the shift types, e.g., different manning levels, salary surcharges, and tasks [24,31].

Of all its concerns, an agent only considers those concerns as being relevant for intention building which do have a significant leisure time interest. This can be interpreted as a simple strategic behaviour because it avoids the effort of a negotiation for unimportant conflicts. A social type dependent threshold sets the relevance. From the remaining concerns, a possible concern with maximum strength is selected as the actual intention at the issue layer, i.e., the issue. Due to the interdependencies between the layers, an issue may become impossible because no partner is found for that issue. In that case, the decision regarding the issue is revised.

5.5   Partner Selection

At the partner layer, the agent selects a promising partner for a negotiation on a given issue. Potential partners are all other available agents that fulfil the requirements of the external constraints. These potential partners are ranked by the partner utility function. The partner utility is strongly influenced by personal and typified experiences likewise. Additionally, every calculation of the partner utility depends on the partners shift plan. The number and the utility of the possible exchanges are taken into account, and the latter is given more importance. The utility of an exchange combines the worth of an exchange with the leisure time preferences of the affected shifts. Similar to the worth of a shift, the worth of an exchange is the difference between the evaluation of the agent's capital stock with and without the exchange. Thus, the worth of an exchange is dependent on the social types.

From all potential partners, the agent selects a possible partner with maximum partner utility as intention of the partner layer. A partner may become impossible because he is currently involved in another negotiation or there has recently been an unsuccessful negotiation on the same issue with this partner. Again, in this case the decision has to be revised.

5.6   Step Selection

The selection of an appropriate next step in a negotiation with a specific partner on a specific issue is subject to the step layer. It is done according to the protocol.

The following applies only to the main negotiation phase, as due to the protocol there is no room for decisions during the pre- and post-negotiation phase. All possible exchanges are desires at the step layer (negotiation options). These desires are ranked by the interactive utility. We calculate this utility as the weighted sum of the agents personal utility and the partner's estimated personal utility. The personal utility corresponds to the utility of an exchange described in the last section. As the individual preferences and leisure time interests of the partners are not known, they are estimated based on the partner's social type. The weights depend on the agent's social type and on its personal and typified experiences. The weight of the partner can be interpreted as concessions towards this partner.

The step selection is realised using strategies and tactics. A tactic generates a single negotiation step for a specific situation, given in the tactics precondition. We assume the set of exchanges that lead to neither agree nor cancel, which is bounded by two lines: the agree line and the cancel line. As the change of the boundaries of the negotiation space heavily influences the flow of the whole negotiation, we call these two lines "strategic lines". A strategy provides a sequence of steps for all situations. In our framework, a strategy is composed of a set of tactics and the two strategic lines. Tactics in a strategy may be weighted. If more then one tactic is applicable in a certain situation, the selection of the tactic to be used is done as follows: tactics without a weight are only considered if the sum of all weights is less than 1. All weights are temporally adjusted so that they sum up to 1. One tactic is chosen randomly and the probability is given by the weights.

Some preconditions of tactics refer to strategic lines. An offer is accepted if the corresponding interactive utility is above the accept line. The negotiation is cancelled if the personal utility of the offered shift is below the cancel line. Because this process is based on two different utility functions, we term it "two-scale-based decision making". Simulation runs show that these definitions are useful, because they avoid situations similar

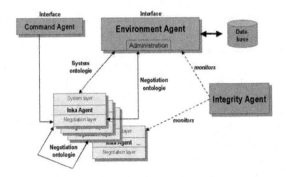

Fig. 4. Core system architecture of the INKA MAS.

to the prisoners' dilemma, which can arise when two "excess altruists"—weighting the partner's utility higher than one's own—are negotiating [28].[17]

6   Implementing the INKA-MAS

The next step in the development cycle is the genuine software engineering job. For the implementation of the INKA system, we have evaluated different multi-agent platforms. One important evaluation criterion was the support of physically distributed agents with individual interfaces. This is necessary for the interactivity experiment. Furthermore, we require a platform that supports complex agent architectures and the modelling of agent communications, e.g., ontology management. We have decided to use the platform JADE, which fulfils these requirements. Using JADE, the configuration of the system can be changed dynamically while the system is running, i.e., agents can enter and exit the system or change the position within the network. Our system is completely implemented in Java; thus, it is independent of the operating system.

Figure 4 visualises the core system architecture of the INKA system. It comprises four types of agents: the environment agent, the INKA agents, the integrity agent and the command agent.

The environment agent is the central element in our system. It provides interfaces to configure and control individual INKA agents as well as the whole system. Additionally, the environment agent provides the access point to the system database that contains all relevant data of the scenario (for details see [31,23,34]). Finally, the environment agent implements the administration, which is the final authority to check and confirm the accordance of negotiated shift exchanges to restrictions set by the formal roles of the involved agents.

The INKA agents are the agents that negotiate on shift exchanges. They consist of two components. The negotiation component implements the negotiation behaviour according to the C-IPS approach described above. The system component cares for

---

[17] There are no impossible desires at the step layer.

the management of the agent's internal knowledge and the processing of request or directives by non-INKA agents, especially by the environment agent.

The integrity agent ensures a safe technical state of the system, especially by coordinating the initialisation of different agents during the start-up process.

The command agent enables us—during system development—to test the C-IPS layers of the INKA agents independently by initiating different types of negotiations: without any guidelines or with a given issue and/or a given partner.

7 Design of Interactivity Experiments

Treating the investigation of hybrid settings as one step of its own in the overall design process for MAS refers to the original Socionics program [32], in which the term hybridisation has been used for all processes of re-entering the computer agents into the real-world domains from which their coordination principles were derived—a process that could broadly be labeled as the 'socialisation' of agents which "incorporate" sociological concepts. In the resulting settings, there is interactivity between technical and human agency, and organisational coordination is based on an entanglement of human and technical sociality (see for these definitions [43]).

As noted earlier, the main challenge at this point is to make an examination of these new settings possible. In order to achieve a methodologically controlled examination, we started with two considerations. As opposed to philosophical definitions of what is the 'true nature' of an agent's agency, we defined the following: if the mutual impact of technical entities as well as their relations to human actors can sensefully be described as social interaction, we will talk of hybrid settings. And as opposed to the often overgeneralised and highly speculative notions of technical agency (e.g., in actor-network theory; see [44]), we developed a methodologically controlled approach to an examination of the theoretical problem of hybridisation.

7.1 An Experimental Approach

The main issue under discussion is: How can we analyse and examine the interactivity between human agency and technical agency in the early phases of system development in a methodologically adequate way? Because the changes to be examined are processual in nature and a variety of parameters are involved, an experimental procedure seems to be appropriate where the examination can be restricted to assumed effects of independent variables on one single variable. By this we draw on a narrow understanding of "laboratory experiments" in sociological methodology and socio-psychological experiments about group behaviour ([40, pp. 289ff.]) which are commonly defined as consisting of three parts:

1. The formulation of precise hypotheses concerning the relationships between the variables involved in the phenomena to be examined.
2. The creation of an examination setting that provides optimal conditions for testing each hypothesis (cf. [5, pp. 204ff.], [57, pp. 32ff.]).
3. The explicit control of the validity of the experimental results, e.g., by introducing control groups or by repetition of series of experiments.

7.2   Hypotheses

In the INKA-project, processes of hybridisation are to be examined in the context of successful organisational coordination based on practical roles. By this we aim at exploring the "social chemistry" (see Section 4.4) and its change through the introduction of sociologically grounded agents. So we focus on patterned variations of social types and their effects on shift negotiations. In an artificial setting, it will be examined whether different optimal shift-plans are the outcome of the negotiations of humans and agents. These changes may, of course, have different time frames. In the following sections, we only describe a static interactivity experiment which is designed for a short-time adaption to an equilibrium of social types.

The coordinational effects that different mixing ratios generate are operationalised with three hypotheses:

1. The precondition of balancing formal and practical roles is that homogenisation limits the productive use of social difference because the scope of activities is smaller. In our domain we assume that resisting the tendency towards homogenisation makes shift-plans with a poor quality more unlikely. The corresponding hypothesis is: *A non restrictive set of social types achieves better results with regard to the quality of shift-plans than a restrictive set of social types.*
2. It can be assumed that a productive use of social difference does not only depend on the sheer number of types but in the first place on a smooth fit of the types involved. Therefore we are not only interested in the mixing ratio of social types but also in the patterns of distribution of types. The corresponding hypothesis is: *The pattern of distribution is the essential factor for the quality of shift-plans, independent from the social types involved.*
3. Even if agents are modeled on social mechanisms, they still are technical creatures and thus differ from humans in nature. Therefore, it has to be assumed that there are different stable mixing ratios reflecting various interdependencies. The results depend on the type of negotiation partners. The corresponding hypothesis is: *There are various stable mixing ratios of social types depending on the nature of negotiation partners—if they are only agents, only humans, or if they are mixed.*

7.3   Indicators

In experimental runs, these hypotheses will be ultimately proved by the quality of the new shift-plans that are the result of the negotiation process. But as the quality is a collective aggregate, it is by no means clear how this quality can be measured at the outset. Using statistical methods, we developed the following indicators to measure a collective quality.

Collective satisfaction with the negotiated shift-plans: Individual satisfaction can be expressed as the percentage of leisure-time interest every single individual can realise. As a collective measure, we define the following: The degree of collective satisfaction is high if the majority of staff reaches an individual satisfaction that is higher than the above-average satisfaction, and at the same time the dispersion of individual satisfaction is small. We weight the results on an ordinal-scale from 1 to 10. A shift-plan that produces a high mean and a small dispersion of satisfaction is scored as the best result.

Frustration caused by the negotiated shift-plans: The individual interest in efficient shift negotiations is defined in negative terms. The measure is the individual frustration which is the ratio of unsuccessful negotiations of that individual to all negotiations it was involved in. A negotiation is unsuccessful if it is canceled because it takes too long. The degree of collective frustration can be defined to be small if the average of the staff shows little frustration and the dispersion of individual frustrations is small. In statistical terms, the best result is composed of a small mean and a small dispersion of individual frustrations.

Organisational perspective to negotiated shift-plans: The organisation at large has a strong interest in a minimum of rotation of the employers concerning the different shift types (early-, late- and night-shift) because in case of accident every employee needs to know the specific workflows of every shift in order to get all the incidental jobs done. We calculate this minimal organisational request in the following way: An individual employee who covers all the different shift types in the common accounting period gets the value 1. If he fails to do this he gets the value 0 what means that he is sanctioned by the organisation. For the collective measure we defined different thresholds. If only 75 percent or less of the staff fulfil this request of minimal rotation, the whole shift plan will be dropped by the organisation. Such a shift-plan gets the value 0, and it will simply be refused by the organisation whatever the values for satisfaction and frustration are. If 75–89 percent of the staff fulfil the rotation conditions, we multiply with 0,8. In the optimal case of 90–100 percent we multiply with 1.

The collective results of these three indicators are calculated in the following way: *(Score satisfaction + score frustration) × value of organisational perspective = score for the quality of shift plan.*
Initial computations show that this mode of statistical evaluation offers good distinctive features for a measurement of the quality of shift-plans based on the constellation of social types.

7.4 Experimental Setting

Because under experimental conditions, the test-persons can concentrate solely on negotiation task, these negotiations will lead to rapid results. Therefore, a considerable amount of single negotiations with different starting conditions and different exercises can be run in relatively short time (we plan a two day experiment). The concrete setting can be described as follows: The test-persons sitting isolated at computers are in a black-box situation because they do not know if the other negotiation partners are humans or agents. Every test-person gets specific negotiation jobs and a list of the social types of the other participants involved. For putting this experimental situation to work, we have to choose professionals working in a hospital as test-persons because they need to have experience with the various social types and their behaviours.

For the analysis of the experiment, we can draw on two different data sources: the negotiation protocols, which are compiled by the computer, and the new shift-plans that are resulting from negotiation. As we are only interested in the results of negotiations, these data are sufficient for a check of hypothesis and an interpretation with the indicators mentioned above.

7.5   Ensuring the Validity of Experimental Results

Experiments in the social sciences call for internal validation criteria. We adopt the proposal of a "pretest-posttest control group design" ([16, p. 248]). The pretest has to assure that the measured effects are not only an outcome of the instrument (or the experimental setting) itself; therefore, running the whole procedure without agents is one good test. Additionally, we systematically compose control groups of humans and agents likewise and deploy them in every phase of the experiment.

7.6   Outline of Dynamic Interactivity Experiments

We designed a second type of interactivity experiments for an examination of dynamic changes that arise from hybridisation over a longer period. As with any introduction of a technical system in an organisation, the introduction of our MAS can be expected to cause effects on two different levels of scale: on the level of interaction, we will analyse the emergence of negotiation routines from interaction and from interactivity; on the level of the organisation at large, we will analyse the emergence of coalitions and "communities of practice" in the overall context of organisational learning. Extending the experimental approach to dynamic processes calls for a different setting and duration of the experiments.[18] As the specification of these experiments is future work, we, in this article, only present the general outline of the extension to the organisational level at the end of the following section.

8   Discussion: Constructing MAS and Social Levels of Scale

In the previous sections, we have introduced the modelling principles, the implementation, and the experimental use of our MAS. Each of these subsequent steps tries to tackle the challenges that arise from the practical rationality of organisational coordination, and utilise the concept of social roles for the design of a MAS. With this approach, the capability to enact social roles is directly built into the agents architecture, in other words: mechanisms and data sets from the levels of groups (practical roles) and organisational subunits (formal roles) are "incorporated" into the single agents. For this reason, our approach is not intended to work for high numbers (to be sure: for millions) of agents or interactions; the approach is located at a middle level of scale from the very beginning. But the issue of scalability is about spanning different levels of scale, especially from the micro- to the macro-level. How does our approach contribute to this issue? Beside being located at a middle level of scale, the basic idea about role based perception and action is the reduction of complexity at the interaction level—and this can be discussed with respect to different kinds of scales. Before we address some of the dimensions in which our MAS is meant—and in some respect in fact turned out—to be scalable, we first have to outline our understanding of scalability.

---

[18] It will be necessary to bring the system to the real world-context of the test-persons who will daily negotiate via and with the MAS for at least one month.

8.1 Dimensions of Scalability

Generally speaking, the scalability of a system is related to a scale where the system can be located. To scale, then, means to relocate the system without—this is the crucial point—negatively affecting or even destroying the overall functionality of the system. In MAS research, the most prominent example for such a relocation is the increase of the number of agents within the system. As the contributions in this volume show (especially Paetow, Schmitt, and Malsch), in the Socionics program there are many relevant scales which can be grouped in different dimensions. Even with respect to the "quantitative dimension if scalability" (Schimank in this volume), there typically exist different scales. That means that the sheer number of agents is only one relevant aspect; scales as number of interactions, size of environmental parameters, or number of messages sent between the agents can be equally important. Furthermore, the "qualitative dimension of scalability" (ibid.) is at least of equal importance, which means that the complexity of the agent architectures or the basic parameters of the interaction processes have to be chosen with respect to the level of scale of social coordination that the overall design is aiming at.[19] Qualitative scaling, then, is not only defined as any change in these complexities, but also inherently linked to pre-given levels of scale from the social world.

Seen from the level of system design, all of these possible scales do interfere with one another, and, of course, have an impact on the overall functionality of the system. In our understanding, any scaling operation has to be measured in the light of the problems to be tackled or by the required properties of the system at hand. These properties might be senseful and immediate reactions of the system, length and desired outcome of interactions, or the fact that the system after some time reaches a stable state. With this focus on a given technical system, two different meanings of scalability should be distinguished which build on one another. The first meaning is that the system is built in such a way that it can be easily relocated. The question, then, is whether it is possible to make changes at any of the scales mentioned without major changes of the system or even without stopping the system. This is an architectural prerequisite for the second meaning of scalability which asks whether scaling in fact negatively influences the functionality of the system. Due to this second definition, a system is scalable if an increase on one scale does not affect the property of the system, or whether the property remains within an acceptable range.

8.2 Scales and Scalability in the INKA System

On the basis of the definitions given, we now can summarise the most important features of our system that allow (or even call for) scaling. Furthermore, we summarise some of the results from simulations that show how scalability in fact can be achieved with the system.

Qualitative Dimension. With our approach, we aim at enhancing the modelling of MAS at the micro-level by the introduction of meso-level concepts. We hope that the

---

[19] This is not surprising because from sociology we know that the mechanisms of coordination on the level of interaction are different from those on the levels of groups, the level of organisations, and the level of society at large.

previous sections showed that meso-level knowledge about human social systems, represented by social types, can be successfully utilised in MAS design. By giving our agents an understanding of empirically relevant social types, they can adapt their behaviour not only based on individual experiences but also based on knowledge that has emerged in the human social life. Because this knowledge is generalised in nature, we are able to address and test two more special aspects of qualitative scalability. We are able to increase or decrease the sophistication of the agents' negotiation strategies and adapt the latter to the required properties, especially to a sufficient number of successful negotiations within an acceptable range of time. Moreover, with the layered architecture of the C-IPS framework (see Section 5) we are able to test the single layers of the agents' internal calculations stepwise. This reduction of the complexity of the overall negotiation behaviour turned out to be very useful, not only for testing purposes, but also for a better understanding of the aggregated outcome of the agents' interactions.

Quantitative Dimension. To use generalised knowledge for micro-level interactions (in our case: negotiations) is not only of interest for issues of agent architecture, but also for the change of the sheer number of parameters involved. In our case the, most important quantitative scale is the number of agents.[20] Our system, first of all, is designed to allow the increase of the number agents without stopping the system—many agents can enter or exit the system dynamically without causing technical problems or the necessity to restart the system.[21] With this prerequisite given we tested how the increase of the number of agents effects the rate of successful negotiations and the negotiations' length[22]. If the agents would calculate without generalised knowledge, the sheer number of negotiations would increase to the second, thus lengthening the whole negotiation process and resulting in a strong decrease of the probability of successful negotiations. In our system, on the contrary, there is only a slight increase of the number of negotiations, and the rate of successful negotiations stays within an acceptable range. But it turned out that there is another critical factor: scaling up the number of agents too much leads to an enormous amount of messages exchanged due to the number of possible negotiations—a kind of "information overload" seems to limit the scaling possibilities.

Nonetheless, the "incorporation" of generalised knowledge in a MAS seems to point to some match between the quantitative and the qualitative dimensions of scalability. Our purely numerical findings could be interpreted in terms of "social experiences" the agents make, and these experiences do bring about a positive reduction of complexity. The argument goes as follows: Social types, by definition, provide a way to classify agents, and this allows the generalisation of experiences made with individual agents to all agents of its class. This procedure becomes critical if the number of agents in the system increases because the agents' costs (investments in, for example, time) to gather

---

[20] Additional scalable parameters are from the data environment of the agents, e.g., the size of the shift plan or the number of tasks, i.e. leisure time interests, to solve.

[21] From our approach, it should be clear that we are talking about small numbers of agents (up to 20).

[22] Acceptable length of the negotiations is part of the definition of success, thus constituting another scale; see our formalisation of "frustration" from negotiations that take too much time in Section 7.3.

reliable experiences about other agents explode. Applying social types simply works against this paralysing complexity, and thus increases the probability of successful negotiations.

Dimension of Hybridisation. The re-entry of the MAS into a real organisation does not simply add more entities to the system, but multiplies the relations and the parameters involved. In the context of scalability, this means that hybridisation constitutes another relevant scale. At this last stage of our development cycle, the utilisation of meso-level concepts is of special importance. Giving our agents an "understanding" of social types, derived from the human social reality they are now confronted with, makes a compatibility of the different "experiences" more likely, and by this decreases the unpredictability of the whole process.[23] Moreover, the C-IPS agent architecture allows to switch between different degrees of autonomy of the agents' decision making, thus enabling MAS designers to scale this degree—this can be very important for the achievement of an overall functionality of the whole setting. Doing this dynamically in a hybrid system, one can smoothly change the ratio of decisions done by humans versus decisions done by artificial agents. In our view, this is the technical prerequisite for a better reflexion of the usage of MAS in the real world because we can stepwise transform a human social system with computer-supported interaction to a hybrid system.

8.3 Extending the Approach on Different Levels of Scale

Any modelling and implementation of a computer system bears its own limitations. In our case, this is especially obvious with respect to the dynamic interactivity experiments (see Section 7.6). This makes some major extensions of the modelling and the implementation necessary, extensions which, again, can be located on different levels of scale.

Introducing Negotiation Routines. As outlined above, the test of the quantitative scalability of our approach pointed to the problem of information overload by the sheer number of messages exchanged. This calls for a generalisation of "experiences" by the single agents themselves, in other words: to an extension on the interaction level. It seems that the agents' enactment of practical roles would be incomplete without the capabilities of learning and following routines. We are trying to achieve this by introducing Case-Based Reasoning (CBR). CBR [1,30] is, generally speaking, a structured approach to machine learning that stores and provides former experiences as single cases, and uses known cases as a solution for new but resembling situations where the solution is not evident. Those cases with the most similar problems are retrieved from

---

[23] In our approach social types are also used to measure the final output of the hybrid system (see our statistical evaluation Section 7.3). Here, the interplay of many of the scales mentioned has to be considered because the goal fulfilment in open (or even in closed) systems where agents and humans interact, calls for an aggregation of individual goals. Arrow's theorem raises doubts about the existence of a unique aggregation [4]. Criteria already developed for isolated negotiations (e.g., [47]) cannot be applied when working with many interdependent negotiations which we use in the INKA project.

the case-base and their positive solutions are used to solve the current problem. The main questions are: What defines a situation as to be able to recognise "resembling" situations? And how could we conceptualise negotiation strategies to allow the agents to routinely act on behalf of anticipated negotiation results?

Introducing Coalition-Building. The necessary reduction of interactions' complexity can also take place on the level of groups. Especially coalitions can, as we know from sociology, drastically reduce the costs of negotiating by delegating parts of the individual interests to a group. The dynamic interactivity experiment is planned to cover a time-span long enough to allow an examination of coalitions emerging.[24] In our context, the main questions are: Does the introduction of the MAS result in hybrid coalitions of humans and agents? And what does this mean for the efficiency and flexibility of the organisation's PEP procedures?

Introducing Organisational Learning. For an overall picture of organisational co-ordination, one aspect of practice-based coalition building is of special interest: the emergence of "communities of practice" (cf. [55]) which are composed of the members of the organisation who care collectively about practical problems of the organisation, without having the official duty to do so. This can be viewed as a special type of organisational learning because it leads to a dynamic re-balancing of formal structure and practical rationality in the organisation at large. In our context, this practical problem is the efficiency and fairness of the distribution of shifts. We focus on the question: Does the introduction of the MAS result in hybrid communities, and what are the organisational consequences of this strengthening of practical coordination?

These extensions require additional conceptual work, and they have to be translated into concrete hypotheses and indicators in order to enable a methodologically controlled examination. In some respect, this starts the development cycle anew. But on this basis it will be possible to achieve a full-fledged approach to the investigation of hybridisation processes, thus closing our version of the Socionics' development cycle.

Acknowledgement

The financial support from the German Research Foundation (DFG) is gratefully acknowledged. We would like to thank two anonymous reviewers and Hans-Dieter Burkhard, Gabriela Lindemann, Werner Rammert and Ingo Schulz-Schaeffer for helpful comments. Team members Dagmar Monett Diaz, Michael Hahne, Alexandre Hanft, Eric Lettkemann, Robin Malitz, Alexander Osherenko and Christian Wiech contributed to the conceptualisation and implementation.

---

[24] Patterns of coalition building are also of great interest for the modelling and validation of complex decision making in computer science; see cf. [29].

References

1. Aamodt, A., Plaza, E. (1984). Case-Based Reasoning: Foundational issues, methodological variations, and system approaches. In: Artificial Intelligence Communications 7(1), pp. 39-59.
2. Aldrich, H. (1999). Organizations evolving. Sage Publications, London, Thousand Oaks.
3. Almog, O. (1998). The Problem of Social Type: A Review. In: Electronic Journal of Sociology, http://www.sociology.org/content/vol003.004/almog.html (12.11.2002).
4. Arrow, K.J. (1963). Social choice and individual values. 2nd ed., Wiley, New York.
5. Atteslander, P. (1993). Methoden der empirischen Sozialforschung. Berlin, de Gruyter.
6. Beer, M., d'Inverno, M., Luck, M., Jennings, N., Preist, C., Schroeder, M. (1999). Negotiation in multi-agent systems. In: Knowledge Engineering Review, 14(3), pp. 285-289.
7. Berg, M., Toussaint, P. (2001). The mantra of modelling and the forgotten powers of paper: A sociotechnical view on the development of process-oriented ICT in health care. http://www.bmg.eur.nl/smw/publications/mantra.pdf (06.08.2002).
8. Bourdieu, P. (1983). Ökonomisches Kapital, kulturelles Kapital, soziales Kapital. In: Kreckel, R. (ed.) Soziale Ungleichheiten. Schwartz, Göttingen, pp. 183-198.
9. Bourdieu, P. (1985). Sozialer Raum und Klassen/ Lecon sur la Lecon. Zwei Vorlesungen. Suhrkamp, Frankfurt a.M.
10. Bourdieu, P. (1990). The logic of practice. Stanford University Press, Stanford.
11. Burkhard, H.-D. (2000). Software-Agenten. In: Görz, G., Rollinger, C.R., Schneeberger, J. (eds.) Handbuch der künstlichen Intelligenz. Oldenbourg Wissenschaftsverlag, München, 3rd edition, pp. 981-986.
12. Burkhard, H.-D., Rammert, W. (2000). Integration kooperationsfähiger Agenten in komplexen Organisationen. Möglichkeiten und Grenzen der Gestaltung hybrider offener Systeme. Technical University – Technology Studies Working Papers, TUTS-WP-1-2001. Institut für Sozialwissenschaften, TU Berlin.
13. Bowker, G.C., Star, S.L., Turner, W., and Gasser, L. (Eds.). Social science, technical systems, and cooperative work. Beyond the great divide. Lawrence Earlbaum, Hillsdale, NY.
14. Castelfranchi, C. (2003). Formalising the informal? Dynamic social order, bottom-up social control, and spontaneous normative relations. Nordic Journal of Philosophical Logic. http://alfebiite.ee.ic.ac.uk/docs/papers/D3/1.Castel-Deon.pdf (20.11.2003).
15. Cohen, M.D., March, J.G., Olsen, J.P. (1972). A garbage can model of organizational choice. In: Administrative Science Quarterly 17 (1), pp. 1-25.
16. Campbell, D.T. (1970). Factors relevant to the validity of experiments in social settings. In: Denzin, N. (Ed.) Sociological Methods: A Sourcebook. Aldine, Chicago, pp. 243-263.
17. Dahrendorf, R. (1974). Homo Sociologicus: Versuch zur Geschichte, Bedeutung und Kritik der Kategorie der sozialen Rolle. Westdeutscher Verlag, Opladen.
18. DiMaggio, P.J., Powell, W.W. (1983). The iron cage revisited: Institutional isomorphism and collective rationality in organizational fields. In: American Sociological Review 48 (2), pp. 147-160.
19. Eisenführ, F. (1994). Rationales Entscheiden. 2nd revised edition, Springer, Berlin.
20. Esser, H. (1999). Soziologie – Spezielle Grundlagen. Band 1: Situationslogik und Handeln. Campus, Frankfurt a.M.
21. Fischer, K., Müller, J.P., Pischel, M. (1998). A pragmatic BDI architecture. In: Huhns, M.N., Singh, M.P. (eds.): Readings in Agents. Morgan Kaufmann Publishers, San Francisco, CA, pp. 217-224.
22. Geller, H. (1994). Position, Rolle, Situation. Zur Aktualisierung soziologischer Analyseinstrumente. Westdeutscher Verlag, Opladen.

23. Gerstl, R., Osherenko, A., Lindemann, G. (2002). The description of formal roles in hospital environments. In: Lindemann, G., Moldt, D., Polucci, M., Yu, B. (eds.): Proceedings of the RASTA'02 Workshop: International Workshop on Regulated Agent-Based Social Systems: Theories and Applications, Hamburg, Germany, pp. 123-130.
24. Gonzales Campanini, I., Holler, G. (1993). Die Neuordnung des Pflegedienstes in einem städtischen Krankenhaus. Ergebnisse der wissenschaftlichen Begleitung in den Städtischen Kliniken Frankfurt a.M.-Höchst. Universität Hannover.
25. Gotsch, W. (1987). Soziale Steuerung – zum fehlenden Konzept einer Debatte. In: Glagow, M., Willke, H. (eds.): Dezentrale Gesellschaftssteuerung: Probleme der Integration polyzentrischer Gesellschaften. Centaurus, Pfaffenweiler, pp. 27-44.
26. Janning, F. (2002). Abschied von der Hierarchie? Dezentralisierung in mittelständischen Unternehmen. Rainer Hampp Verlag, München.
27. Jennings, N.R., Faratin, P., Lomuscio, A.R., Parsons, S., Sierra, C., Wooldridge, M. (2000). Automated negotiation: Prospects, methods and challenges. In: International Journal of Group Decision and Negotiation 10 (2), pp. 199-215.
28. Landesman, C. 1995). The voluntary provision of public goods. PhD thesis, Princeton University. http://www.nonprofits.org/parlor/acknow/landesman/vpopg.html, (access date: 11,20,2003).
29. Laux, H. (1998). Entscheidungstheorie. Springer, Berlin.
30. Lenz, M. (1999). Case retrieval nets as a model for building flexible information systems. Dissertation, Humboldt University Berlin.
31. Lettkemann, E., Meister, M., Hanft, A., Schröter, K., Malitz, R. (2002). The description of practical roles in hospital environments. In: Lindemann, G., Jonker, C., Timm, I.J. (eds.): Proceedings of the MASHO Workshop: Modelling Artificial Societies and Hybrid Organizations. 25th German Conference on Artificial Intelligence, Aachen, Germany, pp. 29-36.
32. Malsch, T. (2001). Naming the unnamable: Socionics or the sociological turn of/ to distributed artificial intelligence. In: Autonomous Agents and Multi-Agent Systems 4 (3), pp. 155-186.
33. March, J.G., Simon, H. (1958). Organizations. Wiley, New York.
34. Meister, M., Urbig, D., Gerstl, R., Lettkemann, E., Osherenko, A., Schröter, K. (2002). Die Modellierung praktischer Rollen für Verhandlungssysteme in Organisationen. Wie die Komplexität von Multiagentensystemen durch Rollenkonzeptionen erhöht werden kann. Working paper tuts-wp-6-2002, Technical University – Technology Studies, Berlin.
35. Merton, R.K. (1957). The role-set: Problems in sociological theory. In: British Journal of Sociology 8, pp. 106-120.
36. Meyer, J.W., Rowan, B. (1977). Institutionalized organizations: Formal structure as myth and ceremony. In: American Journal of Sociology 83, pp. 340-363.
37. Morgan, M., Morrison, M. (1999). Models as mediators. Perspectives on natural and social sciences. Cambridge University Press, Cambridge, Mass.
38. Mueller, J. (1996). The design of intelligent agents: A layered approach. Volume 1177 of Lecture Notes in Artificial Intelligence. Springer, Berlin.
39. Orlikowski, W.J. (1992). The duality of technology: Rethinking the concept of technology in organizations. In: Organization Science 3 (3), pp. 398-427.
40. Pages, R. (1974). Das Experiment in der Soziologie. In: König, R. (ed.) Handbuch der empirischen Sozialforschung. Ferdinand Enke Verlag, Stuttgart, pp. 273-342.
41. Popitz, H. (1967). Der Begriff der sozialen Rolle als Element der soziologischen Theorie. J.C.B. Mohr ,Tübingen.
42. Prinz, W., Jarke, M., Rogers, Y., Schmidt, K., Wulf, V. (eds.). ECSCW 2001. Proceedings of the Seventh European Conference on Computer Supported Cooperative Work, 16-20 September 2001, Bonn, Germany. Kluver, Dordrecht.

43. Rammert, W. (2002). Technik als verteilte Aktion. Wie technisches Wirken als Agentur in hybriden Aktionszusammenhängen gedeutet werden kann. Working paper tuts-wp-3-2002, Technical University – Technology Studies, Berlin.
44. Rammert, W., Schulz-Schaeffer, I. (2002). Technik und Handeln. Wenn soziales Handeln sich auf menschliches Verhalten und technische Abläufe verteilt. In: Rammert, W., Schulz-Schaeffer, I. (eds.): Können Maschinen handeln? Soziologische Beiträge zum Verhältnis von Mensch und Technik. Campus, Frankfurt a.M., pp. 11-64.
45. Rao, A.S., Georgeff, M.P. (1991). Modeling rational agents within a BDI architecture. In: Fikes, R., and Sandewall, E. (eds.): Proceedings of Knowledge Representation and Reasoning (KRR-91), San Mateo, CA, pp. 473-484.
46. Rohde, J. (1974). Soziologie des Krankenhauses. Zur Einführung in die Soziologie der Medizin. Ferdinand Enke Verlag, Stuttgart.
47. Rosenschein, J.S., Zlotkin, G. (1994). Rules of Encounter. The MIT Press, Cambridge, Mass.
48. Scharpf, F. (2000). Interaktionsformen. Akteurzentrierter Institutionalismus in der Politikforschung. Leske und Budrich, Opladen.
49. Schulz-Schaeffer, I. (2000). Sozialtheorie der Technik. Campus, Frankfurt a.M.
50. Schulz-Schaeffer, I. (2001). Enrolling software agents in human organizations. The exploration of hybrid organizations within the Socionics research program. In: Saam, N.J., Schmidt, B. (eds.): Cooperative agents. Applications in the social sciences. Kluver Academic Press: Dordrecht, pp. 149-163.
51. Strübing, J. (1998). Bridging the Gap: On the collaboration between Symbolic Interactionism and Distributed Artificial Intelligence in the field of Multi-Agent Systems Research. In: Symbolic Interaction 21(4), pp. 441-464.
52. Suchman, L. (1987). Plans and situated actions. The problem of man-machine communication. Cambridge University Press: Cambridge, UK.
53. Turner, R.H. (1962). Role-taking: Process versus conformity. In: Rose, A.M. (ed.): Human behavior and social process. An interactionist perspective. Routledge, London, pp. 20-40.
54. Urbig, D., Monett Díaz, D., Schröter, K. (2003). The C-IPS Agent Architecture for modelling negotiating social agents. In: Schillo, M., Klusch, M., Müller, J., Tianfield, H. (eds.) Proceeding of the First German Conference on Multiagent System Technologies (MATES 2003), LNAI 2831. Springer, Heidelberg, pp. 217-228.
55. Wenger, E. (1998). Communities of practice: Learning, meaning and identity. Cambridge University Press, Cambridge, Mass.
56. Wooldridge, M., Jennings, N.R. (1995). Intelligent agents: Theory and practice. In: Knowledge Engineering Review 10 (2), pp. 115-162.
57. Zimmermann, E. (1972). Das Experiment in den Sozialwissenschaften. Teubner, Stuttgart.

Scalability, Scaling Processes, and the Management of Complexity. A System Theoretical Approach

Kai Paetow, Marco Schmitt, and Thomas Malsch

Hamburg University of Technology, Department of Technology Assessment
Schwarzenbergstr. 95, 21071 Hamburg, Germany
(kai.paetow, marco.schmitt, malsch)@tu-harburg.de

Abstract. This work proposes a system theoretical framework for analyzing scalability and scaling processes. Our aim is to clarify the vocabulary used in the debate on scalability issues in multi-agent systems. We, therefore, refer to the terminology of Niklas Luhmann's sociological system theory and general complexity science. To evaluate the heuristic strength of the analytical framework, it is applied to a particular socionic model of a scalable system. Finally, we introduce some proposals for the modelling of scalable multi-agent systems from a sociological point of view. More specifically and system theoretically seen, such a scalable system has to be conceptualized as an organized multi-system system.

1 Introduction

This work proposes a system theoretical framework for analysing scalability and scaling processes.[1] The starting point for our analysis is the observation that the debate on scalability lacks an adequate vocabulary to describe the diverse properties of the concept of scalability. Furthermore, it seems that more theoretical reasoning about the issue is urgently needed.

In *Section 2*, we try to demonstrate how inconsistently the concept of scalability is used in computer science and especially in the research on multi-agent systems (MAS). It is quite hard to point out similarities between the concepts applied. Nonetheless, there are distinctions worth working with: mainly the distinction between scalability as a systemic property and the scaling process as an up- and down-sizing of the system. A second promising insight with conceptual potential is the differentiation of architecture levels on which scaling processes may take place.

Section 3 is guided by a sociological approach to scalability and scaling processes. We outline a complexity theoretical reconstruction of the topic based on Niklas Luhmann's theory of social systems. Scalability and scaling are asserted to be sociologically valuable terms. It is roughly shown in what way interactions and organizations are scalable systems. However, the main focus is put on the development of a heuristics for the sociological analysis of such systems. That instrument is built on basic distinctions like element/relation, quantitative/qualitative, and system/environment.

---

[1] See also the basic work by Paetow/Schmitt in [1]. This article can be understood as a theoretical extension and further clarification of the ideas developed there.

K. Fischer, M. Florian, and T. Malsch (Eds.): Socionics. LNAI 3413, pp. 132–154, 2005.

The usefulness and heuristic quality of the instrument is demonstrated in *Section 4*. Our analytical framework is applied to a specific socionic model of a scalable system not developed in the context of our project work. Our aim is not to criticize that model but to show the general applicability of our heuristics. The scalability and the scaling methods of that socionic model are not only evaluated with elucidating results, it is also possible to reveal its further scaling potentials, not having been explicated by the designers so far.

In the section, we put forward an organization theoretical framework that differentiates a micro-logical and a macro-logical perspective on organized MAS, focusing interactions on the one side and the organization as a socially integrating system on the other. We argue that scaling processes occur within the systemic management of complexity. Problems of scalability are reformulated as problems of reaching an adequate level of system complexity. Processes of scaling by which complexity is managed are led by strategic intent; the outcome of these processes, however, is an evolutionary product.

2 Scalability and the Process of Scaling

In the field of computer science and software engineering, scalability is a topic of major interest. Given the possibilities and necessities of advanced information technology, there is a strong incentive to build systems that are able to grow and to adapt themselves easily to changing circumstances. Especially e-commerce and modern enterprises are in urgent need of software systems that are flexibly adaptable to handle large and complex workloads. One could not agree more: "scalability is arguably the *raison d'être* for interconnection networks" [2, p. 1]. Not surprisingly, even leading software companies like Microsoft and Sun pay much attention to issues of scalability. From a MAS independent, more business-oriented software engineering perspective, Microsoft outlines four essential characteristics of achieving high-levels of scalability to promote its Windows 2000 server family: A scalable system should be able to manage large workloads, deliver high levels of performance, grow easily and quickly, and realize a competitive price/performance ratio [3]. For Sun Corporation, scalability is a top management challenge to be faced by IT solutions for the Web [4].

From a computer science perspective, scalability, also, is an upcoming focal point of research. According to Esposito, an IT-consultant and journalist, the adjective scalable has become "the preferred 'tool' to qualify the features of any sort of software technology for distributed environments" [5, p. 1]. Additionally, he defines that in "general terms, scalability refers to the ability of a system to maintain, if not improve, its average performance as the number of clients grows" [5, p. 2].

There seem to be two common usages of the term scalability in information technology: The first usage refers to the ability of a computer application or product to continue functioning well as it or its context has changed in size or volume; the second usage states a stronger claim when referring scalability not only to the ability to function well in a rescaled situation, but to actually take advantage of it by showing a better performance. [2]

---

[2] These two definitions were found through a search request on the TechTarget site search390.com.

A closer look into publications, however, reveals that there is no consensus among scientists about the meaning of scalability. To give evidence, some quotations are listed in an unsystematic, hence only illustrative way:

In an enquiry concerning complexity measurement in real-time systems, scalability has been conceived as the "property that describes the ease of extension of small to large. Scalability includes both the extension of actual small systems to larger systems and application of small systems techniques inappropriately to the large system domain" [6, p. 29].

As one of the forefathers of Distributed Artificial Intelligence put it, scalability "is the ability to perform Joint Activities in such a way that they can be increased in scale to perform larger projects" [7, pp. 14–15].

A couple of more divergent conceptualizations of scalability can be found in the current MAS science:

Scalability is a many-sided property which can be captured in a scalability metric that balances cost, volume, timeliness and other attributes (sic!) of value in the system, as a function of its size" [8, p. 234].

"[T]he concept scalability denotes the possibility (sic!) to exactly up- and down-size an object. In the field of software systems the degree of scalability of a system architecture can be used to describe how its problem solving behavior reacts on resource modifications" [9, p. 16].

"Scalability requires increasing numbers of new agents and resources to have no noticeable effect on performance nor to increase administrative complexity" [10, p. 121].

"To disambiguate scalable (noting that the term has several different meanings in computer science), the facets we are concerned with are those that refer to the relationship between collective computational resource needs of the agents and the population size" [11, p. 247].

Obviously, scalability denotes very different aspects of a system's extension. A clear definition of the concept that is shared by the community of researchers can hardly be discovered. Scalability is referred to the systemic ability to grow and to perform larger projects in cooperation. Also, it is considered to be a correlation of different system variables like cost and time with size. For some, it describes the correlative relationship of the system's resource endowment and its problem-solving capacity. Furthermore, scalability means that the system can manage the participation of new agents entering the system without additional organizational effort while keeping a stable performance. Scalability, therefore, is understood as a relational term that refers the size of the agent population to the agents requiring a collectively usable computational power.

Thus, as one can easily learn from these quotations, it is obvious that the concept of scalability is far from being clear and coherent in its meaning. There is quite a confusing array of dimensions and levels scalability is brought in connection with: Internet applications, agent architectures, agent societies, and workloads - to name just a few. From this point of view, it is necessary to further clarify the references of scalability and to re-conceptualize the term itself. Moreover, a term is needed that expresses the processual quality of influencing a system's scalable properties. Hence, the term of scaling process seems to be appropriate to denote that quality. Within the literature on MAS scalability, it seems that a distinction between the scaling process inside the MAS (or to put it simple, the variation of the affected scales) and the scalability of the MAS, which is always tightly coupled to some performance metric, is only implicitly drawn. Analytically seen, that distinction is quite promising because it separates the variations in the dimensions of scaling from the abilities to cope with these variations.

To start with the concept of the scaling process, it has to be outlined on which architecture levels a system can be scaled [3]:

- On the *hardware level*, scaling is referred to the technical bedrock of the system that has to be improved. That means, it is tried to enhance the speed and indirectly the performance.
- On the *global structure level*[4], the scaling dimensions range from structural and specialization issues to concerns about resource control and the migration-induced changes of the agent population.
- On the *communication level*, scaling refers to the different communication processes and mechanisms that can be applied and influenced by the system.
- On the *agent model level*, several properties can be scaled, for example, the complexity of the knowledge representation, the inference capabilities, the usage of learning, resource bounded and anytime planning algorithms, the complexity of perception functionality as well as inter-module communication.

There cannot be put enough stress on the major aspect: It has to be clearly stated on what levels and within which dimensions scaling processes are realized. Otherwise, the concept of the scaling process will not gain any theoretical clarity and stridency. It would rest "wishy-washy" and of no avail to serious research. Also, the concept of scalability has to be re-conceptualized in a way that it becomes conceivable what could be described as the constitutive components and the desiderata that are associated with the possibilities of scaling a system. Speaking of desiderata, it should be possible to point out the essential features of a scalable system. Scalability is a technically demanding state and not always easy to realize; furthermore, scalability needs ends the system can operate toward. In a nutshell, only a scalable system can scale itself, whatever the basis of that scalability is. [5] These preconditions of scalability enable and back the system's survivability and functionality. Some evidence has to be brought up to mark out these implicitly used preconditions and desiderata.

The central question in clarifying scalability is: How can the scalability of a system be fostered? What are the techniques that computer scientists and engineers propose?

---

[3] Except for the hardware level, this scheme is borrowed from a proposal for dissertation by Gerber [9]. A quite similar proposal stems from Rana/Wagner/Greenberg/Purvis [12]. Their notions of the different infrastructure levels are: "implementation level", "co-ordination and communication level", "multi-agent behavior level", and "organisation level". See also Wijngaards/Overeinder/van Steen/Brazier [13] where two levels are discriminated: the agent level, that implies also the availability of resources, and the system level. Furthermore, they state the possibility of scaling the agents' functionalities; they reformulate this approach as "extensible functionality".

[4] Gerber denotes this level as agent society level [9].

[5] This aspect has to be explained later.

Intuitively, it makes sense to hypothesize that a system needs self-building and adaptability when it has to cope with masses of participating agents and fluctuation, i.e., agents coming in and leaving the system [11]. The applicable approaches, therefore, determine the most appropriate organizational structure at run-time, on the one hand, and change the structure in compliance with new environmental demands or even turbulences, on the other hand.

Some more ready-made techniques enable agents to work on other tasks while waiting for responses (hiding communication latencies) to segment or distribute the workloads, to replicate strained agents, to use batch requests, to minimize the number of database connections needed by reusing the existing ones, and to cache, i.e., to reduce the path length used by traversing requests and responses as well as the consumption of resources. On the hardware level, scalability can be achieved by using faster machines, clustering machines, and by optimizing servers for specific functions [14, pp. 9 –10; 3, p. 44].

Hence, scalability can gain from improving software and hardware components: First, by optimizing the system at the design level, second, by privileging "the built-in features of a certain mixture of hardware and software", and third, by leaving the responsibility of scalability up to the tools [5, p. 1]. It has to be elaborated which aims those techniques could possibly be applied to.

Scalability is often conceptually connected to notions like robustness, flexibility, and some performance standard [15]. A sensible proposal could be to use these notions as generic terms for desirable system conditions. It does not need any further prove to contend that robust and flexible systems are the ultimate goal of any multi-agent software engineering. In the following, we have to flesh out those terms and their uses in the MAS research.

2.1   Robustness

Robustness is a key element in achieving scalability. A robust system is able to cope with structural inconsistencies and operational uncertainties as well as with component failures and performance degradations. The system's capability to overcome such internal difficulties can be interpreted as its robustness - a kind of performance stability under deteriorating circumstances. A tenable and convincing definition would be: "[R]obustness is the ability of a system to maintain 'safety responsibilities', even though events happen that are able to disturb the system" [16, p. 1]. What are central properties that constitute robustness? *Redundancy* is such a property, that means the system is able to substitute malfunctioning components and to compensate entire functional breakdowns by activating other resources. A second property is *resistance*, the systems vigour to secure its internal operations against harmful or disturbing external influences. Within open multi-agent systems, some common disturbances a robust system has to deal with are, for instance, increases in the population size, changes of the task profile, intrusions of malicious or non-compliant agents, drop-outs of agents, unreliable infrastructures, and emergent dysfunctions [16,17].

2.2   Flexibility

One decisive feature of multi-agent systems, a feature that makes them very distinctive from other forms of software systems, is their flexibility. That flexibility is fundamentally grounded in the autonomy of the individual agents. A system's flexibility can be specified as its adaptability or readiness for structural change. If the notion of flexibility is thematized in the research, it is mostly associated with agent or machine learning [18]. Also, software companies emphasize flexibility as a system's capability. So does Microsoft: "[T]he ability to respond quickly to rapidly shifting business conditions requires systems and platforms that offer the highest levels of flexibility" [3, p. 1]. A scalable system, therefore, has to be flexible and ready to learn.

From a scalability perspective, robustness and flexibility are prerequisites *and* desiderata in one. Facing increasing workloads and information throughput, scalable systems have to be robust and must operate flexibly to perform well. Therefore, it seems advisable to distinguish between robustness and flexibility as preconditions and as goals that have to be achieved by scaling the system.

There have been different attempts at measuring scalability by construing scales and metrics. Gerber, for example, proposes ordinary scales as they are also used in statistics that are nominal, ordinal, and cardinal scales [9, pp. 15–16]. Yet, only cardinal scales are applicable to exact measurements of scaling processes; for instance, agent numbers are cardinally measurable. Additionally, levels of complexity could also be measured. There is a variety of complexity metrics used in computer science. To state just a few, there are metrics for information flow, for the complexity of the system design, for cohesion, and coupling. One of the more prominent metrics is the so-called McCabe's Complexity Metric, "a graph-theoretic metric which measures complexity in terms of linearly independent paths through the code" (cyclomatic complexity) and which also measures "how much the complexity of a program module can be reduced by conversion of a single-entry/single-exit ... subgraphs to vertices (subroutine calls)" (essential complexity) [6, p. 11]. Metrics not only enable designer to compare different states of the system's development or the functioning of different systems but also to determine if the system is operating economically and in the desired fashion after it has been forced to grow internally. Those metrics give hint at a need to correct the system's level of complexity.

To fully measure the process of scaling, it is sufficient to focus on complexity; however, to measure scalability the performance of the system has to be taken into account. The simple reason is that "[s]calability problems generally manifest themselves as performance problems" [10]. Hence, scalability has always be referred to performance in order to indicate a need to scale a system. Also, to meet performance criteria is the *conditio sine qua non* for scalability, that is, scaling is only desirable if those criteria are still be reached. It holds true: "For a system to be scalable, it must meet certain requirements to ensure that nodes can be added to the system without placing an undue burden on overall performance" [19]. A performance function could measure the system's productivity in terms of time consumption and output quantity and quality [9, p. 16]. Combining performance and complexity metrics, scalability could be evaluated by capturing "the expected performance loss at a given load value" [20, p. 47]. That metric measures the likelihood of performance non-scalability (Performance Non-Scalability Likelihood [PNL] metric).

To conclude, it is very advisable to work with a clear differentiation of the notions 'scalability' and 'scaling process'. Systems must be able to scale in order to deal with new demands by the environment. *Scalability* is the ability of the system to grow, to increase in agents participating, to build new structures that coordinate the agents' interactions, or to acquire new tasks. The *scaling process* is the actual process of that growth happening within the system. It uses the system's scalability to let the system develop itself. Scaling is a circular process that constitutively requires the preconditions of scalability to realize the desiderata of scalability. How is this imaginable? To clarify our own approach that takes off at this point of the discussion, we have to introduce a few more concepts that are borrowed form a sociological analysis of complexity issues in social systems. We aim at a further terminological sharpening of the analytical tools to reflect on scalability. Thus, it has to be demonstrated that the scalability debate in computer science can profit from a sociological re-interpretation.

3   Scalability and Scaling Processes, Sociologically Seen

Frankly speaking, scalability is not a topic that has been of interest within the wide field of sociological research. Nonetheless, we believe that computer science can learn from sociology in order to develop a more concise picture of scalability issues. One of the strengths of sociological theorizing is the analysis of social phenomena in broader contexts, especially in the contexts of other disciplines which are often tried to be integrated into the own sociological approach. In this section, we try to invent a sociological concept of scalability and the scaling process that is informed not only by sociology itself but also by complexity science and organization theory. The theory of social systems developed and propagated by Niklas Luhmann serves as theoretical fundament from which we depart with our own thoughts and proposals for a conceptual reframing of the whole topic.

Two main aspects have to be worked out. First, we describe two social settings or entities that have to deal with problems analogous to those scalable software systems face. Especially interaction systems get into trouble when they have to include an increasing number of participating persons and several topics of talk as well as a heavy load of individual contributions. Organizations, the other entity we refer to, have to engage enough and, of course, adequately skilled members to get the work done. They have to concentrate on assignments that are manageable by as many people as needed. There are limits of integration and work coordination. So, how can the organization make sure that it fulfils its goals without getting too complex or losing its flexibility? How can it meet the expectations of society, clients, its external stakeholders or even of its own members when those change and, thereby, urge the organization to structurally change as well? The second aspect is *a new terminology for scaling processes* within real-life and artificial social systems. The main distinctions we introduce are elements and relations, system and environment, and two dimensions of the scaling process, i.e., quantity and quality. These simple distinctions can be conceptually coupled and thus help to develop two matrices just as simple of four different scaling references each.

3.1 Interaction

Do everyday interactions like encounters on the street, family dinners, or group discussions face problems that resemble scalability problems in MAS? For sociologists, it seems quite obvious that it is difficult for interactions to integrate more and more participants. Also, interactions are mostly centralized on one theme at once. Topics to talk about have to follow each other sequentially because interactions are unable to process parallel communications. Thus interactions are systems of small-scale. Their internal complexity cannot rise above a certain level; otherwise the system is compelled to differentiate socially - or to vanish. These problems are quite similar to those of MAS that are mostly based on some mode of interaction, as one can easily see. We have to focus on interactions from a sociological perspective, in our case from the standpoint of systems theory, more thoroughly to distinguish their main characteristics [21,22,23].

Reflexive perception has to be considered as the minimal prerequisite of the constitution of interaction systems. It is some kind of pre-communicative sociality [23, pp. 117–118], communication without verbalization, without the use of language as medium of communication. Personal presence is another prerequisite for interactions to get started. Interactions as autonomous and operationally closed systems [6] are triggered by a double process of perception and communication, hence, by a tight coupling of psychic and social system processes. Interaction, per definition, is communication among persons being present. Thus the difference of presence and absence becomes the fundamental distinction that interactions use to out-differentiate themselves. Presence itself is the principle of border construction. Within the boundary, communication refers to communication; the outside is everything the system differentiates itself from, especially society and other interactions. Interactions are personalized systems, that means, it is always possible to identify the persons participating. Persons are not entire individuals or humans; they have to be understood as communicative constructions, instead. As some form of social structure, they are part of the system. They are topics as well as addressees and addresses of communication.

No matter if interactions take place in everyday situations or in the professional contexts, they are confronted with the necessity of building up complexity. Complexity is a multi-dimensional phenomenon that contains information about the variety of themes and communicative contributions acceptable in the situation (factual, *sachliche* complexity) as well as information about the persons included (social complexity) and about the implicit temporal order of communicative turn-taking (temporal complexity). In real life, interactions are social systems that have only rudimentary capacities to deal with an increase of its complexity. Such an increase maybe propelled by having to integrate more participants into the interaction, by intertwining different topics of talk, or by restraining talkative persons that enervate their counterparts. Moreover, interactions must be able to motivate personal contributions, and sometimes they must be flexible enough to allow a shift of communication themes if it should last over a period of time.

---

[6] It has to be mentioned that there are different levels of social system construction. Luhmann distinguishes interaction from organization and society as different types of social systems. This differentiation is widely accepted within system theoretical research.

3.2   Organization

Organizations, also, are autonomous and self-referentially operating systems. Generally, organizations are goal-oriented systems that distribute assignments to members. Inclusion/exclusion of members is the principle of systemic border construction. Other main characteristics are division of labor and a systemic interest in a long existential duration, its ability of self-reproduction. Decision making is the basic operational unit. Thus organizations should be described as decision-making systems [24,25]. The "domestication" of decisional behavior is one of the most substantial problems organizations have to solve. In other words, the organization has to structure the internal processes by deciding on decision premises supposed to orient further operations. These premises could be foregoing decisions, decision makers as persons, or organization-specific structural forms like communication channels, roles, decision programs, and organizational culture. Interactions occurring within an organization could refer implicitly to those premises in order to reduce their own structural complexity. To facilitate interactions and their structural orientation in the organization, the organization itself has to guarantee an internal level of complexity in order to structure the organizational behavior in a more rational fashion and in order to make use of organizationally framed interactions for itself, for purposes of self-reproduction and goal attainment. However, an organization does not only build internal complexity to structure and to facilitate its inner operations, mainly decisions, but it also needs an adequate level of complexity in comparison to the environmental complexity. It is the organization that decides solely on the adequacy of its complexity whose ultimate criterion is the survivability of the system.

3.3   Complexity

Our contention is that complexity and scalability are issues of much conceptual resemblance. This striking homology leads us to the conclusion that scalability problems should be sociologically analysed by using a terminology borrowed from system theoretical and general complexity science. Computer scientists interested in scalability issues should notice: "Complexity is on the cutting edge of science" [26, p. 57]. It is, for instance, the pivotal feature in the science of the so-called "complex adaptive systems" that entered the research agendas in the seventies. Therefore, one should investigate that promising field of research a little further.

An early definition of complexity that was introduced by LaPorte can be stated as an excellent point of departure for our own intention to construe tools for complexity analysis: "The degree of complexity of organized social systems (Q) is a function of a *number* of system components (C_i), the relative *differentiation* or variety of these components (D_j), and the degree of *interdependence* among these components (I_k). Then, by definition, the greater C_i, D_j, and I_k, the greater the complexity of the organized system (Q)" [27, p. 6]. As one can easily see, the analytic view on phenomena of complexity can be sharpened by introducing a relatively simple distinction, the distinction of components and their interdependencies.

Similarly, Morin speaks of complexity as an "organization of diversity". Organizing diversity renders possible an increase of complexity, that is, first, an increase in the number and diversity of the component parts, and, second, increased flexibility and complication of the interrelations. Moreover, higher complexity entails a decrease of determinism of the interrelations, a win of relational freedom, so to speak [28, p. 558].

Our own approach draws heavily on Luhmann's system theoretical definition of complexity. The difference of system and environment is the most profound distinction system theory is build on. Without environment, a system could not out-differentiate. In order to operate, a system has to draw a clear line between itself and its outside world. "[B]oundary maintenance is system maintenance", as Luhmann says [22, p. 17]. Furthermore, a second "equally constitutive difference" has to be introduced, the difference between elements and relations [22, p. 20]. Instead of components and their interrelations, we prefer speaking of elements and relations as major concepts in the research of complexity phenomena. Systems are the spheres that have to relate elements. Elements are the smallest unit of a system that are not further dissolvable. Relations function as connections between the elements. They organize the system. In some systems like social systems, relations are modifiable. By changing the relations between elements, the system can re-organize itself; it can change. For Luhmann, "an interconnected collection of elements (is) 'complex' when, because of immanent constraints in the elements connective capacities, it is no longer possible at any moment to connect every element with every other element" [22, p. 24]. Thus, complexity can be defined as selective relations among elements. Selective relations, however, are contingent; i.e., they are whether necessary, nor impossible; they could be different, "also being possible otherwise" [22, p. 25]. The system is self-responsible in relating its elements; it is the bearer of risk.

The system has to build an adequate level of complexity, a level that secures the system's survivability, its self-maintenance. System complexity is the most obvious fact that a system has out-differentiated. The boundary setting between system and environment establishes a gap between their levels of complexity. There must not be a point-for-point correspondence between occurrences in the environment and within the system. "The systems inferiority in complexity must be counter-balanced by strategies of selection" [22, p. 25]. Not every event in the environment must irritate the system, must become relevant information. In a second sense, complexity is also a "measure" of the informational deficiencies and indeterminacies. Complexity informs the system about its inability to fully grasp the environmental as well as its own complexity. Therefore, "[t]he system produces and reacts to an unclear picture of itself" [22, p. 28]. One has to ask how a system can influence that picture of itself [7], its complex internal state.

3.4 Forms of Scaling

A complex system builds and reduces its internal complexity by scaling up and down. We argue that complexity is steered by systemic self-scaling. If complexity has to be conceptualized as a selection of relations among elements, then a scaling process can happen in two different fashions, first, as a scaling of elements and, second, as a scaling

---

[7] "Picture of itself" - in another word, its hyper-complexity. A system becomes hyper-complex if it describes itself as complex.

of relations. Furthermore, the scaling process can occur in two dimensions: quantitatively and qualitatively oriented, referred to either numbers or variety. Thus, we can propose a new terminology for the description of scaling processes. More specifically, the heuristic we develop here differentiates forms of scaling, processes that operationalize either elements or relations in a quantitative or qualitative fashion from scaling references, the states in which the system under observation actualizes its momentary level of complexity. Forms of scaling denote mainly temporal aspects of the scaling process, while scaling references focus on factual aspects, the real and observable consequences scaling processes bring about.

Four distinguishable forms of scaling can be construed:

- *Quantitative scaling of elements*: This most simple form of scaling differentiates between more or less elements.
- *Qualitative scaling of elements*: The difference of homogenous and heterogeneous elements is the basis of this form of scaling. The system determines the level of its elementary variety.
- *Quantitative scaling of relations*: More/less relations is the difference of relevance within this form of scaling.
- *Qualitative scaling of relations*: The homogeneity/heterogeneity of relations leads this form of scaling. The system wields influence upon the variety of the elementary couplings.

These forms of scaling are built through a combination of the two fundamental distinctions element/relation and quantitative/qualitative that can be organized in a four-field-matrix. By this matrix, the references of the scaling processes can be outlined evidently. Scaling references denote different pathways to scale a system.

	Elements	Relations
Quantitative Dimension	Number of Elements	Number of Couplings
Qualitative Dimension	Diversity	Multiplexity

Table 1. Scaling References I

This differentiation of scaling references is not yet sufficient. From a system perspective, at least four references can be added. A system exists as a unity of related elements. This unity can be evaluated in its quantitative and qualitative dimensions. Quantitatively, the unity of the difference of elements and relations is describable as the density of the network. Qualitatively, the scaling reference is appropriately denoted by the term "selectivity". Density refers to the interconnectedness of the network, to the actual quantity of relations in comparison to the mathematically possible couplings, whereas selectivity means the actual forms of coupled elements in relation to other forms possible. Two more scaling references are formable by referring to the distinction of system and environment. For the system, environment is not scalable. Yet, the system has to define for itself the operationally relevant parts of its environment, in other words, it has to construe its own environment. [8] The system experiences its environment in a quantitative dimension as irritability and in a qualitative dimension as problems the system has to cope with. These scaling references, irritability and problemacy, rest on the interdependency between system and environment. The first one means the system's openness to environmental disturbances and the second stands for the different problems ascribed to the environment. The additional scaling references can also be summarized in a matrix:

	Element/Relation	System/Environment
Quantitative Dimension	Density	Irritability
Qualitative Dimension	Selectivity	Problemacy

Table 2. Scaling References II

In accordance with these additional references, the list of scaling forms has to be augmented so that four more forms of system scaling can be introduced:

- *Quantitative self-referential system scaling*: This kind of scaling refers to the amount of related elements and their internal interconnectedness in the system. This form of scaling could also be denoted as network scaling.
- *Qualitative self-referential system scaling*: Here, scaling refers to the actualized forms of related elements. These forms differentiate a variety of contingent patterns of operational couplings.
- *Quantitative other-referential system scaling*: The system scales the amount of disturbing occurrences it observes in its environment.
- *Qualitative other-referential system scaling*: This form of scaling is oriented toward the relevance of the environmental perturbations, the challenge they impose on the systemic reproduction or success.

To illustrate this differentiation of scaling references, we have to focus once more on the social systems of interaction and organization. Interactions scale on their element level by determining the amount of communicative contributions the participants can offer or by restraining or extending the variance of communicative mediation by communication symbols (i.e., the variety of acceptable communicative forms). A quantitative scaling of relations within interactions is a process of influencing the communicative references toward each other. It determines which connecting points, *Andockstellen*, further communications can refer to. A qualitative scaling of relations, on the other hand, determines the variety of operational couplings, that is the intermingling of communications within the system. Self-referential scaling of the interaction system can happen as a determination of the system's mutual references the communication actualizes, on the one side, and as an introduction of a theme and the switching of themes, on the other. Hence on this level, the system wields influence on its internal network of

---

[8] In the sense of Weick's concept of enactment [29].

communication and on its selectivity, that is the bandwidth of possible communicative contributions. Other-referential system scaling in interactions has to be understood as influencing the system's reactivity toward environmental "noise", utterances produced by other interactions or single non-participants observing the system. The second other-referential form of system scaling defines whether environmental occurrences will be of systemic relevance and, if it is the case, in what way they have to be self-referentially processed within the system, that means, in what way they have to become a problem the system has to solve.

In contrast to interactions, organizations do have much higher capacities to scale not only on different operational and structural levels but also in quite a plethora of specific communicative forms. Here, we only can give a few abstract examples to illustrate scaling processes within organizations. On the elementary scaling level, organizations try to influence the quantity of communications that can be read or interpreted as decisions within the system. Qualitatively, organizations scale the variety of communicative forms on the elementary level. There might be scientifically oriented communication in the R & D compartment, law-oriented communication among the firm's lawyers or political and economic discussion about careers and higher wages between union members and top-management representatives. Quantitative scaling of relations refers to the operational couplings between decisions and, as the reading of interactions occurring within the organization as decisions. The qualitative variant refers to the variety of couplings, which can be confusing because decisions can refer to a cornucopia of decisional premises. The structural embedding by decision premises not only realizes a multiplexity of relational forms but it also defines the selectivity of these forms by allowing and constraining communicative activities. Organizations also scale systemically by interrelating its elements in dense or less connective ways. In regard to their environments, organizations scale other-referentially by extending or limiting their openness to outside information. Quantitatively, many things can happen, turbulences on markets or political upheavals endangering the overall economic situation, that can lead organizations to react upon. They have to scale their exogenous irritability which can be high, for example, for companies like brokerage firms, or less, like German universities or highly bureaucratized state organizations. Qualitatively, organizations scale relations to their environment by determining what problems the environment confronts them with. Simply put, they have to define what are their jobs and what are the external, especially societal expectations toward them.

3.5 Desiderata of Scalability

Sociologically, it is a truism that social systems are scalable. There is no scalability problem as such for social systems; they simply cannot abstain from constantly realigning their constitutive elements and relations. In other words, they permanently have to manage their complexity. Hence, it is not the question whether social systems are able to scale internally; from a sociological point of view, it is scientifically more fruitful to investigate how and by which basic forms systems scale and if there are limits of scalability. The main problem, however, has to be seen in the quest of adequacy of overall system complexity.

Moreover, scaling processes do not occur without reason. If they are intentionally oriented, which is obviously the fact within organizations, they need targets or states that shall be operationally reached. Scaling processes need and should have desiderata to let the system function well. These desiderata can be developed conceptually by querying normative functional preconditions in organizations in the economy, that is, in companies. These preconditions can be interpreted as highly generalizable aims that do not orient the day-by-day operations, that, however, are prerequisites of the system's survivability. We would propose that these desiderata are robustness, flexibility, efficacy, and efficiency. These notions have to be fleshed out.

Robustness: A robust system is able to survive under changing circumstances. More theoretically, a system is able to reproduce itself during internal processes of self-adaptation and change. In system theoretical terms, a system can perpetuate its operations, its autopoiesis. Organizations are robust if they realize stability in the course of crisis and operational endangerment. Under conditions of turbulent markets and accelerated product innovations that are brought to the market, the robustness of a company organization shows itself when the company is able to secure its position in the market. According to modern management literature, organizations, in the long run, can profit if they concentrate on their core competencies, their operational strengths that let them stand out form the masses and gives them a unique competitive advantage [30]. Thus, robustness rests in a system's self-confidence to be able to refrain from environmental "noise", disturbances that inhibit the system's functionality. Boundary maintenance, i.e., the stabilization of a complexity gap between a system and its environment, seems to be the kernel of systemic robustness.

Flexibility: Yet, the system's boundary does not only have to be secured and maintained, the system also must be adaptable to new environmental challenges. There are a couple of synonyms for flexibility, for instance, adaptability, changeability, readiness to learn, and informational openness. A flexible system is structurally and, in the second place, operationally changeable. Organizations are described as flexible if they are able to react adequately to environmental changes that could affect the entire system and its success. In order to keep track of the changes on global markets, companies have to innovate, that is most of the time, to introduce new or modernized products. Flexibility, also, means the ability to go new ways of production, especially in organizational cooperations like strategic networks. In a wide sense, structural reversibility has to be considered as the bedrock of a system's flexibility.

Efficacy: An effectively operating system achieves its goals or fulfils its function, respectively. Generally, efficacy means goal attainment, i.e., it has to fulfil its purpose constantly. The system's output, the products or services a company delivers, is hereby in the center of interest; it has to be realized in a way that the organization's as well as the customers' expectations are met.

Efficiency: The system's efficiency is measured on the basis of some sort of means-end-rationality. The operations have to be in compliance with economical calculations. The system has to find an economical input/output relation. Thus, a system operates efficiently when it is able to produce its output in a way that a minimal input is needed. The aim is to produce a maximum of output by consuming as less resources as possible (minimax rule). Companies are interested in the realization of efficiency because inputs are costs.

As a result, two forms of scales can be distinguished. On the one hand, we developed eight forms of scaling that are useable as complexity metrics. On the other hand, there are the four performance scales as described before. We propose that scalability is only measurable entirely when these two forms of scales are combined because scalability always refers to some state of complexity compared to certain standards of functionality.

As mentioned above, these notions, robustness, flexibility, efficacy, and efficiency are not only desiderata of systemic processes of scaling, but also preconditions that build the fundamental of scalability. In order to react flexibly, a system has to be robust to some degree, for instance. The crucial point, is nonetheless, how these desiderata can be reached by systemic self-steering that is in our approach, self-scaling. Up to this point, we just have explicated the analytical framework that researchers can use to determine a system's scalability and its actual processes of scaling. Before we turn to our own approach, we want to demonstrate the heuristic value of the tools outlined here. Therefore, we focus on a socionic project that has major interest in issues of scalability. Compared to our own approach, this project is quite different in its theoretical orientation. Nonetheless, we try to find points of connections to our analytical instrument. It is our goal to illustrate our heuristics by applying it to this clearly structured approach that models different levels on which scalability can be analyzed.

4   Scalability in One Selected Socionic Model

This whole section focuses on the analysis of a model that has been developed within a socionic project, a project in which computer scientists and sociologists co-operate to build software systems. Socionics as a new-established area of research tries to model systems informed by social theory [31]. Scalability is a major issue in all projects that belong to the field of socionic research; it is expected, especially by computer scientists, that the import of sociological knowledge can bring forth solutions to scalability problems. Apparently, sociologists are considered to be specialized in analysing large-scale systems like society, since one of their main topics is the inquiry of the societal evolution of social order.

Before we turn to our analysis, we shortly have to sketch out our investigative procedure. First, the theoretical background of the project has to be briefly explicated. What is the main research interest? What are the questions raised? What is expected to be demonstrated by the pure model or by simulations? Second, we investigate the scalability and the actual scaling processes by referring to the analytical tool already outlined above. Therefore, we use the schemas element/relation and quantitative/qualitative to decompose social actions and systemic processes in order to find out in what way the model is scalable and what forms of scaling can be activated (even if the designers are not aware of or do not pay attention to these forms). No question, the model we choose to demonstrate our heuristic could be alternatively interpreted in some parts. We concede that sometimes our interpretation might be called quite creative. Yet, we are able to point out which forms of scaling can be found and which scaling references are central, peripheral, or non-applicable. Furthermore, we can evaluate the centrality and significance of those references within the model. Third, we can give some hints if there are desiderata connected to scaling processes. What effects do the scaling processes in the system have on its robustness, flexibility, efficacy, and efficiency? Our conclusion is a short critical review.

The model we come to talk about is quite different from all other socionic projects, because it has a strong application focus [32,33,34]. The project models the task allocation by transportation firms and transportation agents in a MAS. In modelling agents and organizational forms, it draws on the habitus-field-theory of the French sociologist Pierre Bourdieu. Agents are developed by their endowment with certain forms of capital, the task allocation refers to mechanisms of delegation, and the organizational forms are constructed as fields with specific positional features. Trying to bridge the micro-macro divide discussed within sociology and DAI, the introduction of some meso-level is proposed, a level that manifests itself in a variety of organizational forms using different coordination mechanisms to allocate tasks among agents.

Which forms of scaling can be deduced from that model?

Scaling of elements: Undisputedly, this is an agent-oriented model: agents are the systemic element to be scaled in a quantitative and qualitative way. Qualitatively seen, two types of agents can be generally differentiated: body agents who work on single tasks and head agents who represent collections of agents. Also and more specifically, agents are differentiated by their unequal and diversified endowments with forms of capital.

Scaling of relations: The relational structure of the system is built by the delegation of tasks and agents' positions, that both can be quantitatively scaled. The notion of delegation has to be qualitatively differentiated in two separate forms: the delegation of tasks and the social delegation of positions (which is currently only the head positions). The delegations can further be analytically divided by the mechanisms that create the relations between the agents. Four mechanisms are proposed: economic exchange, gift exchange, authority, and voting.

Self-referential system scaling: Based on the difference of elements and relations elucidated above, we propose that the system as a whole is quantitatively scalable as a network of agents connected through delegations. This interconnectedness could be more or less dense. In the qualitative sense, the internal social world of the system can be further differentiated in several organizational forms as special selective and structurally determining patterns. The system scales itself qualitatively by choosing and establishing the appropriate organizational form. Currently, these forms are strategic networks, virtual enterprises, co-operations, and single firms.

Other-referential system scaling: Quantitatively seen, the system has to scale in response to either new customers' requests, e.g., new tasks for the system to cope with, or special environmental occurrences like traffic delays and false shipments. These permanently changing outside factors force the system to adjust internally. The allocation of tasks in a transport industry and the differences in the quality of the tasks that have to be handled by the system are the form of qualitative scaling of the system. Therefore, these tasks have to be interpreted as the other-referential moments of the system scaling.

In our view, the entire approach to scalability is focused on the qualitative dimension of scaling. The scaling of the system happens by self-organization, that means, the agents group themselves to organizational forms by delegating tasks and positions to each other. The scaling, therefore, affects mostly the *multiplexity* and *selectivity* of the system. The introduction of organizational forms increases the selectivity of the system but may have ambivalent effects on the multiplexity because it is unclear whether the new structural forms substitute the old mechanisms of delegation or whether they are added to the existing range of relations. The *number of couplings* rises with the establishment of organizational forms in the system, whereas the *number of elements* is left unaffected. The diversity of agent positions increases, because every organizational form offers new positions in a field and the emergence of head agents. The effects on *density* are hardly to evaluate since agents are coupled more durably and less frequently differently in the organizational forms. Presumably, the *irritability* of the system stays constant after the self-organizing process, because it is solely the customer determining the task load. Irritability is a given factor to the system. The specialization of the system rendered possibly by the organizational forms may result in a decrease of the *problemacy*, which means that the allocation of tasks would be organized more effectively.

Thus, the *effective* and *efficient* organization of the task delegation is a desideratum of first rank. Moreover, the system's *robustness* is enhanced through the self-organization processes by which persistent forms of task allocation are realized. *Flexibility* is achieved on two levels: on the first level through the dynamic adaptability of the operations of delegation and on the second level through the differentiation of organizational forms with specific advantages like minimal communicative expense in the integrated firm or the high adaptability of the strategic network. The introduction and stabilization of *organizational forms* within a system can result in an extended internal differentiation and task distribution to specialized agents. This structuring on the meso-level can be considered as clear global organization of work to be done in organizational forms additional agents can cling to if they are needed by the system.

Evidently, this model encompasses scalability and processes of scaling in a wide range. Our impression is that this model has been thoroughly reflected, because not only the subject and the purpose of the modelling is clearly given, also the theoretical groundwork and the terminological definitions are well done so that the transition into our own heuristics was relatively easy, although the project bases on a different and competing theoretical approach.

5   Scalability in Organized Multi-system Systems

In this section, we try to outline very shortly some architectural features that seem to be relevant and practicable for the development of scalable systems. Those proposals are mainly of conceptual nature that are additionally developed, that means they are not directly inferable from our analytical framework.

The MAS we have in mind has to be conceptualized as an organization, that means, not as an interaction, a collection of interactions, or a whole society.[9] Basically, the

---

[9] For a more thorough theoretical elaboration of organized MAS see [1].

MAS has to be designed as a system instead, encapsulating operations that are functionally differentiated in several specific tasks to be fulfilled. As mentioned in *Section 3*, organizations are decision-making systems that process this form of communication solely. By establishing decision premises, the organization tries to wield influence on its internal operations that have to occur in a structured fashion to really become functionally integrated. Thus, we have at least two systemic levels encompassed by the organization, namely the organization itself and its internal environment consisting of interactions of different functional specification. Taking this point seriously and clinging to the analogy between organizations and most MAS, we propose to consider MAS as multi-system systems (MSS), composed of a decision-making system, a lot of interaction systems, and individual agents contributing to the work processes. Consequently, there are two distinguishable perspectives on such a MSS: a macro-logical and a micrological one. The macro-perspective focuses on the socially integrating decision system, the organization. The micro-perspective is centered on all forms of interaction within the organization; forms that can be typified as work, information exchange, negotiations, trials of strength (Hewitt), and social conflicts. This perspective, also, is oriented toward informal processes, whereas the macro-logical view mainly focuses on formally executed interactions, that is, interactions which refer to organizational structures set by the organization to regulate the internal communications, interactions, and decisions alike.[10]

An additional system belonging to such a MSS would be a mirror [35]. The mirror, we would like to put forward, operates as the management of the entire organization vested with special functions. These functions are global observation and information gathering, generalizing knowledge and decision premises, and implementing structures that have to orient the internal operations. Speaking in terms of system theory, this kind of mirror functions as a personalizable observer of second order [36]. This management is a system that observes and reflects the organization from within having also a specialized view on the external environment, whereby it gathers information and looks out for opportunities and necessities of interventions. As an intervening entity, the management operates not as a system-internal dictator that can program the communication processes, but as a "perturbator" trying to influence internal interactions by instituting structures as conditioning contexts that lend orientation.

If a MSS, as described, is a goal-attaining system, it needs some sort of operational direction. In real life, organizations are provided with a management system making executive decisions about the organization of work and the operational procedures by which the system's ends shall be reached. Management, therefore, has crucial impact on the structuring and the operations of the system. Although it is normally not considered to be a specific management function, trying to find and to stabilize an adequate level of internal complexity is one of the main challenges for any management. Our contention is that management has to be management of complexity to a large extent. Who, if not the management, the strategic apex of the system, is in charge of dealing with complex-

---

[10] By the way, this differentiation between these two levels of observation can also be used in another heuristically productive way, that is, as a schematic difference for the analysis of scalability and scaling processes in MSS. One could try to find out if a MSS scales differently on the level of internal interactions and on the level of the organizational decision system.

ity? No one. Every system within the organization only has the duty to fulfil what is expected from it. Complexity is always managed in some way where communications occur; however, problems due to over-complexity or due to operational uncertainties in structurally unclear and ambiguous situations, for instance, are issues to be handled elsewhere, namely where strategic decisions are made. We argue that a management of complexity functions as systemic self-scaling, wherein the management as a mirror plays a pivotal role.

The management of the organization is a strategically operating system whose duty is to guarantee goal attainment and efficient work processes. Hence, the management we describe is largely strategic management eager to orient and control all internal operations. It also is in charge to stabilize an adequate level of system complexity. This level is sufficiently precise in its structural determination, but nonetheless allows enough flexibility. Operations cannot happen in any way; they have to get organized, that means they have to occur in accordance with organizational structures. The systemic complexity is organized complexity. In our view, one of the main functions of the strategic management is structuring complexity. Essentially, the management tries to influence the selective relating of elements with each other by conditioning those selective processes.

As a global observer, the management has to construe a "picture" of what is going on within the system. It needs a description of system complexity. This kind of description that is also an evaluation can be understood as hyper-complexity. A system is hyper-complex if at least one self-description of the entire system exists and is processed within it that denotes the system as complex [37, p. 876]. That managerially construed hyper-complexity can be used as starting point for excogitating ways to organize the complexity that, however, can never be fully comprehended. Strategies of selection are needed. We argue that these have to be conceptualized as scaling strategies, namely strategies that propose up- and down-scaling in different forms. Scaling strategies contain performance objectives backed by certain forms of scaling that have to be operationally implemented. System theoretically spoken, they are networks of expectations that set forth a margin of goals for the system to gain operational and structural orientation. That means, scaling strategies restrain operationally while directing the system globally. Strategies work as highly generalized forms of control-knowledge processed in the system.

To give a few examples for possible scaling strategies: Systemic flexibility could be increased if the system is equipped with a large variety of structural forms that can couple a wide range of diverse operations (increased diversity through increased multiplexity). Systemic efficiency could be enhanced by reducing the communicative load, on the one side, and by minimizing the ways possible communication processes may follow on the other (scaling up the system's selectivity and scaling down the element number). Systemic robustness could be fostered by lowering the possibility of getting environmentally perturbated and by strengthening the structural consistency as well as the self-adaptation of the system (higher selectivity and lower irritability). As one can easily see from these examples, many scaling strategies could be built by the management. [11] Furthermore, it is obvious that scaling strategies operationalize the desiderata

---

[11] A more detailed list of possible strategies is provided by Paetow and Schmitt in [38].

of scalability through different forms of scaling whose operational implementation shall bring about a certain level of complexity. How are scaling strategies promulgated in the system? What impact can they have on the systemic processes of self-organization? According to the concept of a Communication-Based Social System Mirror (CBSSM), the strategies are published on the mirror's blackboard, observable by every agent employed by the system. No agent is coerced to follow the strategies, and no interaction could be determined by the management strategies. Interactions are free to refer to their own structures, resting on an informal level, while the agents are supposed to reason autonomously and to decide on the basis of their own reasoning process. Hence, the operational basis constitutes a social reality *sui generis*; a reality the management can only try to influence by setting conditions without instruments to fully control the informal processes occurring there. The actual scaling process comes about as a mixture of intentional management strategies and the informal strategies that emerge out of the interactions. Therefore, the mirror has to take into account the potential resistance of the operational basis, while construing an intended strategy. Strategies are not so much formulated, but more formed in evolutionary processes that intermingle micro- and macro-scaling strategies.[12] From a macro-logical perspective, scaling strategies are decision premises of a special kind functioning as explicit hints for the operational complexity management; whereas from the micro-logical perspective, these strategies can be referred by interactions as decision premises to overcome uncertainties about topics to focus, agents to include, tasks to handle, or other operational complexity problems. Could there be an ultimate aim presumably capable of directing systemic self-scaling? We are apt to presume such an aim. A closer look into the science of complexity reveals that complex adaptive systems being stable and flexible at the same time seem to be paradoxically constituted: They are able to stabilize their instability. This system state could be termed "bounded instability": "[W]hen nonlinear feedback (system) operates in a state poised at the edge of instability its behavior is paradoxically both stable and instable at the same time: there is instability in the sense that specific behavior is inherently unpredictable over the long term, but there is also stability in the sense that "there is qualitative structure to that behavior and also short-term outcomes are predictable" [40, p. 482]. We argue that the moment of instability and flexibility is given by the interactions occurring on the inside of the system, whereas the organization as a structuring system guarantees stability by setting formal frames directing the internal operations. Two main attractors cause diverging effects within the system: interactions as dynamic operations, partly anarchic partly ordered, and the organization as the integrating system obliged to give direction and structure to the interactions relevant for securing the reproduction, i.e. the decision-making processes. The boundedness controls the system's instability, and the instability controls the structural binding of itself. This constitutes the paradox: The system is simultaneously stable and instable. Moreover, the system that is stable allows instability; and it is instable because it preserves stability. The main point is that it is highly crucial to combine those systemic characteristics of stability and instability, robustness and flexibility to use the terms introduced above.

Thus, an organizational MSS is a proto-typical system of bounded instability. The micro-logical perspective focuses mainly on the organizational dynamics at the opera-

---

[12] Our strategy formation model is quite similar to the model Mintzberg proposes [39].

tional basis of the system, while the macro-logical view is centered on the system trying to implement structures that lead the entire system toward its goals or its purpose. The macro-logical perspective, also, analyzes the self-scaling activities of the management representing the organization. Scaling strategies promulgated by the system's management are one factor of stability, whereas the internal communicative reactions to them bring about a dynamic possibly resulting in creative and innovative developments. All scaling endeavours, therefore, have to aim at realizing robustness in the center of the system and flexibility at its fringes. To sustain and further develop core competencies permitting outstanding performances could be a viable strategy, a competitive strategy also propagated in management science [30].

The great challenge for a self-scaling system lies in the problem to maintain a level of complexity that stabilizes the system at the edge of chaos [41]. Effective systemic self-scaling manages complexity by strategic intent, i.e., the intent to realize robustness, flexibility, efficacy, and efficiency. Consequently, scaling processes strive for the nearly impossible: reaching bounded instability that sets creativity and innovativeness free on the one hand, and realizing functionality and economic rationality on the other. In this article, we tried to prove that computer scientists working on issues of scalability can profit extensively from studying complexity science, organization theory, and the bunch of literature connecting both fields of research. [13]

References

1. Paetow, K., Schmitt, M.: Das Multiagentensystem als Organisation im Medium der Technik. In Kron, T., ed.: Luhmann modelliert: Sozionische Ansätze zur Simulation von Kommunikationssystemen. Leske+Budrich, Opladen (2002) 55–113
2. Leong, T.J., Lim, M.: Network Topology Scalability (undated) http://cva.stanford.edu/ee482/research/tjleong.pdf.
3. N., N.: Scalability: Expand IT Capabilities to Meet Business Requirements (2002) wysiwyp://164/http://Microsoft.com/enterprise/articles/scalability.asp.
4. N., N.: Managing Application Services: A Progressive Approach. Manage the Service, Not the Server (undated) http://sun.com/software/cluster/wp-servicemgmt.
5. Esposito, D.: Scalability, Sweet Scalability (2001) wysiwyg://fraContent.fraRightFrames.175...ndive/html/data03082001.asp?frame=true.
6. Preckshot, G.G.: Real-Time Systems Complexity and Scalability (1993) http://fessp.llnl.gov/csrc/files/114566.pdf.
7. Hewitt, C.E.: Towards Open Information Systems Semantics. Part I, Chapter 2. In: Proceedings of the 10th International Workshop on Distributed Artificial Intelligence, Bandera, Texas (1990) 121–126 MCC Technical Report Number ACT-AI-355-90.

---

[13] For an overview and a critical discussion see [42]. It could be shown that the system theoretical heuristics for the analysis of scalability and scaling processes presented here offers quite revealing insights into the issues related to the scalability debate. The heuristic power of elucidation of our analytic tools has been demonstrated by analyzing the scalability of a specific socionic model. Our contention is that these tools can further be sharpened by an organization theoretical embedding, as we sketched out in this last section.

8. Woodside, M.: Metrics and Analysis of Mobile Agent Systems. In Wagner, T., Rana, O.F., eds.: Infrastructure for Agents, Multi-Agent Systems, and Scalable Multi-Agent Systems. Proceedings of the International Workshop for Scalable Multi-Agent Systems, Barcelona, Springer (2001) 234–245

9. Gerber, C.: Scalability of Multi-Agent Systems. Proposal for a Dissertation. Technical report, Deutsches Forschungszentrum für Künstliche Intelligenz, Saarbrücken (1997) TM-97-02.

10. Brazier, F., van Steen, M., Wijgaards, N.J.E.: On MAS Scalability. In Wagner, T., Rana, O.F., eds.: Proceedings of the Second International Workshop on Infrastructure for Agents, MAS, and Scalable MAS, Montreal (2001) 121–126

11. Turner, P.J., Jennings, N.R.: Improving the Scalability of Multi-Agent Systems. In Wagner, T., Rana, O.F., eds.: Infrastructure for Agents, Multi-Agent Systems, and Scalable Multi-Agent Systems. Proceedings of the International Workshop for Scalable Multi-Agent Systems, Barcelona, Springer (2001) 246–262

12. Rana, O.F., Wagner, T., Greenber, M.S., Purvis, M.K.: On MAS Scalability. In Wagner, T., Rana, O.F., eds.: Infrastructure for Agents, Multi-Agent Systems, and Scalable Multi-Agent Systems. Proceedings of the International Workshop for Scalable Multi-Agent Systems, Barcelona, Springer (2001) 304–308

13. Wijngaards, N.J.E., Overeinder, B.J., van Steen, M., Brazier, F.M.T.: Supporting Internet-Scale Multi-Agent Systems (2001) http://www.iids.org/publications/bnaic2002_dke.pdf.

14. Team, H.V.W.S.: A Design for Scalability (2001) http://www7b.software.ibm.com/wsdd/library/techarticles/hvws/scalability.html.

15. Wagner, T., Rana, O.R., eds.: Infrastructure for Agents, Multi-Agent Systems, and Scalable Multi-Agent Systems. Proceedings of the International Workshop for Scalable Multi-Agent Systems, Barcelona, Springer (2001)

16. Schillo, M., Bürckert, H.J., Fischer, K., Klusch, M.: Towards a Definition of Robustness for Market-Style Open Multi-Agent Systems (2000) www.virtosphere.de/data/publications/conferences/2001Schillo+.Robustness.AA01.pdf.

17. Klein, M., Dellarocas, C.: Domain-Independent Exception Handling Services That Increase Robustness in Open Multi-Agent Systems (2000) http://ccs.mit.edu/ases.

18. Weiss, G., ed.: Distributed Artificial Intelligence Meets Machine Learning. Springer, Berlin et al. (1997)

19. Noel, R.: Scale Up in Distributed Databases: A Key Design Goal for Distributed Systems (1996)   http://www.cs.rpi.edu/ñoel/distr_scaleup/distributed.html.

20. Weyuker, E.J., Avritzer, A.: A Metric for Predicting the Performance of an Application under a Growing Workload. IBM Systems Journal **41** (2002) 45–54

21. Luhmann, N.: Einfache Sozialsysteme. In: Soziologische Aufklärung 2. 2 edn. Westdeutscher Verlag (1982) 21–38

22. Luhmann, N.: Social Systems. 2. edn. Stanford University Press, Stanford, Cal. (1999)

23. Kieserling, A.: Kommunikation unter Anwesenden: Studien über Interaktionssysteme. Suhrkamp, Frankfurt/M. (1999)

24. Luhmann, N.: Organisation und Entscheidung. Westdeutscher Verlag, Opladen (2000)

25. Baecker, D.: Organisation als System. Suhrkamp, Frankfurt/M. (1999)

26. Byrne, D.S.: Complexity Theory and the Social Sciences: An Introduction. Routledge, London et al. (1998)

27. La Porte, T.: Organized Social Complexity: Challenge to Politics and Policy. Princeton University Press, Princeton (1975)

28. Morin, E.: Complexity. International Social Science Journal **26** (1974) 555–582

29. Weick, K.E.: The Psychology of Organizing. Addison-Wesley, New York (1979)

30. Hamel, G., Prahalad, C.K.: Competing for the Future. Harvard University Press, Boston (1994)
31. Malsch, T.: Naming the Unnamable: Socionics Turn of/to Distributed Artificial Intelligence. Autonomous Agents and Multi-Agent Systems **4** (2001) 155–186
32. Hillebrandt, F.: Flexible Holonen zur Aggregation höherer Ebenen künstlicher Sozialität (2002) Talk held on the yearly summit of the socionics SPP.
33. Schillo, M., Fischer, K., Klein, C.: The Micro-Macro-Link in DAI and Sociology. In Moss, S., Davidsson, P., eds.: Multi-Agent Based Simulation: Second International Workshop on Multi-Agent Based Simulation, Boston (2001)
34. Schillo, M., Fley, B., Hillebrandt, F., Hinck, D.: Self-Organization in Multiagent Systems: From Agent Interaction to Agent Organization. In: Proceedings of the Third International Workshop on Modelling Artificial Societies and Hybrid Organizations MASHO, Aachen (2002) http://www.tu-harburg.de/tbg/Deutsch/Projekte/Sozionik2/UntitledFrame.htm.
35. Lorentzen, K.F., Nickles, M.: Ordnung aus Chaos – Prolegomena zu einer Luhmann'schen Modellierung deentropisierender Strukturbildung in Multiagentensystemen. In Kron, T., ed.: Luhmann modelliert: Sozionische Ansätze zur Simulation von Kommunikationssystemen. Leske+Budrich, Opladen (2002) 55–113
36. Baecker, D.: Die Form des Unternehmens. Suhrkamp, Frankfurt/M. (1993)
37. Luhmann, N.: Die Gesellschaft der Gesellschaft. Suhrkamp, Frankfurt/M. (1997)
38. Paetow, K., Schmitt, M.: Komplexitätsmangement durch systemische Selbstskalierung. Technical Report 9, Technology Assessment and Design, Technical University Hamburg-Harburg, Hamburg (2003)
39. Mintzberg, H.: The Rise and Fall of Strategic Planning. Prentice Hall, New York et al. (1994)
40. Stacy, R.D.: The Science of Complexity: An Alternative Perspective for Strategic Change Processes. Strategic Management Journal **16** (1995) 477–495
41. Holland, J.H.: Hidden Order: How Adaptation Builds Complexity. Helix and Perseus, Cambridge, Mass. (1996)
42. Kappelhoff, P. In: Komplexitätstheorie: Neues Paradigma für die Managmentforschung, Wuppertal (2002) 49–101

On the Organisation of Agent Experience: Scaling Up Social Cognition[*]

Michael Rovatsos[1] and Kai Paetow[2]

[1] School of Informatics, The University of Edinburgh
Edinburgh EH8 9LE, Edinburgh, United Kingdom
mrovatso@inf.ed.ac.uk
[2] Department of Technology Assessment, Technical University of Hamburg
21071 Hamburg, Germany
kai.paetow@tu-harburg.de

Abstract. This paper introduces "micro-scalability" as a novel design objective for social reasoning architectures operating in open multiagent systems. Micro-scalability is based on the idea that social reasoning algorithms should be devised in a way that allows for social complexity reduction, and that this can be achieved by operationalising principles of interactionist sociology. We first present a formal model of InFFrA agents called m^2InFFrA that utilises two corner-stones of micro-scalability, the principles of *social abstraction* and *transient social optimality*. Then, we exemplify the usefulness of these concepts by presenting experimental results with a novel opponent classification heuristic ADHOC that has been developed using the InFFrA social reasoning architecture. These results prove that micro-scalability deserves further investigation as a useful aspect of socionic research.

1 Introduction

The development of methods to improve the scalability of multiagent systems (MAS) is one of the central themes on the Socionics [4] research agenda. With the rapid growth of the Internet and of mobile communication technologies in recent years, large-scale *open systems* [5,6] are becoming reality, and since scalability is a major concern in this kind of systems, it has the potential of becoming a key issue in MAS research in the next years. Roughly speaking, the various aspects of complexity in MAS that call for scalability fall into two categories [7]: (i) quantitative aspects that depend on the number of agents, interactions, etc. in a system and (ii) qualitative aspects such as the complexity of interactions and the heterogeneity of agents. According to the definition of Paetow, Schmitt and Malsch [7], scalability can be understood as the "operationalisation of complexity", i.e. the capacity of a system to manage complexity. Thus, a system scales well if it is capable of responding to increasing complexity appropriately, rather than "degrading ungracefully" or even collapsing. When complexity management is

---

[*] This work was supported by DFG (German National Science Foundation) under contracts no. Br609/11-2 and MA759/4-2. The research reported on in this article has continued since the time of writing. Accounts of more recent results can be found in [1,2,3].

K. Fischer, M. Florian, and T. Malsch (Eds.): Socionics, LNAI 3413, pp. 155–175, 2005.

effective, it might even be possible to exploit increasing complexity rather than suffer from it.

A core theme in our own research has been to study the impact of using different social theories such as Luhmann's systems theory [8] and symbolic interactionism [9,10,11] as a "construction manual" for building different kinds of MAS with a particular focus on scalability properties of the resulting systems. While work on system-theoretic MAS architectures [12] can comment on arbitrary aspects of scalability, be it at the micro-, meso- or macro-level of social systems, multiagent research that seeks to exploit the principles of interactionism [13] has to focus on more specific aspects. Interactionist theories are, generally speaking, concerned with how social structures affect interaction between humans in a society, how individuals process social knowledge and how social sense is continually re-produced and potentially re-constructed through ongoing interaction. Interaction is seen as an exchange of symbols whose meaning is socially pre-determined, but needs to be re-affirmed by the actors who use these symbols to communicate. In a constant "struggle over signs", it also undergoes changes. Quite naturally, as interactionism is concerned with how actors deal with social meaning, its focus lies not in the study of "mass phenomena", the functioning of entire societies, or macro-characteristics of social life. So how can such a theory contribute to the construction of scalable MAS?

In this paper, we claim that MAS built using interactionist principles can provide substantial contributions to solving scalability problems through the concept of *micro-scalability*. Micro-scalability is the capacity of social reasoning methods to deal with heterogeneity and complexity in the social behaviour of other agents appropriately. Thus, micro-scalable agent architectures operationalise aspects of the complexity of interaction situations by using social cognition as an instrument to manage it. To achieve micro-scalability, we have to improve the ways social knowledge is processed at the cognitive level, and we discuss two principles that serve this purpose and that are both inspired by interactionism: the first one is *social abstraction*, a transition from the "opponent modelling" attitude (one of the main social reasoning perspectives traditionally assumed in MAS research) to a "modelling interaction situations" stance that abstracts from the mental properties of agents interacted with in favour of categorising situations and developing learning strategies to cope with these. The second is *transient social optimality*, which somewhat contradicts classical agent research principles of (constant) optimality. It means that in order to be comprehensible, socially intelligent agents have to abandon optimal strategies from time to time (in the long run, of course, their behaviour should still converge to optimal strategies). Both methods were developed using interactionist theories, and they pave the way for further research on the subject.

The remainder of this paper is structured as follows: in section 2 we provide an overview of the social reasoning architecture InFFrA that serves as a general framework for developing micro-scalable agents. Section 3 introduces a formal model of InFFrA that is useful to formally describe social abstraction and transient social optimality. Then, in section 4, we present the opponent classification heuristic ADHOC based on InFFrA and discuss experimental results that prove the usefulness of the two principles empirically. Some conclusions are drawn in section 5.

2   The InFFrA Social Reasoning Architecture

The Interaction Frames and Framing Architecture InFFrA is a framework for building social learning and reasoning architectures based on the notions of "interaction frames" and "framing". Both are central concepts in the micro-sociological works of Erving Goffman [10], and InFFrA is an attempt to operationalise them for use with computational agents. Essentially, interaction frames describe classes of interaction situations and provide guidance to the agent about how to behave in a particular social context. Framing, on the other hand, signifies the process of applying frames in interaction situations appropriately. As Goffman puts it, framing is the process of answering the question *"what is going on here?"* in a given interaction situation—it enables the agent to act in a competent, routine fashion. Since the InFFrA framework has been described in detail elsewhere [13,14,15], we shall restrict ourselves to a fairly superficial description here.

2.1   Interaction Frames

In InFFrA, a frame is a data structure that contains information about

- possible courses of interaction (so-called *trajectories*) that are characteristic of the class of interactions described by the frame,
- *roles and relationships* between the parties involved in an interaction of this type (actors that fill certain roles, groups, representatives, etc.),
- *contexts* within which the interaction may take place (states of affairs before, during, and after an interaction is carried out) and
- *beliefs*, i.e. epistemic states of the interacting parties.

A graphical representation of an interaction frame is given in figure 1, with examples for possible contents of the four "slots" of information listed above. The "roles and relationships" slot contains, for example, graphical representations of groups (boxes) and relationships (arrows). The trajectory is represented by a protocol-like model of concurrent agent actions (in principle, though, trajectories may be given in any form of behavioural description). In the "context" slot, the trajectory model is "embedded" in boxes that contain preconditions, postconditions and maintenance conditions—these are propositions about properties of the environment that have to hold before, during, or after execution of the trajectory. A semantic network and a belief network are shown as two possible representations of ontological and causal knowledge in the "beliefs" slot, where shaded boxes define which parts of the networks are known to which participant of the frame.

It is characteristic of frames that certain attributes of the above must be assumed to be shared knowledge among interactants (so-called *common attributes*) for the frame to be carried out properly while others may be private knowledge of the agent who "owns" the frame (*private attributes*). Private attributes are mainly used by agents to store their personal experience with a frame, e.g. utilities associated with previous frame enactments and instance values for the variables used in generic representations that describe past enactments ("histories"), inter-frame relationships ("links") etc.

An important thing to stress about the semantics of such a frame is that the trajectory slot constitutes its core element, because it describes *how* interactions following this frame will be carried out. All the other elements of the frame serve only as "side information" about conditions that will hold when this type of interaction occurs.

For example, a frame that describes wedding ceremonies contains information about the participating actors (bride, groom, best man, parents, guests, priest, etc.) and their relationships with each other (e.g. kinship between parents of bride and groom), conditions (pre-conditions: groom proposed to bride, invitations were sent out, etc. post-conditions: legal fact of "being married", honeymoon; maintenance conditions: neither groom nor bride abandon the scene during the ceremony), and beliefs (love among bridal pair, agreement of parents, etc.). But although all this information is supplied, the ultimate use of the frame is to correctly interpret the actions that are observed in the ceremony, and—if in the position of one of the "active" participants—to act appropriately.

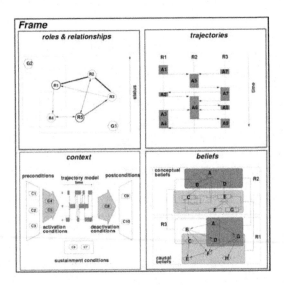

Fig. 1. An interaction frame.

2.2   Framing

The second main element of InFFrA is the framing control flow model for social reasoning and social adaptation. It maintains interaction frames, modifies them with incoming observations if necessary, and applies the most suitable frame in a given interaction situation. In order to describe the steps performed in each framing cycle, some data structures need to be introduced. These are

- the *active frame*, the unique frame currently activated,
- the *perceived frame*, an interpretation of the currently observed state of affairs,
- the *difference model* that contains the differences between perceived frame and active frame,
- the *trial frame*, used when alternatives to the current frame are sought for,
- and the *frame repository*, in which the agent locally stores its frame knowledge.

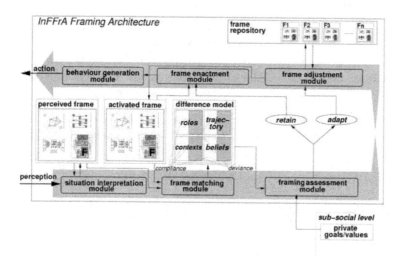

Fig. 2. An overview of the framing process in InFFrA with sub-processes and data structures.

Using these frame data structures, the framing component performs the following steps in each reasoning cycle during an interaction encounter:

1. *Interpretation & Matching:* Update the perceived frame, and compare it with the active frame (the normative picture of what the interaction should be like).
2. *Assessment:* Assess the usability of the current active frame in terms of
   (i) adequacy (compliance with the conditions of the active frame),
   (ii) validity (the degree to which the active frame trajectory matches the perceived encounter) and
   (iii) desirability (depending on whether the implications of the frame correspond to the agent's private goals).
3. *Framing decision:* If the active frame seems appropriate, continue with 6. Else, proceed with 4. to find a better frame.
4. *Re-framing:* Search the frame repository for better frames. "Mock-activate" them as trial frames iteratively and go back to 1; if no suitable frame is found, proceed with 5.
5. *Adaptation:* Iteratively modify frames in the frame repository and continue with 4.
6. *Enactment:* Influence action decisions by applying the active frame. Return to 1.

The entire framing process is visualised in figure 2. Apart from linking functional modules for each of the steps to the data structures on which these are performed, it connects the sub-social reasoning (e.g. BDI [16]) level to the InFFrA layer by taking agent's goals and preferences into consideration in the *frame assessment* phase.

InFFrA provides a unifying view for various perspectives on social learning at the interaction level, and has many features that allow to focus on the core aspects of developing social reasoning architectures. In particular, it assists the designer of such algorithms in focusing on the core issues, such as

- what representation to use for frames in a given application domain,
- how to store, retrieve and modify frames efficiently,
- how to intertwine local goal-directed reasoning with social commitment,
- which operators to provide for creative construction of frames by agents themselves,

and allows for integrating different outlooks on interaction, such as the machine learning perspective [15] and the agent communication semantics perspective [17].

2.3   Social Abstraction and Transient Social Optimality

Before describing the concepts of *social abstraction* and *transient social optimality* in terms of a formal model of InFFrA, we should informally explain the intuition behind them using the above elements of InFFrA.

The principle of *social abstraction* is fairly obvious in the above framework, since it is embodied by the very notion of interaction frames. By definition, these are thought to abstract from particular situations so as to capture the central distinctions between *classes* of these situations. More specifically, they abstract from particular interaction partners, specific world states, and may even coerce different actions in the trajectories into action types (e.g. by varying the content in speech acts with the same performative).

There are two principal arguments in favour of permitting such abstraction. Firstly, the argument from "pre-structuration" states that even though the possibilities for different interactions abound, there is only a certain number of relevant categories of interactions that occur over and over again. These are determined by the action and reasoning capabilities of the agents in a society, by the distribution of resources and by the available communication channels. By the second (much more practical) argument from "bounded rationality", agents have no other *choice* than to generalise from particular interactions for two reasons: (1) It is not reasonable to assume that they have arbitrarily elaborate reasoning capabilities to store all interaction experience and to consider all of that information to act optimally in a new encounter. (2) Even if this were the case, it seems unlikely that information could be directly re-used, given that (especially in open systems) encounters with the same interaction partners under the same circumstances are only occasional (in the best case—in the worst, they are one-time experiences).

As concerns *transient social optimality*, this point is somewhat harder to make. From the InFFrA architecture, it is obvious that optimal social decisions strongly rely on making the right assessments regarding the adequacy, validity and desirability of a candidate frame at the right time. However, in making the right framing choices, there are two conflicting goals that the agent needs to balance, namely (1) *predictability* and (2) optimal *utility*. On the one hand, an InFFrA agent wants to be able to predict others' imminent actions, and, on the other hand, it cannot stick to a particular predictable pattern of interaction if this is sub-optimal utility-wise.

In terms of the framing process outlined above, this conflict arises when adequacy, validity and desirability measures in frame assessment yield contradictory values. A standard way to proceed in that case would be to somehow weigh the importance of these measures so as to achieve an overall evaluation of candidate frames.

But since the agent's own framing choice also affects the reactions of other parties involved in the interaction, things are not that simple. If we assume that other agents are at least as socially intelligent as the agent in question, they will also record interaction experience and apply it strategically. So if we *deviate* from a given, established expectation (in the form of a "safe", well-known, stable frame), because its consequences are not desirable in the current state of affairs for the sake of "trying something new", it is very probable that we will not obtain predictable results. This is because peer interactants will be confused and unable to figure out how the interaction will turn out. So, even if—in the best case—others react in a way that is profitable for oneself, this will only happen at haphazard, i.e. it is not something the agent can rely on in decision making.

Transient social optimality is one answer to this problem that is based on neglecting promising alternatives occasionally for the sake of being "socially comprehensible" for others. In the framing process, this simply means that we trade desirability for validity and adequacy. Thus, the agent can hope to ensure predictability by sacrificing short-term utility, because it is better to have predictable opponents who maybe do not act as nicely as one would wish, rather than constantly trying to make optimal moves while the other might apply the same kind of strategic reasoning.

Goffman, in fact, stresses the strategic aspect of interaction, but it is taken to a level different from, e.g. the traditional decision-theoretic notion of "strategy optimisation" by assuming that agents *adopt* socially established procedures in a strategic fashion rather than to select particular actions in a utility-maximising fashion. To put it differently, behaviour during interactions is only rarely optimised by an individual by completely deviating from expectations; but choosing which of the different expectation patterns to activate is a highly strategic process in which agents compute optimal strategies before taking action.

In the formal model we will now present (section 3), we shall see that this can be formalised by avoiding "redundant" framing cycles unless major problems arise during an encounter. In section 4, the effectiveness of this approach will be underpinned by experimental results.

3   A Formal Model of InFFrA

m^2InFFrA is a full formal model of a specific kind of "simple" InFFrA agents that extends the model of "minimal" agents introduced in [17]. One of its most important aspects is that it enables us to formalise framing as a two-level Markov Decision Process (hence the m^2 in the name), through which the concept of transient social optimality can be defined more precisely. For lack of space, we will not present the model in full detail here (the interested reader should consult [18]) but focus on its core elements.

3.1   Basics

For starters, we assume the existence of two formal languages $\mathcal{L}$ and $\mathcal{M}$. $\mathcal{L}$ is a propositional logical language consisting of (i) atomic propositions $p, q(X, s), \ldots$ that may contain (implicitly universally quantified) variables and (ii) the usual connectives $\vee$, $\wedge$, $\rightarrow$ and $\neg$, the logical constants "true" and "false", and braces () for grouping sub-expressions together. Interpretations of formulae and entailment $\models$ in a *knowledge base* $KB \in 2^{\mathcal{L}}$ are defined in the usual way. We assume that m^2InFFrA agents maintain such a local knowledge base that is revised with incoming percepts and that they have sound and complete inference mechanisms for this logic at their disposal.

$\mathcal{M}$, on the other hand, is a language of message patterns (or templates). As in [17], messages observed in the system can be either physical messages ("real" actions) of the format $\text{do}(a, ac)$ where a is the executing agent and ac is a symbol used for a physical action, or "non-physical" messages $performative(a, b, c)$ sent from a to b with content c. Both sender/recipient and content slots of messages may contain variables for agents, physical actions and content, but not for performatives. As we will soon show, this is useful to abstract from different observed messages. To discriminate between these patterns and actual messages, we write $\mathcal{M}_c$ for the language of *concrete*, variable-free messages.

As to the content c of a non-physical action, this can either be (i) an atomic proposition, (ii) a message term or physical action term, or (iii) a logical formula formed out of these elements. Effectively, this yields a variant of $\mathcal{L}$ as a content language that contains "propositions" for messages/actions (in the sense of "events"). Note that messages in $\mathcal{M}_c$ may, of course, still contain variables in the content slot that are variables in the sense of logical propositions. For the remainder of this paper, we will exclude this kind of logical variables from our considerations when talking about "variables" in the InF-FrA sense. The interested reader can find full definitions of the languages $\mathcal{L}$, $\mathcal{M}$ and $\mathcal{M}_c$ in [19] in this volume.

3.2   Interaction Frames

m^2InFFrA agents are agents that engage in discrete, turn-taking conversations between two parties, and maintain a frame repository $\mathcal{F} = \{F_1, \ldots, F_n\}$ in which they record knowledge about past interactions to apply this knowledge strategically in future encounters. These frames are defined as follows:

Definition 1. A frame *is a quadruple* $F = (T, C, \Theta, h)$, *where*

- $T = \langle p_1, p_2, \ldots, p_n \rangle$ *is the* trajectory *of the frame, a sequence of message terms (patterns)* $p_i \in \mathcal{M}$;
- $\Theta = \langle \vartheta_1, \ldots \vartheta_m \rangle$ *is an ordered list of substitutions* $\vartheta_j = \langle [v_1/t_1], \ldots, [v_k/t_k] \rangle$ *where each* ϑ_j *substitutes variables* v_l *by terms* t_l;
- $C = \langle c_1, \ldots c_m \rangle$ *is an ordered list of condition sets (sets of logical formulae) such that* $c_j \in 2^{\mathcal{L}}$ *is the condition set relevant under substitution* ϑ_j;

– $h \in \mathbb{N}^{|T|}$ *is an* occurrence counter *list counting the occurrence of each member of the trajectory T in previous encounters.*

The semantics of such a frame can be informally described as follows: the agent who "owns" F has experienced $h(p_1)$ encounters which started with a message matching the first element of the trajectory $p_1 = T(F)[1]$ (we write $T(F)$, $\Theta(F)$, $C(F)$ and $h(F)$ for functions that return the respective elements of F). $h(p_2)$ of these encounters continued with a message matching p_2, and so on. (This implies that there was no encounter with prefix $p_1 \cdots p_n$ that continued after p_n according to F.) We will sometimes use the abbreviated syntax $T_h(F) = \xrightarrow{h_1} p_1 \xrightarrow{h_2} p_2 \cdots \xrightarrow{h_n} p_n$ (where $h_n = h(p_n)$) to combine $T(F)$ and $h(F)$ in one expression.

Out of the h_n encounters that included the whole trajectory, exactly one substitution ϑ_j and one condition set c_j held true in the j-th of these encounters. This means that $C(F)$ and $\Theta(F)$ capture the history of past encounters, in which the frame was executed as a whole; it also keeps track of "prefix-matching encounters" that ended after some initial portion of the trajectory, but does not maintain conditions and substitutions for these.

Note that the elements of frames introduced in Section 2 are present in this model, even if it has been simplified somewhat to admit formally rigorous treatment: Roles and relationships, context and beliefs are all captured in the condition sets in C. The trajectory is reduced to a simple sequence T of message templates; the history of the frame (and of its previous successful completions) is stored in C, Θ and h, and links between frames are implicitly maintained by cross-counting occurrence of prefixes of T.

Instead of going into the details of the formal semantics, an example shall illustrate what a frame means:

$$F = \Big\langle \big\langle \xrightarrow{5} \text{propose}(A, B, X) \xrightarrow{3} \text{accept}(B, A, X) \xrightarrow{2} \text{do}(A, X) \big\rangle,$$
$$\langle \{self(A), other(B), can(A, X)\},$$
$$\{agent(A), agent(B), action(X)\} \rangle,$$
$$\langle \langle [A/\text{agent\_1}], [B/\text{agent\_2}], [X/\text{pay\_price}] \rangle,$$
$$\langle [A/\text{agent\_3}], [B/\text{agent\_1}], [X/\text{deliver\_goods}] \rangle \rangle \Big\rangle$$

According to this frame (we use the syntax $\langle T_h(F), C, \Theta \rangle$ instead of (T, C, Θ, h) for convenience), 5 encounters started with a message matching $\text{propose}(A, B, X)$, three of them continued with $\text{accept}(B, A, X)$ and two out of these were concluded by agent A performing physical action X. Thus, another two encounters may have terminated after the first message or were continued with a message that does not match $\text{accept}(B, A, X)$, as is the case for the encounter that turned out differently after the second message. Also, the agent has stored the two conditions and respective substitutions under which this frame has occurred ($h(T)[|h(T)|] = |C(T)| = |\Theta(T)|$).

3.3   Frame Semantics

The semantics of a frame in m²InFFrA are given by the so-called *enactment constraint*, which is assumed to hold whenever a frame $F = (T, C, \Theta, h)$ exists. This constraint can be interpreted in two different ways: as a *retrospective* enactment constraint, that states how often certain transitions between messages have occurred in past encounters, and as a *prospective* enactment constraint, that provides an estimate for the probability with which an arbitrary message sequence is going to occur in the future.

Since the retrospective view is only used to make knowledge base inferences, we will restrict ourselves to a description of the prospective enactment constraint. Roughly speaking, it should express that we expect the future probability of a message sequence to be equal to the frequency with which it has been observed in the past. This could be achieved by simply computing transition frequencies h_{i+1}/h_i in all frames, and keeping track of the total number of encounters experienced so far. However, this would preclude any ability to generalise, since the probability of any message sequence never experienced before would be zero. Therefore, we introduce a real-valued *similarity* measure on message (pattern) sequences $\sigma : \mathcal{M}^* \times \mathcal{M}^* \to \mathbb{R}$ that adds a "case-based" flavour to frames and postulate that

$$\sigma(\vartheta, F) = \frac{1}{|\Theta(F)|} \sum_i \sigma(T(F)\vartheta, T(F)\Theta(F)[i]) \tag{1}$$

$$P(\vartheta|F) = \frac{\sigma(\vartheta, F)}{\sum_\chi \sigma(\chi, F)} \tag{2}$$

So the probability with which an arbitrary substitution ϑ is expected to occur if F is enacted is the expected similarity of ϑ determined using the past frequencies of the cases stored in F, normalised over all other possible substitutions χ. In other words, the more similar a substitution is to previous "samples" of F, the more likely it is to occur. This very much resembles the logic of case-based reasoning [20], because previous cases are combined and weighed according to their similarity with the current case in a way that resembles "nearest neighbour" heuristics.

Rather than knowing how probable ϑ is, we would like to know the probability of particular message sequences, if F is to provide any concrete guidance. For this purpose, we can compute

$$P(w) = \sum_{F \in \mathcal{F}, w = T(F)\vartheta} P(\vartheta|F)P(F) \tag{3}$$

where $P(F)$ is the posterior probability with which an encounter has matched an encounter.

With these definitions, we have formally defined a way to apply the principle of *social abstraction* when forming expectations about social behaviour. However, the above constraints only provide "observer semantics", and do not explain what m^2InFFrA agents who are actively involved in encounters should actually *do*.

3.4   Framing Agents

The following definitions provide the basis for describing the decision-making algorithm of a "framing" m^2InFFrA agent:

Definition 2. *An agent is a structure* $a = (\mathcal{L}, \mathcal{M}, \mathcal{E}, n, u, f, \kappa, \sigma)$ *where*

- $\mathcal{L}, \mathcal{M}$ *are the formal languages used for logical expressions and messages,*
- $\mathcal{E}$ *is a set of encounter identifiers,* $n \in \mathbb{N}$ *is the total number of encounters so far,*
- $u : 2^{\mathcal{L}} \times \mathcal{M}_c^* \to \mathbb{R}$ *is the agent's utility function estimate, where* $u(KB, w)$ *is the estimated utility of* w *being executed with knowledge base KB;*
- $f : \Phi \times \mathcal{M}_c^* \to \Phi$ *transforms any possible frame repository* $\mathcal{F} \in \Phi$ *to a new repository upon experience of an encounter* $e \in \mathcal{M}^*$ (Φ *is the set of all frame repositories);*
- $\kappa : 2^{\mathcal{L}} \times \mathcal{M}_c^* \to 2^{\mathcal{L}}$ *transforms knowledge base contents after an encounter;*
- *and* $\sigma : \mathcal{M}^* \times \mathcal{M}^* \to \mathbb{R}$ *is a similarity measure for variable substitutions.*

These rather complex definitions express that an agent is given by formal languages it uses for communication and reasoning and by utility estimates of communication (and action) sequences depending on his state of knowledge. Further, definition of an agent should specify how the agent transforms his frame repository and knowledge base upon experience of a new encounter, and what similarity function σ he uses to make predictions about future communications.

Given this agent design, the framing state $[a]$ of an agent who is currently experiencing an encounter starting with sequence w is a probability distribution over all potential consequences envisaged by a given his knowledge base and frame repository contents. Defining $[a]$ is, of course, a prerequisite for the application of decision-theoretic principles (such as expected utility maximisation) in the design of m²InFFrA agents. Also, the definition of $[a]$ embodies the empirical, constructivist and consequentialist view of communication semantics proclaimed in [17] in a single formula.

Definition 3. *Let* $a = (\mathcal{L}, \mathcal{M}, u, f, \kappa, \sigma)$ *an agent. A* framing state *of agent* a *is a function* $[a] : \Phi \times 2^{\mathcal{L}} \times \mathcal{M}_c^* \to \Delta(\mathcal{M}_c^*)$ *which maps every*

- *frame repository* $\mathcal{F} \in \Phi$,
- *current encounter prefix sequence* $w \in \mathcal{M}_c^*$,
- *current knowledge base* $KB \in 2^{\mathcal{L}}$

to a finite-support probability distribution $P \in \Delta(\mathcal{M}_c^*)$ *over future message sequences.*

To define $[a]$ in such a way that allows computation of an agent state in accordance with the semantics of m²InFFrA frames, we exploit

- the fact that only frames whose trajectories match recently perceived messages need to be considered,
- current knowledge base contents to reduce the search space to those frames that are applicable in the current situation,
- information about substitutions already applied during the current encounter that restricts degrees of freedom in substituting variables,
- similarities of these substitutions to past cases stored in frames

to derive probabilities for future message sequences.

For lack of space, we cannot present the details of the derivation of $[a]$ here and have to refer the interested reader to [18]. However, we can briefly sketch some general ideas:

If the sequence w has just been observed, this implies that under any $F \in \mathcal{F}$ that prefix-matches w some substitution has to be applied to perform this matching. For any such matching F, this will restrict "still possible" substitutions to a set $\Theta_{poss}(F, KB, w)$. These are all substitutions that provide values for the variables still free in the remaining steps of $T(F)$, under which

1. the remaining steps of $T(F)$ can still be (physically) executed,
2. there is at least one $c = C(F)[i]$ that can be satisfied by the contents of KB,

and which contain the smallest number of variables with this respect (this is necessary to implement a least commitment strategy).

With this, we can redefine equation 1 to obtain

$$P(\vartheta | F, w) = \frac{\sigma(\vartheta, F)}{\sum_{\chi \in \Theta_{poss}(F, KB, w)} \sigma(\chi, F)}$$

where

$$\vartheta \notin \Theta_{poss}(F, KB, w) \Rightarrow \sigma(\vartheta, F) = 0$$

such that the probability estimate is never positive if ϑ cannot be applied anymore.

Thus, after w,

$$P(w' | w) = \sum_{F \in \mathcal{F}, ww' = T(F)\vartheta} P(\vartheta | F, w) P(F | w) \tag{4}$$

yields the probability with which an encounter that started with w will be concluded with w'. As concerns estimates for $P(F|w)$, we can use the frequency with which the frame was carried out as a whole given all runs of F:

$$P(F | w) = \begin{cases} \frac{h(F)[|h(F)|]}{h(F)[|w|]} & \text{if } w \text{ can be unified with the first } |w| \text{ messages of } T(F) \\ 0 & \text{else} \end{cases} \tag{5}$$

Note that, if $w = \varepsilon$, the agent can also use this formula to check whether it is profitable to start an encounter, and what the best choice would be.

3.5   Transient Social Optimality in m^2InFFrA

The main advantage of m^2InFFrA is that it enables us to describe how frame-based design implements transient social optimality, and this is done by re-interpreting action selection in encounters as a Markov Decision Process (MDP) (see, e.g. [21]) and identifying two levels of decision-making in this MDP.

Formally, a (single-level) *Markov Decision problem* is given by a finite set of states S, a finite set of actions A, reward function $R : S \times A \rightarrow \mathbb{R}$ and a *transition probability function* $P \in \Delta(S \times A \times S)$. The intuition is as follows: in a sequence of stages, an agent observes the current state $s \in \mathcal{S}$, executes an action $a \in A$ and receives an immediate payoff $R(s, a)$. With probability $P(s'|s, a)$, the next state the agent finds himself in will be s'. A (so-called *stationary* and *stochastic*) *policy* is a mapping $\pi \in$

$\Delta(S \times A)$ which specifies that the agent executes action a in state s with probability $\pi(s, a)$. The goal of an agent in an MDP is to maximise its long-term payoff, and a criterion that is often applied to define this goal is that of *infinite-horizon expected utility maximisation*, i.e. maximisation of the quantity

$$V^\pi(s) = E\left[\sum_{i=0}^{\infty} \gamma^i r_{t+i} \middle| \pi, s_t = s\right] \qquad (6)$$

where $\gamma < 1$ is a discount factor, $E[\cdot]$ denotes the expected value, and r_t is the reward achieved at the t-th step by applying π.

The MDP formalism has been very popular in recent years, and has to lead to the development of *reinforcement learning* [22] methods which provide algorithms for learning optimal policies from experience (i.e. executing actions and observing feedback values $R(s, a)$ and state transitions (s, a, s')). However, for realistic application domains it suffers from the problem of having to deal with huge state spaces S which leads to long convergence times for learning algorithms since every action has to be executed in every state (at least once) to be able to discern policies that are optimal.

Hierarchical reinforcement learning methods ([23] provides a survey of the state of the art), on the other hand, attempt to abstract from the state space of the "core" MDP in such a way that smaller state spaces are obtained at a higher level of abstraction.

With the concept of transient social optimality in mind, it only seems natural to view frames in a similar way, as "macro"-actions during the execution of which agents do not truly optimise overall their possible action choices in each step. So while equation 4 in the previous section can be basically decomposed to obtain a transition model similar to that of a ("flat") MDP, we can also use a frame as a *hierarchical abstraction of a reasonable course of interaction*. This view not only reduces decision-making complexity but also makes the decision-making agent comprehensible for its peers.

To develop this view, we have found the *options* framework [24] to be most suitable for application to m²lnFFrA. In short, the framework considers "options" $\langle \mathcal{I}, \pi, \beta \rangle$ where $\mathcal{I} \subseteq S$ is the so-called *initiation set*, π is the policy of the option, and $\beta : S^+ \rightarrow [0; 1]$ is a stochastic termination condition. The idea is that an option is available at time t if and only if $s_t \in \mathcal{I}$. If it is chosen, then a_{t+1} is selected according to π, and $\beta(s_{t+1})$ determines whether execution of the option is terminated (whereupon the agent gets to choose a new option).

The concepts used to define options carry over to frames quite naturally:

- $\mathcal{I}$ is the set of states in which a frame can be used, which depends on its conditions and on whether it matches the current encounter prefix;
- π is given by the messages/actions the agent is supposed to execute according to the frame at specific points in time; of course, because of Θ_{poss}, each frame is not a single strategy, but a *set* of strategies, which are quite similar to each other;
- β is the criterion for "re-framing"—it depends on whether
  - the active frame still matches the perceived encounter,
  - the remaining active frame steps are still (physically) executable, and
  - on whether these remaining steps still appear desirable.

Looking at frames as options now enables us to apply standard reinforcement learning techniques such as Q-learning [25] to learn a *framing* strategy, while the freedom of choice at the level of substitutions from Θ_{poss} allows us to optimise during frame execution to find an optimal *action* strategy within the boundaries of a frame. Again, we are not able to go into the details of how this is achieved in practice. They can be found in [18].

To summarise, viewed from a decision-theoretic perspective, the concept of transient social optimality leads to a hierarchical view of decision-making and learning. Trying to stick to a "routine" so that others can understand what one is doing is, in other words, just a simplification of the process of making optimal decisions, since we deliberately disregard information which is available from experience for the sake of promoting stable patterns of interaction.

We believe it is one of the most interesting aspects of the work reported on here that the application of sociological concepts in the design of socially intelligent agents can be shown to parallel existing AI notions, such as "being hierarchical" about MDPs.

4   Micro-scalability in ADHOC

The ADaptive Heuristic for Opponent Classification ADHOC is an implementation of InFFrA that addresses the problem of learning opponent models in the presence of large numbers of opponents in game-theoretic interaction situations. It constitutes a first implementation of InFFrA in which we studied how agents can classify opponents they confront in fixed-length Iterated Prisoners' Dilemma ((I)PD) [26] games so as to learn optimal strategies against these opponent classes. If they succeed in classifying opponents quickly during the encounter, this would guarantee that they can behave optimally against unknown opponents.

A detailed description of ADHOC can be found in [15]. Here, we only provide an informal overview of the algorithms and concentrate on its relationship to m^2InFFrA and, in particular, on social abstraction and transient social optimality.

4.1   Overview

In the ADHOC interaction setting, agents from a growing population are randomly matched in pairs to play a fixed number (say, 10) of PD iterations. No agent knows the duration of each encounter, and, initially, all agents are unknown to each other. The goal of these agents is to maximise their cumulative utility over time, where one-shot payoffs are as in table 1. To this end, they evolve a (bounded) number of opponent classes from scratch that are the interaction frames of ADHOC. Each of these classes contains

1. A deterministic finite automaton (DFA) that represents the opponent's strategy in "strategic" mode, and the agent's own strategy in "comprehensible" mode.
2. A "support" of agents that belong to this class, i.e. that have played according to the DFA in past encounters.

a_j	C	D
a_i		
C	(3,3)	(0,5)
D	(5,0)	(1,1)

Table 1. Prisoner's Dilemma payoff matrix. Matrix entries (u_i, u_j) contain the payoff values for agents a_i and a_j for a given combination of row/column action choices, respectively. C stands for each player's "cooperate" option, D stands for "defect".

3. A set of past encounters ("samples") with members of this class that is used to train the DFA. To learn a DFA from sequences of actions, we apply the model-based learning method *US-L** proposed by Carmel and Markovitch [27].
4. A table of Q-values [25] that is updated using received payoffs in order to learn an optimal strategy against the DFA, as in *US-L**.

Also, ADHOC agents maintain a similarity function between agents and opponent classes that guides re-classification.

The ADHOC algorithm proceeds as follows: Given an opponent that the framing agent is currently interacting with, the behaviour of both agents in the current encounter (we assume that ADHOC is called after the encounter is over) and an upper bound on the maximal number of frames, the agent matches the current sequence of opponent moves with the behavioural models of the frames (situation interpretation and matching). It then determines the most appropriate class for the adversary (assessment) using the similarity function between adversaries and classes. After an encounter, the agent may have to revise its framing decision: If the current class does not cater for the current encounter, the class has to be modified (frame adaptation), or a better class has to be retrieved (re-framing). If no adequate alternative is found or frame adaptation seems inappropriate, a new class has to be generated that matches the current encounter. In order to determine its own next action, the agent applies the counter-strategy learned for this particular opponent model (behaviour generation). Feedback obtained from the encounter is used to update the hypothesis about the agent's optimal strategy towards the current opponent class.

In "strategic" mode (the normal case), actions are selected in the following way: if an unknown peer is encountered, the agent determines the optimal class to be chosen after *each move* in the iterated game, possibly revising its choice over and over again in every step of the encounter. Else, the agent uses its experience with the peer by simply applying the counter-strategy suggested by the class this peer had previously been assigned to. This reflects the intuition that the agent puts much more effort into classification in case it interacts with a new adversary it knows very little about.

"Comprehensible" mode, on the other hand, is relevant when an agent discovers that the opponent is not pursuing any discernible strategy whatsoever, i.e. appears to be behaving randomly. This can be verified by checking whether the automaton of a class is constantly modified during many consecutive games. In this case, the ADHOC agent plays some fixed strategy for a fixed number of games, and then returns to strategic mode. So an agent takes the initiative to come up with a reasonable strategy, if his adversary's behaviour makes no sense. In other words, he tries to become "learnable" himself in the hope that an adaptive opponent will develop some strategy that can be learned in turn.

4.2 ADHOC and m^2InFFrA

Although ADHOC complies with the formal model of m^2InFFrA for the most part, some aspects of InFFrA have been realised in it at a higher level of complexity (marked with $\oplus$ below) and some in a much simpler fashion (marked with $\ominus$). These deviations from the formal model are due to the properties of the interaction scenario:

$\ominus$ $\mathcal{M}_c$ is reduced to two actions C(ooperate) and D(efect), since there are no more actions in the (I)PD game. Both of these messages are also physical actions that always yield payoffs to the players.

$\oplus$ Trajectories are modelled as deterministic finite automata (DFA) rather than simple trajectories. This way, trajectory models are much more expressive[1], and this is computationally feasible because there are only two actions. Note, however, that these DFA only define the strategy of *one* party while the other party is *free* to behave in arbitrary ways without breaking a frame.

$\ominus$ Condition sets in frames are only used to discriminate between "strategic" and "comprehensible" mode, i.e. any frame can only be activated in one of these modes. Otherwise, there are no restrictions as to when an opponent class/frame might be assigned to an opponent.

$\ominus$ Substitutions only refer to agent names (since messages C and D cannot be parametrised), and all substitutions of a frame/opponent class are identical. Consequently, the similarity measure σ can be re-defined to directly compare an opponent to an entire opponent class.

$\oplus$ Private attributes are more elaborate than in standard m^2InFFrA. Apart from a fixed number of encounter samples that agents store with each frame, they also maintain a membership function that assigns each agent to a class. Moreover, all agents' similarity with all classes is constantly tracked. Utility experience is stored in a Q-table, which is also used to guide action in strategic mode.

$\oplus$ ADHOC agents generate frames (opponent classes) from scratch, and the architecture not only defines how frames are modified with experience, but also when new frames should be created, merged or deleted.

$\oplus$ In comprehensible mode, the agent plays the fixed strategy represented by the DFA of the frame activated. In strategic mode, however, the agent is free to optimise its behaviour, and selects actions according to the exploration/exploitation factors of the Q-table that belongs to the class the opponent has been assigned to.

Placing ADHOC in the m^2InFFrA context in this way allows for a more precise identification of the social abstraction and transient social optimality properties of ADHOC.

---

[1] Note that, since encounters have a fixed length, the DFA-frame could be replaced by a number of frames with sequence trajectories that are semantically linked with each other to express that they pertain to the same strategy.

Social Abstraction. This is achieved by viewing frames (opponent classes) as possible social behaviours that do not depend on the particular agent who employs them. Experimental results prove that this is not only a reasonable strategy in the light of bounded rationality that allows agents to maintain a bounded number of opponent models although they are faced with huge numbers of opponents. Much more than this, coercing different opponents into the same class even leads to an *accelerated* learning process. As shown in figure 3, ADHOC agents converge much more quickly to high payoffs than agents who maintain one model per opponent.

This is yet another advantage of social abstraction: by categorising interaction situations appropriately, an agent can learn optimal strategies for his own behaviour much easier, because more "data-per-model" is available (in ADHOC, this means that the Q-tables are updated much more often, and thus converge to optimal strategies more quickly). This plot also shows, however, that it is not possible to combine all the be-

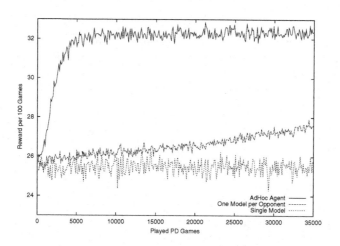

Fig. 3. Comparison of cumulative rewards between an ADHOC agent, an agent that maintains one model for each opponent and an agent that has only a single model for all opponents.

haviours into just one opponent model, as long as more than one strategy is around. Figure 4 provides further evidence for the facts that ADHOC learns exactly as many classes as are present in the long term. Here, ADHOC agents are shown to converge to four opponent classes in a setting where opponent agents use any one of four fixed strategies (ALL C, ALL D, TIT FOR TAT or TIT FOR TWO TATS). In terms of scalability, this is a very important result, because it means that ADHOC agents are capable of evolving a suitable set of opponent classes regardless of the size of the agent population, as long as the number of strategies employed by adversaries is limited (and in most applications, this will be reasonable to assume). A particular challenge in developing the heuristic in a way that guarantees this convergence is, of course, to ensure that sim-

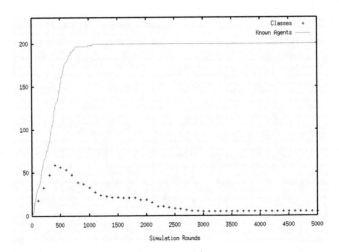

Fig. 4. Number of agent classes an ADHOC agent creates over time in contrast to the total number of known (fixed-strategy) opponents (which is increased by 40 in rounds 150, 300 and 450). As can be seen, the number of identified classes converges to the actual (four) strategies.

ilar classes are merged in the long run, so that unnecessary "temporary" classes can be erased (these are generated when encountering new agents or when the DFA-learning algorithm makes a wrong guess).

Transient Social Optimality. This aspect of micro-scalability appears in ADHOC in a twofold way. Firstly, it is embodied in the strategy of "blindly" selecting a frame that an agent has been assigned to, if that agent is encountered again (which is followed until that opponent deviates from his previous strategy). Assuming that the ADHOC agent has been using this frame for a while, he will learn to play an optimal strategy against it, and his own behaviour towards this class of opponents will be stable. Thus, implicitly, he can "inform" his opponents about the strategy he will settle on if they keep behaving the same way, so that he becomes more predictable for these agents in turn. If an unknown agent is encountered, this strategy (e.g. picking an arbitrary frame) would be too risky, so transient optimality cannot be applied in this case, and the agent must select the best-matching class in each round to make an optimal move.

In terms of m^2InFFrA, this means that the criterion of whether to activate the frame with the highest expected utility is "in each move" if the opponent is unknown and "only at the beginning of the encounter" if the agent is acquainted with the current adversary.

But there is a second, much more important aspect of transient optimality in AD-HOC, and this is the process of switching between strategic and comprehensible modes. This process has been elaborated after initial experiments with ADHOC agents playing agents each other (rather than playing against simple agents with fixed strategies as above), where agents appeared to behave randomly throughout. This was due to the fact that, if they want to learn optimal strategies, this will involve some form of exploration. Unfortunately, whenever agents perform exploratory actions their behaviour can no more be represented as a DFA, and can therefore not be classified by their opponents.

To alleviate this problem, agents were made to switch to a fixed strategy for a while, whenever they cannot understand what their opponent is doing. As the results in figure 5 show, this was sufficient to achieve effective patterns of interaction in the "ADHOC vs. ADHOC" case. So, by abandoning optimality as a foremost goal in certain situations,

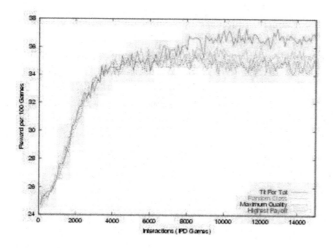

Fig. 5. Comparison of agent performance in "ADHOC vs. ADHOC" simulations and different selection methods for the strategy chosen if the opponent exhibits random behaviour. TIT FOR TAT can be shown to perform slightly better when chosen as an interim fixed strategy, while other heuristics were based on generating random DFA, choosing the DFA from the opponent class with maximum payoff, or that with highest "quality" (a heuristic function).

an ADHOC agent becomes comprehensible, his opponents settle on a counter-strategy, and so does the first agent after he switches back to strategic mode.

Returning to the m^{2}InFFrA model, we can see that frame activation does not depend on (payoff) optimality *at all* in this case. Instead, some heuristic is used to determine the activated frame, and this frame remains activated without making a new framing decision for a while. A final interesting property of these simulations is that, although TIT FOR TAT outperformed other strategies as a choice for the comprehensible strategy (which is not surprising because TIT FOR TAT is very powerful against a variety of counter-strategies), the result of achieving fruitful coordination does not depend on the interim fixed strategy choice. This suggests that being comprehensible at all is much more important for framing agents than the short-term payoffs ensured by following an effective comprehensible strategy.

5 Conclusions

This paper introduced "micro-scalability" as a new concept for social reasoning architectures based on the principles of *social abstraction* and *transient social optimality*. Micro-scalability constitutes the central contribution of MAS architectures derived from interactionist social theories to the scalability aspect of the Socionics endeavour. Starting from the social reasoning architecture InFFrA that is inspired by Goffmanian concepts, we provided an informal description of these notions. Then, they were made precise by introducing a formal model of InFFrA, and set into the context of simulation experiments obtained in the development of the opponent classification heuristic AdHoc.

Eventually, we hope that learning algorithms that are currently being developed using the m^2InFFrA model will prove scalable in more realistic applications, and we are currently working toward this goal. Other interesting implications are the evolution of stable empirical agent communication semantics using frame-learning, and a deeper investigation into the macro-effects of using micro-scalable social reasoning architectures.

References

1. Fischer, F., Rovatsos, M.: An Empirical Semantics Approach to Reasoning About Communication. Engineering Applications of Artificial Intelligence **18** (to appear, 2005)
2. Fischer, F., Rovatsos, M., Weiß, G.: Acquiring and Adapting Probabilistic Models of Agent Conversations. In: Proceedings of the Fourth International Joint Conference on Agents and Multiagent Systems (AAMAS-05), Utrecht, The Netherlands (to appear, 2005)
3. Rovatsos, M.: Computational Interaction Frames. PhD thesis, Department of Informatics, Technical University of Munich (2004)
4. Malsch, T.: Naming the Unnamable: Socionics or the Sociological Turn of/to Distributed Artificial Intelligence. Autonomous Agents and Multi-Agent Systems **4** (2001) 155–186
5. Gasser, L.: Social conceptions of knowledge and action: DAI foundations and open systems semantics. Artificial Intelligence **47** (1991) 107–138
6. Hewitt, C.: Open information sytems semantics for distributed artificial intelligence. Artificial Intelligence **47** (1991) 79–106
7. Paetow, K., Schmitt, M., Malsch, T.: (Scalability, Scaling Processes, and the Management of Complexity. a system theoretical approach) In this volume.
8. Luhmann, N.: Social Systems. Stanford University Press, Palo Alto, CA (1995)
9. Blumer, H.: Society as Symbolic Interaction. In Rose, A.M., ed.: Human Behavior and Social Process. Routledge and Kegan Paul, London (1962)
10. Goffman, E.: Frame Analysis: An Essay on the Organisation of Experience. Harper and Row, New York, NY (1974) Reprinted 1990 by Northeastern University Press.
11. Mead, G.H.: Mind, Self, and Society. University of Chicago Press, Chicago, IL (1934)
12. Nickles, M., Weiss, G.: (Multiagent Systems without Agents – Mirror-Holons for the Compilcation and Enactment of Communication Structures) In this volume.
13. Paetow, K., Rovatsos, M.: Grundlagen einer interaktionistischen Sozionik ("Foundations of Interactionist Socionics"). Research Report RR-8, Department of Technology Assessment, Technical University of Hamburg, Hamburg (2003)
14. Rovatsos, M.: Interaction frames for artificial agents. Technical Report Research Report FKI-244-01, Department of Informatics, Technical University of Munich (2001)

15. Rovatsos, M., Weiß, G., Wolf, M.: Multiagent Learning for Open Systems: A Study in Opponent Classification. In Alonso, E., Kazakov, D., Kudenko, D., eds.: Adaptive Agents and Multi-Agent Systems. Volume 2636 of Lecture Notes in Artificial Intelligence. Springer-Verlag, Berlin (2003)

16. Rao, A.S., Georgeff, M.P.: BDI agents: From theory to practice. In: Proceedings of the First International Conference on Multi-Agent Systems (ICMAS-95). (1995) 312–319

17. Rovatsos, M., Nickles, M., Weiß, G.: Interaction is Meaning: A New Model for Communication in Open Systems. In Rosenschein, J.S., Sandholm, T., Wooldridge, M., Yokoo, M., eds.: Proceedings of the Second International Joint Conference on Autonomous Agents and Multiagent Systems (AAMAS-03), Melbourne, Australia (2003)

18. Fischer, F.: Frame-Based Learning and Generalisation for Multiagent Communication. Diploma Thesis, Department of Informatics, Technical University of Munich, Munich, Germany (2003)

19. Nickles, M., Rovatsos, M.: (Communication Systems: A Unified Model of Socially Intelligent Systems) In this volume.

20. Kolodner, J.L.: Case-Based Reasoning. Morgan Kaufmann, San Francisco (1993)

21. Puterman, M.L.: Markov Decision Problems. John Wiley & Sons, New York, NY (1994)

22. Sutton, R., Barto, A.: Reinforcement Learning. An Introduction. The MIT Press/A Bradford Book, Cambridge, MA (1998)

23. Barto, A., Mahadevan, S.: Recent Advances in Hierarchical Reinforcement Learning. Discrete Event Systems **13** (2003) 41–77

24. Sutton, R.S., Precup, D., Singh, S.: Between MDPs and semi-MDPs: A Framework for Temporal Abstraction in Reinforcement Learning. Artificial Intelligence **112** (1999) 181–211

25. Watkins, C., Dayan, P.: Q-learning. Machine Learning **8** (1992) 279–292

26. Luce, R.D., Raiffa, H.: Games and Decisions. John Wiley & Sons, New York, NY (1957)

27. Carmel, D., Markovitch, S.: Learning and using opponent models in adversary search. Technical Report 9609, Technion (1996)

Trust and the Economy of Symbolic Goods: A Contribution to the Scalability of Open Multi-agent Systems

Bettina Fley and Michael Florian

Hamburg University of Technology
Department of Technology Assessment
Schwarzenbergstrasse 95, 21071 Hamburg, Germany
{bettina.fley, florian}@tu-harburg.de
http://www.tu-harburg.de/tbg/

Abstract. Today, the importance of trust to issues of social coordination seems to be largely accepted in Distributed AI and sociology. This paper suggests a sociological multi-level concept of trust to provide suitable solutions to problems of large-scale open multi-agent systems (MAS). For this purpose, we firstly analyze DAI concepts dealing with the notion of trust and examine effects of trust on the scalability of MAS. We argue that trust itself must be modeled as a social mechanism that allows the scaling up of agent coordination in open MAS. Secondly, we summarize sociological conceptions of trust and outline problems concerning the build-up and diffusion of trust from a sociological perspective. Finally, we introduce a multi-level approach to trust by referring to sociologist Pierre Bourdieu's concept of the economy of symbolic goods including basic social mechanisms in order to cope with the coordination of large numbers of heterogeneous agents.

1 Introduction

Almost 20 years ago, Hewitt [1] already considered the challenge of scalability in open information systems. His notion of "large-scale open information system" refers to both, *size* in the sense of projects that "cover a large geography over a long period of time with many mutual dependencies with overlapping subprojects" ([2, p. 80]) and *openness*, i.e., unanticipated outcomes as well as possible input of new information at any time (cf. [2]). Hewitt provides a preliminary view of scalability that refers not only to changes of numerical size, to distribution across space and time, or to aspects of resource economy, but also to the problem of social order when he both pursues the question of "global coherence" and defines scalability explicitly as "activities to increase the scale of commitments"([2, p. 100]). A basic definition of scalability in distributed systems has then been provided by Neuman [3] who recommends that a system is said to be *scalable*, "if it can handle the addition of users and resources without suffering a noticeable loss of performance or increase in administrative complexity." Even though Neuman does not explicitly refer to distributed artificial intelligence (DAI) and multi-agent systems (MAS), his suggestion to connect scalability with effects on performance and his distinction between different dimensions of scale seems to be helpful for MAS-design (cf., e.g., [4]).

K. Fischer, M. Florian, and T. Malsch (Eds.): Socionics, LNAI 3413, pp. 176–198, 2005.

The importance of self-organization to improve the scalability of MAS has been stressed by Turner and Jennings [5]. When they refer to scalable MAS, they also take particular requirements of open systems into account. The application of MAS in open systems like the Internet does not only entail a large number of agents, but also confronts designers with dynamic changes of the agent population during run-time. Hence, the notion of scalability focuses on the "relationship between the collective computational resource needs of the agents and the population size" ([5]). Since MAS should be "self-building (able to determine the most appropriate organizational structure for the system by themselves at run-time) and adaptive (able to change this structure as their environment changes)" ([5, p. 246]), Turner and Jennings "believe that an MAS that can both operate with different population sizes and deal with dynamic changes to population during operation, is more scalable" ([5, p. 247]). Accordingly, they do not only refer to aspects of resource economy (i.e., when an MAS deals successfully with larger population sizes despite predefined limits to the availability of computational resources), but also consider aspects of MAS self-organization based on the distinction between "agent interactions" and "organizational forms" to improve the scalability of MAS.

The problem of scalability of MAS largely refers to undesirable *effects on performance* (or output) when a certain parameter of an MAS, which should be measured numerical (e.g., number of agents, heterogeneity of agents, size of the task load, heterogeneity of tasks), is altered along a scale. The unwanted effects of scaling can firstly be a decrease of outcome or a loss of performance at global level, whereas different performance measures exist (e.g., the rate of successful accomplished tasks in task-assignment MAS). Secondly, aspects of resource economy are discussed (i.e., the input of resources required). Moreover, some authors not only address quantitative effects, but stress *qualitative* aspects of scaling system parameters (e.g., administrative complexity [3], agent complexity, or institutionalized behavior patterns and regularities on different levels of sociality, cf. Schillo and Spresny in this volume). Durfee [6] has recently discussed several DAI concepts with regard to scaling up agent coordination strategies. The DAI problem is that agent coordination strategies which scale well to the numerical change of agent population size, "tend to deal poorly with other confounding dimensions" ([6, p. 42]). Agent coordination strategies must consider characteristics of the agent population (e.g., the complexity or heterogeneity) as well as the task environment and solution properties (in terms of quality, robustness, and overhead limitations). Although Durfee has revealed some scalability dilemmas of coordination concepts, he has not considered the restrictions of dealing with social coordination from a micro-social point of view. We expect, however, that including meso- and macro-social perspectives on coordination, and hence trust, would provide a promising way to face the challenge of scalability.

In summary, an MAS is considered to be scalable, if the scaling of certain parameters does not lead to an unwanted rise of input and to an undesirable decrease of output or performance. Interestingly, several approaches connect the problem of scalability to problems of open systems (cf. [1,2,3,7,5,4,8]. Large-scale open agent systems, however, do currently not exist. Often, in agent-based simulation systems, "the agents involved are kept small and/or simple (to facilitate simulation)" ([4]). Openness is defined by Davidsson (in [9]) with regard to the possibilities of agents to join artificial societies. Accordingly, there are no restrictions to gain access to *open* agent societies, while in *semi-open* systems "any agent can join the society given that it follows some well-specified restrictions (or, at least, promises to do so)". Unfortunately, making and keeping a promise are two different things. If the Internet will sometime be populated by a vast number of information agents, which are potentially able to communicate and interact with each other, it would be unrealistic to assume that these agents will be benevolent and willing to cooperate in an altruistic fashion (cf. [10]). Especially in electronic commerce and business applications, where autonomous and self-interested agents as well as open (or semi-open) MAS are desired, it will be difficult (if not impossible) to "engineer agent societies in a top-down manner" [10] in order to provide some kind of central control, and to gain comprehensive control of agents' behaviors.

Hence, the use of open MAS in dynamic environments like the Internet does not only implicate large numbers of agents, but also faces designers with the problem of dynamically changing population size during operation (cf. [5]). In addition, openness will confront designers and users with a varying number of *malicious* agents that may not only be self-interested, competitive and reject collaboration, but may even pursue their goals opportunistically by means of deception, and fraud. Since interaction between agents is considered to be an approach to realize a global outcome efficiently (what implies that agents need to take into account the actions of other agents somehow so that a desirable global outcome can be realized), open MAS easily lead to problems of efficient agent coordination. In open systems, autonomous agents may provide other agents (and human users as well) with incomplete, deceitful, or false information. If agents are able to deceive, i.e., intentionally pretend to carry out actions they will not complete in the end, other agents become misled or undertake inefficient actions due to false assumptions about their interaction partners. Consequently, the performance of the MAS will decrease and the desired global outcome will not be realized. Under these conditions, open (and semi-open) MAS must be able to cope with large and changing numbers of malicious agents to tackle the problem of scalability. The crucial question is, whether MAS can handle the growing complexity of both, assessing agents and social interactions (in terms of uncertainty, deception and fraud) and managing appropriate reactions to agent's deviations. Hence, deception and fraud require further mechanisms to ensure efficient coordination and cooperation. In open environments, where agents can break contracts, computational models of *trust* are required to determine the reliability of interaction partners, to support the communication process by assessing the seriousness of commitments, and to reduce the set of issues so that they do not need to be fixed in contracts meticulously (cf. [11]).

In recent years, trust has attracted much attention in DAI to adapt MAS to the demands of open systems (cf. [12,13,14,15]). The DAI-literature mainly relates the term trust firstly to the existence of malicious behavior of both human users and artificial agents acting autonomously on behalf of humans, and secondly, to resulting problems when MAS are deployed in large-scaled open computer networks like the Internet (e.g., electronic commerce). Trust has turned out to be an essential property to increase the robustness of open MAS by detecting deceitful agents and excluding malicious agents from interaction (cf. [16,17]). Nevertheless, little attention has been paid to the likeliness that different models of trust may have various effects on the scalability of multi-agent systems. A major problem is that the mainstream of MAS work deals with systems "in which agents are peers of each other" [5], i.e., systems where agent interactions are pure social micro-phenomena from a sociological point of view. It seems unlikely that artificial social systems that are designed for peer-to-peer relations and which show structures (e.g., acquaintance topologies) that do not exceed a social micro-level are appropriate for large-scaled MAS with a dynamically changing population composed of hundreds or even thousands of agents (cf. [5]). In DAI, some metaphors from human societies have already been used to support MAS design with structures on higher levels of social aggregation (e.g., organizations). Nevertheless, trust has not been discovered as such a meso- or macro-phenomenon by DAI (with the exception of [18] who consider "trust contagion" a macro-level phenomenon). We assume that sociology itself is the reason for this, since some sociological theorists (e.g., [19]) support an understanding of trust as mere interpersonal expectations, although they state that trust is essential for the build-up of social order. However, other theories suggest that trust is not only based on personal relations, but as well on phenomena on the meso and macro-level of sociality (cf., e.g., [20,21,22]). In the following, we argue that the social diffusion and generalization of trust on different levels of sociality is relevant to the scalability of MAS. Moreover, we argue that models of trust in DAI need to improve the "scaling up" of the trust mechanism itself (i.e., the build-up of trust on higher levels of sociality to improve social coordination).

In sociology, trust is considered to be an important factor for the emergence of the macro phenomenon of social order since trust reduces social complexity and uncertainty (cf. [19,20,23]). As we both are sociologists, no technical solutions should be expected from our paper. Although DAI has borrowed ideas from social theory repeatedly, this exploratory paper is motivated by the conviction that only an approach with deep insights into sociological theories is useful to overcome problems of agent societies. We hope to contribute to the transformation of sociological concepts into models of artificial social systems that are suitable for technological requirements of DAI by giving these insights with regard to trust.

In the remainder of the paper we will explore both opportunities and limitations of a multi-level approach to trust as an important mechanism of social coordination. Especially in open MAS, quantitative scaling as well as an increase of the heterogeneity and complexity affect social coordination by trust. Interpersonal trust will hardly be practicable when the population size is growing and the properties of other agents are unknown or uncertain. In the following sections we will discuss, whether trust is suitable for social coordination at multiple levels of sociality and how far the trust mechanism is able to support scalability in open MAS. For this purpose we firstly analyze DAI concepts dealing with the notion of trust and examine effects of trust on issues of scalability in MAS (Section 2). Secondly, we summarize sociological conceptions of trust and outline problems concerning the increase and expansion of trust from a sociological perspective (Section 3). Finally, we introduce a multi-level approach to trust by referring to sociologist Pierre Bourdieu's concept of the economy of symbolic goods including basic social mechanisms (gift-exchange, social delegation, social and symbolic capital) to cope with large numbers of heterogeneous agents which may possibly turn out to be malicious (Section 4).

2   Conceptions of Trust in Distributed AI

Marsh [24] was one of the first DAI-researchers who adopted the idea from sociological theory to conceive trust as a coordination mechanism that allows agents to deal with uncertainty about other agent's behavior in a somehow controlled way. His conception of trust can be considered as an alternative to control mechanisms (i.e., security devices or sanctions against deviant behavior), which are intended as solutions to problems of malicious behavior open MAS are confronted with. In essence, he regards trust as a particular probability an agent ascribes another agent that the latter will behave cooperatively in a certain situation. Trust allows agents to decide whether to interact with other agents and with whom. Even though there is no ultimate certainty, if the other agent will behave maliciously in the end, interacting only with agents which are perceived as trustworthy in certain situations reduces the risk of carrying out an action that does not pay (either from the perspective of a self-interested agent or from the view of the entire system). *Trust is not meant to eliminate uncertainty about maliciousness completely (like security devices), but allows to deal with uncertainty in a reflected way.*

At first glance, this makes trust an attractive coordination mechanism in terms of scalability for two reasons: firstly, the output of an MAS does not need to drop unavoidably when the agent population or heterogeneity of agents in an open system augments, because interaction between agents still takes place despite of the uncertainty about the outcome. Note that deception and fraud not only diminish a systems' output, if they occur in a system *de facto*. Agents interact with other agents either implicitly or explicitly on the basis of the benefit an interaction produces regarding their individual or joint goals. If agents cannot reason about the utility of an intended action, because of uncertainty about the risk whether an agent cheats, they may dispense with interaction. *Interaction with malicious agents produces no benefit, but no interaction produces no benefit as well.* There exists a trade-off between too many interactions (i.e., too much damage from malicious behavior) and too few interactions (i.e., less benefit than possible). Secondly, the resource consumption is not likely to be as costly as for security tools that aim at the utmost prevention of harm. The input of resources does not need to rise as much when certain parameters scale (e.g., agent population). *However, we hypothesize that it depends on the modeling of the sources of trust or rather on the mechanisms of trust building, whether trust really improves the scalability of MAS.*

Much research on mechanisms of trust building and adaptation has been undertaken since the foundational work on trust in DAI by [24]. A large number of conceptions in DAI refers to the utilitarian paradigm in social sciences (cf. [25,26,27,24,17,28]). Here, trust is associated with interactions, where material and immaterial goods (e.g., affection) that have a certain utility, are exchanged between transaction partners that rationally maximize their value by calculating costs and benefits of the interaction. Trust is considered a subjective probability whether a transaction partner (trustee) will cooperate or not. Marsh [24] concentrated on a precise formalization of different components of which the subjective probability (trust value) about the trustworthiness of another agent is composed and on definitions of a cooperation threshold when to place trust. DAI-researchers following Marsh rather focused on sources and dynamics of trust. Similar to utilitarian trust conceptions, they consider experience [27] and/or reputation ([25,17,29,28]) as primary sources of trust and the adaptation of trust to changing conditions.

With respect to the scalability of open MAS, trust building by mere *experience* is quite problematic concerning the initiation of trust building and the adaptation of trust. Firstly, at the beginning of exchange relations with agents that newly entered a system, 'blind' trust (i.e., mere confidence without reason) has to be placed. Otherwise, exchange does not take place and no experience could be made. For this reason, a basic trust value is used for unknown agents in Marsh's concept [24]. In Birk's conception, agents are labeled with different colors. When an agent is initialized, it has certain interaction preferences regarding the color of the labels of other agents. However, these labels are no indicators of benevolence. Once trust is built, the labels are redundant [26]. Secondly, in order to adapt a certain (basic) trust value on the basis of experience, it is necessary to interact with other agents before their real trustworthiness can be estimated. Hence, in a system where the agent population may change due to entries and exits at a large number, a lot of risky interactions have to be carried out without any safeguards against harm from malicious behavior to find out about the trustworthiness of potential transaction partners. Moreover, risky transactions have to be made continuously since trusted agents may leave the system and experiences already made may become useless and new transaction partners need to be found. *Great losses might be the consequence from the viewpoint of the agents and with respect to the outcome of the entire system* (because, e.g., tasks are not completed).

Some authors attempt to solve the problem of too many harmful interactions by using *reputation* as a mechanism to spread trust values within an agent population in order to build trust more quickly than by mere experience. While Abdul-Rahman and Hailes [25] concentrate on the development of a recommendation protocol without specifying the sources of trust of the recommending agents, other work combines the mechanisms of reputation and experience ([30,17,29,28]). Moreover, the latter concepts do not only use reputation as a solution to gain trust in other agents more quickly and with less potential loss. They also optimize the process of spreading information with respect to input (communication costs) and output (correctness of information) by building networks between trusting agents. Thereby two problems have to be solved. Firstly, the decentralized spreading of information requires a great amount of communication in case that any agent exchanges information with anybody else in order to acquire the maximum data available. Secondly, the estimations of trust values of other agents and the recommendations by other agents are only helpful information, if the recommenders are trustworthy themselves, i.e., do not spread false information. The work of Schillo et al. [17] mainly deals with the second problem whether a third party is trustworthy concerning the trustworthiness of other agents. Two types of trust are distinguished: trust in the honesty of a witness and trust in the cooperativeness concerning other interactions. The first type (trust in the honesty of a witness) allows the emergence of a peer-to-peer (P2P) network among witnesses in which reliable information about the experience with other agents is spread. Venkatraman, Yu, and Singh use the idea of small-world networks to optimize communication effort [29]. In their model agents can build P2P-sub communities consisting of a small fraction of the entire agent population. All member agents of a sub community are allowed to exchange information with each other member whereas only one pivotal agent exchanges information with other communities (i.e., their pivotal agent). Metzger et al. [30], who applied the idea of small-world networks to the problem of efficient spam-filtering, showed that the building of sub communities or organizations by using holonic architectures indeed reduces input (communication), while the distribution of information (outcome) is effected quickly and efficiently with respect to the detection of spam-mail. This work concentrates on the process of both trust building and the self-organized building of organizations. Organizations, to which agents commit themselves for longer-termed periods, are built during run-time, if a certain trust value between agents exceeds a threshold.

From a sociological perspective, these approaches are quite relevant to scalability, because network building represents a shift from micro- to meso-level and reputation contributes to the generalization and abstraction of trust from interpersonal relations. Nevertheless, these approaches do not solve the following problems completely that relate to the question of how to "upscale" trust: how can agents built enough reliable trust in other agents when the agent population, the heterogeneity of agents, and their motives of action, etc. scales without an excessive increase of resource consumption or unproportionate losses of performance?

Initial trust values. Models which use reputation ([17,29,28]) do not resolve the problem that no realistic trust values are available for new agents and 'blind' trust has to be placed initially.[1] Some agents have to start to interact with new agents to acquire experience that afterwards can be spread as reputation in the system. If the number of unknown agents rises due to the openness of a system, too little qualified information may be available, so that the system's performance in terms of outcome (e.g., exchange, successful completed tasks) may decrease. Although trust can be considered as a mechanism that may improve the scalability of open MAS, a major problem is to build reliable trust values when a number of new agents enter a system. Thus, one problem to be solved is the "up-scaling" of trust itself (i.e., the diffusion and generalization of trust on different levels of sociality). *With reference to sociological theory, we assume that the problem of generalizing trust can be solved, if incoming unknown agents have a mechanism that allows them to signal their trustworthiness.* This signal would be of no value with respect to outcome, if agents could use it in order to pretend cooperativeness, but afterwards exploit the cooperativeness of the trustor. Rather these signals have to create a certain commitment to behave accordingly, they need to effect rules of reciprocity. With rules of reciprocity we mean the mutual obligation between agents to compensate for the willingness to exchange some kind of good.[2]

---

[1] An exception is the work of Metzger et al. [30] where information about spam is exchanged to prove trustworthiness of other agents repeatedly before using information of those agents to filter spam. However, it still has to be proved whether this concept can be applied to other application scenarios (e.g., electronic commerce).

[2] Within DAI-research on trust, some authors refer to the utilitarian notion of reciprocity, or more precisely, game theory (cf. e.g., [31,17]). Within this model of social interaction, the signaling of willingness to cooperate does not create any commitment to act accordingly. Signaling of the

Apart from the problem of how to receive initial trust values, concepts that use reputation are confronted with problems concerning the complexity of motives of action.

Generalization of trustworthiness. In open systems agents may act on behalf of human users whose intentions and interests are more diverse than those of agents in experiments. The work of Schillo et al. [17] in particular emphasizes that a trust model that uses recommendations of third parties needs to cope with the problem of the trustworthiness of third parties themselves. However, the trustworthiness and honesty of an agent (A1) who recommends another agent (A2) does not guarantee that the experience made with the recommended agent (A2) will be transferable to transactions between other agents (An) and the recommended agent (A2) as suggested by [17]. The malevolence or benevolence of an agent may vary with each transaction partner. *From a sociological perspective, reputation is only an advantageous mechanism with respect to scalability, if criteria exist under which conditions experiences made with agents or situations can be generalized for other transactions with other agents.*

Continuity of a trusting relationship. Another problem is that it can not be assumed that a trustee will behave in any situation trustworthy once a reciprocal relation towards a trustor has been built. Interests and goals may change. Moreover, trustworthiness may differ with the trust or distrust showed by a trustor. Probably, experience, reputation, and even symbols of trustworthiness that have been signaled at the beginning may not be sufficient to sort out malicious behavior, because agents may decide to behave opportunistically just after a while. The work of Castelfranchi and Falcone concentrates on the self-enforcing dynamics of trust (cf. [18]) and the complexity of human goals and beliefs [33]. They suggest that trust in DAI should not be reduced to a simple subjective probability derived from experience or reputation. Instead, a trustor needs to have a theory of the mind of the trusted agent to place trust appropriately. With respect to scalability, their conception may be inefficient regarding the system resources required because they propose that a trustor should not only estimate one parameter (the trust value of a trustee), but seven mental attitudes. However, they do not specify how a trustor can find out about these attitudes. We hypothesize that mechanisms which enable estimations about these great numbers of mental attitudes are very costly with respect to resources. Costs may augment unproportionally when the agent population increases. *Therefore, we propose to look for a mechanism that enables a reliable and continuing signaling of trustworthiness in order to indicate the state of a relationship between a trusting and a trusted party.*

Sources of trust on higher levels of social aggregation. Another concept of Castelfranchi and Falcone proposes to combine trust and control mechanisms in task-assignment domains and in case of a turbulent environment where the outcome of a transaction may not be beneficial due to various reasons [21]. They suggest that control may not only create distrust, but can support trust building. Therefore, they propose to imple-

---

intended action in this scenario only may be used as a starting point or indication to decide with whom to play the first game (like, e.g., in [17]). Sen [32] criticizes that the iterated prisoner's dilemma and game theory are unrealistic because of the likeliness of asymmetrical costs and benefits for all involved parties and the unlikeliness to play games in the same constellation continually. We argue that these asymmetries of costs, benefits, and situations are crucial so that only certain signals may produce reciprocity (see section 4).

ment certain possibilities of surveillance (in the course from the delegation of a task until its completion) to correct a decision about the delegation of a task to a particular agent. However, we agree with Luhmann ([20,34]) that the existence of norms and sanctions may be a source of trust. Nevertheless, the threat of sanctions (e.g., the withdrawal of a delegated task from a particular agent) has to be latent in order not to create distrust, i.e., sanction mechanisms already need to exist before a transaction takes place and independently from the single interaction. *We suggest that such sources of trust that exist independently from an actual interaction between agents and their intentions (i.e., meso- or macro-level sources of trust) may support the generalization and continuity of trust relationships.* However, since establishing centralized control opposes the decentralized approach of MAS to AI [35] and is hardly feasible in open systems, the question is how trust and sources of trust on levels of social aggregation that exceed mere interaction can emerge in a system.

In summary, much research on mechanisms of trust building and adaptation has been done in DAI. Nevertheless, to meet the requirements of large-scale open systems mechanisms for building and adapting trust are still confronted with problems. They range from initial trust values to criteria for the extrapolation of past experiences to the future (e.g., reciprocal relations) and for the generalization of experiences and trust values. We argue that social mechanisms for the diffusion and generalization of trust must be taken into consideration in order to provide solutions to the scalability problem of MAS. In the following section, we argue that sociological theory provides further aspects of the trust phenomenon that can help overcoming these challenges.

3   A Sociological Multi-level Approach to Trust

From a sociological perspective, the *"up-scaling" of trust* (i.e., a sufficient build-up of trust as a basis of social practice independently from population size) requires conceiving trust as a phenomenon that is not restricted to interpersonal relations but also has its foundations on the meso- and macro-level of sociality. Taking into account the discussion of DAI-concepts in Section 2, a sociological conception of trust to improve the scalability of MAS needs to satisfy the following conditions: on the interpersonal level, such a concept must firstly explain the deduction of trustworthiness from signals when new agents enter a system and, secondly, explicate indications of trustworthiness in on-going exchange relations. These signals themselves have to be reliable, i.e., they must not be usable in an opportunistic way, but create obligations and commitments without replacing trust by control. Moreover, the distribution and generalization of trust itself requires the identification of conditions whether interpersonal trust is transferable to other social relations. We hypothesize that a generalization of trust necessitates the possibility to place trust in individuals as well as in aggregations of agents on the meso-level of sociality (networks, groups, organizations). Additionally, this permits the exploitation of the potential of holonic architectures for scalability issues (cf. [Schillo/Spresny and Hillebrandt in this volume]) regarding the efficiency of reputation mechanisms. Last not least, we hypothesize that the potential of trust for the scalability of MAS depends on whether trust towards individuals, networks, groups, and organizations becomes generalized on the macro-level of an artificial society. We suggest that this can be achieved by means of institutionalization of accepted or accredited signals of trustworthiness.[3] With the following discussion of sociological concepts of trust, we aim at expounding their advantages and insufficiencies concerning the mentioned requirements that a sociological concept of trust needs to meet to be instructive for DAI. However, space restrictions do not allow a comprehensive review of the sociological literature.

3.1 From Subjective Probability to Social Relation

In the recent two decades, trust has developed a topic of mainstream sociology. Comparable to other central sociological categories like power or authority, a broad range of trust conceptions has been developed to date. The only common denominator of the various sociological contributions is that trust is considered to be a certain expectation of an agent about (social) events in the future. This expectation is decisive for the agent's present actions and behavior since these events have either negative or positive consequences for it. The differences between the various trust conceptions in sociology relate to questions regarding (1) the degree of awareness about that expectation respectively the rationality of decisions based on this expectation, (2) the sources of this expectation (information, experience, norms and possibilities of sanctioning, shared background assumptions, group affiliation, signals, etc.) or rather the mechanisms to dynamically build trust, (3) the interdependencies with other social phenomena (power, control), (4) the objects of trust (individuals, corporative agents, institutions, or systems), and (5) the effects or functions of trust. Along these aspects three major approaches of trust can be distinguished: an ultiliarian, a normativistic, and a social-relationalistic view.

The *utilitarian perspective* on trust (cf. [19,37]) that is based on the assumption that social interaction generally is a form of exchange of goods that have certain utilities between agents which rationally maximize their value by calculating costs and benefits. This point of view had a lasting influence on DAI since Marsh's [24] adoption. However, the disadvantages of this perspective with respect to a multi-level approach of trust are similar to the weaknesses of those DAI models that have been derived from this conception (Section 3). Since a trusting expectation within this approach is considered a *calculable, subjectively estimated probability* of an agent whether a trustee in an interaction will cooperate, the dynamics of trust in social relations are rather neglected. Hence, trust is considered to be a mechanism that has only effects on the degree to which an agent exposes itself to the risk of opportunism, but not on the prevention of opportunism itself. Explanations of how subjective probability is obtained are rather underdeveloped. Only information about a potential trustee and interpersonal reputation are taken into consideration as sources of trust, but no meso- or macro-phenomena of sociality, so that trust remains a mere interpersonal mechanism, even though Coleman extends interpersonal trust from dyads to systems of trust (cf. [19]).

Within the *normativistic paradigm* a unified and elaborated trust conception does not exist. However, trust is not completely neglected within this complementary ap-

---

[3] Bachmann [36] argues that macro-sociological conceptions of trust based on institutional arrangements can not adequately be modeled with simple reference to micro-sociological concepts. However, [36] does not provide an appropriate model to link interpersonal relations of trust and institution-based trust and neglects alternative options of trust beyond the misleading dichotomy between rational calculation and normative obligation.

proach to the utilitarian perspective (cf. [38,39]). Normativists hypothesize that the actions of agents become reciprocally predictable because of shared valid and obligatory norms. Trust is needed regarding the reliability and validness of norms so that agents can orientate their actions towards others [39]. However, trust, i.e., the expectations about norm conform behavior of others, is not considered to be a calculable probability, but a feeling that becomes stronger with the density of interaction [38]. Münch emphasizes that the validity of norms is bound to societal groups, because firstly norms may differ between societies or social groups. Norms have to be known to serve as trusted expectations. Secondly, the validity of norms requires the unified reaction of a group in cases of norm violation [38]. With respect to Zucker's distinction of different sources of trust on different levels of sociality (cf. [40]), the normativistic view is advantageous with respect to explanations how characteristics like the affiliation in certain societal group produces trust because trust in one affiliate can be generalized for all affiliates. A major disadvantage is that this understanding of trust does not explain the selection or discrimination of particular options of action within a group due to conflicting interests (i.e., all affiliates are to the same extent trustworthy) or between groups which do not share common norms. Trust is considered a mixture between familiarity with norms and confidence in the preservation of those norms by the group.

Other work takes into consideration that trust is a *"social relationship"* ([20, p. 6]), which is neither explicable by the existence of social norms nor by utilities desired to be realized. Especially Luhmann, who presented one of the most comprehensive conception of trust (cf. [20,34]), as well as Granovetter [41] *pay attention to the fact that trust is build in social processes among trusting and trusted parties and generates reciprocal commitments between these parties.*

Granovetter [41] rather focuses on explanations of trustworthiness than trust itself. He argues that transactions between two parties are not only about the value of the particular object of exchange, but about a set of interrelated aspects, i.e., social content (friendship, status, reputation), crosscutting ties, and relations to other agents or groups. The longer a relation lasts, the more contents are added to that relationship, the more interdependencies with other relationships build up, and hence the more an agent looses, if he or she exploits the given trust opportunistically for the sake of short-sighted utility. Consequently, benevolent or moral behavior is not explained by either the internalization of norms or the general willingness of actors to act conform to norms, but by the *embeddedness of interaction* in particular networks of relations. Within this approach, trust is not only considered an expectation that enables the realization of benefits, but rather a *resource that needs to be accumulated in the course of ongoing transactions.* Granovetter's argumentation is particularly helpful to explain the generalization of trust within networks due to interconnections of reciprocal ties and interests. However, the scope of his explanation is restricted to a certain phenomenon of the meso-level (i.e., networks comprised of individuals).

Luhmann's trust conception (cf. [20,34]) has several advantages with respect to the requirements of a multi-level approach to trust mentioned above. Firstly, his conception provides a clear-cut definition of trust as a *specific solution to risks.* Trust neither has to be confound with familiarity, i.e., an unaware belief about the continuity of a social environment (including certain behaviors of other agents), nor with confidence (i.e., an attitude when risks are recognized, but their prevention does not seem to be feasible by the agent) [34]. Secondly, Luhmann does not ignore effects of social macro-phenomena (e.g., norms, law, authority, control). Trust is neither a calculable probability nor placed 'blindly' without any reason. Although Luhmann considers trust only as necessary in situations where the outcome of interaction is neither calculable nor guaranteed by norms, placing trust does not mean ignoring indications of trustworthiness (available information, existing norms or social structures). However, the announcement of potential sanctions creates distrust. Thus, it is necessary that thoughts about a possibly harmful action remain latent, so that a trusting relationship may work out. Thirdly, Luhmann explains that trust not only enables, but also constrains interaction. An agent or party that wishes to be trusted, so that an interaction takes place, may use trust tactically. Therefore, the trusted party may present itself trustworthy by *signals* and *symbols* with respect to the assumed expectations of others. This produces obligations to behave conform to the presentation of oneself because a trustee most likely would not destroy the image of himself and devaluate the effort made to generate that image (cf. [20, pp. 65]). This does not only apply to trust relations between individuals. Luhmann distinguishes between trust in persons and trust in systems (just like Giddens in [23]). However, since he refers with his notion of system trust to "symbolic generalized communication media" (e.g., law, money, power) (cf. [20]), he disregards aggregations of social entities on the meso-level such as networks and social groups as sources and objects of trust.

In the following section, we suggest that elements of the theory of practice developed by Pierre Bourdieu are more suitable to integrate the advantages of those approaches that consider trust as a *social relation*. Furthermore, it facilitates the extension of trust from social networks to other meso-level phenomena (groups, organizations) and to macro-level phenomena as well. We assume Bourdieu's treatises on the economy of symbolic goods as a fruitful approach to explain the generalization and abstraction of trust from interpersonal relations.

3.2   Trust and the Economy of Symbolic Goods

Trust has never been an analytical category within Bourdieu's theory nor has he explicitly analyzed this phenomenon in his work either. Nevertheless, the term *trust* is repeatedly mentioned in his treatises about the generation and accumulation of *social* and *symbolic capital* by the symbolic exchange of goods (cf. [42, p. 261], [43, p. 192]).[4] The

---

[4] Bourdieu considers "capital" as "accumulated labor (in its materialized form or its 'incorporated', embodied form)" ([44, p. 241]), i.e., a social force inscribed in objective and subjective structures. The "structure of the distribution of the different types and subtypes of capital at a given moment in time represents the immanent structure of the social world, i.e., the set of constraints (...) which govern its functioning in a durable way, determining the chances of success for practices" (ibid.). *Social capital* "is the sum of the resources, actual or virtual, that accrue to an individual or a group by virtue of possessing a durable network of more or less institutionalized relationships of mutual acquaintance and recognition" ([45, p. 119]). *Symbolic capital* (perceived as social prestige, honor, or reputation) is the form that other capital takes "when it is grasped through categories of perception that recognize its specific logic, or, if you prefer, misrecognize the arbitrariness of its possession and accumulation" (ibid.). Due to space

generation of *social capital* relates to the problem of cooperation among self-interested agents (cf. [43, p. 197]). On the one hand, Bourdieu assumes agents to be self-interested in the sense of a *selfishness* that is socially conditioned (cf. [47]) and that is supposed to be generally oriented towards achieving a higher social position in the social space or different social fields by increasing available resources ("capital"). Thus, the relations between agents in a field are characterized by competition. On the other hand, Bourdieu presumes that long-termed mutual commitments and binding relations (symmetrical relations of reciprocity and solidarity as well as asymmetrical relations of domination and loyalty) can be generated in absence of possibilities to enforce the adherence to commitments by means of control, unconcealed sanctions, or physical force. Yet, Bourdieu does not follow the explanations of methodological individualism to derive *social order* from the deliberate and voluntary exchange of power or property rights. Vice versa, Bourdieu does not explain cooperation or solidarity by mere internalization of a given *normative* social order—even though the incorporation of a historically arbitrary and apparently self-evident social order into the cognitive structures of agents ("habitus") is considered to be an important factor for the reproduction of binding social relations in absence of overt violence. A central rationale for the apparently unforced generation and reproduction of cooperative symmetrical or asymmetrical relations between social parties (individual, collective, or corporative agents) is the *symbolic*, hence gentle and invisible violence of honor, recognition, and prestige that is exerted by a practice of perpetual *symbolic exchange* of gifts. The giving of a gift symbolizes, on the one hand, unselfishness and the abdication of the competitive pursuit of own interests and creates, on the other hand, gratitude, debt and obligations to reciprocate the gift to be respectable, and hence, produces binding relations for the future (social capital). The recognition of the connotations of a gift by an agent is due to the fact that symbolic exchange, similarly to economic exchange, is a *social institution*. In contrast to economic exchange, which underlies the principle of obvious material self-interest, the practice of gift exchange has a twofold truth: the objective logic of exchange (i.e., the reciprocation of a gift) and the necessity of a subjective and collective denial of self-interest including the belief in the gratuitous, unrequited generosity of both parties. In other words, the effects produced by the exchange of symbolic goods result from the fact that *an economy or market of symbolic goods* exists "in the form of a system of objective probabilities of profit [...], a set of 'collective expectations' that can be counted on" ([43, p. 192])—based upon a collective *production of (common) beliefs* (Bourdieu).   .

These profits are not only social capital and at least received counter-gifts (minus the gifts given). The twofold truth of symbolic exchange effects the generation of another sort of capital as well: *symbolic capital*, since *reputation* as the ascription of certain characteristics to individual or corporative agents by symbols and the legitimate acquisition of certain recognized symbols, can be regarded as a *resource*. The apparently gratuitous giving of goods produces different symbolic profits: (1) the recognition of the materialistically unselfish act (this recognition of 'fair' behavior is important to legitimate asymmetrical relations), (2) the accentuation of economic power and the disposal over material guarantees, since gift-giving requires economic capital, and (3) the

---

restrictions, we can not give a detailed summary of the basic theoretical elements of the theory of practice. For an abstract of the theory see ([46,47]).

accentuation of the social capital accumulated by gift-exchange in form of warrantors and the affiliation to certain networks, groups, or organizations.

The theory of practice considers *social* and *symbolic* capital, which have been generated and accumulated in an economy of symbolic goods, as major sources of trust. As shown in the previous sections, trust refers to both the selection or discrimination of alternative options of action in the face of the arbitrariness of human behavior (e.g., malicious behavior) and to the expectations about the cooperative behavior of other social parties concerning own actions and interests. With respect to the theory of practice, *trust can be defined as a practical expectation tied to symbolic relations of the denial of self-interest and competition between agents (individuals as well as collective and corporative agents)* (cf. [43, p. 192]). With "practical" we refer to the central hypothesis of the theory of Bourdieu that agents do not act on the basis of purposeful, intentional calculations, even though they are self-interested. Their actions are partially unconscious, effected by their dispositions of perception, recognition, and action (their habitus), and they follow a "logic of practice" that seems to be *practically* "rational" in the sense that these actions are practicable, satisfactory, and conclusive regarding the "objective" requirements of situations that are typical of certain social positions. In the following, we show that these two forms of capital represent basic links between micro- and macro-level trust.

4   Suggestions for a Multi-level Approach to Trust in MAS

In order to describe the effects of an economy of symbolic goods with respect to the build-up and distribution of trust on different levels of sociality, we start with our analysis at the micro-level of sociality (see Table 1). This does not mean that we assume a kind of presocial, primitive state where social order emerges from the socially unstructured actions of agents. With respect to MAS, this means that agents need to possess at least the ability to recognize certain behaviors of other agents in their common social meaning, i.e., to recognize a gift as a gift and not as a foolish act of lavishness.

4.1   Process-Based Trust[5]

A crucial practice for the accumulation of social and symbolic capital is the *dyadic interpersonal exchange of gifts*. One central argument of how gift-exchange produces binding relations is that a gift may remain unreciprocated. A gift is subjectively and collectively meant to be gratuitous, thus an equivalent refund in form of a counter-gift can not be explicitly asked. Since the "logic" of the economy of symbolic goods is to deny self-interest, a certain time has to elapse before a counter-gift can be made, so that the subjective and collective self-deception about the logic of exchange is not revealed. Moreover, the material value of gifts must not be obvious, and a counter-gift must be different from the initial gift with respect to form and size. Even though there is a high probability that a gift will be reciprocated due to the institutionalization of

---

[5] Note that our notion of process-based trust (gift exchange) differs from the usage of the term in [40]. A first prototype of an MAS, in which agents exchange gifts, has already been implemented in the context of our socionics project (cf. [46]).

gift-exchange, "the shift from the highest probability to absolute certainty is a qualitative leap out of proportion to the numerical difference" ([42, p. 191]). The second important argument for the binding power of gift-exchange is that a counter-gift not only compensates for the initial gift, but incurs new obligations, since every gift (initial or counter-gift) is subjectively perceived as a voluntary act of a free will. *A counter-gift does not terminate, but continues the relation of (mutual) obligation.* Yet, there is always the possibility that sometime a gift will not be reciprocated, since selfish agents do not exchange gifts indiscriminately with everyone because their economic resources to produce social and symbolic profits are finite.

With respect to the scalability of MAS, interpersonal gift-exchange has two major advantages. Firstly, *an initial gift is a reliable and valid signal of trustworthiness*, especially under the premise of self-interested, unacquainted agents. A gift incurs costs and risks. If an agent gave a signal that has not any value, he would loose nothing, if he behaved completely different next time or exploited the trust of the other agent. Since a gift is a kind of investment in social capital that requires economic resources of the donor, the gift commits an agent, because his resources are finite. If he used the signal to exploit the trust of another agent, he would loose at least his investment and probably the symbolic recognition of his status position, too. On the contrary, even in case a gift is not recognized as such, and is exploited by another agent 'opportunistically', it is likely that the material loss is less than, e.g., the loss in an economic transaction when blind trust is placed. This is because the profits of gift-exchange are symbolic ones and initial gifts (at least in case of symmetrical gift-exchange) are usually of a size that does not exceed the resources of the receiver to give a counter-gift. Secondly, gift-exchange reliably indicates the *transferability of trust between both agents in a dyadic exchange to the future* as long as the reciprocal interest of the social relation is confirmed by a perpetual process of exchanging gifts.

However, on the micro-level of sociological analysis, gift-exchange produces no symbolic profits recognized by third parties yet[6], and mutual obligations are restricted to the two parties of exchange. Hence, trust can not be generalized regarding third parties.

4.2   Network-Based Trust

The generalization of trusting expectations to third parties requires the extension of analysis to the meso-level of sociality, i.e., the embeddedness of the agents of a dyadic exchange in networks of reciprocal relations (cf. [41]). According to Bourdieu, the social capital of an agent is not only the sum of dyadic relations to which can be fallen back, but the *totality of actual and potential resources that are tied to a durable network of mutual knowledge and recognition* [44]. These networks are built and maintained by the perpetual labor of symbolic exchange. On this level of sociality, the formerly accumulated social capital is deployed as *symbolic capital* in the process of establishing reciprocal ties with third parties (cf. [42, p. 208]). Agents, to whom relations of mutual obligations exist, are acting as guarantors of the unselfishness of the parties that aim at

---

[6] With micro-level we mean a perspective of sociological analysis that does not exist in absence of other levels. The symbolic dimension in general produces effects on all levels simultaneously.

building reciprocal ties with each other by symbolic exchange for the first time. Step by step, a network of intertwined and even entangled obligations is produced. Hence, agents belonging to this network are urged to act unselfish to the greatest possible extent towards all affiliates of a network in order not to risk their symbolic and social capital. Therefore, trusting expectations can be generalized for each agent of a network, even though interpersonal symbolic exchange never took place between certain agents of the network.

However, this generalization of trusting expectations on the level of networks is only valid between affiliates of such a network for two reasons: Firstly, as long as a network is not vivid to the environment (e.g., by obvious distinctive marks) as a social entity, the potential positive or negative symbolic capital (good or bad reputation concerning selfishness) of this network can not be transferred to an affiliate. Secondly, a disadvantage with respect to population size and heterogeneity is that the placement of trust demands knowledge of the agents belonging to a network, what is obviously only possible in small networks.

4.3   Group-Based Trust

A precondition for the generalization of trust from persons to networks and the transfer of the ascribed characteristics of the network to its affiliates respectively is the appearance of a network as a recognized social entity to which certain characteristics can be ascribed in its totality. Hence, the further generalization of trust requires analyzing another phenomenon of the meso-level: the institutionalization of a *social group*, i.e., the processes that transform either an ensemble of unrelated agents (a "class", cf. [48, pp. 127]) or a network of more or less equal affiliates (cf. [44]) into a *collective agent*, which is defined by its ability to act like 'one' person.

The transformation of a network into a group requires both the existence of recognized criteria and symbols of affiliation and the designation of at least one representative who speaks for the group and symbolizes it. Thus, the process of generating such a collective agent can not be explained by the mechanism of symbolic exchange only. A further mechanism, *social delegation* (i.e., the process and act of appointing an agent as representative, cf. [22]) has to be added to the analysis. Social delegation entails more than the advantage of making a group vivid to others. Even though a representative is engaged to act unselfish in the interest of the group, he may use the resources of the group for his own interests. Symbolic exchange is important with respect to delegation in two aspects: firstly, a delegate may try to prove his unselfishness by gift-exchange to legitimate his power. "An unbroken progression leads from the symmetry of gift exchange to the asymmetry of conspicuous redistribution that is the basis of the constitution of political authority ([42, p. 215])". Secondly, a representative will not be selected randomly out of the number of group members, but due to his power within the group. Since agents are competitive, it is likely that a process of vertical differentiation between affiliates takes place in a network of more or less equal agents before a network becomes a collective agent. As the solidarity within a network does not allow selfishness, asymmetrical gift-exchange (i.e., the giving of gifts which can not be reciprocated adequately due to their size) may be used to produce trust in the appropriateness of an agent as representative or to convince the members to pass the ministry of representation as a counter-gift to the donor. Trust between representatives of a group and its members is hence rather based on domination and loyalty than on reciprocity and solidarity.

However, with respect to the generalization of trust, group-based trust is still not satisfying. Reasons for outsiders to trust a group and its members because of their affiliation in that group may only be derived from the symbolic capital a group has accumulated as a collective agent. As long as no direct relations of mutual obligations of a trusting outsider with the group have been tied, the only reason to behave trustworthy towards outsiders is the possible loss of the symbolic capital. If an outsider is not considered as powerful enough to destroy the symbolic capital, there is no serious reason for solidarity with him.

4.4   Organization-Based Trust

Organizations differ from groups because of their degree of formalization and legal regulation. Membership and the task of representation are based on economic exchange (wage, salary) and are regulated by contracts of employment. Loyalty with dominating agents is hence enforceable by authority including sanctions like the resolution of contracts in case of a breech. In contrast to groups, we consider organizations as *corporative, not collective agents*. Trust of non-members in organizations or in their members respectively is to a great extent depersonalized, since trust in organizations is not based on personal obligations. Trust in a corporative agent represents trust in a system, based on the latent possibility to enforce contracts. Even trust in members has to be considered as a depersonalized type of trust. Members represent "access points" [23] to the trusted system because members are obliged to act according to their organizational position. Hence, the symbolic capital an organization has accumulated is reliable to a great extent and thus a generalizable source of trust. However, according to Bourdieu, organizations are no apparatuses, but social fields, i.e., fields of social forces and struggles. Agents may deviate in their practice from the interests of the corporative agent for competitive aims. Since sanctions can not be applied to any action due to a lack of resources to carry them out, symbolic exchange hence may substitute and supplement control and contracts to generate loyalty and solidarity. However, the production of trust by symbolic exchange in the context of organizations is rather difficult since economic interests are hard to conceal.

4.5   Institution-Based Trust

Even though organizations contribute to the generalization and depersonalization to a great extent, they are phenomena of the meso-level of sociality. This implicates that they are only capable to generalize trust with respect to themselves and their members. The generalization of signs and symbols, which ascribe certain trust promoting characteristics (e.g., skills, abilities, obedience to a certain code of conduct) to agents (individuals as well as collective or corporative agents) in a valid and reliable way and independently of any affiliation in a certain group or organization, requires phenomena of the macro-level of sociality. According to Bourdieu (cf. [42]), we consider institutions or institutionalized mechanisms as such phenomena. Symbolic exchange on the micro-

and on the meso-level is not "scalable" to any extent, since gift-exchange requires economic resources and cannot be carried out with too many agents. With respect to the generalization of trust in open systems, institutions that contribute to the accumulation and distribution of generalized symbolic capital are necessary. In the context of the theory of practice, institutions can be defined as relatively stable and permanent regularities of practice, which are based on objectified history and are recognized as legitimate, explicit, or implicit rules within certain social fields. Institutions correspond on the side of agents with their cognitive structure (habitus) and need to be reproduced by the practice of agents. Institutions concerning cultural and symbolic capital are, e.g., titles of education (diploma) or certificates that attribute certain qualities to organizations. Within the process of generating institutions, the state plays an important role (cf. [43, p. 175]) by establishing definite differences between legitimate and illegitimate practices, e.g., by awarding the title as medical doctor. Moreover, mass media contributes to the generation of institutional rules.

Table 1. The generalization of trust expectations on different levels of sociality.

	Micro-level	Meso-level			Macro-level
	Process-based trust	Network (NW) -based trust	Group-based trust	Organization-based trust	Institutional-based trust
Social mechanism	• Dyadic gift-exchange (GE)	• Interpersonal GE in NW	• Asymmetrical GE • Social Delegation by GE	• Authority, control, contract • GE possible	• Redistributive GE (legitimating)
Source	• Symmetrical Social Capital (SoC)	• NW of SoC • Symbolic Capital (SyC) tied to person	• Asymmetrical SoC • SyC tied to group	• SyC tied to organization • SoC (Loyalty)	• SyC tied to intermediary third parties • SoC (Loyalty)
Practical reasons of trust	Dyadic Reciprocity	Solidarity, collective reciprocity	Solidarity, legitimate "unselfish" domination, loyalty	Possibility to enforce claims, sanctions	Legitimacy of institutions (public utility, public opinion)
Social Area of trust validity	Dyadic Relation	Generalization for affiliates inside NW	Generalization for affiliates & group, partial transferability to interaction with outsiders	Generalization for organization & members, transferability to interaction with outsiders	SyC recognized and available in entire society, not dependent on affiliation or membership

Degree of Generalization &
Depersonalization of Trust Expectations

However, the trust in symbolic capital produced by institutions depends to a great extent on the trust and legitimacy of those third parties (e.g., governmental authorities; certain newspapers) that act as intermediary parties and ascribe symbols of an institution to an individual, corporative, or collective agent (e.g., by certification). The legitimacy of those intermediary parties depends to a great extent on the collective belief that they act in the interest of a community or society respectively and not on behalf of certain pressure groups or dominating classes. The redistribution of public (e.g., student's grants) or private (e.g., financing of 'disinterested' foundations, donations to hospitals) capital serves this legitimization. Hence, the logic of the gift and the economy of symbolic goods are also effective on the macro-level of sociality to generate trust. On the one hand, *symbolic exchange produces trust in institutions and intermediary third parties*. On the other hand, *institutions ascribe certain symbols and characteristics* to individual, collective, and corporative agents and, hence, enable a diffusion of trusting expectations within a society that is not necessarily tied to affiliation or membership in forms of social aggregation of the meso-level.

After sketching these trust creating mechanisms on different levels of sociality (see Table 1 for an overview), it may appear questionable, if all the required elements of this trust concept (the different mechanisms, representations of social and symbolic capital, organizations, and institutions) can be implemented in an agent system, and whether this model has beneficial effects on the distribution and generalization of trust as well as the scalability of the entire MAS. All these elements will require a lot of system resources when implemented. Regarding the question, if this concept technically can be implemented, we hope that this is possible. We consider this paper a supplementary approach to the conception of improving scalability of MAS by flexible holonic structures (cf. [46], Schillo/Spresny and Hillebrandt, in this volume), which has been inspired by the theory of Bourdieu as well. Implementations of this concept already consist of mechanisms for social delegation, simple forms of gift-exchange and allow agents to build organizations and networks during run-time. However, a general answer to the question, if this model will indeed improve the scalability of open MAS, can not be given in general, but has to be examined by experimentation (i.e., social simulation). Although this concept has been presented with regard to any kind of MAS in which cooperation between self-interested agents plays an important role, the development of this multi-level trust model was influenced by work on task-assignment MAS in a market-based scenario (electronic market place for transportation orders) where self-interested agents engage in interaction with other agents to distribute tasks according to costs, competence, and task load. E-commerce platforms in the World Wide Web are an application field for MAS where malicious behavior is a more severe problem than in systems that use MAS in the sense of a software engineering paradigm for building complex, but closed software systems. Since the prevention of malicious behavior and trust are crucial for the performance of an open MAS, the resource consumption of the suggested trust building mechanisms may be justified.

5   Conclusion

In recent years, issues of trust and scalability have attracted increasing attention in DAI. Although trust has been regarded as an important mechanism of social coordination, the distribution and generalization of trust itself as well as differences in the way trust is operating on the micro, meso, and macro-level of social aggregation have been largely neglected. We argued that sociological concepts will support DAI in adapting MAS both to the challenges of scalability and to the issues of trust as well. Contributions from DAI to trust issues have been analyzed and compared with sociological conceptions concerning trust on different levels of sociality. The relationship between trust and scalability was discussed with reference to conceptions of trust prevailing both in DAI as well as in sociology. Finally, a multilevel approach to the distribution and generalization of trust was introduced using sociological concepts provided by Pierre Bourdieu. Gift-exchange, social delegation, social and symbolic capital were identified as basic social mechanisms of building trust in large-scaled open systems. We argued that these mechanisms (1) facilitate the "scalability" of trust due to their signaling of cooperativeness and (2) enable a conception of trust as social relation that includes the idea of reciprocity, and (3) therefore supports both the formation of social networks and the diffusion of trust on the macro-level of society. According to Bourdieu, the framework of an economy of symbolic goods facilitates different models of trust situated on multiple levels of sociality as a basic condition to scale trust in MAS. Our ideas and proposals are, of course, determined by our sociological point of view. This may explain our neglect to reason about the technical practicability in favor of exploring unknown scientific terrain. Nevertheless, we hope to contribute to the transformation of sociological concepts into models of artificial social systems that are also suitable for technological requirements of DAI.

6   Acknowledgments

We are indebted to Dr. Frank Hillebrandt, Daniela Spresny, Dr. Klaus Fischer and Michael Schillo for many fruitful discussions. This work was funded by Deutsche Forschungsgemeinschaft (DFG) under contract FL 336/1-2.

References

1. Hewitt, C.E.: The challenge of open systems. Byte **10** (1985) 223–242
2. Hewitt, C.E.: Open Information Systems Semantics for Distributed Artificial Intelligence. Artificial Intelligence **47** (1991) 79–106
3. Neuman, B.: Scale in distributed systems. In Casavant, T., Singhal, M., eds.: Readings in Distributed Computing Systems. IEEE Computer Society Press, Los Alamitos, CA. (1994) 463–489
4. Wijngaards, N., Overeinder, B., Steen, M.v., Brazier, F.: Supporting Internet-Scale Multi-Agent Systems. Data and Knowledge Engineering **41** (2002) 229–245
5. Turner, P., Jennings, N.: Improving the Scalability of Multi-agent Systems. In Wagner, T., Rana, O., eds.: Infrastructure for Agent, Multi-Agent Systems, and Scalable Multi-Agent Systems, Berlin (2001) 246–262
6. Durfee, E.: Scaling Up Agent Coordination Strategies. IEEE Computer **34** (2001) 39–46
7. Gerber, C.: Self-Adaptation and Scalability in Multi-Agent Societies. PhD thesis, Universität des Saarlandes (1999)
8. Rana, O., Stout, K.: What is scalability in Multi-Agent Systems? In Sierra, C., Gini, M., Rosenschein, J.S., eds.: Proceedings of the Fourth International Conference on Autonomous Agents. Barcelona, Catalonia, Spain,, New York, ACM Press (2000) 56–63

9. Davidsson, P.: Categories of Artificial Societies. In Omicini, A., Petta, P., Tolksdorf, R., eds.: Engineering Societies in the Agents World II. Second International Workshop, ESAW 2001, Prague, Czech Republic, Revised Papers. Volume 2203 of Lecture Notes in Computer Science/Lecture Notes in Artificial Intelligence., Berlin et al., Springer (2001) 1–9

10. Davidsson, P.: Emergent Societies of Information Agents. In Klusch, M., Kerschberg, L., eds.: Cooperative Information Agents IV: The Future of Information Agents in Cyberspace. Volume 1860 of Lecture Notes in Computer Science/Lecture Notes in Artificial Intelligence. Springer, Berlin et al. (2000) 143–153

11. Ramchurn, S., Sierra, Godo, L., Jennings, N.: A Computational Trust Model for Multi-Agent Interactions based on Confidence and Reputation. In: Proceedings of the Sixth International Workshop of Deception, Fraud and Trust in Agent Societies, Melbourne, Australia. (2003) 69–75

12. Castelfranchi, C., Tan, Y., Falcone, R., Firozabadi, B., eds.: Special Issue on Deception, Fraud and Trust in Agent Societies. Part 2. Volume 14. Applied Artificial Intelligence Journal (2000)

13. Castelfranchi, C., Tan, Y., eds.: Trust and Deception in Virtual Societies. Kluwer Academic Publishers, Dordrecht (2001)

14. Castelfranchi, C., Tan, Y., Falcone, R., Firozabadi, B., eds.: Special Issue on Deception, Fraud and Trust in Agent Societies. Part 1. Volume 14. Applied Artificial Intelligence Journal (2000)

15. Falcone, R., Singh, M., Tan, Y., eds.: Trust in Cyber Societies. Integrating the Human and Artificial Perspectives. Volume 2246 of Lecture Notes in Computer Science/Lecture Notes in Artificial Intelligence. Springer, Berlin et al. (2001)

16. Schillo, M., Bürckert, H., Fischer, K., Klusch, M.: Towards a Definition of Robustness for Market-Style Open Multi-Agent Systems. In: Proceedings of the Fifth International Conference on Autonomous Agents (AA'01). (2001) 75–76

17. Schillo, M., Rovatsos, M., Funk, P.: Using Trust for Detecting Deceitful Agents in Artificial Societies. [14] 825–848

18. Falcone, R., Castelfranchi, C.: The Socio-cognitive Dynamics of Trust. Does Trust Create Trust? [15] 55–72

19. Coleman, J.: Foundations of Social Theory. Belknap Press, Cambridge, Massachusetts, London (1990)

20. Luhmann, N.: Trust and Power. John Wiley & Sons, Chichester, New York, Brisbane, Toronto (1979)

21. Castelfranchi, C., Falcone, R.: Trust and Control. A Dialectic Link. [14] 799–823

22. Bourdieu, P.: Delegation and Political Fetishism. Thesis Eleven (1984/1985) 56–70

23. Giddens, A.: The consequences of modernity. Stanford University Press, Stanford (1990)

24. Marsh, S.: Formalising Trust as a Computational Concept. PhD thesis, University of Stirling, Department of Computing Science (1994)

25. Abdul-Rahman, A., Hailes, S.: Supporting Trust in Virtual Communities. In: Proceedings of the 33rd Hawaii International Conference on System Sciences. Volume 6., Maui, Hawaii, IEEE (2000) http://csdl.computer.org/comp/proceedings/hicss/2000/0493/06/04936007.pdf.

26. Birk, A.: Learning to Trust. [15] 133–144

27. Jonker, C.M., Treur, J.: Formal Analysis of Models for the Dynamics of Trust based on Experiences. In Garijo, F.J., Boman, M., eds.: Multi-Agent System Engineering. Proceedings of the 9th European Workshop on Modelling Autonomous Agents in a Multi-Agent World, MAAMAW'99. Volume 1647 of Lecture Notes in Computer Science/Lecture Notes in Artificial Intelligence., Berlin et al., Springer (1999) 221–232

28. Yu, S., Singh, M.: An evidential model of distributed reputation management. In: Proceedings of the First International Joint Conference on Autonomous Agents and Multiagent Systems 2002. Bologna, Italy, New York, ACM Press (2002) 294–301

29. Venkatraman, M., Yu, S., Singh, M.:   Trust and Reputation Management in a Small-World Network (Poster). In: Proceedings of Fourth International Conference on Multiagent Systems, ICMAS-2000, Boston, Massachusetts, IEEE (2000) 449–450 http://csdl.computer.org/comp/proceedings/icmas/2000/0625/00/06250449abs.htm.
30. Metzger, J., Schillo, M., Fischer, K.: A multiagent-based peer-to-peer network in java for distributed spam filtering. In Maik, V.and Müller, J., Pchouek, M., eds.: Multi-Agent Systems and Applications III. Proceedings of the 3rd International Central and Eastern European Conference on Multi-Agent Systems, CEEMAS 2003, Prague, Czech Republic. Volume 2691 of Lecture Notes in Computer Science/Lecture Notes in Artificial Intelligence., Berlin et al. (2003) 616–625
31. Axelrod, R.: The Evolution of Cooperation. Basic Books, New York (1984)
32. Sandip, S.: Reciprocity: A foundational principle for promoting cooperative behavior among self-interested agents. In: Proceedings of the Second International Conference on Multiagent Systems, ICMAS-1996. Menlo Park, CA, AAAI Press (1996) 322–329
33. Castelfranchi, C., Falcone, R.: Trust Is Much More than Subjective Probability. Mental Components and Sources of Trust. In: Proceedings of the 33rd Hawaii International Conference on System Sciences. Volume 6., Maui, Hawaii, IEEE (2000) http://csdl.computer.org/comp/proceedings/hicss/2000/0493/06/04936008.pdf.
34. Luhmann, N.:   Confidence, Trust. Problems and Alternatives.   In Gambetta, D., ed.: Trust. Making and Breaking Cooperative Relations.   Electronic edn., http://www.sociology.ox.ac.uk/papers/gambetta213-237.pdf (2000) 94–107
35. Gasser, L.: Social Conceptions of Knowledge and Action. DAI Foundations and Open Systems Semantics. Artificial Intelligence 47 (1991) 107–138
36. Bachmann, R.: Kooperation, Vertrauen und Macht in Systemen Verteilter Künstlicher Intelligenz. Eine Vorstudie zum Verhältnis von soziologischer Theorie und technischer Modellierung. In Malsch, T., ed.: Sozionik - Soziologische Ansichten über künstliche Sozialität. Sigma, Berlin (1998) 197–234
37. Gambetta, D.: 'Can We Trust Trust?'. In Gambetta, D., ed.: Trust. Making and Breaking Cooperative Relations. Electronic edn., http://www.sociology.ox.ac.uk/papers/gambetta213-237.pdf (2000) 213–237
38. Münch, R.: Rational Choice - Grenzen der Erklärungskraft. In Müller, H.P., Schmid, M., eds.: Norm, Herrschaft und Vertrauen. Beiträge zu James S. Colemans Grundlagen der Sozialtheorie. Westdeutscher Verlag, Opladen, Wiesbaden (1998) 79–91
39. Popitz, H.: Die normative Konstruktion der Gesellschaft. Mohr, Tübingen (1980)
40. Zucker, L.G.: Production of Trust. Institutional Sources of Economic Structure, 1840-1920. Research in Organizational Behavior 8 (1986) 53–111
41. Granovetter, M.: Problems of Explanation in Economic Sociology. In Nohira, N., Eccles, R.G., eds.: Networks and Organizations. Structure, Form, and Action. Harvard Business School Press, Boston (1992) 25–56
42. Bourdieu, P.: Selections from The Logic of Practice. In Schrift, A.D., ed.: The Logic of the Gift. Toward an Ethic of Generosity. Routledge, London, New York (1997) 190–230
43. Bourdieu, P.: Pascalian Meditations. Polity Press, Cambridge, UK/Oxford, UK (2000)
44. Bourdieu, P.: The (three) Forms of Capital. In Richardson, J.G., ed.: Handbook of Theory and Research in the Sociology of Education. Greenwood Press, New York, London (1986) 241–258
45. Bourdieu, P., Wacquant, L.: An Invitation to Reflexive Sociology. Polity Press, Chicago (1992)
46. Schillo, M., Fischer, K., Fley, B., Florian, M., Hillebrandt, F., Spresny, D.: FORM - A Sociologically Founded Framework for Designing Self-Organization of Multiagent Systems. In Lindemann, G., Moldt, D., Paolucci, M., eds.: Regulated Agent Based Social Systems. First

International Workshop, RASTA 2002, Bologna, Italy, Revised Selected and Invited Papers. Volume 2934 of Lecture Notes in Computer Science/Lecture Notes in Artificial Intelligence., Berlin et al., Springer (2004) 156–175

47. Schillo, M., Fischer, K., Hillebrandt, F., Florian, M., Dederichs, A.: Bounded social rationality. Modelling self-organization and adaptation using habitus-field theory. In: Proceedings of the Workshop on Modelling Artificial Societies and Hybrid Organizations, MASHO'00. (2000) 112–122

48. Bourdieu, P.: In Other Words. Essays Towards a Reflexive Sociology. University Press/Polity Press, Stanford, Cal./Cambridge, UK (1990)

Coordination in Scaling Actor Constellations
The Advantages of Small-World Networks

Christian W.G. Lasarczyk[1] and Thomas Kron[2]

[1] Computer Science, University of Dortmund
christian.lasarczyk@udo.edu
[2] Institute for Sociology, Open University of Hagen
thomas.kron@fernuni-hagen.de

Abstract. The emergence of order in systems with many actors or agents is an interesting problem for sociology as well as for computer science. Starting the from sociological theory of the dyadic "situation of double contingency", our main focus is on large actor populations and their capability to produce order depending on different actors' constellations. Based on the theory for dyadic actor constellations we present our model of the actor. We do not want the actors to identify one another, so we do not need to modify this model if we scale up population size next and introduce constellations. Thereby we take regular, random and small–world constellations into account. After describing our measures of order we study emergence of order in different constellations for varying population sizes. By means of simulation experiments we show that systems with small–worlds exhibit highest order on large populations which gently decreases on increasing population sizes.

1 The Production of Social Order as a Coordination Problem

The explanation of how social order is generated, stabilised, and eventually changed by itself, is a main topic of sociology. The cause can probably be seen in the "annoying fact of society" (Dahrendorf), that humans have to deal with each other and from this social situations just develop. The reason for this relies in a parametric distribution of control and interests at certain resources, which forces the actors into one–sided or mutual dependencies. The actors are forced to process and accomplish their intention interferences [1].

The structural connection as the background of social acting [2] — the connection over mutual control of interesting resources — can be modelled by three basic types of social, strategic situations (co–ordination, dilemma, conflict). The *co–ordination problem* consists of the fact that the actors must find a tuning, which makes it possible, for all involved actors, to receive the possible utility. The interests of the actors converge here. For example, if some actors like to meet, but they do not know yet, in which place. If the individual and collective interests differ, then there is a *dilemma*. Who cleans the dwelling today, you or I? However, under certain conditions there are still cooperative solutions. This is no longer the case within a *conflict*, when the individual interests come apart completely. You always want to see soap operas whereas I want to see sports. This all has been examined thoroughly by sociology, and a few proposals have been made

K. Fischer, M. Florian. and T. Malsch (Eds.): Socionics, LNAI 3413, pp. 199–217, 2005.

to solve this problem: social order is generated by a powerful state, the Leviathan [3]; by an "invisible hand" [4]; by norms [5], which are legitimated by values located in a cultural system of a society [6,7]; or by rational action choices in consideration of a long common future [8].

In this contribution we just want to deal with the coordination problem, and within this problem class we deal with a specific problem that has to be solved: the difficulty of producing social order by solving the co–ordination problem *within scaling actor constellations*[1].

To repeat: the coordination problem is the simplest problem of the formation of social order. Hence many sociologists think that this problem has been investigated in all its problem dimensions. Particularly the rational choice theory assumes that dilemmas and conflicts are more interesting fields of scientific activity than coordination problems. Our suspicion is that simulation experiments open up new vistas which are ignored otherwise because there is simply a lack of the respective "analysis tool".

1.1   The Problem of Scaling in Coordination

The problem of scaling is an old issue in sociology. Already the German sociologist George Simmel has devoted the second chapter of his famous "Sociology" of 1908 to the "quantitative definiteness of the group". There he emphasised that on the one hand threshold levels of a group size just make certain social formation possible at all. On the other hand an increasing group size can make realisation of such formations more difficult. As an example he refers to a specific problem of social order: "So one can e.g. ascertain that total or approximated socialistic orders always have been accomplishable in small circles, but always have been abortive in great ones"[9]. In fact, Simmel has analysed the formal consequences of the scaling of the group size less than the influence on the relation of society — personality (individuality). Nevertheless we can find arguments in his scripts for the relevance of the *Zahlbestimmheit* in the arrangement of the group in subgroups, whereby (local) independency and mobility on the one hand and on the other hand (global) coherence are possible at the same time (one speaks of "glocalisation"). Those were not only first clues for the sociological concept of "social differentiation"[10], but also, as we will see, first precursors for the model of small–world networks.

To point out the difficulties with scalings on the co–ordination problem we will take a game–theoretical view. Game–theoretically formulated we have a commonness of the interests in a succeeding co–operation with a missing dominant strategy, and the existence of several equilibriums as well as a (pareto-) optimum of a once found solution.

Without reference points the actors can build mutual action forecasts in an infinite recourse without arriving at a result, particularly if the number of action alternatives is high. In small communities where everybody can observe the other's actions, the actors will be able to find a solution in a while by trial and error, or they can talk with each other and find an all–side accepted "focal–point". But this will not be possible if

---

[1] So, in this article we are just considering one of the two relevant scaling dimensions (see Schimank in this anthology).

$$
\begin{array}{c}
\text{B} \\
\begin{array}{cc} 1 & 2 \end{array}
\end{array}
$$

$$
\text{A} \quad
\begin{array}{c|cc}
1 & 4,4 & 0 \\
\\
2 & 0 & 4,4
\end{array}
$$

Table 1. Game–Theoretical Modeling of the Co–Ordination Problem

the actor constellation exists of a such a great number of actors that the conditions of mutual observability and suggestibility as well as the dependency of the actor on the success of the cooperation is no longer given. Then at least[2] the coordination problem reemerges.

1.2 Double Contingency

The absence of the important starting point as the main difficulty of the co–ordination problem within the emergence of order is known in sociology as the "problem of double contingency". Talcott Parsons [11], has formulated this problem as follows[3]:"The crucial reference points for analysing interaction are two: (1) Each actor is both acting agent and object of orientation both to himself and to the others; and (2) that, while acting, the agent orients to himself and to others, in all primary modes of aspects. The actor is knower and object of cognition, utiliser of instrumental means and a means himself, emotionally attached to others and an object of attachment, evaluator and object of evaluation, interpreter of symbols and himself a symbol." According to Parsons, Niklas Luhmann[14] identified the problem of double contingency as the main problem of producing social order. The problematic situation is this: two entities[4] meet each other. How should they act, if they want to solve the problem of contingency, that is, if necessities and impossibilities are excluded?[5]

---

[2] Furthermore, there could be a qualitative step from the coordination problem to a dilemma if one assumes that there are only *rational* actors. Then the scaling means that everybody thinks of the own cost–value–ratio if he participates in solving the problem: the costs are for sure, but the own contribution to the solution is getting lower the more actors are involved. And if one will decide to participate nevertheless, how can he be sure that the other will do so, too? The result is, that nobody will participate but waits for a free–riding possibility.

[3] In an earlier version, Parsons' [12] solution for the problem of double contingency had a much more economical bias. See also Münch [13].

[4] The term "entity" denotes what Luhmann[14] called "Ego" and "Alter", and Parsons called "actor".

[5] One of Luhmann's basic assumptions is that both actors are interested in solving this problem. Luhmann[14]: "No social system can get off the ground, if the one who begins with communication, cannot know or would not be interested in whether his partner reacts positively or negatively." But the question remains: Where does the motivation (interest) come from? According to Luhmann, an answer should not consider actor characteristics (like intentions) as starting point for system theory. We think that Luhmann falls back to his earlier anthropological position (see Schimank [15,16]) and assumes a basic necessity of "expectation–certainty",

Luhmann's assumptions for the solution of the problem of double contingency refer to self–organisation processes in the dimension of time. In a first step an actor begins to act tentatively, e.g., with a glance or a gesture. Subsequent steps referring to this first step are contingency reducing activities, so that the entities are enabled to build up expectations. As a consequence, a system history develops. Beginning from this starting point further mechanisms could be instituted to generate order, such as confidence or symbolic generalised media.[6] Thus in this perspective, social structures, social order, or social systems are first of all structures of mutual expectations. That is, every actor expects that the other actor has expectations about its next activity. In this paper we act on the assumption of the situation of double contingency as the origin of social order referring to co–ordination problems[7].

Summarised, the solution of the problem of double contingency presupposes at least the motivation of the actors by expectation–certainty as well as their possibilities of forming expectations over expectations. Accordingly we model our simulation scenario, we now want to describe briefly.

2   Modelling the Situation of Double Contingency

The basis model of the simulation scenario consists of agents, able to mutually signal themselves N different symbols. The same number of $|N|$ different symbols is available for each agent and determines the scope of action and thus the contingency. These symbols are sent successively, individually, and alternately. There is no predisposed relationship or metrics between the symbols, represented as numbers. In the course of a simulation relations can develop by the way agents use the symbols. Two agents, chosen from the entire population, transmit in turn a symbol to each other[8] , so a situation of mutual observation exists. We take each symbol by an action, whereas each action is represented by a symbol one–to–one.

2.1   Action Motivation

Which motivations do the agents have for the selection of the symbols? According to the sociological analysis of the problem of double contingent situations explained above, we assume only two basal motivations[9]:

---

that is, that Alter and Ego want to know what is going on in this situation. A fundamental uncertainty still remains and takes further effect in the emerged systems as an autocatalytic factor. See also the approach to formulate "double contingency" from the perspective of a communication network as provided by Leydesdorff [17].

[6] For new simulation experiments about the genesis of symbolic generalised media, see Papendick/Wellner [18].

[7] We have done this before (see [19,20,21]).

[8] Because the agents do not differentiate explicitly between information and message, we do not model Luhmann's communication term, which consists of a three–way selection from information, message, and understanding.

[9] Further possible motivations, e.g. an interest in possible resources, remain unconsidered in the model. We particularly follow Luhmann, who considers intentions as too sophisticated

- Expectation–certainty, i.e., the agents want to predict the reactions of the other agents to own activities as well as possible. In other words, the agents want, that their expectations will not become disappointed by the reactions of other agents.
- Expectation–expectation, i.e., the agents want to accomplish the expectations of the other agents as well as possible.

2.2 Memory

The memory serves as a storage of action/reaction–combinations in the past. From this information the agents compute expectations to the future. We use a square matrix X as the agent memory, which is stretched by the quantity of possible activities and reactions. All values of the matrix are initialised with a very small positive value

$$0 < x^{\text{init}}_{\text{action,reaction}} \ll 1 \ . \tag{1}$$

The agent learns a reaction following an activity by raising the according value within the matrix by one

$$x^{\text{new}}_{\text{action,reaction}} = x^{\text{old}}_{\text{action,reaction}} + 1 \ . \tag{2}$$

The value of a matrix entry rises at the rate the appropriate action/reaction–combination occurs in interactions of the agent.

Learning is associated with forgetting. For this reason, there is the possibility of selecting a value r_{forget} (forgetting rate), which is added after learning to each matrix entry

$$x^{\text{new}}_{i,j} = x^{\text{old}}_{i,j} + r_{\text{forget}}, \quad \forall x_{i,j} \in X \ . \tag{3}$$

So the value r_{forget} determines the rate at which the matrix entries assimilate.[10]

2.3 Choosing an Action

Starting point of choosing an action a is the last action b of the other agent[11]. So you can always interpret an action as a reaction, which is performed by the agent in the following steps:

1. Calculate for each action a the action value $AV_b(a)$ as a combination of expectation–certainty and expectation–expectation.
2. Select a reaction on the basis of these action values.
3. (Re-)Act and if necessary[12] store the reaction.

We will explain these steps now.

---

for modelling the situation of double contingency: the pursuit of the own use is a much to fastidious attitude, than one could generally presuppose it [14].

[10] Without becoming equal as a result of this increase.

[11] The agents store their last action and send this one first if they meet another agent. At the beginning this action is chosen randomly.

[12] The own activity as reaction is only stored explicitly if the Ego–memory is used.

Calculation of the Expectation-Certainty (EC). As already suggested, the expectation–certainty corresponds to the desire of being able to estimate the reaction of the interaction partner. For this it is important, that the other agents reacted unambiguously to a symbol in the past. If each possible reaction takes place with same probability, then the consequences of an activity are not foreseeable. As a measurement for expectation–certainty we take the so called Shannon–entropy [22] from the field of information theory. In order to be able to determine the expectation–certainty for an activity a we take the vector x_a from our memory matrix X. This stores the frequency of all reactions plus the added forgetting constant r_{forget}. We normalise this vector and interpret its entries as probabilities for the possible reactions to activity a. So, the expectation–certainty for activity a is computed as

$$EC(a) = 1 + \sum_{i \in x_a} i \log_{|N|} i \quad . \tag{4}$$

This value is independent from action b the agent has to react to.

Calculation of the Expectation-Expectation (EE). By the inclusion of expectation–expectation agent A considers the own desire for certainty (as expectation) as well as the expectation of the other actors, agent A is interacting with.

Also this calculation is based on the agent's memory, in which agent A stores the reaction of the other agents to agent A's action. This leads to agent A's expectation, that the other agents expect the same reaction agent A expects from them[13].

Starting from the action b of the interaction partner the associated vector x_b gets normalised. Its entries $x_{b,a}$ are interpreted as the probability the interaction partner expects activity a:

$$EE_b(a) = x_{b,a} \quad . \tag{5}$$

Combination of Expectation-Certainty and Expectation-Expectation. The computed expectation–certainty EC and expectation–expectation EE for every possible action a now have to be combined to an action value AV. To which parts the single values enter the action value, is determined by a factor $\alpha \in [0, 1]$

$$AV_b(a) = (1 - \alpha) \cdot EE_b(a) + \alpha \cdot ES(a) + \epsilon \quad . \tag{6}$$

The small value ϵ is added in order to ensure that no action value becomes zero. If an action value becomes zero, this action won't be taken into consideration. Therefore we construct our model in a way that all symbols are always possible alternatives for the action selection. This corresponds to latent uncertainty of the agents mentioned above as an autocatalytic factor.

---

[13] If the computation is done on the Ego–memory (instead of the so called Alter–memory), which only serves for the storage of own reactions to other agents actions, then the agent acts in the same way, as it already did in its past as a reaction to the activities of the others.

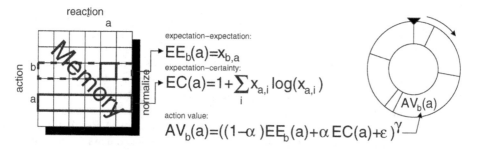

Fig. 1. This figure shows schematically the steps necessary to set the probability with which action a is chosen as reaction to symbol b.

Action Selection. Before the actual selection of the activity is done, all action values again will be taken to the power of γ and then be normalised. This proceeding makes a continuous transition possible between the random selection of actions ($\gamma = 0$), the proportional selection ($\gamma = 1$), and the maximising selection [14] ($\gamma \gg 1$). Finally, the action is selected proportionally to the action value exponentiated with γ. Figure 1 shows a summary of the single steps to the activity choice.

2.4   Observers

In our basic simulation model two agents interact with one another, who are selected randomly from the quantity of all agents. In addition, we are able to annul the anonymity of the interaction by permitting observers. These take part in interactions in the sense of participation, but not actively. So observers learn from the behaviour of the other agents.

3   Modeling General Actor Constellations

We place the agents into parameterised small–world networks[15]. The scientific origin of small–world networks goes back to an experiment of Milgram [29], who had discovered that two arbitrary persons in this world are separated on the average only by six other humans[16]. The question is, how "six degrees of separation" are possible. The graph–theoretical formulation of the problem reads: How can one connect several billion of vertices with edges, so that starting from any point A, one can reach any point B just by following the edges without more than six intermediate steps in average? The Hungarian mathematician Paul Erdös discovered, that independently of the number of

---

[14] For the relevance of the logic of selection for a sociological explanation see Esser [23,24].

[15] See [25,26,27,28], for an actual overview and further developments.

[16] Few years ago the German journal 'Die Zeit' had looked for the shortest connection of an Falafel–lunch–owner in Berlin with Marlon Brando. Not more than six intermediate steps were necessary. The New York Times repeated this play, that was called "Six Degrees of Monica" (Monica Lewinsky was meant) with the same result.

points a relatively small percentage of coincidentally distributed connections (edges) are sufficient in order to get a completely connected graph. And the larger the number of vertices becomes, the more this percentage is reduced. The problem her is, that social relations in a social world are not random. Family and friends do not represent random graphs. Here Granovetter [30] points out that there are not only strong but weak relations too, which can have a strong influence (for instance for job procurement). Weak relations could build social bridges[17].

Thus Granovetter shows that weak social relations can produce social structures with properties similar to small–world structures (job offers by acquaintances lead to small characteristic path lengths, while a circle of friends leads to high clustering). So Granovetter owes an explanation of the mechanism to create such structures, too. But how can we reconstruct such networks?

Here begins the work of Watts and Strogatz [31,32,33] , who have developed a model, which is suitable for the production of static small–world networks. We now present this model briefly and describe a little modification.

Dissatisfied with the fact that network topologies are modelled either as totally co-incidental or as completely arranged (regularly)[18], while most biological, technical, and also social networks [34,35] lie between these two extremes, Watts and Strogatz [31] have developed a model, which makes the interpolation between these two topologies possible. By doing so, structures develop with high clustering, comparably with the regular lattices, and with small characteristic path lengths, as can be found in random graphs. They call the developing structures small–world networks.

Starting point is a regular lattice with n vertices arranged in a circle. Everyone of those vertices is connected by k edges to $k/2$ vertices on the left and $k/2$ vertices on the right. This regular lattice is cyclically gone through $k/2$–times. First the edges to the direct circle neighbour of a side are rewritten with the probability p, i.e., the connection to the circle neighbour is solved and the regarded vertex is connected with any other vertex, it has not been connected to yet. In the following round the next circle neighbour is regarded and so on.

With this kind of the construction one receives the regular lattice for $p = 0$, for $p = 1$ a random graph. Watts and Strogatz are interested in the structural characteristics of nets with $0 < p < 1$, the range between order and randomness. Against p they investigate the characteristic path length[19] $L(p)$ as a global characteristic of the nets and the cluster coefficient[20] $C(p)$ as a local characteristic. It turned out that for a small

---

[17] Behind Granovetter's argument hides the picture of socialisation, which is characterised by strongly connected clusters, from which only few connections penetrate the cluster environment. This structure is an accumulation of complete graphs, in which each vertex is connected with each other vertex within the cluster, and in which only a few relations connect the different clusters. One can recognise the picture of society as an accumulation of autopoietic, structural coupled systems, too.

[18] Regular graphs are characterised by the fact that each vertex owns accurately the same number of edges. In contrast to this the edges are completely random within the random graph.

[19] The average path length of the shortest path between two vertices is called characteristic path length.

[20] The cluster coefficient is to quantitatively show the tendency for clustering. If k_i is the degree of a vertex i and $E_i \subseteq E$ is the set of the edges, which connect the vertices of its neigh-

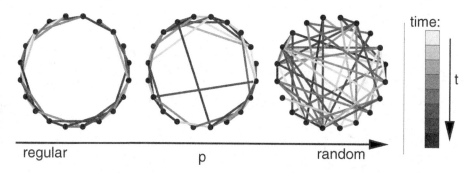

time:

t

regular   p   random

Fig. 2. Possible sequence of interactions depending on probability p for edge rewriting.

interval of p nets occur, whose characteristic path length $L(p)$ is comparable with those by random graphs, while the cluster coefficient $C(p)$ corresponds still approximately to that of the regular lattice. That is a characteristic, which is provable in many biological, technical, and social nets and which allows a high speed for signal propagation and synchronisation in dynamic systems.

We are of the opinion that in a small population, where no local separation exists, every agent is able to meet every other agent. But nevertheless preferences exist, which lead to small–world like constellations. This contrasts to Watts' and Strogatz' static modelling of small–world networks. Once the edge rewriting procedure is finished, possible connections are fixed.

For this reason we extended our model so that the interaction structure in one time period corresponds to a small–world network, however though each agent still has the possibility of interacting with every agent. On the basis of the original model by Watts/Strogatz we approximate that the probability $p(e_{xy})$ for the existence of an edge between the vertices x and y is proportional to

$$
p(e_{xy}) = \begin{cases} 1 - \beta \left(1 - \frac{p}{n-k)}\right)^{k-2d_{xy}+2} , & d_{xy} \leq k/2 \\ 1 - \left(1 - \frac{p}{n-k)}\right)^{k} , & \text{otherwise} \end{cases} \tag{7}
$$

The variables p, k and n have the same meaning as in the previous model. Within this model every agent can still interact with every other agent, but the probability to do so depends on its distance d_{xy} on the circle. The first of the two interacting agents is selected randomly, the probability of the second agent is proportional to $p(e_{xy})$. Observers are selected proportionally to the sum of both $p(e_{xy})$ values. For random agent constellations we use a pseudo random number generator. Figure 2 shows possible interactions between the agents located on a circle during a longer period of time, exemplary.

---

bourhood among each other, then its cluster coefficient amounts to $C_i = |E_i| / \binom{k_i}{2}$. This coefficient reflects the relationship between existing and possible edges in the neighbourhood. The average of the coefficient of all vertices is the cluster coefficient of the graph.

4   Measures of Order

Before we present the results, we first explain our measure of order. It might have become clear that it concerns the achieved order, but how can order be measured? Sociology offers only few concrete references (for an overview see [36,37]). According to these we suggest two measures[21], with which we measure the order achieved.

4.1   Systemic Integration

A rather macroscopic measure of order is *systemic integration*. It represents the certainty of the "average agent"

$$\overline{C}(b) = 1 + \sum_{\forall a \in N} \overline{AV_b}(a) \cdot \log_{|N|} \overline{AV_b}(a) \ . \tag{8}$$

reacting to a symbol b weighted by the frequency $p(b)$ with which this symbol is used in the past. This leads to a systemic integration of

$$I = \sum_{\forall b \in N} \overline{C}(b) \cdot p(b) \ . \tag{9}$$

4.2   Weighted Systemic Integration

Obviously it is easy to achieve a high systemic integration in systems if the number of factually communicated symbols has been reduced to two or three after a while. To uprate highly integrated systems and a large number of symbols we weight the systemic integration with the number of communicated symbols in the preceding time interval. In other words: the *weighted systemic integration* of a system A is higher than the *weighted systemic integration* of a system B if both systems have the same systemic integration but system A is able to cope with a higher contingency (larger number of symbols) at the same time.

5   Results

Table 2 shows the settings of the parameters described above.

We measure systemic order for different population sizes in the three described agent constellations (random, small–world network, regular). Starting with a population size of 64 agents we double the number of agents three times. We choose the simulation

---

[21] We have tested and used further measures in other places, e.g. reduction. We counted the number of different symbols, which were selected in a certain time interval by the agents. The smaller the number of selected symbols, the larger the achieved *reduction* of the agents, and the larger the order. This is a macroscopic order perspective. *Certainty* is a microscopic measure for the emergence of order measuring the certainty of the agents over actions selected by them. A high value represents high certainty and thus a high degree of order. To calculate certainty we use the entropy over all normalised action values of possible actions in reaction to symbol b.

Parameter	Value	Parameter	Value
number of agents	64–512	number of symbols $|N|$	50
weight α (EE–EC)	0.5	selection exponent γ	2
avg. nr. of time steps per agent	5.000	interactions per step	5
neighbourhood k	6	observer	2
forget rate r_{forget}	10^{-3}		
$p_{regular} = 0$		$p_{SWN} = 0.1$	

Table 2. Parameter settings used in our simulation runs.

duration such that every agent in average actively takes part in 5000 interactions. This means that we simulate 160.000 steps for a population size of 64 agents, 320.000 steps for a population size of 128 agents, 640.000 steps for a population size of 256 agents, and we simulate 1.280.000 steps for a population of 512 agents. We carried out 30 runs for each combination of population size and agent constellation and describe the average results. Figure 3 shows the dependency between the average weighted systemic order at the end of simulation and the number of agents for all three constellations.

As you can see, no order originates within large populations within a random constellation. Nevertheless, order rises for smaller populations sizes. The random constellation differs from all the others inasmuch as emerging order is *here* a time–consuming task. Figure 4, showing the time dependent emergence of order for different constellations with 128 agents, clarifies this fact. Agents within such a random constellation minimise the number of communicated symbols. This leads to a higher certainty in choosing a reaction because factually fewer symbols come into question. This simplifies the creation of order. High systemic order with many symbols is possible, too, and we have to rate this order differently than systemic order arising from a reduced number of symbols. For that reason we weight systemic order with the number of used symbols, as mentioned above.

Past research [38,21] shows that emergence of order in random constellations is not only a time consuming task but also happens only if the system is not perturbed or perturbation is low. This condition is fulfilled here.

If you compare weighted systemic order of random and other constellations while scaling up agent population size, you see that order emerges in regular and small–world constellations; even though it decreases for larger populations. Thereby you find higher order within small–worlds in comparison to regular structures.

The main aggregation affect we concentrate on is the emergence of order in large agent populations for *some* constellations. We ascribe this to the vision range of the agents. While agents in regular constellations only interact with their neighbourhood, agents in small–world constellations primarily but not exclusively interact with their neighbourhood, whereas in random constellations agents choose their interaction partner arbitrarily.

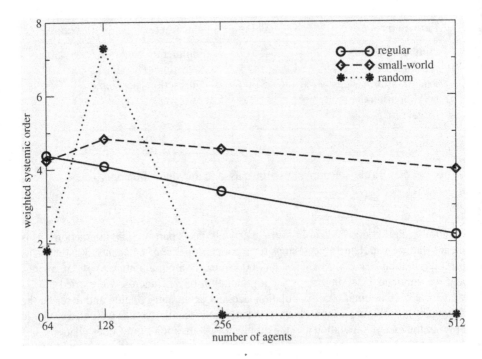

Fig. 3. Average systemic order of 30 independent runs for regular, random and small–world constellations and four different population sizes. We connect the measure points for optical reasons.

The agents have no possibility to shape individual expectations at all, so their expectations refer to a "generalised agent"[22] in populations with $N > 2$. The word "generalised" denotes, that the agents expect, the other agents react like the average of all agents they gained experience with before (through interaction or observation).

Expectations towards such a generalised interaction partner are build up in the memory of all agents. This happens to agents within a neighbourhood of regular or small–world networks on the base of comparable experiences, so their expectations equalise in the course of time. From a sociological point of view a mutual fulfilment of (expectation-) expectations evolves.

By increasing the size of the neighbourhood the process of adaptation is getting more difficult. Or to restate this sociologically: By increasing the size of "community", "collective consciousness" (*Kollektivbewusstsein*) gets lost. We think of "collective consciousness" as the ability to adapt expectations and (expectation-) expectations. Within random constellations there is no neighbourhood in the narrower sense because agents may interact with every other random agent. The process of adaptation is difficult right from the beginning. Scaling up populations size makes it difficult to build up expecta-

---

[22] The generalised agent is understood in the sense of a "generalised other" in terms of George Herbert Mead [39] as the sum of expectations of all, which are relevant in a certain situation.

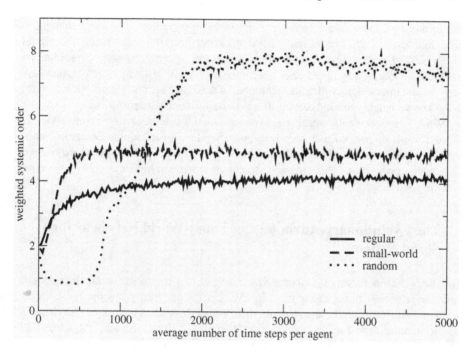

Fig. 4. Emergence of order in regular, small–world and random constellations with 128 agents. Albeit order in random constellations is heigh at the end, it is a time consuming task.

tions by mutual adaptation. In random constellations all properties have global effects. For this reason populations in this kind of structure show a high degree of order if population size allows a gradual convergence, or they do not show any order at all.

As you can see further, with raising numbers of agents systems with regular constellations have a lower degree of weighted systemic order than systems with small–world networks. We call this effect *scaling resistance* of small–world agent constellations and attribute this effect to the small characteristic path length of small–world networks. Remember, that for systemic order the question of how certain an agent reacts to an action plays an important role. To restate this question: Does the agent know the expectations to its action and is it able to expect the reaction of its interaction partner?

Expectations evolve from interaction. Thereby, because of the concept of generalisation mentioned above, interactions with neighbours (or other previous interaction partners) of an agent could have been sufficient to built up expectations that correspond with the behaviour of the agent. In our small–world constellations, arbitrary agents are able to interact with each other. With a low probability these could be distant agents. So agents do not only build up expectations towards the interaction partner, but also towards their generalised neighbourhood. Therefore (after this interaction) the agent is able to live up the expectations of a distant part of the population better than before and furthermore these agents better live up to their expectations. The agent changes its behaviour and so carries these newly build up expectations into its own neighbourhood.

For sure, the adaptation of expectations also happens in regular agent constellations. But here two interacting agents have a big intersection within their past interaction partners. So just interactions with a small number of unknown agents (agents not belonging to the known neighbourhood) benefit from the adjustment of expectations.

While, metaphorically speaking, expectations towards behaviour at the "back of beyond" must be handed over step by step in regular constellations, agents in small–world constellations benefit from the facility to adapt their expectations towards distant parts of the population. Thus, in such structured systems a higher degree of systemic order is possible.

6   The Evolutionary Advantage of Small-World Networks for Social Systems

The thesis that increasing population size can lead to a change of social structures, is common in sociology for a long time. In 1893 Durkheim already saw the cause for the development from simple, segmentarily differentiated societies to complex, division of labour organised societies in a mechanism, that almost drives the actors to specialisation, so that these — as unintended consequence [40] — build up new social structures.

According to Durkheim this unintended aggregation effect is attributed to an increasing population in a limited area and the social density developing from it: "If the society comprehends more individuals which are in close contact at the same time, then the effect [of increasing division of labour] follows necessarily." [41]. Increased social density leads to increased competition. Specialisation by division of labour, so Durkheim referring to Darwin, decreases the competition pressure. Specialisation is the mechanism for occupying ecological niches of the social competition — at least if the demand for relevant resources is smaller at the same time than their offer, and there are no other possibilities to escape the competition. We do not want to examine the plausibility of Durkheim's threads here. We only want to state this as an indication that sociology has seen the increase of population in a quite prominent place as a cause for important changes of social structure within the framework of social development (social evolution).[23]

---

[23] It seems that Durkheim [41] implicitly thought of small–world networks while describing the social–structural changes. He said that the disbandment of segmentary society, which is characterised by high individuality and demarcation of social segments (thus high clustering), leads to the fact that an "interchange of movements between the parts of the social mass, which had not affected each other till then", develops. Thereby the social system "generalises" itself, it will be, we would say today, more global. "The social relations [...] therefore becomes more numerous because they diffuse to all sides over their original borders. Thus the division of labour more and more progresses, the more individuals there are, who keep in touch sufficiently, in order to be able to interact". Durkheim also calls this "dynamical density". Finally, society organised by division of labour is the result of the scaling of the population and the increasing dynamic density: "The division of labour changes in direct relation to the volume and for the density of the societies; thus if it constantly progresses in the course of the social

At this point, we want to ask the question, if small–world structures are the (inescapable?) result of an evolutionary process. Thereby we do not want to describe the single step of evolution, but rather concentrate on those forces, which, as a selection criteria, put pressure on communities and maybe contribute to the establishment of small–world structures. We take advantage of knowing the result of the evolutionary process — small–world structures. Results presented here and in early research let us conclude the reasons, that lead to the establishment of small–world networks.

First, we want to make some assumptions. Our starting point is a regular structure: a multitude of self–contained sets of individuals. Sociologically, we want to interpret them as communities like they occur in real world as families, tribes, or prides. We do not want to take into account how these closed communities arise, for sure another evolutionary process leads to them. In fact many higher life–forms live in such communities, e.g. lactation forces the instantaneous integration of all newborn mammals into a community (see also Kron [42]). We further assume that the territories of communities are not spatially separated, but individuals can meet individuals of other communities, even if they do not want to. In the end, we assume that the encounter of two individuals of different communities can have repercussions to their communities, if the meeting individuals do not have expectations of the behaviour of the other individual (see Münch [43] for this assumption as a starting point of social differentiation). Moreover, we assume in terms of methodological individualism, that each community is finally based on its members. Without extraneous causes — evolution shall be the only force here — the individuals on the one side produce certain characteristics of communities, i.e. certain social structures. On the other side, it's the community forming the action, which penalises its members — if the community is evolutionarily unfit for example. From this point of view, also evolution considers the "duality of action and structure" [44].

The previous assumptions suggest, why the regular starting structures do not endure. Expectation must not inevitably arise from the encounter of two individuals from different communities. Rather than this we can assume, that both individuals mutually guess "bad" motives (see [42,45]), even though they are well disposed to the other. This situation can be harmless, but it also can lead to disadvantages for one or both of the interacting individuals. In this case individuals take advantage of making expectations out of their experiences because these expectations can minimise the disadvantages (e.g., getting killed). It is sufficient if the sow turns tail and runs expecting to become eaten.

After getting clear that expectations can be an advantage, there are two possibilities how individuals can obtain those expectations. Firstly, individuals can form those expectations on the basis of *subjective* experiences, i.e. of their own life story. Or, secondly, those expectations can be imparted *collectively* within the community [24]. We assume here, that these expectations have to be made in lifetime because they are, e.g., too fugacious to emerge by evolution.

Let us look at the first possibility that every individual forms expectations based on subjective experiences. This possibility does not appear to be optimal because the

---

development, so because the societies became regularly more closely and more extensive in general" [41].

[24] This differentiation is purely analytical, whose components empirically should often be inseparably aligned.

primary situations, in which expectations can be formed, can involve the mentioned disadvantages. But even if such situations would always end positively for the participating individuals, it needs plenty of time until all individuals of all communities have formed their expectations. And in fact we have surveyed that the formation of order in random constellations is a longsome process. The situations get worse with increasing variety, which is equivalent to a large population in our model. The reason for the total breakdown in our simulation should be the restricted cognitive capacity of our agents, modelled by the forgetting. But even for *real* actors this is not an improper assumption (the authors speak from their own experiences).

The second possibility is, that every individual of a community forms expectations towards a few individuals outside of the community, and import these expectations to the own community. Thereby it is not important how these expectations are passed on, if by communication, or — as in our case — by mutual observation, so that it changes its behaviour because of adapted expectations. We have modelled this with the small-world constellation. This constellation shows construction efficiency in respect to (information propagation) performance and is the most economic constellation[46] tested here. Agents only occasionally interact with other agents outside of their neighbour-hood/community. Their expectations, which are adapted by the interaction with other agents, are put forth in their own neighbourhood by a modified behaviour. We can observe that in this constellation there is a very rapid formation of order, and that this order is also approximately achieved in a scaling population. Furthermore, this constellation has been proved as very robust against interferences.

We interpret the fact, that expectation structures are able to form a high ordering first of all in those actor constellations, which are already identified in existing communities, as a first indication of their importance.

7   Conclusion and Outlook

Starting from the problem of double contingency following the "classical" definitions by Parsons and Luhmann, it is shown how social order emerges in scaling actor constellations. For this we augment the "simple" coordination–situation with the dimension of different actor constellations (random, regular/neighbourhood, small–world). The main result is that small–world networks evidently have a specific meaning in the formation phase of a social system. In the linear degeneration of small–world actor constellations, while scaling up the degree of actors, you can also see that these are less fragile than other constellations. Finally, we reason that small–world actor constellations are significant in the evolutionary process of social systems (especially if you take into account that small–world networks seem to be very resistant against interferences [38]) and have to be recognised in the explanation of the emergence of social order in scaling actor constellations.

We believe that small–world structures are not only in real world social systems of particular importance, but also in many other systems in which an appropriate ratio of robustness and adaptivity is needed to let a local convergence follow a global convergence.

Multi–agent systems seem to be predestined to profit from constellations similar to small–world networks because they are modelled on social systems based on division of labour.[25] They could take profit of small–worlds in such areas, where mutual adaption by communication and/or observation is needed, while the agents are intransparent otherwise. Adapting the communication system is a promising field here (see [47]).

Acknowledgement

This research was funded by a grant to Wolfgang Banzhaf (BA 1042/7-3) and a grant to Uwe Schimank (Schi 553/1-3) within the DFG program "Sozionik". The authors would like to thank Oliver Flasch, Markus Friese, Frank Rossdeutscher and Lars Winter for proof–reading this article and coding the "Luhmann Simulator".

References

1. Schimank, U.: Handeln und Strukturen. Juventa, Weinheim (2000)
2. Esser, H.: Soziologie. Spezielle Grundlagen. Band 3: Soziales Handeln. Campus, Frankfurt/Main, New York (2000)
3. Hobbes, T.: Leviathan. In Molesworth, W., ed.: Collected English Works of Thomas Hobbes. Volume 3. Taylor and Francis Books Ltd., Aalen (1966, first edn. 1651)
4. Smith, A.: The Wealth of Nations. Oxford Pniversity Press (1985, first edn. 1904)
5. Durkheim, E.: De la division du travail social. Presses Universitaires de France, Paris (1968, first edn. 1893)
6. Parsons, T.: The Structure of Social Action. Free Press, New York (1937)
7. Parsons, T.: The System of Modern Society. Englewood Cliffs (1971)
8. Axelrod, R.: The Evolution of Cooperation. Basic Books, New York (1984)
9. Simmel, G.: Soziologie. Untersuchungen über die Formen der Vergesellschaftung. Suhrkamp, Frankfurt/Main (1992, first edn. 1908)
10. Schimank, U.: Theorien gesellschaftlicher Differenzierung. Leske + Budrich, Opladen (1996)
11. Parsons, T.: Social interaction. In Sills, D.L., ed.: International Encyclopedia of the Social Sciences. Volume 7. MacMillan, New York (1968) 429–441
12. Parsons, T.: The Social System. Free Press, New York (1951)
13. Münch, R.: The American Creed in Sociological Theory: Exchange, Negotiated Order, Accommodated Individualism and Contingency. Sociological Theory 4 (1986) 41–60
14. Luhmann, N.: Soziale Systeme. Grundriß einer allgemeinen Theorie. Suhrkamp, Frankfurt/Main (1984)
15. Schimank, U.: Gesellschaftliche Teilsysteme als Akteurfiktionen. Kölner Zeitschrift für Soziologie und Sozialpsychologie 4 (1988) 619–639
16. Schimank, U.: Erwartungssicherheit und Zielverfolgung. Sozialität zwischen Prisoner's Dilemma und Battle of the Sexes. Soziale Welt 2 (1992) 182–200
17. Leydesdorff, L.: "Structure" / "Action" Contingencies and the Model of Parallel Processing. Journal for the Theory of Social Behaviour 23 (1993) 47–77

---

[25] But also in many other fields of computer science, where the influence of structure is just observed in its extreme value — regular and random — networks, could be interesting research areas for small–world networks.

18. Papendick, S., Wellner, J.: Symbolemergenz und Strukturdifferenzierung. In Kron, T., ed.: Luhmann modelliert. Sozionische Ansätze zur Simulation von Kommunikationssystemen. Leske + Budrich, Opladen (2002) 175–208
19. Dittrich, P., Kron, T., Banzhaf, W.: On the Scalability of Social Order. Modeling the Problem of Double and Multi Contingency Following Luhmann. Journal of Artificial Societies and Social Simulation **6** (2003) http://jasss.soc.surrey.ac.uk/6/1/3.html.
20. Kron, T., Dittrich, P.: Doppelte Kontingenz nach Luhmann – Ein Simulationsexperiment. In Kron, T., ed.: Luhmann modelliert. Ansätze zur Simulation von Kommunikationssystemen. Leske + Buderich, Opladen, Germany (2002) 209 – 251
21. Lasarczyk, C.W.G., Kron, T.: Globale Kohärenz in sozialen Systemen. In Burkhard, H.D., Uthmann, T., Lindemann, G., eds.: Modellierung und Simulation menschlichen Verhaltens. Volume 163 of Informatik Berichte. Humboldt–Universität zu Berlin, Berlin (2003) 77–91
22. Shannon, C.E.: A Mathematical Theory of Communication. Bell System Technical Journal **27** (1948) 379–423, 623–656
23. Esser, H.: Soziologie. Allgemeine Grundlagen. Suhrkamp, Frankfurt/Main, New York (1993)
24. Esser, H.: Soziologie. Spezielle Grundlagen. Bd. 1: Situationslogik und Handeln. Campus, Frankfurt/Main, New York (1999)
25. Barabási, A.L.: Linked. (Perseus Books Group, Cambridge, Massachusetts (2002)
26. Buchanan, M.: Nexus: Small Worlds and the Groundbreaking Science of Networks. (W.W.Norton & Co., New York) (2002)
27. Watts, D.J.: Six Degrees: The Science of a Connected Age. W. W. Norton & Company, New York (2003)
28. Newmann, M.E.J.: Models of the Small World. Journal of Statistical Physics **101** (2000) 819–841
29. Milgram, S.: The Small–World Problem. Psychology Today **1** (1967) 60–67
30. Granovetter, M.: The Strengh of Weak Ties. American Journal of Sociology **78** (1973) 1360–1380
31. Watts, D.J., Strogatzith, S.H.: Collective Dynamics of 'Small-World' Networks. Nature **393** (1998) 440–442
32. Watts, D.J.: Networks, Dynamics and The Small World Phenomenon. American Journal of Sociology **105** (1999) 493–527
33. Watts, D.J.: Small-Worlds. The Dynamics of networks between Order and Randomness. Princeton University–Press, Princeton, NJ (1999)
34. Amaral, L.A.N.: Classes of small-world networks. In: Proc. Natl. Acad. Sci. Volume 97., USA (2000) 11149–11152
35. Erickson, B.: Social Networks: the Value of Variety. Contexts **2** (2003) 25–31
36. Greshoff, R., Kneer, G.: Struktur und Ereignis in theorievergleichender Perspektive. Westdeutscher, Opladen, Wiesbaden (1999)
37. Reckwitz, A.: Struktur. Zur sozialwissenschaftlichen Analyse von Regeln und Regelmäßigkeiten. Westdeutscher, Opladen (1997)
38. Kron, T., Lasarczyk, C.W.G., Schimank, U.: Zur Bedeutung von Netzwerken für Kommunikationssysteme – Ergebnisse einer Simulationsstudie. Zeitschrift für Soziologie **32** (2003)
39. Mead, G.H.: Geist, Identität und Gesellschaft. Suhrkamp, Frankfurt/Main (1973)
40. Merton, R.K.: The Unanticipated Consequences of Purposive Social Action. American Sociological Review **6** (1936) 894–904
41. Durkheim, E.: Über soziale Arbeitsteilung. Studie über die Organisation höherer Gesellschaften. Suhrkamp, Frankfurt/Main (1992)
42. Kron, T.: Moralische Individualität. Leske + Budrich, Opladen (2001)
43. Münch, R.: Dialektik der Kommunikationsgesellschaft. Suhrkamp, Frankfurt/Main (1991)

44. Giddens, A.: The Constitution of Society. Polity Press, Cambridge (1984)
45. Lepperhoff, N.: Dreamscape: Simulation der Entstehung von Normen im Naturzustand mittels eines computerbasierten Modells des Rational-Choice-Ansatzes. Zeitschrift für Soziologie **29** (2000) 463–486
46. Latora, V., Marchiori, M.: Economic small–world behavior in weighted networks. The European Physical Journal B **32** (2003) 249–263
47. Steels, L.: The spontaneous self-organization of an adaptive language. In Muggleton, S., ed.: Machine Intelligence 15. Oxford University Press, Oxford, UK (1996)

From Conditional Commitments to Generalized Media: On Means of Coordination Between Self-Governed Entities

Ingo Schulz-Schaeffer

Technische Universität Berlin
Institut für Soziologie
Franklinstr. 28/29, Sekr FR 2-5, 10587 Berlin, Germany
schulz-schaeffer@tu-berlin.de

Abstract. In the absence of pre-established coordination structures, what can a self-governed entity—i.e. an entity that chooses on its own between its possible actions and cannot be controlled externally—do to evoke another self-governed entity's cooperation? In this paper, the motivating conditional self-commitment is conceived to be the basic mechanism to solve coordination problems of this kind. It will be argued that such commitments have an inherent tendency to become more and more generalized and institutionalised. The sociological concept of generalized symbolic media is reinterpreted as a concept that focuses on this point. The conceptual framework resulting from the considerations is applicable to coordination problems between human actors as well as to coordination problems between artificial agents in open multi-agent systems. Thus, it may help to transfer solutions from one realm to the other.

1 Introduction

Coordination is the central theme for multi-agent research (cf. [1, p. VIII]). The key problem in this research area centres around ensuring coordination between agents (cf. [2, p. 187]). This problem is caused by the basic characteristics of agents: autonomy and pro-activeness. According to a well-known definition, agents are "hardware or (more usually) software-based computer system(s)" (ibid.) with at least these two properties: They operate autonomously "without the direct intervention of humans or others, and have some kind of control over their actions and internal state" (ibid.). And they function pro-actively, meaning that they "do not simply act in response to their environment", but "are able to exhibit goal-directed behaviour by *taking the initiative*" (ibid.). Humans in important respects can also be considered autonomous and pro-active entities and human societies have accumulated some thousand years of experience confronting coordination problems relating to autonomy and pro-activeness. Therefore, it is a promising idea to develop inter-agent coordination in analogy to forms of human interaction, which have proved to be successful.

However, to avoid that this analogy remains only metaphorical, we need to develop sufficiently precise concepts to define the common ground from which coordination in human as well as in agent interaction may evolve. In this paper, a general framework

K. Fischer, M. Florian, and T. Malsch (Eds.): Socionics, LNAI 3413, pp. 218–241, 2005.
© Springer-Verlag Berlin Heidelberg 2005

for dealing with coordination problems between self-governed entities will be provided. The basic suggestion is to conceive the initial situation of double contingency between self-governed entities, whose only means to affect others' behaviour is to make commitments, as this common basis. This paper will show how conditional commitments can be employed by an entity to motivate another self-governed entity into responding cooperatively. Yet, this solution contains many restrictions. In adapting the concept of generalized symbolic media of interaction (or communication) to the problem of coordination, the emergence of generalized and institutionalised forms of commitments will be introduced as a means to overcome some of these restrictions. However, we will see that this general framework does not apply to closed multi-agent systems, since under the condition of closed systems less elaborate ways to deal with coordination problems are available and sufficient. On the other hand, it is all the more important with respect to coordination problems in open multi-agent systems. Here, the analogy based on the common ground assumption works pretty well. In conclusion, I point out to the need for extending the analogy to hybrid systems.

2 Coordination in the Face of Double Contingency: Motivating Conditional Commitments

In the absence of given coordination rules or procedures, self-governed entities—i.e. entities that choose on their own between their possible actions—face a particular coordination problem when they aim to mutually adjusting their actions. This problem is defined by the initial situation of double contingency. Talcott Parsons and collaborators describe this situation with respect to two entities, ego and alter, as follows: "On the one hand ego's gratifications are contingent on his selection among available alternatives. But in turn, alter's reaction will be contingent on ego's selection and will result from a complementary selection on alter's part." ([3, p. 16]). First of all, the behaviour of both parties involved is contingent on their own selections. Moreover, if alter is part of ego's relevant environment and vice versa—that is, part of the environment the respective entity takes into account when choosing its own behaviour—then one entity's selections are contingent on the selections of the other one. Thus, from the perspective of ego—the entity that wants to start a sequence of coordinated interaction—the situation of double contingency implies a double uncertainty: Ego does not know which behaviour to choose because it does not know which behaviour alter will choose in reaction to its action.

With respect to the goal of achieving coordination, the double uncertainty that accompanies situations of double contingency leads to a deadlock. If coordination is defined as establishing situations where two or more entities select their actions in a suitable way to commonly produce certain results, then the effect of this double uncertainty is to prevent coordinated behaviour.[1] Hence, deadlock can only be broken through re-

---

[1] As I will argue below, the coordination problem resulting from the situation of double contingency is not only a problem of harmonizing actions with respect to common or complimentary goals but at first a problem of establishing common or complimentary goals. For this reason, I use the term coordination in a much broader sense than it is used, for example, by Esser ([4, p. 59-71]).

ducing uncertainty. At least the behaviour of one entity must become predictable to a certain degree so the other entity can rely on it while choosing its behaviour. However, one has to remember that we are dealing with self-governed entities. This means only the respective entity itself can make its own behaviour predictable. For a self-governed entity, the only means to do so is through self-commitment. For example, ego may announce:[2] "I commit myself to perform the action P every time I will be in the situation S." From alter's point of view such a self-commitment on the part of ego may or may not be useful: Alter will welcome ego's commitment if ego's action P contributes to what alter wants to achieve in the situation S. But as long as ego makes its commitment under the condition of uncertainty about alter's selections it is more probable that for alter this action P is without use.

From ego's point of view, an even more crucial problem is that this commitment does not—or only by chance—makes alter cooperate with respect to ego's goals. Let us assume that ego is interested in the result produced by the combination of its action P and alter's action Q in the situation S. By fulfilling the self-commitment ego will do its part to bring about this result. But so far there is no reason why this commitment should enhance the probability of alter to react by performing the action Q. Consequently, ego runs the risk of constantly investing resources (by performing action P each time situation S comes around) without achieving its desired results. Upon reflection, ego may avoid this useless waste of resources by narrowing the self-commitment as follows: "I commit myself to perform action P in situation S on condition that you, alter, perform action Q."[3] Does such a conditional commitment solve the coordination problem? The answer is yes, but only if alter as well as ego is interested in the results stemming from the combination of actions P and Q. In this case, if alter estimates ego to be trustworthy, it will perform action Q followed (if this estimation was appropriate) by ego's action P. But without such coinciding interests, again, alter is not inclined to cooperate.

As long as the entities involved cannot rely on given coincidences of interests, there is only one way to solve the remaining coordination problem: by producing such coincidences. But since a self-governed entity can affect the behaviour of other self-governed entities only by making commitments, producing coinciding interests has to be achieved by making commitments. Thus, the general strategy towards producing coinciding interests lies in ego to commit itself to act in the interests of alter (or to commit itself to refrain from acting against alter's interests) on condition that alter does something ego is interested in (or refrains from acting against ego's interests). Let us assume that ego is interested in alter's action Q (which in combination with ego's continued actions will lead to a result it aims at) and that ego has reasons to believe that alter may be interested in its action P (which is, as we as godlike observers of the scene know, an appropriate assumption, since ego's action P in combination with alter's further actions will lead to a result alter aims at). By announcing: "I commit myself to perform action

---

[2] To simplify matters I will assume that the entities in question are able to use a common language. This is obviously a nontrivial assumption. But since the problem at hand is not how a common understanding between self-governed entities can occur but the problem of their coordination, this simplification seems to be justified.

[3] Or if action P has to be performed first: "I commit myself to perform action P in situation S on condition that you, alter, commit yourself to perform action Q."

P on condition that you perform action Q." ego not only makes its own behaviour more predictable to alter but at the same time it tries to make alter's behaviour more predictable to itself. That is, the self-commitment now aims at reducing uncertainty from both sides of the double contingency problem. This is done by transforming the initial situation where only ego has an interest in alter to act in a specific way into a situation where alter has also an interest to act in this way, namely the interest in thereby bringing about ego's action P. And even though ego and alter's interests in alter's action Q are different, they are now coinciding interests in the sense that both parties are interested in alter performing action Q.

However, a number of preconditions have to be met so that such a self-commitment will work as described. First of all, ego requires certain resources at its disposal, resources allowing ego to change the situation in question to alter's advantage or disadvantage (and the same applies to alter with respect to the resources required to meet ego's condition). Second, ego needs sufficiently reliable knowledge about alter's interests. Otherwise ego would not know how to use its resources to alter's advantage or disadvantage. Lastly, alter needs to trust ego's commitment towards the intended action. Alter will only be motivated to react accordingly when alter places confidence in ego's promised behaviour. None of this preconditions is trivial. Ego may or may not possess the resources necessary for motivating alter (and alter may or may not possess the resources required to adopt ego's proposal). And, in the positive case, ego may not know enough about alter's interests to employ its resources successfully. Even when ego holds the relevant resources at its disposal and knows how to motivate alter through the resources, alter could doubt ego's commitment, rendering ego's resources and knowledge useless. As we will see, all these preconditions push towards standardizing, generalizing, and institutionally framing such motivating conditional commitments to become more efficient means of coordination.

3   The General Framework as an Intermediary

When speaking about self-governed entities in the preceding section, I have avoided to specify the nature of the entities I have in mind. So far, I have only defined the entities as those able to choose between possible actions on their own. Speaking about possible actions implies that these entities have certain resources at their disposal that enable them to act in one or another way. The term "action" is only meant to designate a change in the entity's or its environment's state brought about by this entity. The preceding considerations also imply that these entities have interests in the sense that their self-governed behaviour is directed at the attainment or avoidance of certain future states of affairs; that they are able to make plans that include actions on the part of other entities in order to realize or prevent these future states; that to this end they are able to reflect on their own interests as well as on the presumptive interests of other entities; that they are able to employ the concept of self-commitment; and that all interaction takes place under the rule of double contingency, meaning that no given structures guide the interaction.

Defining the initial situation in this way, the main intention was to choose a level of abstraction suitable to serve as a point of departure for dealing with both the problem of coordination between human actors (or corporative actors) as well as with the problem of coordination between autonomous software agents. Moreover, this general framework is intended to act as an intermediary between both realms of coordination problems. To this end it has been conceptualised so as to lie in between both of them. That is, some aspects apply more to human actors than to software agents. For example, pursuing interests and reflecting on presumptive interests of others are properties we usually assume an average competent human actor to possess. In contrast, software agents must first be programmed to possess any capabilities. But today certain agent architectures exist, especially the so called BDI agent architectures (cf. [5]; [6]), that allow for implementing agents, which approximately show such properties. Hence, the assumptions in this respect are not altogether unrealistic.

On the other hand, some aspects of the general framework more appropriately describe the properties of software agents than those of human actors. This is the case with the absence of given structures. Since any structure guiding the agents' interaction must be pre-programmed by the designers of the respective multi-agent system, at first no structures exist that reduce the double contingency problem. Human actors, in contrast, grow up within given societies. From the individual's point of view the society is prior to him or her (cf. [7]). Thus, there are always given social structures (cf. [8]) reducing double contingency and possibly serving as coordination mechanisms. But if we are interested in understanding how such coordination mechanisms once came into existence and since we have all reasons to believe that they are constantly at risk to newly emerging uncertainties, our general framework seems to be a (to a certain degree counterfactual but nonetheless) useful point of departure for analysing the problem of coordination between human actors, too.

4   Motivating Conditional Commitments in Human Interaction

In the following section, I will apply the general framework to the problem of coordination between human actors. I shall counterfactually assume a situation of pure double contingency with respect to coordination issues within a certain population of human actors. In the absence of any pre-established coordination mechanisms, how may one actor (ego) gain another actor's (alter's) cooperation by means of motivating conditional commitments?

One way is to draw upon physical strength as a resource (or upon resources enhancing ego's capabilities to use physical force, such as weapons or other actors ready to fight under ego's command) and to threaten to use it to alter's disadvantage. A respective self-commitment could run as follows: "I commit myself to harm you, unless you obey my orders." If, according to alter's estimation, ego possesses the resources required to make his threat come true (i.e. physical strength or additional resources superior to his own), if alter believes ego will really use them accordingly, if alter possesses the resources required to obey, and if the threatened harm from the point of view of alter is more unfavourable than his obedience, then there is a good chance that alter will choose to obey, so that ego's self-commitment will result in alter's cooperation.

But perhaps ego wants to avoid the risk of alter's retaliation. He or she may be unsure of the own strength compared to alter's or may not see the coordination issue as worth the risk at all. Under these circumstances ego might prefer to motivate alter's cooperation by offering resources in return. Correspondingly, ego could announce: "I commit myself to place certain of my resources at your disposal on condition that you transfer certain of your resources to me." Again, if alter believes that ego really possesses the offered resources and trusts in his or her self-commitment, if alter has the resources at his disposal demanded by ego, and if from the point of view of alter getting those resources of ego serves his interests better than not giving away those resources of his own, then there is a good chance that alter will accept ego's proposal.

However, there are coordination problems of considerable relevance to human actors, which can not easily be solved by exchanging resources or by threat of force. This is the case when coordination requires participants to share common (or complementary) orientations. For example, if ego happens to be attracted to alter, much of their future interaction will depend on whether or not alter comes to feel the same. Or, if ego counts on alter to feel morally obliged to respond to him or her in a certain way, the participants' moral agreement is the basis for their coordination. Otherwise, the coordination rests on alter accepting as true, what ego holds to be true. Even though in these three cases the common (or complementary) orientations are different with respect to their content: truth, values or affective attitudes, the basic coordination problem is the same: To establish a certain kind of common or complementary orientations as a precondition of coordination.

Let us assume a situation without pre-established normative orientations—Parsons' solution to the problem of double contingency (cf. [9, p. 148-151])—and without any other given social structure that might help to solve the coordination problem at hand (such as common knowledge or common affective attitudes). Thus, ego's request to adopt a certain aspect of his world view poses a problem to alter. Even if alter is sufficiently confident to gain his share of a successful cooperation based on his adoption of ego's orientation (this will be a necessary subject of ego's self-commitment), he can not know whether or not he is well advised at all to follow ego's suggestions. Therefore, ego has all reasons to try to convince alter of the truth of his assertions, the moral rightness of his convictions or the veracity of his feelings (you will have recognized the three Habermasian validity claims of communicative action, cf. [10, p. 410-427, Vol. I]).

To achieve this, self-commitments unfortunately are of limited help, since ego's statements are only subjective whereas alter should prefer to obtain objective information. Nevertheless, there is one thing ego by means of self-commitments can do: Demonstrating alter his persuasion concerning the truth, rightness or veracity of his suggestions by committing himself to bear the consequences following from them. With respect to claims of truth this means for ego to commit himself to assume responsibility for the reliability of his assertions, e.g. to commit himself to compensating alter for damages that may occur if his knowledge turns out to have been unreliable. In doing so, ego places a kind of a bet on the reliability of his assertions, thereby disclosing the degree to which he himself is convinced (a strategy already recommended by Kant to assess a person's subjective persuasion, cf. [11, p. B 849f.]; [12]). Under the condition that there is no other way to verify ego's assertions, such a commitment may serve as an auxiliary proof and motivate alter to adopt them. With respect to moral convictions, ego can demonstrate to alter his own persuasion by committing himself to obey to the values he wants to establish and, additionally, by committing himself to treat alter as if he, too, was subject to them. If ego believably exemplifies his moral convictions through his own behaviour and if alter for whatever reasons has an interest in being deemed to be a respectable person according to ego's moral standards, self-commitments of this kind may enhance the chance of alter to adopt ego's convictions. And with respect to feelings of relatedness, affection, and solidarity all ego can do is to make self-commitments to the effect that he will act according to those feelings, hoping thus to motivate alter to reciprocate.

Obviously, the success of all these attempts to initiate coordinated interaction by using motivating conditional commitments depends on many "ifs", particularly when coordination requires commonly shared or complementary orientations. But attempts to coordinate actions by threat of force or by exchange of resources include considerable uncertainties and restrictions, too. Thus, it is reasonable to assume that the chances of success could be enhanced substantially if not all these prerequisites have to be established anew, each time such a self-commitment is made. This is where the concept of generalized symbolic media comes into play.

5   Generalized Symbolic Media of Coordination

Parsons introduces the concept of generalized symbolic media in order to describe a "family of mechanisms" ([13, p. 42]), which have in common that they are "ways of getting results in interaction" (ibid.) by "fac(ing) the object with a decision, calling for a response" (ibid.). According to Parsons, within the social system, this family of mechanisms comprises of four generalized media: money, political power, influence, and value-commitments (cf. [14, p. 94-95]). These "mechanisms are ways of structuring *intentional* attempts to bring about results by eliciting the response of other actors to approaches, suggestions, etc. In the case of money, it is a matter of offers; in the case of power, of communicating decisions that activate obligations; in the case of influence, of giving reasons or 'justifications' for a suggested line of action." ([13, p. 42]) Starting from Parsons' concept of generalized symbolic media of interaction, Luhmann has developed a concept of symbolically generalized media of communication, where he arrives at a somewhat different list: In his opinion, besides money and power, truth and love are the most elaborated generalized media in modern societies. Additionally, he considers religious belief, art and basic civil values to be rudimentary forms (cf. [15, p. 176-179]; [9, p. 222]; [16, p. 332-358]). But with respect to the role they play as mechanisms to coordinate the actors' selections (cf. [16, p. 320]), his view on the generalized media resembles Parsons' perspective: They allow to condition the respective selection "so that it works as a means of motivation, that is, so that it can adequately secure acceptance of the selection" ([9, p. 222]).

Both Parsons' and Luhmann's description correspond to the way in which the motivating conditional commitment works as a means of coordination. Thus, the question arises what is the difference and what is the advantage if an actor draws upon one of the generalized symbolic media when trying to motivate other actors to adopt his or her selections. Indeed, there is a certain similarity to the use of self-commitments as described above. But this is not so amazing, since proposing a selection with reference to one of these media is nothing else but making a motivating conditional commitment. In this respect no difference exists between an actor offering money in exchange for certain goods or services and another actor trying to arrive at the same result through a barter exchange. In both cases the respective actor, ego, attempts to motivate alter to agree to a certain transaction by committing himself or herself to transfer to alter something of value on condition that alter responds according to this request.

In other respects, however, drawing upon generalized symbolic media makes a difference. By referring to them, the possible success of attempting coordinated interaction is considerably enhanced. This is due to two basic properties of these media: generalization and symbolization. As indicated above, the success of the motivating conditional commitment alone is always in danger from the problems and restrictions posed by the particular circumstances of the prospective participants' individual situation. Drawing upon one of the generalized symbolic media, in this respect has the effect of transforming the concrete situation into an instance of a much more general situation, thereby overcoming at least some of these problems and restrictions. The term 'symbolization' refers to the fact that by using one of these media, the means to elicit a certain response is not the relevant resource itself, but a symbolic representation thereof. Again, one effect is decontextualisation, and to the degree this is the case, the generalized symbolic media are symbolically generalized media. Additionally, but not less important, the emergence of symbolic representations of this kind comes along with the emergence of institutional arrangements, whose function is to make sure that these symbolic representations work as if the 'real' resources, they stand for, were present (cf. [14, p. 96]). This, in turn, has the effect of simplifying matters, since some of the prerequisites for successful coordination now no longer have to be brought about by the prospective participants themselves, but can be left to these institutional arrangements.

The paradigmatic case of a generalized symbolic medium is money (cf. [14, p. 94]). In order to illustrate how the media's properties of generalization and symbolization can contribute to overcome problems of coordination, I will look at the case of money first. One of the major problems of barter trade is that the actor, who offers a certain commodity in exchange for another commodity, not only must find someone, who is interested in the offered commodity, but someone, who additionally is capable and ready to provide the desired commodity for exchange (cf. [17, p. 119]; [18, p. 557-558]). Obviously, this problem of "double coincidence of wants" ([17, p. 119]) is the greater the more uncommon the commodities in question are. But basically, this is a problem inherent in each attempt at making a barter exchange since the occurrence of coinciding complementary offers and requests is more or less unlikely on condition that each party is characterized by its own individual constellation of disposable and desired resources.

Money deals with this problem, since money, as Coleman puts it, "enables two parties to break apart the two halves of the double coincidence of a barter transaction. For example, B can engage in one half of the transaction with A, by providing services to A (in return for money), and then engage in the second half with C, who provides B with services 'in return' for those B provides to A (concretely in return for money B earlier received from A). B need not discover a D, who both needs what he can provide and has what he needs." ([17, p. 120]) In this way, money helps overcome a major impediment to economic exchange: "the fact that at any given time and place only one party of a pair who might engage in a transaction has an interest in what the other party has" ([17, p. 121]). When dividing the transaction into two halves, money transforms a situation which is relatively specific and therefore relatively unlikely to occur into a situation that is much more general and therefore much more likely to occur: The resource that is offered in return for the desired commodity is now a resource everyone has an interest in, at least everyone who has interests in any commodities different from the ones already at his or her disposal. This is because the resource offered, a certain amount of money, represents exchange value, that is, the generalized capacity to exchange it for a certain amount of any commodity offered for money. In addition to this property to mediate exchange by serving as a general equivalent form of value (cf. [19, p. 83-85]), money has at least two further properties which by generalization of the situation help to enhance the chances of exchanges to occur: The property to be used as a store of value, and its property to function as a measure of value. The property of money as a store of value allows temporally to separate the single exchanges within an overall transaction: Because of this property an actor may be ready to provide a certain commodity in return for money at a given time even if the exchange for which he wants to employ this money will take place only some time later. Thus, the use of money not only allows to break up the double coincidence of actors complementary offering and looking for certain commodities, but the temporal aspect of this coincidence, too. And last but not least, the property of money as a measure of value "makes goods and services ..., which in other respects such as physical properties are incomparably heterogeneous, comparable" ([14, p. 95]) and therefore much more easy to exchange.

In contrast to commodity money, such as gold, spices, or cigarettes that have been used to represent value, modern money no longer contains its value (in form of its value as a commodity), but merely symbolizes it. "It is symbolic in that, though measuring and thus 'standing for' economic value or utility, it does not itself possess utility in the primary consumption sense—it has no 'value in use' but only 'in exchange', i.e. for possession of things having utility." ([20, p. 236]). Modern fiat money, such as the dollar, is "'valueless' money" ([20, p. 237]), it "has no intrinsic utility, yet signifies commodities that do, in the special sense that it can in certain circumstances be substituted for them" ([13, p. 39]). This feature of modern money—likewise to be abstracted from every commodity by only symbolizing value—"introduces new degrees of freedom" ([13, p. 40]) in economic exchange, for example because "money, unlike virtually all commodities, does not intrinsically deteriorate through time and has minimal, if any, costs of storage" ([13, p. 41]). Hence, in the case of money, the positive effects of generalization are in part effects of symbolic generalization.

Another, but not less important consequence of the evolution of modern money is its dependence upon the co-evolution of certain institutional structures. This is the case, because the property of modern money to symbolize value is based on another symbolic property of money: Its property to serve as a symbolic representation of self-commitments of trusted third parties. This applies to fiat money as well as to its precursor, fiduciary money.[4] Fiduciary money represents a promise from its issuer (e.g. a

---

[4] With respect to the distinction between commodity money, fiduciary money and fiat money see [17, p. 119-120].

bank or a trading house) to balance the debts it stands for, and fiat money is 'good' only as long as the government keeps the "promise to maintain a balance between growth in goods and services and growth in money supply" ([17, p. 121]). Thus, symbolic money requires in one or another way institutional arrangements securing the promise it embodies (i.e. its exchange value). Otherwise no one would accept intrinsically valueless money in exchange for intrinsically valuable commodities. But if trusted third parties of this kind do exist, a part of the commitments, which otherwise would have to be made by those engaged in a transaction can now be substituted by these trusted third parties' promises. Consequently, less trust must be invested in the respective other party involved in the exchange, serving as a further contribution of this generalized symbolic medium to make economic exchange more likely to occur.

If Parsons is right that money is only one, if perhaps the most prominent member of a "much more extensive family of media" ([14, p. 94]), and if it is appropriate to treat these media as media of coordination between actors, [5] then similar effects of generalization and symbolization should also be observable with respect to other media. I will address the issue of power only very briefly, since coordination by means of power is of little importance within multi-agent research, as I will argue below. Afterwards, I will discuss the case of influence in more detail.

Parsons describes power, in line with Weber, to be "the capacity of persons or collectives 'to get things done' effectively, in particular when their goals are obstructed by some kind of human resistance or opposition" ([20, p. 232]). According to him, the difference between an attempt to obtain obedience by threat of force and the respective attempt by exercising power is comparable to the difference between a barter exchange and an exchange mediated by money: "Securing possession of an object of utility by bartering another object for it is not a monetary transaction. Similarly, ... securing compliance with a wish ... simply by threat of superior force, is not an exercise of power. ... The capacity to secure compliance must, if it is to be called power in my sense, be generalized and not solely a function of one particular sanctioning act which the user is in a position to impose, and the medium used must be 'symbolic'." ([20, p. 237-238]) Power, as well as money, has a 'real basis': "For the case of power, the basis of unit security corresponding to economic 'real asset' consists in possession of effective means of enforcing compliance ... through implementing coercive threats or exerting compulsion." ([13, p. 47]) Along with money, power is the generalized symbolic representation of this 'real basis'. It is this generalization and symbolization of physical force that makes binding obligations more likely to occur: "(J)ust as possession of stocks of monetary gold cannot create a highly productive economy, so command of physical force alone cannot guarantee the effective fulfillment of ramified systems of binding obligations." (ibid.)

Without any symbolic representation of physical force, the only way for alter to determine if ego maintains the capability to enforce his compliance is to test ego's physical force. But when ego was right in claiming superiority, the outcome of such a test is a

---

[5] And not only as media of communication in the sense that they mediate the autopoietic emergence of specialized social systems (what is Luhmann's main focus, cf. [16, p. 359-371]) or as media of interchange between the functional subsystems of the society (what for Parsons is of major interest, cf. [21, p. 110-117])

disadvantage to both parties. Alter must face ego's sanctions as consequence to his disobedience, a situation alter would have avoided were he informed in advance. And ego is compelled to employ his force although he would prefer gaining alter's cooperation through deterrence. Power as a means to symbolize capabilities enforcing compliance in a generalized way, a way allowing a comparison between different amounts of such capabilities, helps to overcome such problems by enabling the participants to assess their relative capabilities in advance. However, in one respect, power as a coordination medium is substantially different from money. Power is not a medium in the sense that it intermediates between the parts of an overall transaction (cf. [4, p. 413-414]). Normally, power is not a 'currency' that could be traded in exchange for compliance. Rather, it is a medium only in the sense that it makes it easier to grasp a special kind of relationship between actors: the power relation as the basis of coordination by dominance and submission. With respect to intermediating capacities, influence, the generalized medium I will turn to now, is much more similar to money than power can ever become.

As we have seen, Parsons and Luhmann agree that money and power are generalized symbolic media, but disagree about the remaining media. According to Parsons these are influence and value-commitment, whereas Luhmann holds that truth, love, and to a certain degree, religious belief, art, and basic civil values additionally play the part of generalized media. I will argue—partially in accordance with Parsons ([13, p. 51-58])—that all such media should be viewed as representing different types of influence so that the medium influence constitutes a kind of a sub-family within the media family. Starting from a position that treats the generalized symbolic media as mechanisms to overcome coordination problems in situations where the motivating conditional commitment at first is the only means to initiate coordinated interaction, such an assumption makes some sense. As I have argued above, coordination on the basis of shared assertions of truth, of shared moral (or religious) beliefs, or of mutual feelings of affection (and, to include art: of shared aesthetic feelings) are similar because in each case the establishment of one or another kind of a commonly shared (or complementary) perception of the particular situation at hand is the means to achieve coordination. In the absence of a pre-established common ground this leads to the question of why alter should be motivated to adopt ego's assertions, beliefs, etc. The admittedly unsatisfying answer I gave above refers to ego's degree of persuasiveness. As we will see now, influence of one or another kind generalizes and symbolizes persuasiveness, thereby helping to overcome certain problems and restrictions that arise when alter's cooperation depends on his or her estimation that acting according to ego's definition of the situation lies in his or her own interest.

The crucial problem of coordination through adopting assertions, beliefs, or feelings lies in bringing about "a decision on alter's part to act in a certain way because it is felt to be a 'good thing' *for him*, ... for positive reasons, not because of obligations he would violate through noncompliance" ([13, p. 48]). For example, if it is a matter of adopting a certain information, "there must be some basis on which alter considers ego to be a trustworthy source of information and 'believes' him even though he is not in a position to verify the information independently—or does not want to take the trouble" ([13, p. 48]). As I have argued above, ego's commitment to bear the consequences following alter's adoption of his suggestions may provide such a basis to a certain degree. But these self-commitments' capacities to work in this way are limited: Alter is neither sure not to become subject to ego's fraud, nor can he or she rule out that ego is mistaken even if he himself truly believes what he says. For both reasons, it would make alter's decision easier if he or she could obtain more general knowledge about ego's performance in comparable situations. Thus, it would help alter to assess ego's trustworthiness in both respects, if he or she could relate the actual situation to prior experiences with ego in similar situations, or if he or she could find out to which degree other people feel positive about having adopted ego's suggestions in similar situations. And if such comparisons turn out to confirm ego's trustworthiness, ego will welcome them, since they enhance the persuasiveness of his suggestions. Influence of one or another kind can be understood to be the generalized symbolic medium that represents the accumulated perceptions of certain actors with respect to their trust in another actor's capability and willingness to make suggestions that will improve their situation, if adopted. In this sense, "(i)nfluence is a means of *persuasion*" ([13, p. 48]).

Since space is short, I will illustrate only one type of influence, namely scientific reputation. According to Merton, "graded rewards in the realm of science are distributed principally in the coin of recognition accorded research by fellow-scientists. This recognition is stratified for varying grades of scientific accomplishment, as judged by the scientist's peers."([22, p. 56]) In characterizing recognition by fellow-scientists, that is, reputation within a scientific community, as "the coin of the scientific realm" ([22, p. 644]), Merton implies it to bear analogy to money. The basis of this analogy is the observation that in science reputation has become "symbol and reward for having done one's job well" ([22, p. 640]). This leads to some questions: In which way is reputation a generalized symbolic media in the sense of an intrinsic valueless representation of something else of value? In which way does this medium help to overcome problems of coordination? And what does this currency buy?

In the case of scientific reputation, to have intrinsic value would mean to contain scientific truth, what reputation certainly does not. Rather, reputation contains information about the capability of a scientist to produce information of scientific value, as judged by fellow-scientists. Compared with what the scientist in question concretely has contributed to science, this is a rather general information, since it represents the accumulated recognition of several of this scientist's contributions by several of his fellow-scientists. And reputation is a symbolic representation because it does not somehow recapitulate or summarize the content of this scientist's accomplishments, but merely symbolizes his peers' estimation of how serious his contributions at large should be taken.

According to Luhmann, the "plausibility of reputation" ([23, p. 246]) depends on the assumption that reputation will be attributed according to scientific accomplishment. But as we have seen, reputation does not directly follow from a researcher's contribution to science, but results from his fellow-scientists' perceptions thereof. Hence, the question arises as to how to make sure that reputation sufficiently corresponds with actual accomplishment. One part of the answer lies in the self-adjusting properties of reputation. If fellow-scientists involved in a particular research problem recommend referring to a certain scientist's contributions and other scientists, after following this recommendation came to the conclusion doing so was of no help, this will (at least in the long run) not only affect the recommended scientist's reputation, but those fellow-scientists' reputation, too. The fellow-scientists would appear to have given bad advice. In order not to compromise their reputation, scientists have a certain interest not to claim much more than their research really can contribute, and more general: an interest to live up to the expectations raised by the reputation they have already obtained.[6] The same applies to recognition by fellow-scientists. They, too, must be cautious not to misjudge other scientists' accomplishments, in order to save their own reputation.[7] In addition to this informal institutionalisation of the reputation mechanism, the referee system as a more formal mechanism to attribute scientific reputation has been established (cf. [25]). Like the institutions which are backing money, those informal or formal institutions' function is to make sure that reputation becomes and remains a sufficiently adequate symbol to represent scientific accomplishment.

In which way does reputation as a generalized symbolic medium help to overcome problems of coordination? As we have seen, the answer with respect to influence in general is that this medium communicates information about the presumptive quality of an actor's suggestions, what is useful in situations where on the part of the addressee of such a suggestion it is either impossible or too costly to verify its quality independently. This applies to scientific reputation, too: "Studies of the communication behavior of scientists have shown that, confronted with the growing task of identifying significant work published in their field, scientists search for cues to what they should attend to. One such cue is the professional reputation of the authors. The problem of locating the pertinent research literature and the problem of authors' wanting their work to be noticed and used are symmetrical" ([24, p. 59]): Since the readers' "behaviors in selecting articles" are, to a considerable degree, "based on the identity of the authors" (ibid.), their reputations, scientists must acquire a reputation as a means of producing interest in their research results. To the extent to which reputation is a reliable indicator of scientific accomplishment, referring to it simplifies (cf. [23, p. 249]) the scientists' search for those contributions of other scientists that prospectively are most important to their own work.

Thus, reputation helps to overcome coordination problems by supporting the allocation of scientific findings to those who will need them in their own research. Like money as a medium of economic exchange, reputation, too, enables two parties to break apart the two halves of a double coincidence: the double coincidence that the scientist looking for scientific findings useful for his work finds someone who is capable and ready to provide him with such findings. One half of the overall transaction consists of offering scientific findings to everyone who might be interested, i.e. of publishing them, in order to be rewarded by the fellow-scientists' recognition. The other half of

---

[6] As Merton ([24, p. 57]) observes with respect to Nobel laureates, "the reward system based on recognition for work accomplished tends to induce continued effort, which serves both to validate the judgment that the scientist has unusual capacities and to testify that these capacities have continual potential. ... It is not necessarily the fact that their own Faustian aspirations are ever escalating that keeps eminent scientists at work. More and more is expected of them, and this creates its own measure of motivation and stress. Less often than might be imaged is there repose at the top in science."

[7] This is a major reason of why a considerable part of the citations to be found in scientific texts refer to authors, whose scientific accomplishments are beyond doubt.

the transaction exploits reputation, which those who offer their findings already have accrued, to single out what appears to be most promising contributions and in turn to pay recognition to its authors if their findings actually turn out to be useful. Thus, from the perspective of those who pay recognition, reputation is a means to get authoritative advice with respect to their own scientific work. From the viewpoint of those attaining recognition, it is a means to strengthen their position "within the opportunity structure of science" ([24, p. 57]), that is, their chances of "access to the means of scientific production" (ibid.). In this sense, "status, or recognition from others ... has a characteristic that makes it somewhat like money: The value of a particular act of deference from a person is proportional to his own status. It is as if he has a particular quantity of status and pays out a certain fraction of it through the act of showing deference to another." ([17, p. 130-131])

As we have seen, referring to generalized media has the effect of transforming particular coordination problems into instances of much more general ones, thereby reducing the need to meet the specific preconditions of the particular situation. The parties mutually have to know much less about their individual interests, strategies, capabilities, and trustworthiness, since part of what otherwise had to be negotiated between them now can be left to the respective generalized medium. Consequently, the generalized media are means of "disembedding", that is, of "the 'lifting out' of social relations from local contexts of interaction and their restructuring across indefinite spans of time-space" ([26, p. 21]). By helping to overcome restrictions imposed by local social contexts and the limitations of co-presence, they are powerful means of coordination making even cooperation between complete strangers probable to occur.

6 Bridging the Gap: Generalized Media as Emergent Effects of Conditional Commitments

If we want to draw upon generalized media as a way to overcome problems of coordination between self-governed entities as characterized by the general framework description given above, one major problem still remains: the problem of how generalized media come into existence, starting from an initial situation in which all an entity can do to initiate coordination is to make motivating conditional commitments. It must be shown that from this initial situation at least some development towards generalization (and symbolization) of conditional commitments may occur. Otherwise it would be much less useful as a point of departure for considering solutions to problems of coordination between self-governed entities. Additionally, the general framework would lose much of its relevance as an intermediary, that is, as a basic concept that helps to transfer means of coordination between human actors to the realm of software agents.

Luhmann ([15, p. 174]; [16, p. 316-317]), in particular, emphasizes that generalized media result from self-reinforcing processes and counts on the possibility that such processes can be initiated by nothing more than one first suggestion of an actor to adopt his definition of the situation. This may happen as follows: "In a still uncertain situation alter decides tentatively to act in a certain way, as a first step. He starts with a friendly glance, a gesture, a gift—and then awaits ego's reaction to the definition of the situation thus proposed. In the light of this first step each following action has the determinative effect of reducing contingency—whether it be in a positive or in a negative way." ([9, p. 150]) In the long run, such attempts at testing other actors' reactions to suggestions of one or another kind leads to more reliable expectations of how they typically will react. The generalized media can be understood to represent reliable expectations regarding the prospective reactions of other actors to certain types of suggestions. Thus, the next step towards generalized media is disembedding expectations from their local contexts of origin, that is, their transformation into general patterns of orientation with respect to certain types of coordination problems.

Even this next step can be deduced at least to a certain degree from the initial situation as characterized by the general framework. According to Esser ([18, p. 560-561]), successful solutions to problems are almost automatically adopted by other actors, since they see that they will be better off in doing so. Consequently, a successful selection changes the situation by affecting other selections, thus setting off a process by which general solutions to typical problems are developed and become institutionalised. Carl Menger's outline of an 'organic' development of commodity money, to which Esser refers in this context, follows this pattern of explanation: according to Menger, it takes only a simple observation to solve the problem of double coincidence in barter exchanges, the problem that "not only does A have something that B wants, but it is also true that B has something that A wants, and both want what the other has more than they want what they themselves have, which they are willing to give up in exchange" ([17, p. 119]): Each individual can easily discover that some commodities, in comparison to others, are on greater demand. So, when looking for a certain commodity, it is more likely to find someone, who offers it, among the many, who themselves look for a marketable commodity than among the few, who look for a less marketable item. Thus, it is an obvious idea for anyone who offers a less marketable commodity to exchange it not only for the commodity he looks for, but—if this is not possible—also to exchange it for other commodities which he does not need but for which there is a greater demand than for his own commodity. In this way he gets nearer to his aim, since now he can look among the many, who are in demand for this commodity, for someone who offers what he wants. And if he is successful, a transaction mediated by this demanded commodity has been performed. Based upon this solution of the double coincidence problem, everyone will prefer to possess among the highly demanded commodities those with the highest marketability, the least deterioration, and the best divisibility, thus paving the way for the development of commodity money whose primary function is to be a medium of exchange (cf. [27, p. 174-176]).

In the same way, influence can be understood to result from aggregated and thereby generalized experiences with cooperation on the basis of conditional commitments. At least with respect to influence, as far as it is an informally institutionalised medium of coordination, this can be easily shown. An everyday experience serves as an appropriate example: When you have moved to a new place, how do you find a dentist, in whose skills you hope you can trust? Probably, you will ask your new neighbours or colleagues and follow their recommendations. The rationale behind this strategy is as follows: from the point of view of the neighbours or colleagues, the recommended dentist so far kept his promise to treat their dental problems successfully, otherwise they would not have recommended him. So, it seems likely that this dentist will be capable of dealing with other persons' dental problems as well. Following the neighbours' or colleagues' recommendations means adopting a solution to a problem which has proved to be successful. At the same time, it implies a certain degree of generalization of this solution as a precondition of its transferability. The person who follows such recommendations, concludes from other persons' individual experiences with this dentist's capabilities to his competency in general. Or to put it another way: He refers to this dentist's professional reputation as an indicator of his problem-solving capacity.

To a certain degree even power can be conceived to emerge from the initial situation in which the motivating conditional commitment is the only means of coordination. This can be observed in situations where the physical means to enforce compliance are distributed relatively equally among the parties involved, but their readiness to actually employ them is not. In such situations those more willing to use force will often gain a capacity to secure compliance far beyond their relative physical strength, thus accumulating power as distinct from force. Nevertheless, the emergent qualities of power relations are limited, since the basis of this medium, that is, the "possession of effective means of enforcing compliance" ([13, p. 47]), is less affected by exchanges mediated by power than it is in the case of money or influence because power usually is not a circulating medium[8] in the sense of transferring what it represents. Rather than to be an emergent effect of prior exchanges, the possession of such effective means primarily results from decisions of system-builders, for instance of those who found a company and delegate rights and resources to the different positions within this company. Thus, "designed institutions" rather than "emergent institutions" (cf. [28]) are the basis of coordination mediated by power.

7   Generalized Media of Coordination in Closed Multi-agent Systems?

In early stages of research in multi-agent systems one can already observe the implementation of coordination mechanisms, which at first glance resemble coordination by means of generalized media: The contract net protocol ([29, p. 77]) emulates a simple mechanism of economic exchange. It implements a coordination structure, where the agents involved possess the capabilities to announce tasks they want to be carried out by other agents, to "evaluate their own level of interest" ([29, p. 77]) in performing tasks announced by other agents, to submit bids according to these evaluations, to evaluate received bids and to select between them. Often a certain quality of the task itself—for example the amount of time the bidding agents state they will need to perform it—is used to evaluate them (cf. [30, p. 30-32]), but sometimes a more general measure of value, some kind of money, is used (cf. [31]). In both cases the respective coordination mechanism goes beyond barter exchange in that it employs a more or less generalized medium to make different offers (or different announcements) comparable.

Coordination by identifying the agent that is best suited for performing the respective task in a population of agents with different expertise is another strategy often employed in multi-agent research. An early example of coordination structured by the

---

[8] In this respect, Parsons ([20, p. 245-246]) argues to the contrary.

agents' particular skills is the distributed vehicle monitoring testbed (cf. [32]). In this case, the "spatially-distributed nodes detect the sound of vehicles, and each applies knowledge of vehicle sounds and movements to track a vehicle through its spatial area. Nodes then exchange information about vehicles they have tracked to build up a map of vehicle movements through the entire area." ([33, p. 74]) Another way to use an agent's particular ability as basis of their coordination is not to refer to skills but to willingness. Much of the early multi-agent research starts from the so called benevolent agent assumption: "Agents are assumed to be friendly agents, who wish to do what they are asked to do." ([34, p. 41]) In this case coordination is brought about by the agents quality to be "perfectly willing to accommodate one another" (cf. [35, p. 42]).

Coordination by implementing means to secure compliance seems to play a part in every multi-agent system, but mostly in an implicit way. An explicit suggestion is Shohams and Tennenholtz' idea of imposing social laws on agents. Taking the domain of mobile robots as their example, they argue: "Suppose robots navigate along marked paths, much like cars do along streets. Why not adopt a convention, or, as we'd like to think of it, a social law, according to which each robot keeps to the right of the path? If each robot obeys the convention, we will have avoided all head-on collisions without any need for either a central arbiter or negotiation." ([36, p. 277]) But most multi-agent researchers do not like this idea very much. While they concede that it is indeed an effective way to overcome coordination problems, they fear that pre-programmed conventions or laws of this kind will reduce the autonomy and pro-activeness of the agents (cf. [30, p. 45-48]) and thereby affect what is held to be the distinctive feature of this strand of research: coordination as an emergent effect of interaction between agents without a central authority.

Though these solutions at first glance seem to resemble coordination by means of generalized media, in fact they bear only a poor resemblance because—as Castelfranchi puts it—the respective approaches in multi-agent research "still remain in a world of 'pre-established harmonies'" ([37, p. 50]; cf. [38, p. 268]). At least within closed multi-agent systems, coordination is largely a result of predefined patterns of behaviour: The agents who are subject to rules, conventions, or social laws cannot act otherwise than to comply, the benevolent agents do not possess the option to act malevolently, the spatially or functionally distributed agents interact on the basis of given knowledge about their respective skills, and the agents announcing and bidding for tasks do not possess interests that could interfere with the performance of the overall exchange system.

Closed multi-agent systems are characterized by the fact that the development and implementation of all agents involved as well as of the system's architecture (e.g. inter-agent relations, interaction protocols) are completely in the hands of one designer or designer team (cf. [30, p. 14]). In this case, there is little reason why designers should provide agents with properties which pose impediments to coordination, then being forced to implement coordination mechanisms in order to overcome the coordination problems resulting from these properties. Why should they develop agents that are able to violate obligations, thereby raising the need to develop means to secure compliance? Why should they employ complicated reputation mechanisms to enable agents to evaluate their respective skills, if they possess complete knowledge about their agents' capabilities because they have programmed them and could easily distribute this knowledge among the agents? The answer is, they will not, and they actually do not, when the aim is to develop agents, which efficiently coordinate their actions within closed multi-agent systems. Rather, multi-agent researchers developing closed systems restrict their agents' conduct in a functional way so that collaborative problem-solving necessary results from their pre-programmed patterns of behaviour. Thus, coordination between agents in closed multi-agent systems differs from our general framework in that it heavily relies on pre-established structures. This does not mean that closed multi-agent systems cannot be modelled on human social systems. Since a large part of social interaction between human actors is very successfully governed by given social structures, quite the contrary is true. But it does mean that in closed multi-agent systems there is little need to refer to conditional commitments and to generalized forms of making commitments (i.e. generalized media) in order to ensure coordination.

8   From Conditional Commitments to Generalized Media in Open Multi-agent Systems: The Paradigmatic Case of Reputation

The situation completely changes when we move on from closed to open multi-agent systems. Open multi-agent systems can be pragmatically defined as systems where the behaviour of the agents involved is not developed and is not completely controlled by one designer or one designer team (cf. [39, p. 246]). More precisely, open multi-agent systems are characterized by one or both of the following attributes: They are systems with open membership, in which every designer or user who wants his agent to become a participant, in principal may do so (cf. [30, p. 17-21]). And/or the (or some of the) agents involved may be subject to emergent properties. In other words, in the course of their 'life' agents are able autonomously to change their patterns of behaviour, for instance by 'learning' from prior experiences. The growing interest in research in open multi-agent systems mainly results from the consideration that there will be a lot of promising applications in the domain of agent-based web services, which presuppose open systems at least in the sense that all agents, which are authorized by their users to engage in certain transactions may possibly become cooperation partners.

With respect to the question of inter-agent coordination, the most important consequence of the two aspects related to openness is that agents now are—as Hewitt ([40, p. 322]; [41, p. 81-82]) calls it—"at an *arm's length relationship*". This means that the "internal operation, organization, and state of one computational agent may be unknown and unavailable to another agent" ([40, p. 322]) so that the agents know about one another only what they communicate to others. Since these agents act only according to their respective designers' or users' specifications (or in the case of emergent features: according to their own advancement of such specifications), there is no way to ensure collaboration by means of pre-established structures. Rather, nothing else but the negotiations between the agents account for success or failure of an agent's attempt to initiate coordinative interaction.[9] Thus, agents in open multi-agent systems are confronted with the coordination problem as characterized by our general framework.

---

[9] Again, the only given structure that has to be presupposed is the existence of a common language, that is, of a communication protocol such as KQML (cf. [42]; [43]) or the agent communication language of the FIPA (cf. http.//www.fipa.org), which is being used by all agents

I have argued that in the absence of pre-established coordination structures the only means a self-governed entity has to evoke another self-governed entity's cooperation is to motivate this entity to act in a certain way by making conditional commitments. Additionally, I have tried to show that this solution to coordination problems has an inherent tendency to become more and more generalized and institutionalised, thereby removing some of the restrictions of the initial situation, in which alter when deciding whether to follow a suggestion he is asked to adopt can consider nothing more but ego's conditional commitments. If this is true, similar ideas and efforts should be observed in research on open multi-agent systems.

Indeed, in the last decade we have witnessed a lot of pioneering work in establishing commitment as a basic concept of coordination between agents (see for example [44]; [45]; [46]; [47]). In this period, some researchers have even gone so far as to claim that "(a)ll coordination mechanisms can ultimately be reduced to (joint) commitments and their associated (social) conventions" ([46, p. 234]). Within a few years the concept of coordination through commitments made by agents, according to Castelfranchi and Conte, has become the dominant view: "No preexisting relationships, no objective bases, no specific motivations for cooperation are supposed in the agents, no obligations and constraints, except their free commitments, are thought to be put on them." ([48, p. 537]) Its wide acceptance can be underlined by the somewhat exaggerated assertion that "(t)ypically, multi-agent systems ... use centrally the concept of commitment" ([49, p. 13]).

In accordance with the considerations above regarding the motivating conditional commitment as the first step towards coordination, it has been emphasized that an agent's commitment should be thought of as a social commitment in the sense of a promise to act in a way another agent is interested in (or is interested in to prevent), it is a "(c)ommitment of one agent to another" ([47, p. 41], cf. [47, p. 42-45]) that is based on an "*internal* commitment" ([45, p. 257]): The agent commits itself to act in this way (cf. [46, p. 236]). Likewise, it is seen that "(w)ith respect to coordinating the behavior of multiple agents, the most important feature of commitments is that they enable individuals to make assumptions about the actions of other community members. They provide a degree of predictability to counteract the uncertainty caused by distributed control" ([46, p. 240]), that is, caused by the fact that the agents involved are self-governed entities.

However, most of the early approaches assume 'good faith', postulating that "agents commit only to what they believe themselves capable of, and only if they really mean it" ([5, p. 64]; cf. [2, p. 195]; [47, p. 45]), allowing obligations to be revoked only after "explicit release of the agent by the party to which it is obliged", or when it turns out that the agent "is no longer able to fulfill the obligation" ([5, p. 65]; cf. [45, p. 254-256]). In the meantime it has become widely recognized that in open systems this good faith assumption is as unrealistic as the benevolent agent assumption of the early days was (cf. [50, p. 227]), since it does not take into account the possibility of incompetence or fraud. Consequently, the question of how to enable agents to assess other agents' trustworthiness in order "to make our agents less vulnerable to others' incompetent or

---

participating in communication, to make sure that suggestions and responses are properly understood.

malevolent behavior" ([51, p. 97]), has become a major topic in multi-agent research (see for example [52]). In particular, much research has been done in recent years on reputation mechanisms (cf. [53]).

This interest in reputation has much to do with its emergent properties. For researchers who fear that pre-designed coordination structures might reduce the autonomous problem-solving capacities of interacting agents, but who nevertheless acknowledge that there is a need for means to reduce coordination problems, it is an intriguing idea that such a means of coordination may "emerge from a spontaneous process" ([28]), that is, from the accumulated past experiences one agent has made with another agent, or additionally, from the accumulated recommendations of other agents reflecting their experiences with the performance of this agent. Thus, it is the property of being "an intrinsic enforcing mechanism" that does not need to be "controlled by a given external entity", but is controlled "by the whole group" ([28]), that makes reputation being viewed as a promising means of coordination between autonomous agents. In accordance with the considerations regarding generalized media of cooperation, multi-agent simulations have shown that the effectiveness of the reputation mechanism grows in line with its generalization. For example, [54] have compared two experimental settings with respect to the ability of 'respectful' agents (i.e. those who follow a certain norm) to identify 'cheating' agents (i.e. those who do not). In the first setting the agents learn about other agents' behaviour only from their own experiences, in the second setting they exchange their experiences. The result of the simulation is not surprising (in the second setting the agents are much better in identifying cheaters), but clearly shows the use of accumulating experiences, and that means: the use of transforming individual evaluations into general indicators of agents' performance.

9 Closing Remark: The Need to Hybridise Open Multi-agent Systems

In the previous section I have dealt with the general framework of analysing coordination problems between self-governed entities, starting from commitments as the only means to motivate another self-governed entity's cooperation. I have tried to show how it may enhance our understanding of coordination problems between agents in open multi-agent systems and how it may help to identify impediments to coordination in open systems as well as the respective means of coordination that have emerged in human societies to deal with them. Obviously, in addition to the problem of whether to trust in an agent's commitments, there are a lot of further impediments to coordination posed by the initial situation of double contingency. Thus, identifying processes where more general means of coordination emerge from conditional commitments may in this respect prove to be of help to overcome problems of coordination in open multi-agent systems.

However, modelling coordination mechanisms between agents on conditional commitments and their emergent generalizations raises a problem that should not be ignored. I have argued that an important aspect of the generalized media's capabilities to facilitate cooperation is that they allow to substitute reliance on individual actor's intentions or resources by reliance on institutions. The more these means of coordination are symbolically generalized, the more important (and the more efficient) this institutional background becomes: Fiat money ultimately relies on the capability of the society's central bank to prevent inflation or deflation; political power in the end relies on the capability of the state to hold the legitimate monopoly of force. This leads to the question of how ultimately to ensure the reliability and trustworthiness of the institutions supporting coordination in open multi-agent systems.

So far, this question has been answered with reference to the self-adjusting properties and to the intrinsic enforcing mechanisms of emergent institutions. For example, the agent who does not stick to his commitments in the long run will gain a bad reputation, and, consequently, will be avoided by other agents. But these intrinsic properties fail to prevent certain malpractices: a user might employ the strategy to always kill his or her agent after having gained a bad reputation and create a new one. Or he or she might choose to create additional agents who deceptively recommend this agent's trustworthiness so that it will gain a good reputation (cf. [55]). It should be obvious that malpractices of this kind cannot be avoided by means of coordination mechanisms, which only affect the behaviour of the agents. Rather, institutional arrangements are required to make sure that what affects an agent affects its user as well. To this end, access rules to open systems and rules regarding the users' responsibility for their agents' behaviour have to be established. If only for this reason (in fact, there are other good reasons, too, cf. [56]), research on open multi-agent systems necessarily leads to research on hybrid systems, that is, on systems of interaction among and between computational agents and human actors.

10   Acknowledgments

I am very grateful to Ying Zhu for the revision of my English.

References

1. Van de Velde, W., Perram, J.P.: Preface. In Van de Velde, W., Perram, J.P., eds.: Agents Breaking Away. 7th European Workshop on Modelling Autonomous Agents in a Multi-Agent World, MAAMAW'96, Berlin etc., Springer-Verlag (1996) V–X
2. Jennings, N.R.: Coordination Techniques for Distributed Artificial Intelligence. In Jennings, N.R., ed.: Foundations of Distributed Artificial Intelligence. John Wiley & Sons, New York etc. (1996) 187–210
3. Parsons, T., Shils, E.: Some Fundamental Categories of the Theory of Action. A General Statement. In Parsons, T., Shils, E., eds.: Toward a General Theory of Action. Harvard University Press, Cambridge, Mass. (1951) 3–29
4. Esser, H.: Soziologie. Spezielle Grundlagen. Band 3: Soziales Handeln. Campus, Frankfurt/Main etc. (2000)
5. Shoham, Y.: Agent-oriented Programming. Artificial Intelligence 60 (1993) 51–92
6. Haddadi, A., Sundermeyer, K.: Belief-Desire-Intention Agent Architectures. In Jennings, N.R., ed.: Foundations of Distributed Artificial Intelligence. John Wiley & Sons, New York etc. (1996) 169–210
7. Mead, G.H.: Mind, Self, and Society. From the Standpoint of a Social Behaviorist. 14. impr. edn. Univ. of Chicago Press, Chicago etc. (1967)

8. Durkheim, E.: The Rules of Sociological Method. Free Press, New York etc. (1982)
9. Luhmann, N.: Soziale Systeme. Grundriß einer allgemeinen Theorie. Suhrkamp, Frankfurt/Main (1984)
10. Habermas, J.: Theorie des kommunikativen Handelns. Band 1 und 2. Vierte, durchgesehene Auflage edn. Suhrkamp, Frankfurt/Main (1987)
11. Kant, I.: Kritik der reinen Vernunft. Meiner, Hamburg (1956)
12. Krohn, W.: Das Risiko des (Nicht-)Wissens. Zum Funktionswandel der Wissenschaft in der Wissensgesellschaft. In Böschen, S., Schulz-Schaeffer, I., eds.: Wissenschaft in der Wissensgesellschaft. Westdeutscher Verlag, Wiesbaden (2003) 97–118
13. Parsons, T.: On the Concept of Influence. Public Opinion Quarterly **27** (1963) 37–62
14. Parsons, T.: Social Structure and the Symbolic Media of Interchance. In Blau, P.M., ed.: Approaches to the Study of Social Structure. Free Press etc., New York (1975) 94–120
15. Luhmann, N.: Einführende Bemerkungen zu einer Theorie symbolisch generalisierter Kommunikationsmedien. In Luhmann, N., ed.: Soziologische Aufklärung. Band 2: Aufsätze zur Theorie der Gesellschaft. Westdeutscher Verlag, Opladen (1975) 170–192
16. Luhmann, N.: Die Gesellschaft der Gesellschaft. Suhrkamp, Frankfurt/Main (1997)
17. Coleman, J.S.: Foundations of Social Theory. The Belknap Press of Harvard University Press, Cambridge., Mass. etc. (1990)
18. Esser, H.: Soziologie. Allgemeine Grundlagen. Campus, Frankfurt/Main etc. (1993)
19. Marx, K.: Das Kapital. Kritik der politischen Ökonomie. Erster Band. 4., durchgesehene Auflage, Hamburg 1890 edn. Dietz Verlag, Berlin (1971 <1890>)
20. Parsons, T.: On the Concept of Political Power. Proceedings of the American Philosophical Society **107** (1963) 232–262
21. Schimank, U.: Theorien gesellschaftlicher Differenzierung. 2. Aufl. edn. Leske + Budrich, Opladen (2000)
22. Merton, R.K.: Priorities in Scientific Discovery. American Sociological Review **22** (1957) 635–659
23. Luhmann, N.: Die Wissenschaft der Gesellschaft. Suhrkamp, Frankfurt/Main (1990)
24. Merton, R.K.: The matthew effect in science. Science **159** (1968) 56–63
25. Zuckerman, H., Merton, R.K.: Patterns of Evaluation in Science: Institutionalization, Structure and Functions of the Referee System. Minerva: A Review of Science, Learning and Policy **9** (1971) 66–100
26. Giddens, A.: The Consequences of Modernity. Stanford University Press, Stanford, Ca. (1990)
27. Menger, C.: Ueber das exacte (das atomistische) Verständnis des Ursprungs jener Socialgebilde, welche das unreflectirte Ergebnis gesellschaftlicher Entwickelung sind. In Menger, C., ed.: Untersuchungen über die Methode der Sozialwissenschaften und der politischen Ökonomie insbesondere. Volume Bd. 2 of Gesammelte Werke, hrsg. mit einer Einleitung und einem Schriftenverzeichnis von F. A. Hayek. 2. Aufl. edn. Mohr, Tübingen (1969 <1883>) 171–183
28. Conte, R.: Emergent (Info)Institutions. Cognitive Systems Research **2** (2001) 97–110
29. Davis, R., Smith, R.: Negotiation as a Metaphor for Distributed Problem Solving. Artificial Intelligence **20** (1983) 63–109
30. Schulz-Schaeffer, I.: Vergesellschaftung und Vergemeinschaftung künstlicher Agenten. Sozialvorstellungen in der Multiagenten-Forschung. Research Reports RR 3, Technikbewertung und Technikgestaltung, TU Hamburg-Harburg, Hamburg (2000)
31. Wellman, M.P.: A General-Equilibrium Approach to Distributed Transportation Planning. In Szolovits, P., ed.: AAAI-92. Proceedings of the Tenth National Conference on Artificial Intelligence, San Jose, California, July 1992, Menlo Park etc., AAAI Press/The MIT Press (1992) 282–289

32. Lesser, V.R., Corkhill, D.D.: The distributed vehicle monitoring testbed: A tool for investigating distributed problem solving networks. The AI Magazine **4** (1983) 15–33
33. Durfee, E.H., Lesser, V.R., Corkhill, D.D.: Trends in Cooperative Distributed Problem Solving. IEEE Transactions on Knowledge and Data Engineering **I** (1989) 63–83
34. Martial, F.v.: Coordinating Plans of Autonomous Agents. Springer-Verlag, Berlin etc. (1992)
35. Davis, R.: Report on the Workshop on Distributed AI. Sigart Newsletter **73** (1980) 42–52
36. Shoham, Y., Tennenholtz, M.: On the Synthesis of Useful Social Laws for Artificial Agents Societies (Preliminary Report). In Szolovits, P., ed.: AAAI-92. Proceedings of the Tenth National Conference on Artificial Intelligence, San Jose, California, July 1992, Menlo Park, Ca. etc., AAAI Press/The MIT Press (1992) 276–281
37. Castelfranchi, C.: Social Power. A Point Missed in Multi-Agent, DAI and HCI. In Müller, J.P., ed.: Dezentralized AI. Proceedings of the First European Workshop on Modelling Autonomous Agents in a Multi-Agent World, Amsterdam etc., Elsevier Science Publishers (North-Holland) (1990) 49–63
38. Conte, R., Castelfranchi, C.: Mind is Not Enough: The Cognitive Bases of Social Interaction. In Doran, J., ed.: Simulating Societies. The Computer Simulation of Social Phenomena. UCL-Press, London (1994) 267–286
39. Schulz-Schaeffer, I.: Innovation durch Konzeptübertragung. Der Rückgriff auf Bekanntes bei der Erzeugung, technischer Neuerungen am Beispiel der Multiagentensystem-Forschung. Zeitschrift für Soziologie **31** (2002) 232–251
40. Hewitt, C.E.: Offices are Open Systems. ACM Transactions on Office Information Systems **4** (1986) 271–287
41. Hewitt, C.E.: Open information systems semantics for distributed artificial intelligence. Artificial Intelligence **47** (1991) 79–106
42. Finin, T., Weber, J., Wiederhold, G., Genesereth, M., McKay, D., Fritzson, R., Shapiro, S., Pelavin, R., McGuire, J.: Specification of KQML Agent-Communication Language plus Example Agent Policies and Architectures. (Draft) Working Paper of the DARPA Knowledge Sharing Initiative External Interfaces Working Group (1993)
43. Labrou, Y., Finin, T.: A Proposal for a new KQML Specification. Technical Report TR CS-97-03, Computer Science and Electrical Engineering Department, University of Maryland, Maryland, Baltimore County (1997) MD 21250.
44. Bond, A.H.: A Computational Model for Organization of Cooperating Intelligent Agents. In Lochovsky, F.H., Allen, R.B., eds.: Proceedings of the Conference on Office Information Systems, Cambridge, Massachusetts (1990) 21–30
45. Cohen, P.R., Levesque, H.J.: Intention Is Choice with Commitment. Artifical Intelligence **42** (1990) 213–261
46. Jennings, N.R.: Coordination: Commitment and Conventions: The Foundation of Coordination in Multi-Agent Systems. Knowledge Engineering Review **8** (1993) 223–250
47. Castelfranchi, C.: Commitments: From Individual Intentions to Groups and Organizations. In Lesser, V., ed.: ICMAS-95. Proceedings of the First International Conference on Multi-Agent Systems, June 12-14, 1995 in San Francisco, California, Menlo Park etc., AAAI Press/The MIT Press (1995) 41–48
48. Castelfranchi, C., Conte, R.: Distributed Artificial Intelligence and Social Science: Critical Issues. In Jennings, N.R., ed.: Foundations of Distributed Artificial Intelligence. John Wiley & Sons, New York etc. (1996) 527–542
49. Michel, A., Senteni, A.: Emotions as Commitments Operators: A Foundation for Control Structure in Multi-Agent Systems. In Perram, J.P., ed.: Agents Breaking Away. 7th European Workshop on Modelling Autonomous Agents in a Multi-Agent World, MAAMAW'96, Berlin etc., Springer (1996) 13–25

50. Rosenschein, J.R., Genesereth, M.R.: Deals Among Rational Agents. In Gasser, L., ed.: Readings in Distributed Artificial Intelligence. Morgan Kaufmann Publishers, San Mateo, Ca. (1988) 227–234

51. Marsh, S.: Trust in Distributed Artificial Intelligence. In Werner, E., ed.: Artificial Social Systems. Volume 4th European Workshop on Modelling Autonomous Agents in a Multi-Agent World, MAAMAW'92 of Lecture Notes in Artificial Intelligence 830., Berlin etc., Springer-Verlag (1994) 94–114

52. Castelfranchi, C., Falcone, R.: Principles of Trust for MAS: Cognitive Anatomy, Social Importance, and Quantification. In: ICMAS'98. Proceedings of the International Conference on Multi-Agent Systems, Los Alamitos, Cal., IEEE Computer Society (1998) 72–79

53. Conte, R., Paolucci, M.: Reputation in Artificial Societies. Social Beliefs for Social Order. Kluwer Academic Publishers, Boston (2002)

54. Castelfranchi, C., Conte, R., Paolucci, M.: Normative Reputation and the Costs of Compliance. Journal of Artificial Societies and Social Simulation 1 (1998) http://www.soc.surrey.ac.uk/JASSS/1/3/3.html.

55. online, S.: eBay-Sicherheitsloch: Wie ein Träumer das Bewertungssystem aushebelte. Spiegel Online (2003) http://www.spiegel.de/netzwelt/netzkultur/0,1518,236673,00.html.

56. Schulz-Schaeffer, I.: Enrolling Software Agents in Human Organizations. The Exploration of Hybrid Organizations within the Socionics Research Program. In Saam, N.J., Schmidt, B., eds.: Cooperative Agents. Applications in the Social Sciences. Kluwer Academic Publishers, Dordrecht etc. (2001) 149–163

Scalability and the Social Dynamics of Communication. On Comparing Social Network Analysis and Communication-Oriented Modelling as Models of Communication Networks

Steffen Albrecht[1], Maren Lübcke[1], Thomas Malsch[1], and Christoph Schlieder[2]

[1] Hamburg University of Technology
Department of Technology Assessment
Schwarzenbergstr. 95, 21071 Hamburg, Germany
{steffen.albrecht, maren.luebcke, malsch}@tu-harburg.de
[2] Bamberg University
Department of Applied Computer Science
Feldkirchenstr. 21, 96045 Bamberg, Germany
christoph.schlieder@wiai.uni-bamberg.de

Abstract. Internet communication is a major challenge for anyone claiming to design scalable multiagent systems. Millions of messages are passed every day, referring to one another and thus shaping a gigantic network of communication. In this paper, we compare and discuss two different approaches to modelling and analysing such large-scale networks of communication: Social Network Analysis (SNA) and Communication-Oriented Modelling (COM). We demonstrate that, with regard to scalability, COM offers striking advantages over SNA. Based on this comparison, we identify mechanisms that foster scalability in a broader sense, comprising issues of downscaling as well.

1   Introduction

Internet communication is a very large-scale process with millions of messages passed every day. Uncountable emails are sent and received, websites are visited by growing numbers of users in search for information, and masses of contributions are published in Internet forums such as Usenet discussion groups. With figures like, for instance, the 700.000.000 messages in the Usenet archives on Google's servers,[1] increasing by ca. 150.000.000 messages every year, Internet communication appears to be an ideal case for approaching issues of scalability in multiagent systems (MAS).

In viewing communication as a central element to consider in the design of MAS, we follow the methodology of Communication-Oriented Modelling (COM) that was developed by Malsch and Schlieder [1]. COM is supposed to complement and reinforce agent-oriented modelling (AOM), today the standard approach to distributed artificial intelligence (DAI). In contrast to AOM, COM models communication as a stream of messages connected to one another by references. It does not conceive of communication as a transmission of information from sender to receiver, as it is typical for agent

---

[1] See groups.google.com.

K. Fischer, M. Florian, and T. Malsch (Eds.): Socionics, LNAI 3413, pp. 242–262, 2005.

communication languages in current agent platforms. From the COM perspective, individual agents and their internal operations are only peripheral elements. The focus is on the emergent structural properties of communication.

In this paper, we want to evaluate COM's potential for the design of scalable multiagent systems. We do this by comparing COM to another way of modelling social structures: Social Network Analysis (SNA). Both COM and SNA can be regarded as sociological models, derived from the analysis of social phenomena. Both model communication in the form of networks, thus allowing to analyse and simulate various communicative phenomena in MAS as well as human society. However, while SNA follows an actor-centric approach and is largely static, COM puts communication in the centre of analysis and focuses on its dynamics.

Our hypothesis is that COM is better suited to model communication on a large scale. By systematically exploiting the temporal dimension of dynamic network reproduction, it should be capable of accelerating and up-scaling its message turnover to an extent that meets the demands of real world mass communication in the Internet. In the following section we demonstrate that the small differences between both models actually have a major impact on our ability not only to describe and explain, but also to simulate and empirically analyse large-scale processes of communication in the Internet. Such a potential is also relevant for future perspectives—once a powerful tool has been developed, it can be used to support human beings as well as artificial agents engaged in such processes of communication, and an important step towards the design of large-scale open systems in the sense of Hewitt [2] would be made.

As we think of such practical relevance for the design of MAS, we have to reconsider the notion of scalability. Large numbers, as suggested by much of the literature on scalability, is not the only important aspect. Scaling up is just one option for an MAS to cope with a changing demand. The underlying issue, as we see it, is the ability to react flexibly to changing environments. Scaling down, then, can be important as well, e.g., to concentrate on solving difficult and complex problems. In Section three, we present our new perspective and discuss different strategies to cope with scalability in this sense.

The final section concludes with a reflection on SNA and COM's ability to model scalable communication networks. It summarizes the results of our comparison and highlights the advantages of the COM model. However, as a field of intensive development, new work in SNA proposes to have interesting implications. Cross-fertilization between COM and SNA will be a promising option for future work.

2   SNA and COM as Models for Scalable Communication Systems

One of sociology's central purposes is the construction of models of the social world. Models serve as a link between abstract theories and empirical reality [3]. They translate the social theoretic perspective into a description of the relations between relevant entities, each of which can be tested by observation. In its long tradition, sociology has developed a large number of models at various levels of abstraction and complexity. Some of the sociological models are directly related to specific domains of social phenomena, others claim to be relevant for a broader range of the social world. Due to their generality, the latter can be regarded as methodological tools for describing and analysing social phenomena.

The transfer of concepts and models from sociology to DAI and to the development of MAS is one of the acclaimed outcomes of Socionics [4]. Along the lines of the so-called "computational reference", we examine how sociological models of communication can be used as models for the construction of large-scale communication processes in MAS. While research in DAI has acknowledged the need to move from single messages to sequences of message exchange, i.e., 'conversations' [5], the models we are interested in go one step further, trying to enhance our understanding of communication on the level of agent societies that comprise vast numbers of agents. Such an understanding is the first step towards—and a necessary prerequisite of—using communication structures in the design of MAS.

For this purpose, we have identified two sociological models that seem worth a closer investigation: Social Network Analysis and Communication-Oriented Modelling. Both are rather abstract models, but nevertheless provide means that are precise enough to conceptualize communication processes. SNA has a long tradition of research, but is less specific than COM—a very new approach, outlined only recently. Despite apparent similarities of their visualizations, there is a considerable degree of difference between both. We will present both models and compare them to examine the impact of their differences on their ability to serve as models for scalable communication systems.

2.1   Social Network Analysis: A Guide to Modelling Communication?

Within the social sciences, interest in using Social Network Analysis to describe and analyse social structures has been steadily increasing. In the early days of 'sociometrics' in the 1930s, researchers started to use graph drawings to describe interpersonal structures. This was the birth of the "network perspective" in the social sciences. In the following decades and until today, more and more social phenomena were described with the help of network models: Studies using SNA range from small group research to research into organisational structures as well as the analysis of, e.g., international economic transactions. The results of these studies have proved the viability of applying the network perspective in sociology, so that today, network analysis is seen as "one of the most promising currents in sociological research" [6].

What is it that makes SNA so attractive, and what makes it seem an interesting candidate for modelling large-scale processes of communication? First, a network is a very flexible model for various forms of structural patterns. SNA presupposes only two basic entities, nodes and edges. It offers a number of mathematical methods to derive meaningful information out of the various combinations that can be observed or modelled with these two entities. Second, concerning the analysis of empirically observable networks, SNA offers methods that are highly sophisticated from a mathematical point of view. They build on algorithms forming the state of the art in statistics (e.g., hierarchical clustering, factor analysis) as well as special procedures based directly on graph theory (e.g., triad census) (cf. [7], [8]).

However, SNA should not be seen as a mere toolbox for the quantitative analysis of structural data. This would ignore a vast array of literature trying to make sense of the network phenomenon in theoretical terms. Thus, thirdly - as Wasserman and Faust put it in their seminal textbook on SNA - , "network analysis, rather than being an unrelated collection of methods, is grounded in important social phenomena and theoretical concepts." [7] That is, there is a body of theoretical concepts and hypotheses laying the foundations for structural analysis, and both theory and methods are intimately interwoven with one another.

In this tradition of SNA as a research perspective (rather than a mere set of methods), social network models largely concern sets of actors and their relations. Although in principle, the graph theoretic algorithms of SNA can be applied to whatever basic unit one is interested in, SNA is typically actor-centric, focusing on individual or collective actors as the nodes of the network.[2] Thus, communication networks are conceptualized as exchange networks with a set of actors engaging in the exchange of messages.[3]

There are good reasons to attempt to model processes of communication with the help of SNA. All theories conceive of communication as an intrinsically *relational* phenomenon. Communication establishes ties between actors in turning from utterance to reception and vice versa. SNA seems to be well suited to model communication since it has gained respect particularly for capturing the relational aspects of social structures. Despite being based on such simple constructs as nodes and edges, it has proven to be able to grasp even highly complex structures resulting from the selective combination of these basic elements.

Applying SNA to model especially *large-scale* communication processes is a less evident choice. The research methods of SNA originated in small group research, and still today many algorithms are based on matrix representation that pose difficulties when growing to large scales [14]. However, recent applications of network measures to the graph of the world wide web [15] show that in general it is possible to model and analyse even very large networks. It depends on the methods that need to be applied to the networks whether scale is a problem or not. We will examine this issue more deeply after we have introduced a second way of modelling communication processes: COM.

---

[2] This does not mean that SNA is employing an overly simplistic concept of agency. Actors can be human beings, but also collective actors like families (as in Padgett and Ansell's study on the marriage strategies of the Medici and their peers [9]), organisations, or even nation states (as in a study of the international telephone network [10] and of the Eurovision song contest [11]). But in any of these cases, actors are relatively stable social entities with a certain degree of autonomy in their behaviour. Furthermore, while we do identify SNA with an actor-centric perspective, this does not mean that within the broad community interested in SNA there are no other applications of the network perspective. Examples include information networks (as in citation analysis) or semantic networks. As extensions to the actor-centric perspective of SNA, these are discussed in the final section of this paper.

[3] A typical—even canonical—study of communication networks is Freeman's analysis of an early computer conferencing system [12]. He studies a network of 50 scientists using a CMC system, and measures their relations based on awareness, acquaintanceship and exchange of messages. The structural properties of the network are analysed by looking at the amount of messages exchanged between each pair of actors in a given time. Thus, the scientists and their relational properties are in the centre of analysis, and the author even claims that "in one sense, then, the study of the sociology of science is the study of links among persons." [12] For a similar application of SNA to communication networks, see [13].

2.2   Communication-Oriented Modelling

In contrast to SNA, COM is specifically designed to understand and analyse the complexity and temporality of social communication. It is based on a social theory of communication and provides conceptual means focused on modelling communication processes. COM was proposed as a model for multiagent communication by Malsch and Schlieder [1]. Here, we summarize the theoretical foundations only briefly and concentrate our discussion on issues of large scale.

Theoretical Foundations. As we have noted above, communication in COM is not organised along the lines of agent-to-agent relations as in AOM. In communication on the level of society, as for instance on the Internet, we can observe patterns of communication organised as message-to-message relations. This means that messages refer to other messages in an ongoing process of weaving and reweaving complex webs of communication. Moreover, messages usually are not sent to a specific receiver, but published "to whom it may concern". Thus, whenever a message is published for an audience rather than sent to a receiver, and whenever communication is dominated by messages referring to other messages rather than agents influencing other agents' actions, it is not the agent but the communication that should be considered as the foundational unit of analysis.

Communication consists of two types of operations: reception (understanding a message) and inception (producing a message). Inception and reception are defined as the temporal elements (or elementary operations) of social communication. They are complementary operations. Messages cannot be connected with each other by either a reception or an inception alone. Both operations must be activated and carried out in a temporal order, i.e., a predecessor message must have been received before any successor message can be inceived etc. Defining inception and reception as the ope elements of social communication means to compare them to the elements in biological systems, i.e., biological cells in a living body. These are permanently reproduced and exchanged, and so are communicative operations. Hence, and this is in accordance with what may be called the communicative turn in sociology (cf. [16], [17]), reception and inception are construed as the temporal "stuff" that communication networks are made up of.

In contrast to the transient character of communicative operations, messages can be relatively persistent. Messages are empirical sign-objects and—again in contrast to communicative operations—being empirical, they can be observed. In line with Peirce's semiotics and Mead's concept of symbolic interactions, a message is a perceivable, empirically observable object [18]. It is a meaningful object, or in Mead's terminology, a significant object. Being meaningful and empirically observable, messages point out to communicative operations, which, in turn, are unobservable. Whenever a message refers to another message, we can reasonably assume that the preceding message has been received, and that this reception has triggered the inception of the referring message. Methodologically, we cannot observe communication at the level of its elementary operations. Thus, to draw inferences about the inceptions and receptions actually taking place, we have to observe the pattern of referencing.

In COM, messages are activated, deactivated, or reactivated in a continuous process of selective referencing. There are always messages that are drawn on again and again by more and more subsequent messages. The more a given message is referenced by subsequent messages, the higher its social visibility and the longer its life-span or social persistence. Unless a message is permanently drawn on again and again by successor messages, it will gradually loose its social visibility, although in a physical sense it may still exist. Thus, social persistence and visibility of messages are fostered by referencing while decay and disappearance are induced by constant non-referencing. Viewing message referencing from the macro perspective of large-scale processes, communication networks can be described as patterns of messages emerging from the selective interplay of referencing and non-referencing.

Moreover, a communication network's continuous reproduction depends on massive redundancy, on the permanent production and disappearance of masses of elementary operations and related messages. Selective referencing is based on redundancy. To keep going, a communication network not only must permanently replace and reproduce its operational elements and its operational manifestations in a continuous process, but it must do so on a very large-scale level. The following figure is supposed to give a rough idea of how emergent patterns of communication depend on what could also be called the systematic waste production of huge amounts of communication.

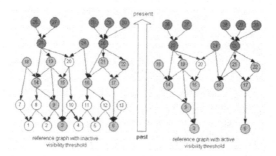

Fig. 1. Referencing graphs without (left) / with visibility threshold (right): nodes with low visibility are displayed in white, nodes with high visibility are displayed in dark colours

In Figure 1 we can see two snapshots of a COM model of a message referencing structure. In COM, nodes are messages and edges are references. The arrows of referencing are directed against the temporal flow of communication. The diagram shows how some messages obtain more social visibility and persistence by being referenced more often, while some others are ignored and remain un-referenced until they disappear from the screen because their visibility sinks below the threshold.

Modelling Communication with COM. Comparing the two snapshots, it becomes apparent that the concept of social visibility is an important factor in shaping the structure of a communication process. Visibility acts as a self-enforcing momentum—only messages with a high degree of visibility are referred to in the course of time, and the visibility of a specific message increases with the number of references directed to it. For modelling communication processes with COM, finding an appropriate visibility function is of central importance for the adequacy of the model (see [1] for an elaboration of this aspect).

Another characteristic of COM models is their inherent temporality. Since COM is conceiving of communication as a dynamic process, there has to be a constant flow of messages and references for the process to go on. The state of the model at each point in time depends on the previous states. And for a message's visibility to become an indicator of its relevance, the dynamics of referencing are crucial. As communication is not only a relational, but also a temporal phenomenon, COM seems well equipped to model communication processes.

2.3   Comparing SNA and COM with Regard to Scalability

Both models seem equally well suited for modelling communication, and we can now concentrate on issues of scalability. At the time being, MAS are developed on a rather small scale, involving just a couple of agents. Current state-of-the-art agent platforms (like JADE, FIPA-OS, etc.) support numbers of up to some hundreds of agents, but not more. There are two reasons why we cannot be satisfied with such a limited scale of MAS. First, one of the most interesting application domains of MAS is the Internet. With many hundreds of millions of users online, any MAS for the Internet has to be of a very large scale, far exceeding today's standards [19]. Second, from the perspective of sociology, we are interested in modelling communication on the level of society. Whereas it is less problematic to reason about and model interpersonal communication, the societal level poses quite the same problems that in computer science are related with "large-scale open systems" [2]. Thus, the models we are interested in must be able to represent empirical phenomena on various scales, from agent-to-agent communication to very large scales .

In DAI, scalability usually amounts to the question: How is it possible to support growing numbers of agents on multiagent platforms, and what can be done to improve a system's problem solving capacity by adding more agents to the system [20], [21]? Hence, the quantity of agents is the crucial independent variable [22]. It is measured against, e.g., the amount of computational operations [23] or the maximum communication load [24]. To achieve scalability, MAS designers have to enable their system to cope with increasing numbers of agents.

However, other factors can also lead to an increase in scale. In the context of Internet communication on a many-to-many-basis, we would like to know how to scale up the number of messages, not only of agents. And when, for instance, some agents are replaced by a different type, the system will become more complex and the dependent dimensions (computational operations, communication load, etc.) are affected as well. Therefore, our comparison of the two models of communication departs from a notion of scalability that views the communication system as the central phenomenon potentially growing to a large scale.

As a complex system, communication might grow in several respects. Basically, we can distinguish two *dimensions* of change - quantity and quality. In each dimension, two kinds of *entities* can change - agents and communication. That is, a communication system grows in scale if ...

...the number of participating agents increases (quantitative change of agents)

...more messages are exchanged (quantitative change of communication)

...different types of agents take part in it (qualitative change of agents)

...different types of communication are involved (qualitative change of communication).

For both models respectively, we will examine how well they are able to model communication under conditions of an increasing complexity of the communication system. According to our strictly systemic perspective, we are only interested in the elements of a system and their relations, not in the internal construction of these elements, as for instance the agent's architecture.[4]

SNA Scaling Up. First, we want to examine SNA's potential to scale up with respect to the number of messages. As mentioned above, communication processes are modelled in SNA as a set of actors (nodes) connected by flows of messages (edges). Increasing the number of messages would not result in a substantial change of the structure of the network. The set of actors remains the same, and once a connection has been established, it will only change qualitatively. More messages will result in a stronger connection between the actors involved. But of course, with more messages being exchanged, the probability that two actors are connected increases also, so that the network might become more complex. Another aspect is the qualitative change of the edges. Edges have to be differentiated according to their strength, depending on the number of messages exchanged between two actors. However, it is easy to translate this quality into a quantity, and introducing a threshold value allows to reduce the complexity of the model. Consequently, the number of messages exchanged can be scaled up to a large degree.

If we think about scaling up realistically, however, it affects not only the number of messages, but also the number of agents involved in the MAS. Agents are modelled as nodes in SNA, and increasing the number of nodes means to put a high burden on the modelling capacity. Due to constraints of computational power in past times, SNA has not been able to cope with large numbers of nodes. Today, the problem of computing power has vanished, but still a fundamental problem remains: every increase in the number of agents implies an increase in the number of *possible* relations between them to the power of two.[5] Since most measures in SNA work with a comparison of actual vs. potential relations between nodes, this means that SNA has to fully cope with

---

[4] For a justification of this narrow view in the analysis of large-scale communication systems, see [1].

[5] This leads us to another general drawback of using SNA to model communication networks: each actor has to be modelled, whether he communicates or not (since he always could be communicating, and thus has to be respected). Due to the high amount of "lurking" observed in computer-mediated communication (see [25], [26], [27]), we can expect that only a small part of the agents is actively involved in the communication process. Agent-based models produce unnecessary overhead and thus appear to be less favourable for modelling such communication processes.

the additional complexity. Thus, scaling up the number of nodes in SNA implies an unproportionally high computational burden.

There are methods to cope with this problem in SNA. One is to exclude all irrelevant actors from the network. In a communication network, all actors that are not communicating can be considered irrelevant. However, in a dynamic social system, one can never be sure whether an actor will become relevant or not, so that this method is only applicable in special circumstances. Another more promising method is to aggregate actors to form collective actors. This amounts to shifting the level of analysis from the individual to groups or other collective actors. The complexity of the network on the higher level will typically be greatly reduced. But as a side effect, a lot of information not only on the individual actors, but also on the relations between them is lost in the process of abstraction.

Taking the types of messages being exchanged into consideration is also posing difficulties to SNA models. Typically, communication networks in SNA ignore the type of messages exchanged. However, one might wish to design different networks for each type of communicative relation (e.g., task-related vs. coordination-related communication). Such multi-relational or multiplex networks consist of multiple matrices, one for each type of relationship. Increasing the types of relations follows a linear scale and is not problematic. However, multiplexity weakens the efficiency of the model to a considerable degree, because the amount of change that is effective (i.e., the additional messages exchanged) is small compared to the amount of data that has to be computed (i.e., an additional matrix for each new type of relation). What is more, existing problems with the number of actors will be multiplied if many matrices have to be modelled.

Finally, we have to consider the case of scaling up the types of actors involved. On this dimension of scalability, SNA is highly scalable, as it is possible to completely ignore the type of actors involved by simply regarding them as uniform nodes. One problem that might arise is that it is difficult for SNA to take into account attributional data together with the relational data. Approaches to solve this problem are currently a topic of research [28]. However, with regard to modelling communication processes in MAS, we can neglect this problem, as in large-scale open systems, we typically have all sorts of agents involved, and from the point of view of a communication system, it would not be wise to attempt to model the individual agents explicitly. The same, of course, holds true for the COM model.

COM Scaling Up. COM models communication by taking messages as the central elements. Thus, one would expect that scaling up the number of messages increases the load of the system substantially. The model has to take into account every new message with all its references to other messages, and the computational burden could easily grow to an unmanageable size. Compared to SNA, which only needs to change the strength of the relations in a given network, COM appears to be less scalable.

However, this problem is already accounted for in the design of COM. By exploiting the selectivity of referencing and the temporal effects of social visibility, COM is able to intelligently reduce the number of messages that actually have to be considered. Only messages with a high degree of visibility need to be taken into account by the model, all other messages are ignored and will not be a burden for further processing. Hence, increasing the number of messages in COM results in a proportionally smaller increase of the computational load of the system. The extra burden is focused on only those messages that are most important for the further proceeding of communication. Moreover, the visibility threshold applied in the model is variable, so that one can regulate the selectivity of the model with respect to the demand in a given situation.

Given a fixed amount of computational resources, a communication network's scalability with regard to the number of message nodes can be enhanced by simply raising its visibility threshold. Raising the visibility threshold implies that the disappearance rate grows and, as a consequence, the network's search space becomes smaller (see Figure 1 for a visualization of this effect). Thus, more messages and references can be processed in the same time. This feature of COM is derived from observations of different types of social communication: message turnover in oral communication, evidently, suffers (or profits) from much higher disappearance rates than textual communication.

Observing real-world communication, points to another social mechanism of reducing complexity despite growing numbers of messages: subforum formation. Subforum formation means that in communication messages typically centre around topics, so that an empirically observable structure emerges. In the message reference graph, we can observe distinct clusters of messages with references to messages on the same topic, but not to messages on other topics. Each of these clusters is a subforum. An example is the citation graph of scientific papers: citations crossing disciplinary boundaries are rare compared to citations within a discipline. Thus, each discipline (and each specialty within a discipline, etc.) can be regarded as a subforum. The emergent hierarchical structure of forums makes it easier for scholars to find papers of interest in the mass of scientific production and to find interested audiences for their publications, respectively.

Incorporating this mechanism in COM means to enable the communication system to dynamically detect the formation of subforums. As a result, larger amounts of messages can be computed, since the hierarchy of forums reduces the search space for individual messages. Subforum formation can be seen as a variant of the well-known "divide and conquer"-strategy: Only messages referring to the specific topic under question need to be taken into account. Thus, together with the visibility thresholds, COM offers two mechanisms to scale up to large numbers of messages.

As for the number of agents involved, scaling up is less problematic than for the number of messages. Since COM was designed specifically for modelling communication processes and takes messages as its basic units, it does abstract from the agents uttering the messages. Increasing the number of agents has almost no effect at all on the model - except for a growing number of messages exchanged between these agents, which is likely to be the consequence. But again, in this case all additional resources are used in a highly effective way to reduce the complexity.

Scaling up the types of messages in COM can be compared to scaling up the types of actors in SNA. One can design the model as completely ignorant of the type of messages, representing each message, whatever its type, as a uniform node. This is the way the model is designed at the moment. In this case, scaling up the type of messages has no effect on the complexity of the model. However, it might seem reasonable to provide an option for representing different types of messages in COM. Analyses of communication processes have shown that turn-taking and sequences of messages are very important for the effectiveness of communication. These can only be modelled adequately if different types of messages, e.g., offer / bid or request / reply can be distinguished. On the other hand, communication theory based on Mead and Peirce shows that it's not the content of a message, but rather its effect in the flow of communication that makes a message meaningful in a particular way.[6] Thus, the simplification done by the COM model rests on a sound theoretical foundation.

Finally, what happens if we wish to scale up the type of agents involved, increasing the heterogeneity of the system's components? First, we would not expect any effect at all arising from an increase in the type of actors. As the COM model abstracts from agents, changing the type of agents should not affect the model's performance. However, we have to think about what it means to model the communication of heterogeneous agent societies. Despite the communication-oriented approach, the agents do not completely vanish from the model. They mark the point where messages are received and new messages are inceived coupling both operations in form of references. In consequence, any change in the heterogeneity of actors will impact the kind of referencing taking place in the process of communication. However, the COM model can account for such effects by its capacity to model dynamically changing flows of communication. Thus, scaling up the type of agents in the MAS would not pose problems to COM's level of scalability.

Results. The comparison of the two models of communication shows that the COM model is favourable for modelling increasingly complex communication systems. With its specific design, derived from a sociological theory of communication, and by help of exploiting the temporal dynamics of processes of communication, COM has less problems to scale up than social network models. Abstracting from the communicating agents and placing the messages in the centre of interest has proved to be advantageous with respect to scalability. As our thought experiment in scalability has shown, the only case in which COM is less scalable than SNA is when the number of messages increases. But taking into account the specific mechanisms of COM, this disadvantage of COM vanishes completely.

SNA models, in contrast, are influenced by issues of scale in two dimensions. As a flexible and rather abstract model of structural patterns, SNA has no problems with an increase in the number of messages or with heterogeneous sets of agents involved in the communication. However, scaling up the number of agents could result in an quadratic growth of the demand of computational power, part of which would not have any effect on the performance of the system. Although there exist some mechanisms to reduce the complexity introduced by large numbers of agents, these are limited in their applicability. Scaling up the heterogeneity of messages and communicative relations would lead to only a small overall increase in computational load, but this increase would be even less effective. Thus, applying social network models to communication processes would likely result in an unnecessary waste of resources.

---

[6] This assumption is also prominent in DAI. As Hewitt pointed out in his classical text on the actor model of computation, this view can be applied to agent communication as well, allowing to abstract from the content of messages by looking at the structure of message flows [29].

Two reasons for this result can be identified. First, SNA, in the form discussed here, is actor-centric, narrowing its scope to social entities like human beings or organisations. This implies that a large part of the tools cannot be applied to communication in the same effective way as to actors. The same criticism that led to the development of COM as a complement to agent-based modelling can be directed towards SNA. Large-scale communication processes are not primarily based on individual agents and their characteristics, but rather show emergent systemic properties best described as message-to-message relations.

Second, SNA is largely static, focusing on established structures without providing sufficient means to analyse dynamic processes. As we have seen, it is precisely the ability to exploit the dynamic aspects of communication that enables COM to cope with a growing scale. Certain social mechanisms to reduce complexity, like, e.g., selective memory and the ability to forget, are inherently temporal. To fully profit from the transfer of sociological concepts to solve the scalability problem, the models employed must be able to encompass the dynamics of social communication.

3   Scalability Reconsidered

3.1   A New Perspective on Scalability

So far, we have regarded scalability from the perspective of large-scale communication systems, considering only the effects of scaling up the system along various dimensions, notably the quantity of agents and communication. However, this view of scalability is not the only one, and, in our opinion, not the most appropriate for reflecting the design of multiagent systems. Whether a multiagent system is big or small says little about its actual performance, that is, its ability to solve the problems it was designed for. Of course, some MAS have to be able to grow to a large number of agents (i.e., Internet marketplaces, etc.), others, however, might operate more efficiently by, e.g., changing their way of approaching problems. Simply to grow is not a strategy that can be employed universally.

We propose to regard scalability in the context of the problems a MAS is designed to solve. The most important aspect of scalability is the ability to react to changing needs in a flexible manner. Thus, adaptability is the prerequisite of scalability. This new view of scalability is more general than the classical view.[7] In the case of our reference example of multi-agent communication, we can identify two problems to be solved: The one is to simply cope with a mass of communication, i.e., processing messages and making them available for reception, the implications of which are discussed above with regard to a large scale. The other problem in communication is to ensure that communication is going on, that messages keep on generating other messages referring to one another, despite the many threats making an interruption of the process of communication likely [16]. Such threats occur for example in conflicts, and the problem of ensuring continuation cannot be solved by scaling up, but rather requires a more intensive treatment.

---

[7] Note that the classical view is included in this general notion as a special case. Coping with large numbers of agents can be one sort of problem a MAS has to solve, e.g., providing matchmaking and facilitation services for individual agents on the Internet.

Thus, what we gain by adopting this problem-oriented perspective is a broader range of solutions to the problem of scalability. Scaling up the number of agents is only one option to cope with increasing problem load, re-organisation, for instance, might be another one. In any case, the important independent variable is not the number of agents, but the problems that are solved. As Laitinen et al. note, "scalability in the context of software engineering is the property of reducing or increasing the scope of methods, processes, and management according to the problem size." [30] Accordingly, the two

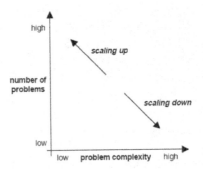

Fig. 2. A problem-oriented view on scalability: A system can either solve many simple problems (upper left corner) or some complex problems (lower right corner). The arrows outline the scalability strategies under conditions of constant resources: scaling up or scaling down

dimensions of quantity and quality have to be applied to the problem domain of the MAS under consideration. In the quantitative dimension, there can be many problems to solve or only a small number. Solving large numbers of problems requires strategies to scale up, as outlined above. Typically, few problems will not pose difficulties to any MAS. However, problems can have different qualities, ranging from simple to complex problems. Again, only the complex problems are hard to tackle. Combining both dimensions, as shown in Figure 2, we can identify two situations that require an MAS to scale, given a fixed amount of computational resources: a large number of simple problems means it is necessary to scale up, and a small number of complex problems requires to scale down[8] (solving a larger number of more complex problems is only possible if resources are added to the system).

---

[8] The notion of scaling 'down' is introduced here to mark the contrast to the well-known notion of scaling 'up'. Against possible intuitions, it does not mean to simply reduce the capacity of a system, but rather to switch from a quantitative scale to a qualitative one. However, as the term 'qualitative scaling' has already been used in relation to upscaling (see Schimank in this book), we chose the notion of 'scaling down' for addressing such qualitative changes.

3.2   Mechanisms for Scaling Down

As we have already discussed how MAS can scale up, we will now focus on mechanisms for scaling down. As outlined above, scaling down means the ability to adapt to a kind of problem solving behaviour that is most suitable for a small number of highly complex problems. For example, we can think of a "problem mode" of the MAS in which all resources available can be concentrated to solve one or a few problems.

Our discussion of mechanisms for scaling down does not follow the model of a one-to-one comparison of SNA and COM. As we will see, both models provide mechanisms to scale down that are complementary rather than competitive. In searching for solutions to the new problem of scaling down, we would be ill-advised to reject any opportunities. Rather, we seek for a constructive cross-fertilization of both approaches. We identify three mechanisms for downscaling: increasing the depth of information, selective memory, and the fusion of subforums.

Scaling Down by Increasing Information Depth.   Both SNA and COM are abstract models of the empirical phenomena that can be described and analysed with their help. By increasing the information depth of these models, we are searching for more complex representations. Adequate representation of the complexity of problems is a precondition and first step to the solution of difficult problems.

Given a social network based on the exchange of communication, there is no direct way to make it more complex without changing the basic factors (number of agents or messages, types of agents or messages). However, the abstract representation of social structure can be replaced by a more detailed one by 'zooming' in on the nodes or the edges of the network, the actors or the relations, respectively. A social actor, for example, can be conceived as a collection of roles, each entertaining specific communicative relationships with other actors. These roles can be analysed or modelled separately to account for a problem in a more detailed way.

In most cases, deconstructing the nodes of a social network in such a way means to decompose the edges as well. For each role, a special type of relationship will exist (e.g., a person can be a mother to her kids and a boss to her employees), resulting in a multiplex network. The result is a more complex network that can be exploited to better solve complicated problems. The negative side of the scaling-down process is that the mathematical methods to deal with such multiplex networks are very complex and resource consumptive. The application of such methods should follow only after a thorough analysis of the problem, and it should be selectively concentrated on the area for which a solution can be expected.

In COM, a similar strategy can be applied to increase the density of information incorporated in the model's representation. The point of departure is that the concept of referencing in COM is abstracting from the underlying difference of inception and reception. In Figure 3, a communication process is shown at two different levels of abstraction. On the left side, the referencing level is shown, on the right side, the same process is depicted at the operational level of reception and inception. At the operational level the process appears to be much more complex and fragile.

As we can see, a message can only be inceived by a single operation, but it can be received multiply. By receiving a message, an agent or actor can be activated to publish another message by carrying out another operation, an inception. Both types of operations together are needed to create a reference. However, both operations are at the same time highly autonomous. An inception is free to process the meaning of a reception, but it is also free not to process at all. This is the interesting point of selective interruption. Distinguishing reception and inception, instead of viewing communication as a single operational element, thus helps to gain more insights into the inherent fragility and contingency of social webs of communication. Furthermore, it opens up possibilities to

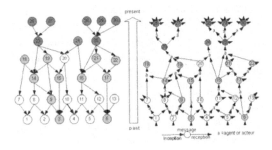

Fig. 3. Levels of abstraction in COM models: referencing (left) and the operational level of inception and reception (right)

influence and modify the flow of communication. By revealing the role of the agent as the crucial link between reception and inception, the operational representation allows to analyse the process to detect where exactly the problem comes up, and to find ways for solving it. The level of detail of this model is a problem for large scales, but it means an advantage for therapy if the system switches in the problem-mode.

However, bridging the gap from reception to inception with agents does not mean that the solution has to be sought in the agent's internal architecture. In order to describe what actually happens when reception triggers inception, we must keep in mind that it would be misleading to attribute continuation values to individual selection alone. Of course, value differences are produced by autonomous operations in the first place. But any value is but an ephemeral selection, a disappearing temporal element of a continuous process of communication. And the emergent outcome of selecting and re-selecting informational content and practical relevance are patterns of social visibility and persistence reinforcing the social selectivity of communication.

Scaling Down by Selective Memory. The identification of such patterns of social visibility and persistence, on the other hand, can be seen as a contribution to developing solutions for highly complex problems. One strategy to deal with complex problems in the course of time is to foster learning by help of memory - exactly contrary to the social process of forgetting caused by visibility thresholds. A communication system, then, can be conceived as a specific form of memory, storing past events and their consequences in form of relatively stable abstract structures. These structures can be used by individual agents as a reference for their decisions, e.g., about where to publish a new message, or which message to reply to first.[9]

But simply storing information in analogy to a library will not help. A communication system as selective memory should be conceived as storing relations rather than a specific content that can be requested. The latter form of memory is only able to store predefined information that can be applied to predefined situations. The first, in addition, supports the capability of producing new information [32]. Thus, the communication system should not be a static storage device, but a dynamic and selective medium, including mechanisms for pattern recognition.

The COM model has already shown to be able to model dynamic structures. It seems possible to model a kind of selective memory with the help of COM techniques. The social visibility function is an example of how such a mechanism could be designed—though it acts in the opposite direction. As mentioned before, SNA has much bigger problems with modelling dynamic phenomena. Messages in a communication network, for instance, are ultra-persistent entities, as the evolving structure is a cumulative one. Paradoxically as it seems, this design for persistence is a barrier for modelling the kind of memory needed for storing problem solutions in a flexible and dynamical way.

Scaling Down by Subforum Fusion. As shown above, COM offers the possibility of reducing the search space of large-scale discussions by identifying subforums based on shared topics. This differentiation of a communication network is not a one-way process. Subforums can as well be combined to build one larger forum, e.g., if the topics are very similar, or if the communication in two or more subforums converges. We will call such a process of subforums merging together "subforum fusion".

A similar mechanism is employed in the identification of cohesive subgroups in SNA. Cohesive subgroups are sets of actors that are densely related to one another—the relations within the subgroup have to be stronger than the relations to actors on the outside. To identify such subgroups, SNA offers an algorithm based on hierarchical clustering techniques. It is possible to flexibly choose the strength of cohesion required for the identification of a subgroup. Thus, a network can consist of only one "sub"group at the one extreme and as many subgroups as there are actors at the other extreme, depending on the threshold chosen.

Switching from a higher threshold value to a lower value will result in a similar fusion as in COM. The difference is that in SNA we are combining actors based on the relations they have, instead of thematic forums as in COM. The effect, however, is in both cases the same. The search space grows larger as the differentiation between the forums / groups disappears. What has been considered a problem for scaling up is a solution for scaling down: if the problems become more complex, a solution is harder to find. Thus, increasing the search space will be a sensible strategy.

The identification of mechanisms to scale down shows that COM is also well prepared to face scalability in a more general sense than commonly used. Although COM at the moment is not ready to model all of them, we have demonstrated that the social

---

[9] In DAI, several methods to use knowledge encoded in structures have been developed under the umbrella of research in "case-based reasoning" (e.g., [31]).

theoretical foundation in communication theory and the dynamic approach to modelling enable COM to incorporate such extensions without having to change the model significantly.

4   Conclusions and Future Work

In this paper, we have shown that COM's claim to be particularly useful for modelling scalable communication is justified. Compared to one of the most attractive methods of contemporary sociology, Social Network Analysis, COM seems to be better able to cope with communication processes of large scale. We have already identified two reasons for this result: COM focuses on messages as the central elements of communication, contrary to SNA's actor-centrism. And whereas SNA is often criticised as being overly static, COM models communication networks as a dynamic flow of messages being only loosely connected by references. As a third reason, we might add that COM profits from a sound theoretical foundation in a theory of communication specialised on large-scale processes. SNA, in contrast, is criticised as lacking a thorough theoretical foundation [33]. Studies in SNA typically employ an exchange theoretic framework [34], but work in communication theory has pointed out the limitations of such an approach to communication.

Our results have implications for the design of multiagent systems as they point out some drawbacks of agent-oriented modelling techniques. In large-scale communication, messages are not addressed to a specific receiver, but are posted to be read by anybody who shows interest. In Usenet discussion groups, for instance, all messages follow a "to whom it may concern" fashion. The address, then, is one of many possible topics, but not an individual or a group of agents. This is in striking contrast to the classical message-sending paradigm employed in AOM.

Another characteristic not accounted for in that paradigm is the "open system"-character of large-scale communication processes. Life and death of communication in a Usenet discussion group is to a large degree independent of the life and death of the individual agents participating in the discussion. As is typical for open systems, agents come and go and return whenever they like, some leaving traces, others remaining passive. In some cases, it might even be impossible to disclose the true identity of an agent, e.g., if one agent uses multiple pseudonyms or if many agents share one address. Consequently, we cannot assume to have insights into the internal operations of agents, and fluctuation among the members of the system will be high.

Models centring on the agent as the basic unit of a system, like AOM or SNA, face severe problems once communication leaves the level of small groups and grows to larger scales. As a consequence, one of the objectives of MAS design according to the agent-oriented methodology is to reduce communication as much as possible, e.g., by trying to avoid redundancy. However, as sociologists have come to realise, the vast redundancy and waste production in social communication has important functions for the reproduction of society. Thus, COM tries not to avoid communication, but to model it in a way scaling up to large numbers of messages being exchanged.

Our reflection on the notion of scalability as a theoretical term in Socionics and DAI has shown that issues of scalability should not be regarded from a system-oriented view, but from a problem-oriented view. This brings the necessity of scaling down into play - an important mechanism for MAS to cope with changing environments. Concentrating resources on the solution of a small number of problems might seem to contradict the practical imperative of MAS design to use resources efficiently. However, as we have argued, there are empirical cases that make it necessary to draw on resource consumptive procedures. e.g., in a conflict laden discussion, it may be important to consider receptions independently from whether they trigger an inception or not. The crucial point is not to avoid modelling conflictive situations, but to realise what is required in a given situation: scaling down to fine-grained computation at the operational level of reception and inception, or scaling up and reducing complexity by applying reference graphs.

Concerning future work on the COM model, we have found that despite being well suited for modelling scalable communication networks, COM can still learn from the concepts developed in the tradition of SNA. For example, COM would profit from methods of abstraction that allow to consider more than just the two levels of operations and references discussed in this paper. Messages usually do not follow each other randomly but according to specific patterns of communication. Such patterns can be represented by more abstract objects at a higher level of aggregation. In fact, human society relies heavily on social mechanisms of abstraction and aggregation. To operationalise such abstract objects, COM could learn from SNA by drawing on work on subgroup identification, as mentioned above (cf. [35], [36]), and multilevel modelling [37]. The gain in scalability would be twofold: abstract objects reduce complexity when scaling up, and as techniques of pattern recognition, they help building a selective memory for scaling down.

There are other currents within SNA that are related to the COM approach in their attempt to overcome the actor-centrism, e.g., a small number of studies in communication research uses SNA methods to analyse semantic relations or event sequences by help of networks built from message-to-message relations in which "the 'node' is the comment or message, and the relationships are the references among the posted messages." ([38], cf. [39], [40]) In some SNA-oriented works in citation analysis [41] and in content analysis of discourses [42], the interest is not in the authors and their relations, but in the utterances (journals, articles or statements, respectively) as nodes and their references to one another. Although this small body of literature supports the COM view that the essential aspect of communication is the relation between messages, it still shares with SNA the static view of communication that has been rejected above. Furthermore, these studies suffer from being restricted to very small scales and cannot be applied to the large-scale communication (citation analysis is an exception in this regard).

Finally, researchers in SNA together with physicists and others have begun to analyse structural properties of networks in general, with social networks being only one case among others, e.g., biological networks [43]. A related trend is that more and more SNA researchers interested in the dynamic aspects of social networks turn towards the computer sciences to cope with the complexity of relational processes. For example, the most promising approaches to dynamic networks use simulation models that rely heavily on computer programs [44], [45]. This trend has lead to a fruitful interchange between SNA and computer science. Researchers have explicitly mentioned the field of DAI as a potential source of inspiration for modelling dynamic social networks [46]. Furthermore, some simulation studies have proved the viability of modelling networks by help of agent technology [47], thereby avoiding some of the problems of a purely graph-theoretic approach without having to give up the network perspective. In building on these approaches and in parallel in turning from actors to communication, COM could advance our understanding of communication processes significantly.

References

1. Malsch, T., Schlieder, C.:   Communication without Agents? From Agent-Oriented to Communication-Oriented Modeling. In Lindemann, G., Moldt, D., Paolucci, M., eds.: Regulated Agent-Based Social Systems. LNAI 2934. Springer, Berlin, Heidelberg (2004) 113–133

2. Hewitt, C.:   Open Information Systems Semantics for Distributed Artificial Intelligence. Artificial Intelligence **47** (1991) 79–106

3. Morgan, M., Morrison, M.E.: Models as Mediators. Perspectives on Natural and Social Science. Cambridge University Press, Cambridge et al. (1999)

4. Malsch, T.: Naming the Unnamable: Socionics or the Sociological Turn of/to Distributed Artificial Intelligence. Autonomous Agents and Multi-Agent Systems **4** (2001) 155–186

5. Dignum, F., Greaves, M.: Issues in Agent Communication: An Introduction. In Dignum, F., Greaves, M., eds.: Issues in Agent Communication. LNAI 1916. Springer-Verlag, Berlin, Heidelberg, New York (2000) 1–16

6. Emirbayer, M., Goodwin, J.: Network Analysis, Culture, and the Problem of Agency. Am. Journal of Sociology **99** (1994) 1411–1454

7. Wasserman, S., Faust, K.: Social Network Analysis. Methods and Applications. Cambridge University Press, Cambridge et al. (1994)

8. Jansen, D.: Einführung in die Netzwerkanalyse. Grundlagen, Methoden, Anwendungen. Leske und Budrich, Opladen (1999)

9. Padgett, J., Ansell, C.: Robust Action and the Rise of the Medici, 1400-1434. Am. Journal of Sociology **98** (1993) 1259–1319

10. Barnett, G.A.: A Longitudinal Analysis of the International Telecommunication Network 1978-1996. Am. Behavioral Scientist **44** (2001) 1638–1655

11. Yair, G.: "Unite Unite Europe". The Political and Cultural Structures of Europe as Reflected in the Eurovision Song Contest. Social Networks **17** (1995) 147–161

12. Freeman, L.: The Impact of Computer Based Communication on the Social Structure of an Emerging Scientific Specialty. Social Networks **6** (1984) 201–221

13. Albrecht, S., Lübcke, M.: Communicational Patterns as Basis of Organizational Structures. In Lindemann, G., Moldt, D., Paolucci, M., eds.: Regulated Agent-Based Social Systems. LNAI 2934. Springer, Berlin, Heidelberg (2004) 16–30

14. Batagelj, V., Mrvar, A.: Pajek Program for Large Network Analysis. Connections **21** (1998) 47–57

15. Broder, A., Kumar, R., Maghoull, F., Raghavan, P., Rajagopalan, S., Stata, R., Tomkins, A., Wiener, J.: Graph structure in the web. In: Proc. of the 9th Int. World Wide Web Conference, Amsterdam (2000) 309–320

16. Luhmann, N.: Social Systems. Stanford University Press, Stanford, CA (1995)

17. Stichweh, R.: System Theory as an Alternative to Action Theory? The Rise of 'Communication' as a Theoretical Option. Acta Sociologica **43** (2000) 5–13

18. Mead, G.: Mind, Self and Society from the Standpoint of a Social Behaviorist. University of Chicago Press, Chicago (1996 [1934])
19. Finkelstein, A., Kramer, J.: Software Engineering: A Roadmap. In Finkelstein, A., ed.: The Future of Software Engineering. Proc. of the Conference on the Future of Software Engineering, Limerick, Ireland, New York, ACM Press (2000) 3–22
20. Brazier, F., van Steen, M., Wijngaards, N.: On MAS Scalability. In Wagner, T., Rana, O., eds.: Proc. of the 2nd Int. Workshop on Infrastructure for Agents, MAS, and Scalable MAS, Montreal, Canada, AAAI (2001) 121–126
21. Hewitt, C.: Towards Open Information Systems Semantics. In: Proc. of the 10th International Workshop on Distributed Artificial Intelligence. MCC Technical Report No. ACT-AI-355-90, Bandera, Texas, USA (1990)
22. Rana, O.F., Wagner, T., S, M., Greenberg, Purvis, M.K.: Infrastructure Issues and Themes for Scalable Multi-Agent Systems. In Wagner, T., Rana, O., eds.: Infrastructure for Agents, Multi-Agent Systems, and Scalable Multi-Agent Systems. LNAI 1887. Springer-Verlag, Berlin, Heidelberg, New York (2001) 304–308
23. Turner, P., Jennings, N.: Improving the Scalability of Multiagent Systems. In Wagner, T., Rana, O., eds.: Infrastructure for Agents, Multi-Agent Systems, and Scalable Multi-Agent Systems. LNAI 1887. Springer-Verlag, Berlin, Heidelberg, New York (2001) 246–262
24. Wilde, P.d., Nwana, H., Lee, L.: Stability, Fairness and Scalability of Multi-Agent Systems. Int. Journal of Knowledge-Based Intelligent Engineering Systems 3 (1999) 84–91
25. Nonnecke, B., Preece, J.: Lurker Demographics: Counting the Silent. In: Proceedings of CHI 2000. ACM, The Hague (2000) 73–80
26. Stegbauer, C., Rausch, A.: Die schweigende Mehrheit - "Lurker" in internetbasierten Diskussionsforen. Zeitschrift für Soziologie 30 (2001) 48–64
27. Smith, M.: Invisible Crowds in Cyberspace: Measuring and Mapping the Social Structure of USENET. In Smith, M., Kollock, P., eds.: Communities in Cyberspace. Routledge, London (1999) 195–219
28. Chiesi, A.: Network Analysis. In Smelser, N., Baltes, P., eds.: International Encyclopedia of the Social and Behavioral Sciences. Elsevier, Amsterdam et al. (2001) 10501–10504
29. Hewitt, C.: Viewing Control Structures as Patterns of Passing Messages. Artificial Intelligence 8 (1977) 323–364
30. Laitinen, M., Fayad, M., Ward, R.: The Problem with Scalability. Comm. of the ACM 43 (2000) 105–107
31. Leake, D., ed.: Case-Based Reasoning. Experiences, Lessons & Future Directions. AAAI Press, Menlo Park, CA (1996)
32. Esposito, E.: Soziales Vergessen. Formen und Medien des Gedächtnisses der Gesellschaft. Suhrkamp, Frankfurt/M (2002)
33. Granovetter, M.: The Theory-Gap in Social Network Analysis. In Holland, P., Leinhardt, S., eds.: Perspectives on Social Network Research. Academic Press, New York et al. (1979) 501–518
34. Cook, K., Whitmeyer, J.: Two Approaches to Structure: Exchange Theory and Network Analysis. Ann. Rev. of Sociology 18 (1992) 109–127
35. Frank, K., Yasumoto, J.: Embedding Subgroups in the Sociogram: Linking Theory and Image. Connections 19 (1996) 43–57
36. Frank, K., Yasumoto, J.: Linking Action to Social Structure within a System: Social Capital within and between Subgroups. Am. Journal of Sociology 104 (1998) 642–686
37. Snijders, T., Baerveldt, C.: A Multilevel Network Study of the Effects of Delinquent Behavior on Friendship Evolution. Journal of Mathematical Sociology 27 (2003) 123–151
38. Rice, R.: Network Analysis and Computer-Mediated Communication Systems. In Wasserman, S., Galaskiewicz, J., eds.: Advances in Social Network Analysis. Research in the Social and Behavioral Sciences. Sage, Thousand Oaks, London, New Delhi (1994) 167–203

39. Danowsky, J.: Computer-Mediated Communication. A Network Based Content Analysis Using a CBBS Conference. Communication Yearbook **6** (1982) 905–924

40. Jeong, A.: The Sequential Analysis of Group Interaction and Critical Thinking in Online Threaded Discussions. Am. Journal of Distance Education **17** (2003) 25–43

41. Cronin, B., Atkins, H.B.: The Web of Knowledge. A Festschrift in Honor of Eugene Garfield. Information Today, Medford, NJ (2000)

42. Vedres, B., Csigó, P.: The Discourse of Consolidation: Network Analysis of Four Months of Economic Policy Discourse. In: Paper presented at the Sunbelt XVIII and Fifth European International Social Networks Conference, May 28 - May 31, Sitges, Spain (1998) 73–80

43. Watts, D.: Six Degrees: The Science of a Connected Age. W.W. Norton & Company, New York (2000)

44. Snijders, T., van Duijn, M.: Simulation for Statistical Inference in Dynamic Network Models. In Conte, R., Hegselmann, R., Terna, P., eds.: Simulating Social Phenomena. Springer-Verlag, Berlin, Heidelberg, New York (1997) 493–512

45. Zeggelink, E., Stokman, F., van de Bunt, G.: The Emergence of Groups in the Evolution of Friendship Networks. In Doreian, P., Stokman, F.N., eds.: Evolution of Social Networks. Gordon and Breach, Amsterdam (1997) 45–71

46. Stokman, F.N., Doreian, P.: Evolution of Social Networks: Processes and Principles. In Doreian, P., Stokman, F.N., eds.: Evolution of Social Networks. Gordon and Breach, Amsterdam (1997) 233–250

47. Macy, M., Willer, R.: From Factors to Actors. Computational Sociology and Agent-Based Modeling. Ann. Revue of Sociology **28** (2002) 143–66

Multiagent Systems Without Agents — *Mirror-Holons* for the Compilation and Enactment of Communication Structures*

Matthias Nickles and Gerhard Weiß

AI/Cognition Group, Department of Informatics, Technical University of Munich
D-85748 Garching bei München, Germany,
{nickles,weissg}@model.informatik.tu-muenchen.de

Abstract. It is widely accepted in Distributed Artificial Intelligence that a crucial property of artificial agents is their *autonomy*. Whereas agent autonomy enables features of agent-based applications like flexibility, robustness and emergence of novel solutions, autonomy might be also the reason for undesired or even chaotic agent behavior, and unmanageable system complexity. As a conceptual approach to the solution for this "autonomy dilemma" of agent-based software engineering, this work introduces the *HolOMAS* framework for open multiagent systems based on special meta-agents, so-called *Mirror-Holons*. Instead of restricting agent autonomy by means of normative constraints and defined organizational structures as usual, Mirror-Holons allow for the gradual *uncoupling* of agent interaction and *emergent* system functionality. Their main purpose is the derivation and adaption of *social structure knowledge* and evolving stochastical *social programs* from the observation and compilation of agent communication and additional design objectives. Social programs can either be executed by the Mirror-Holons themselves, or communicated to the agents and the system designer, similar to the functionality of mass media like television or newspapers in human societies.

Keywords: Multiagent Systems, Holons, Agent Communication, Cybernetics, Artificial Sociality, Autonomous Computing, Multiagent Coordination Media

1 Introduction

In [8,9,12], a novel approach to the design and control of open systems with truly autonomous agents has been introduced, which aimed at the establishment of mechanisms for autonomy-preserving self-control of the system by means of the *reflection* and propagation of social *expectation structures*. The main component of this architecture is the so-called *Social System Mirror*, a MAS-middleware component which continuously observes agent communications, derives generalized social structures from these observations (plus additional normative design objectives if required), and communicates ("reflects") these structures back to the agents. Leaning on *Social Systems Theory* [2,8], interaction structures like organizational structures [4], norms and agent roles

---

* This work is supported by Deutsche Forschungsgemeinschaft (DFG) under contracts no. Br609/11-2 and MA759/4-2.

are always the regularities (*structures*) of communication processes which have to be represented as adaptive and normative *expectations* [8,12] regarding the continuations of these processes. The goals of a Social System Mirror (or "mirror" for short) are the indirect, autonomy-preserving influencing of agent behavior by means of the system-wide propagation of social structures towards quicker structure evolution and higher coherence of communication structures without restricting agent autonomy, and the provision of an evolutionary model of social structures for the MAS designer. While a Social System Mirror models a single communication system and remains (apart from the propagation of expectations) passively, the successor architecture *HolOMAS*, which we introduce in this work, is able to model multiple communication systems at the same time through multiple *Mirror-Holons* in order to model large, heterogeneous systems. In addition, Mirror-Holons can take action themselves by means of the execution of emergent social programs which are generated from expectation structures.

A Mirror-Holon can be characterized informally as a

higher-order agent which "impersonates" an entire distributed, social program via the synchronous or asynchronous execution of extrapolated multi-agent interaction trajectories learned and revised i.a. by observation of multi-agent interactions.

Other agents, including other Mirror-Holons, can (besides their contribution of learning examples via their communications) optionally be involved in this execution process as effectors, which execute commands in social programs in their respective environmental domain, if they do not prefer to deny the respective command. In any case they can influence the social programs accommodated by the Mirror-Holon through their communication with peer agents. In addition, a Mirror-Holon can use given structures in addition to learned structures also (e.g., norms and protocols).

Since Mirror-Holons are agents that in some sense comprise "lower-level" agents and can be comprised recursively by higher-level, similarly constructed Mirror-Holons themselves recursively (forming a so-called *holarchie*), HolOMAS is strongly related to the *Holon* concept [27]. Nevertheless, there is an important difference between Mirror-Holons and traditional agent holons (e.g. [24]): A Mirror-Holon does not contain sets of *agents*, but instead actively represents a certain *social functionality* which is identified in form of regularities in the observed communications, without disregarding the autonomy of his adjoint lower-order actors. This allows for a flexible, more or less loose coupling of desired system functionality and lower-order agent behavior (although a governing of lower-order agents by means of social norms and sanctions is also optionally possible).
Since the holon concept of HolOMAS is based on the observation of agent interactions which can be used to coordinate agents behavior in turn, HolOMAS is also related to the theory of *coordination spaces* [25].

We expect that the concept of Mirror-Holons opens up prospects of autonomous software systems where on the one hand agent autonomy should not (or can not) be restricted, and on the other hand a fast, reliable system behavior is required (so to speak "real-time multiagent systems"). They are also expected to provide consistent, reliable and homogenous computational representations of open systems (e.g., virtual organizations) which otherwise can not **guarantee** such properties due to; e.g., internal conflicts and incoherencies.

The further sections of this paper are organized as follows: The next section introduces the basic concepts of Mirror-Holons. Section 3 outlines the central aspect of our framework, the empirical derivation of expectation structures (represented as so-called *expectation networks*), Section 4 describes how holon programs can be induced from empirically obtained social structures, and Section 5 outlines how multiple Mirror-Holons emerge and communicate. Finally, Section 6 points out open research problems and motivates future work.

2   Mirror-Holons

Since symbolic, deniable communications with a more or less indefinite result in terms of subsequent actions is the only way for truly autonomous agents to overcome their opaqueness, agent sociality can be modeled in terms of emergent, evolving expectation structures of communication processes *only* [8]. Because ultimatively the meaning of communications lies in their expected consequences, in [8,9,19,12] we have therefore introduced expectation structures regarding communicative actions (therefore, sometimes called "communication structures") as a universal means for the modeling of social structures. Such (social) expectation structures integrate both normative expectations (expectations which describe how someone *should* behave) and adaptive expectations derived empirically from the actual behavior, which might be in open systems with a heterogeneous, fluctuating set of black-box-agents the only way to determine communication semantics. According to the concept of *autopoiesis* [2], expectation structures of social systems are more or less stable and reproduce themselves in order to provide a context for further communication despite the mental opaqueness of actors.

A formal framework for the representation of expectation structures can be found in [19] and (in a revised, abbreviated version, together with a learning algorithm) in [11].

A Mirror-Holon is a higher-order agent that comprises the behavioral spectrum of multiple lower-order yet intelligent and autonomous agents. To distinguish "ordinary" agency from such higher-order-agency, we introduce the taxonomy below of social structures in terms of the sort of agent communications that contribute to these structures. Social expectation structures model sets of communication processes, which are, in our usage of this term, sequences of elementary communications coupled by a relation called *communicative adjacency*. Communicative adjacency indicates that communication subsequent to another communication expresses implicitly or explicitly the understanding and referencing of the preceding communications. Communication processes can, from an observers perspective, be identified as trajectories of communication acts (especially utterances using some formal communication language). Since communication processes are the most elementary kind of observable sociality, we use them as the empirical evidence for the modeling of social systems [2], and in particular of so-called *spheres of communication* (cf. Section 3).

Social expectation structures and the communications they are modeling can be given a (informal) hierarchy as follows:

First-order expectation structures are social expectation structures which describe the inner coherence and correlations of communication processes, but not their boundaries of validity. Unaware of latent information about the participating agents respectively their hidden intentions and goals, and if agents do not contradict themselves, first-order expectation structures can only describe expectations which are communicated explicitly, because agents aim for a consistent, justified and reliable communicational behavior towards other agents temporarily. First-order expectation structures are thus not able to model phenomena like insincerity or fraudulence as long as they are not communicated explicitly. Typical examples for first-order expectation structures are *spheres of commitment* [7] and closed-system structures like simple virtual organizations. E.g., an auction protocol which is not aware of insincere agents that might break contracts (and consequently does not provide counter-measures like sanctions) can be considered as a first-order expectation structure.

Higher-order expectation structures are social structures that model first-order (second-order...) social structures we call second-order (third-order...) social structures. If an observer models processes of higher-order communications, and he trusts the communicated propositions (about other communications), then she can easily obtain higher-order expectation structures from the message content.

An example for the use of second-order expectation structures is the following scenario: In a discussion, employees of some organization hold opinion A. Suddenly their boss steps into the office. In the continuation of the discussion, the employees hold opinion $\neg A$. Whereas the discussion before and after the appearance of the boss would be modeled using two mutually inconsistent first-order expectation structures, second-order expectation structures would relate both first-order structures and explain the transition from one to the other with the entry of the boss into the office.

Seemingly, from the *passive* modeling of communication processes in order to forecast the interactional behavior of a set of agents to the *active* participation it is only a small step. We could describe an active higher-order agent as an entity that derives so-called *actual* expectation structures from empirical observations, maintains an other set of expectation structures (so-called *goal structures*, e.g. predefined by the system designer or empirically obtained also), and aims at a minimization of the differences of these two sets of expectation structures in a rational way by taking action himself (especially by means of communication) in one or both of these two agents domains (actual and goal).[1] Doing so, Mirror-Holons are not only emergent from lower-order agents' behavior, but they can be goal-directed with goals emergent from observed behavior also. A Mirror-Holon is thus also an agent with the peculiar feature that its social belief and its goals are (at least partially, depending from the type of Mirror-Holon, as explained below) obtained at run-time in form of emergent expectation structures. Therefore, Mirror-Holons can be used to influence a multiagent system *from out of itself* instead of an external instance like in usual approaches to multiagent control (for example, in [9], we have shown how a Social System *Mirror* (a simple kind of Mirror-Holon, cf. below) can be used as a CASE-tool for agent-oriented software development for the purpose of the derivation and propagation of expectation structures in an evolutionary MAS design process). In some sense, this concept is a reversal of the concept of "cognitive" agents that are enabled to interact socially (e.g., [16]), since the cognition and acting of Mirror-Holons are seen as an outcome of observed communications and not the other way round as usual.

This concept of *goal structures* emerging from *actual structures* (the actual, empirical social communication structures of the MAS at a certain time) would be of no use if the goal structures and the actual structures were identical. There are several possibilities to obtain goal structures different from actual structures, e.g. by

- *Synthesization* of goal structures from the informational contributions of multiple, heterogenous communication sources (either agents or peers in open P2P networks). Using techniques like *social reification* [13,14,15], this synthesization can provide reasonable results even in case of inconsistent informational input (e.g. conflictive behavior). Possible applications are, e.g., the propagation of the resulting structures in order to improve the social reasoning of agents and/or the system designer (similar to the effect of public *mass media* like television or books on human societies.). This improvement is especially useful for the unveiling of *social conflicts* [26]. Examples for the application of synthesized social structures are *Open Ontologies* and *Open Knowledge Bases*, which—in contrast to traditional information media—maintain, weigh and socially reify semantically conflictive (conceptual or instantiated) knowledge computationally [13,14,15].

- *Biasing* of actual, empirical structures by means of normative structures which were predefined by the system designer in order to filter out undesired behavior and strengthen desired behavior using sanctions or argumentation. Such structures can result from schemes like *RNS* [18].

- *Simplification and acceleration* of communication structures. Goal structures can be obtained from the compilation of actual expectation structures using modifications in order to make them more simple, fast and reliable. If the respective

---

[1] Acting in order to manipulate the agents domain "physically" and directly (not using symbolic interactions) can be modeled as a certain kind of *indirect* communication, too. So "ordinary", non-interactive acting is included within this rational social behavior, too, as long as the "physical actions" have a significant impact on behavior of the other agents.

Mirror-Holon is sufficiently powerful, it could even enact observed communication processes (for a certain period of time) in its domain *without* the further participation of the agents that contributed to these processes, whereas a "weaker" Mirror-Holon could act as a "communication catalyzer" that makes use of the agents as *effectors* to put physical actions occurring in these processes into action. In both cases, the Mirror-Holon would act as a more or less complete replacement of the observed multiagent system (we speak about a *Functional Mirror-Holon* (cf. Section 2) in this case).

– *Merging* of the structures of multiple social systems.

This list is not exhaustive, and combinations of these approaches are also imaginable.

Each Mirror-Holon possesses two communication *ports*: The unidirectional *source port* is used to observe communications that occur in the *source domain* (goals), whereas the bidirectional *target port* is used to both, observe communication and participate actively in communication in the *targeted domain*. We use the term "domain" in a quite broad sense, denoting observable events generated by agents during interaction and physical phenomena. For a Mirror-Holon, a certain "physical" domain is of course only indirectly accessible by means of the observation of communications. Source and targeted communications are typically generated by different sets of agents (including other Mirror-Holons), but as with the original Social System Mirror, it might be reasonable to have a non-empty intersection (i.e., an interaction domain influences itself). From the input obtained from these ports the Mirror-Holon derives two *expectation networks* (ENs) [8,9,19,11,12]. An EN is a concrete, graph-based formal representation form for expectation structures (cf. below for details). Participating using the target port means communication with the aim to reduce the difference of the expectation structures obtained from source and target port by means of taking action using the target port (more precisely: minimizing the probability that the expected continuation of agent communication observed via the target port deviates from the expected source port communications). The concrete goals of a Mirror-Holon is thus determined at run-time from the source port—a Mirror-Holon acts towards his targeted audience like a representant of the source structures. In addition, each Mirror-Holon is optionally equipped with a number of normative expectation structures which serve as an a-priori presetting for the source expectation structures build in by the system designer.

2.1 Expectation Networks

Expectation networks, introduced in [8], are graphs that represent expectation structures formally—specifically, they represent the empirically obtained probability distribution of all significant future event sequences resulting from the observance of the agents and their environment. They can also be used to pre-define expectation structures designed manually by the system designer, modeling e.g. normative expectations directed to the agents in order to restrict their behavior. Expectation networks may need to be adapted if unexpected newly observed events occur, and might subsume communicative actions as well as non-symbolic "physical" events. Expectation networks can be modeled in

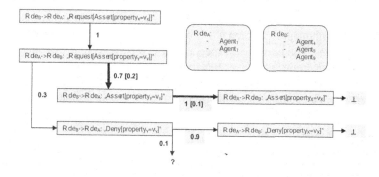

Fig. 1. An expectation network

multiple levels of generalization to enable the description of under-specified utterances, communication patterns, collaboration-emergent meaning (e.g., shared opinions of agent groups) and agent roles (which are basically generalized agent behavior patterns). Expectation networks also provide a common ground which contextualizes an communication act within a discourse. They are furthermore able to represent not only dynamic (i.e. adaptable) expectation, but also *normative* expectations (e.g. laws), which remain stable even if they contradict actual behavior. Please refer to [12,19] for a detailed, formal description of expectation networks.

Figure 1 shows a very simple expectation network that represents the structure of a discourse of two agents (or two agent roles, respectively). For simplicity, we use a graphical notation which is slightly different compared to the full notation. Nodes (depicted as squares) are labeled with message templates (in a formal agent communication language) or the special symbols "⊥" (denoting the end of a conversation) and "?" (denoting an unknown or uninteresting continuation). Nodes are connected by edges (shown as arrows) labeled with numerical *expectabilities*, which denote the probability that the respective message(s) occur subsequently. These probabilities are derived from observed frequencies of the respective message sequences in the past. The thickness of edges represents the *normativeness* of the respective expectability and the numerical value in square brackets denotes its *deviancy*. An edge with high normativeness (thick arrow) represents an expectation which has proved itself as empirically stable in the long term, which is a typical property of expectations obtained from laws and other social norms. The deviancy is the difference of long-term and short-term expectability, corresponding to the expectability of agent behavior which deviates from a social norm. Substitution lists appear in rounded boxes. A substitution list denotes a social *role* the listed agents can impersonate. For this purpose, the message templates contain role variables ($Role_A$ and $Role_B$) that can be bounded to each of the list entries, provided this bounding is done in a consistent way along the respective network path. An expectation network can be *generalized* in two ways: First, a single expectation network might describe the expectations regarding multiple message sequences due to different instantiations of role variables (a Mirror-Holon might be able to obtain these roles automatically from the unification of syntactically matching message sequences observed for different agents as described in [8,12]). Second, each message sequence is expected to be repeatable without precondition if the root of the corresponding path does not have any incoming edges. The numerical expectabilities correspond to the *frequency* of observed message trajectories in the past that unify syntactically with the respective paths. Theoretically, an expectation network must contain a path for every possible sequence of messages, but in practice, edges with a very low or unknown probability are omitted.

2.2   Structure Enactment and Execution

Likewise there are multiple ways to obtain holon goal structures from actual empirical structures (social programs, mainly), there are also multiple possibilities for the enactment of goal (i.e. source) structures by means of Mirror-Holon communication using the target port:

- *Influencing through information* aims for a change of the behavior of agents (in the targeted domain) by means of informing them about otherwise tacit social structures (in a way similar to the influence *mass media* have in human societies). These information depend from the source structures obtained from the source port, but do not necessarily be exhaustive or true (e.g., a Mirror-Holon might be able to lie in order to influence the target domain).

- *Argumentation, negotiation and sanctioning* are discourse practices of social agents which can be likewise performed by Mirror-Holons. Since Mirror-Holons are primarily thought as control instruments used by the system designer, a Mirror-Holon usually has more power in terms of the enactment of positive or negative sanctions it can impose on "ordinary" agents.

- *Direct enactment* of goal structures requires that the Mirror-Holon has direct access to the target domain. In this case, the Mirror-Holon puts speech acts and other events into action *instead of* or in collaboration with the agents within the target domain.

In general, Mirror-Holons have the following architecture (cf. fig. 2). As we'll see later, this general architecture, which is influenced from *Social Systems Theory* [2] and *Second-Order Cybernetics* [28], allows for a lot of variety.

Definition. A (general) *Mirror-Holon* is defined as a structure

$$(sourceKB, targetKB, defaultKB, sourceUpdate, targetUpdate) \text{ where}$$

- $sourceKB : EN$ is the current model of the source domain ("KB" stands for knowledge base, which means here a set of social structures, i.e. *social knowledge*). This model is given as an expectation network (EN) or some stochastically equivalent representation formalism which represents a probability distribution of events (especially communicative actions) that is incrementally updated from observed messages.

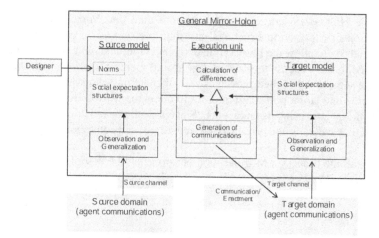

Fig. 2. General Mirror-Holon

- $targetKB : EN$ is the current model of the targeted domain. It is also represented as an expectation network, and adapted dynamically. Some types of Mirror-Holons do not use this model (cf. below).

- $defaultKB : EN$ is the initial content of $sourceKB$. It serves as a normative, a priory bias for the learning of $sourceKB$ from observations, and helps to avoid the bootstrapping problem which might occur otherwise in case no reasonable, structurally relevant input can be accumulated through the source port initially.

- $sourceUpdate : EN \times ACL \rightarrow EN$ is a function which updates the source model after the observance of a message $m \in ACL$, whereby ACL is some agent communication language. This process of source model adaptation is called *generalization* (of observed communication processes). It has the following two aspects: *Timely generalization*, i.e., the extrapolation of communication trajectories into the future, and *role/social program generalization*, i.e., the abstraction of behavioral patterns from concrete agents.

- $targetUpdate : EN \times ACL \rightarrow EN$ likewise updates the target model (including events the respective Mirror-Holon has generated by itself).

We provide two different functions for the update of source and target model in order to allow different algorithms. E.g., it might be useful to do strong filtering and generalization of the source model to obtain consistent, stable goal structures, whereas the targeted domain is modeled as accurate as possible to enable an effective influencing of the targeted audience.

If at least one Mirror-Holon appears in a multiagent system, we talk about a *HolO-MAS* ("Holonic Open Multiagent System").

A single HolOMAS can accommodate more than one Mirror-Holon to enable diversification of expectation structures into multiple *spheres of communication* (cf. Section 3 and 5). To allow the observation of agent communication, the Mirror-Holons are supposed to have access to some sort of shared memory (*whiteboard*) the agents use to make some or all of their messages and other actions observable for the Mirror-Holon (source and target port), and in order to allow the Mirror-Holon to emit events directed to the agents (using its target port). Since it would be rather off-topic, we do not consider technical details and privacy issues regarding such communication media here.

In general, the process a Mirror-Holon performs can be described as follows (the so-called *Mirror-Holon Cycle*):

1. $targetKB := \varnothing$

2. $sourceKB := defaultKB$

3. $message_{source} := pull(sourcedomain)$

4. $sourceKB := sourceUpdate(sourceKB, message_{source})$

5. $message_{target} := pull(targeteddomain)$

6. $targetKB := targetUpdate(targetKB, message_{target})$

7. $subst := unifier(sourceKB, targetKB)$

8. $\Delta := subst(sourceKB) - targetKB$

9. $put(targetdomain, \Delta)$

10. go to step 3

whereby the following additional procedures are used: *pull* denotes a function which waits for and reads the latest event (e.g. message) that occurred in the respective domain. *unifier* computes a list of role variable and agent name substitutions such that the application of this substitutions list as a function *subst* on $sourceKB$ makes this expectation network as similar as possible to $targetKB$ by means of an appropriate renaming of variables and agent names, i.e., *unifier* finds the most general unifier for the matching parts of the two expectation networks. The infix function '$-$' (step 8) calculates the difference of two expectation networks and results in a list of subsequent Mirror-Holon communications which minimizes this difference of $sourceKB$ and $targetKB$ with the highest probability using the lowest number of single communications. *put* emits this communication sequence to the targeted audience. "Difference" means the graphical tree-distance of the two ENs here.

As a simple example, imagine a source model which contains the following expectation network paths (we use a textual representation here instead of the graphical notation that should be self-explanatory):

$Role_A \rightarrow Role_B : DeliverGoods(...)$
$\dashrightarrow (0.9)\ Role_B \rightarrow Role_A : FulfillPayment(...)$
$\dashrightarrow (0.1)\ Role_B \rightarrow Role_A : DenyPayment(...)$

For some trading scenario, this course of events can be considered as ideal (just 1% expectation of denial of payment). These expectations might have been obtained in a closed source domain with sincere and reliable trading agents, or could have been predefined via *defaultKB* by the MAS designer. In contrast, the target model shall contain the following structures:

$Role_X \rightarrow Role_Y : DeliverGoods(...)$
$\dashrightarrow (0.5)\ Role_Y \rightarrow Role_X : FulfillPayment(...)$
$\dashrightarrow (0.5)\ Role_Y \rightarrow Role_X : DenyPayment(...)$

A Mirror-Holon with the task to correct undesired behavior occurring in the target domain would find a high deviancy of the target expectation network in comparison with the source structures, and should perform appropriate sanctions as follows:

$Agent_Y \rightarrow Agent_X : DenyPayment(...)$
$\dashrightarrow (1)\ MirrorHolon \rightarrow Agent_Y : Sanctioning(...)$ where the $Agent_{...}$ are instances of the respective agent roles.

In the case target and source domain are equal, and $Role_Y$ (respectively the instancing agents) deviates from its expected behavior because it is unaware of some fact (e.g., legal powers), the Mirror-Holon could alternatively (or in addition) act as a Social System Mirror and just inform $Role_Y$ about the possible consequences of its behavior.

However, after some cycles, the influence of the Mirror-Holon should lead to reasonably adapted target structures, e.g.:

$Role_X \rightarrow Role_Y : DeliverGoods(...)$
$\dashrightarrow (0.8)\ Role_Y \rightarrow Role_X : FulfillPayment(...)$
$\dashrightarrow (0.2)\ Role_Y \rightarrow Role_X : DenyPayment(...)$

2.3 Special Mirror-Holons

Obviously, the computation of function '−' within the Mirror-Holon Cycle is problematic, and we doubt that it can be computed efficiently for the general case.[2] It is also not completely clear yet what "minimizing the difference" of two expectation networks means. For now, we can define this only for special cases: If − results in a sequence of holonic communications that makes the target communication equal to the source communication, the Mirror-Holon surly succeeded in obtaining its goal at least temporary.

For these reasons, we introduce in the following more "manageable" Mirror-Holon subtypes derived from the general case described above.

Social System Mirror (cf. Figure 3)

A Social System Mirror [8,9] is a Mirror-Holon with the following specific properties:

- *The targeted domain is a part of its source domain*, i.e. a domain influences itself at least to some degree. Such influencing mimics *mass media* like television, books and newspapers in human societies, where information (possibly strongly biased by norms and a-priory knowledge) appear to be related to the needs and the behavior of persons who do not necessarily have been involved directly in the creation of these information (e.g. readers of a newspaper). In the special case the targeted domain is the same as the source domain, and $defaultKB = \varnothing$, we would obtain a truly self-influencing of the domain.

- *The Mirror-Holon emits meta-communications (communications about communications) only* (i.e., technically, the content of the generated utterances consist of information about expectation structures only. In particular, a Social System Mirror does not "impersonate" the acting within the source domain.)

- *A Social System Mirror does not impose sanctions on its targeted domain.* In the most basic case, the target port even works in one direction (emit messages) only, and the holon simply generates mass communication $(1 : n;$ where n is the number of agents in the targeted domain). The idea behind this is that the targeted audience should select relevant information from the mirror communication itself, electively querying a "socially-aware, open knowledge base" [13,14,15].
  Of course, this property could be omitted or relaxed, if necessary, and in any case, a Social System Mirror is able to *inform* about sanction and social norms.

---

[2] Of course, we could incrementally compute random Mirror-Holon behavior e.g. using a genetic algorithm, and hope that this eventually leads to the desired structures.

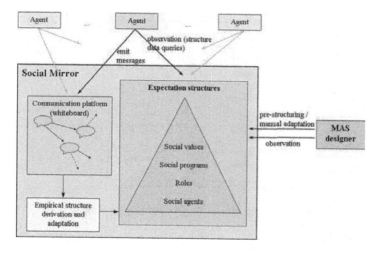

Fig. 3. Social System Mirror

The two main purposes of Social System Mirrors are 1) the informational influencing of evolving open agent systems during the design phase [9], comparable to a CASE tool, and 2) the enhancement of the social capabilities of the targeted agents by means of enhancing their knowledge about the social system structures.

Normative Mirror-Holon A *Normative Mirror-Holon* (a subtype of the Social System Mirror) does not make use of its source port (*sourceUpdate* does nothing), and *defaultKB* is not empty. Thus it is a means for the propagation of social norms and static knowledge. It can be used, e.g., to communicate normative action constraints to autonomous agents (if the scheme can be translated into expectation networks as it is possible for role-based obligation schemes like RNS [18]). Optionally, it can be equipped with the ability to argue and/or impose sanctions for norm-deviant agent behavior.

Functional Mirror-Holons are Mirror-Holons which represent suitable social structures (*social programs* [2,8,9]) as executable programs, which are inductively derived, evaluated and adopted during run-time of the MAS. We call both the original social structures and the derived computational programs "social programs".[3]

Synchronous-Functional Mirror-Holon (SFMH) (cf. Figure 4)
    A SFMH is a Functional Mirror-Holon that works as a functional representation of social expectation structures. Its functionality is based on the interpretation of expectation structures as social programs. These can e.g. be ENs (executed by means of stochastic simulation, cf. Section 4), or declarative,

---

[3] The term "functional" is used to emphasize the priority of social functionality over non-functional, redundant structural determination according to [2].

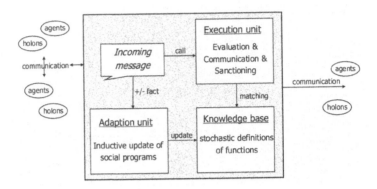

Fig. 4. Synchronous-Functional Mirror-Holon

functional programs in the computer-scientific sense. In the latter case (which can only be sketched here for lack of space), each SFMH represents its *sourceKB* as an adaptive set of function definitions, which are continuously and inductively learned from observed communication acts (in the context of other communication acts and other observable events). Each function represents a certain generalized sequence of correlated agent action events, similar to the paths in the expectation network.

The SFMH communicates the content of *sourceKB* to the agents in the same way a Social System Mirror communicates expectation structures to enhance or update their own social belief. But in addition, the agents can also *call* the inductively learned "social functions" like communications macros, and the evaluation of each function can in turn create "calls" of further agent behavior. Therefore, a SFMH works in interaction with other agents with the aim to make their social behavior more efficient.

Asynchronous-Functional Mirror-Holon (AFMH) (cf. Figure 5)

An AFMH is a variant of the SFMH, with the important difference that it separates the process of continuous observation and learning of expectation structures on the one hand, and the execution of the derived social programs on the other (in Figure 5 called "evaluation") timely and organizationally. Following Social Systems Theory, the loose coupling between these two processes is called *irritation* (of the structures represented by the social programs).

An AFMH does not inform the targeted agents to put the inductively derived action functions into practice, but instead performs the recorded and extrapolated sequences of agent actions by itself, or, alternatively, *forces* the targeted agents to execute them by means of normative power.

AFMHs have the big advantage that they do not require a model of the target domain and thus do not need to calculate the difference of source and target model to obtain optimal target communications—instead, they more or less

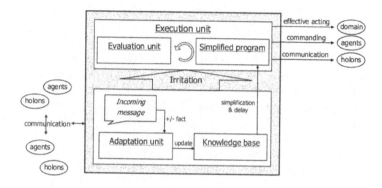

Fig. 5. Asynchronous-Functional Mirror-Holon

copy and replace the observed MAS. More specifically, the calculation of the difference of source and target model is trivial, because it always results in the source model. However, usually an AFMH simplifies and speeds up the source structures before execution. AFMHs are most useful if the Mirror-Holon just needs to execute communicative acts which have a physical impact and not just a symbolic meaning.

Because of their simplicity and generality, we have chosen AFMHs for this work as the concrete example type for Mirror-Holons in the next sections, whereas we do not go into detail about the other types.

3   Empirical Semantics

As we have seen, a Mirror-Holon can be thought as an acting impersonator of expectation structures. Therefore, the by far most important task for a Mirror-Holon is the derivation of communication meaning. In this section, we provide only an informal overview of the central aspects of our communication model. Please consult [11,17] for details and a formal framework.

Although many approaches to the semantics of agent communication languages (ACL) have already been proposed, it is widely realized in distributed artificial intelligence that a comprehensive understanding of agent communication is still outstanding. While it is relatively easy to define a proper formal semantics for the so-called "content level" of agent languages (in contrast to the speech act illocution encoded by means of performatives), like it has been done for, e.g., KIF [20], there is still no general model of the actual *effects* of utterances in social encounters, a field which is traditionally studied in linguistical pragmatics and sociological theories. Currently, two major speech-act-based [21,22,23] approaches to this aspect of agent communication (i.e. "semantics" in a broader sense, covering both traditional linguistic sentence semantics and pragmatics) exist, if we do not count plain interaction protocols (in some sense

278 Matthias Nickles and Gerhard Weiß

primitive social semantics) and other low-level formalisms like message passing. The older *mentalistic* approach (e.g. [6,3]) specifies the meaning of utterances by means of a description of the mental states of the respective agents (i.e., their beliefs and intentions), while the more recent approaches to ACL semantics (e.g. [5,1]) try to determine communication from an *objectivistic* point of view, focussing on public language rules. The former approach has two well-known shortcomings, which eventually led to the development of the latter: At least in open multiagent systems, agents appear more or less as black boxes, which makes it in general impossible to impose and verify a semantic described in terms of cognition. Furthermore, they make simplifying but unrealistic assumptions to ensure mental homogeneity among the agents, for example that the interacting agents were benevolent and sincere. Objectivist semantics in contrast is fully verifiable, it achieves a big deal of complexity reduction through limiting itself to a small set of normative rules, and has therefore been a significant step ahead. But it oversimplifies social processes, and it does not have a concept of semantics dynamics and evolution. In general, we doubt that the predominately normative, static and definite concepts of current approaches to ACL semantics, borrowed from the study of programming languages and interaction protocols, are adequate to cope with concepts crucial for the successful deployment of agents to heterogeneous, open environments with changing populations like the internet. Of course, this issue is less problematic for particular environments, where agent benevolence and sincerity can be presumed and agent behavior is relatively restricted, but for upcoming information-rich environments like the Semantic Web, three particular communication-related properties, which are traditionally associated with human sociality, deserve increased attention: 1) meaning is usually the *result* of multiple heterogeneous, possibly indefinite and conflicting communications, 2) benevolence and sincerity can not be assumed, and 3) homogenous mental architectures and thus the uniform processing of communicated information cannot be assumed also.

The meaning of utterances has two dimensions that need to be covered by a comprehensive approach to the semantics of agent communication (the term "semantics" here always in the broader computer scientific meaning including pragmatics, not just the more abstract linguistic sentence meaning): First, the sentence level, which is the aspect of meaning that is traditionally subject of linguistical semantics. This aspect of meaning is contextualized with an environmental description in the form of a (assumably) consented ontology. In addition, a calculus to describe objects and events within the environment the respective utterance refers to has to be provided, for example predicate logic and temporal modalities. The second dimension of meaning, its pragmatics (i.e., the actual use and effect of utterances in social encounters), contributes by far the most difficulties to current distributed artificial intelligence. This is mainly due to agent autonomy, which makes it extremely difficult to obtain deterministic descriptions of agent behavior. Thus, current objectivist approaches either deliberatively avoid pragmatics at all, or try to impose pragmatical rules in a normative manner (leaving beside mentalistic approaches, which are not suitable for black- or gray-box agents in open system for obvious reasons).

The communication model we propose is grounded in *Social Systems Theory* [2], as it has been adopted for the modeling of expectation structures of artificial agents [8]

Note 1. The term "agent" always shall denote both ordinary agents and Mirror-Holons..

In our communication models [8,19,11,17], called *Empirical Semantics* and *Empirical-Rational Semantics*, which we can only outline here, a single communication attempt can be seen as a request to act in conformance with the information expressed by the utterance, or respectively to establish a requested future state (this includes both assertions of propositional information and requests to perform actions). In contrast to non-communicative events, an utterance has no (significant) direct impact on the physical environment. Instead, its consequences are achieved socially, and, most important, the addressee is free to deny the communicated proposition. Since an utterance is always explicitly produced by a self-interested agent to influence the addressee, communicated content can not be "believed" directly (except in the case the addressee could have derived its truth/usefulness herself and a communication would thus be rather unnecessary), but needs to be accompanied with social reasons given to the addressee to increase the probability of an acceptance of the communicated content. This can be done either explicitly by previous or subsequent communications (e.g., "If you comply, I'll comply too"), or implicitly by means of generalizations from past events (e.g., trust). The expected communication events which are triggered by a communication (in the context of the preceding communication process) in order to support the aims of this communication we call (informally) the *rational hull* of the triggering communication. The rational hulls of communications specify i.a. the rational social relationships which steer the acceptance or denial of communicated content according the public communication attitudes (their public intentional stances, so to say) the agents exhibit, e.g. by argumentation and sanctioning. Typically, a rational hull is initially very indefinite and becomes increasingly definite in the course of interaction, provided that the agents work towards mutual understanding (whereat understanding of course does not necessarily entails consent).

Our model is centered around the following terms, which we propose primarily as empirical replacements and supplements for terms used in traditional ACL semantics, like message content and commitment.

Social expectation structures (communication structures) As already described, social expectation structures are the part of the expectation structures consisting of social expectations that result from communication processes and constrain future communications. The visible effect a certain utterance brings about in the social expectation structures is the semantics of this utterance if no a-priori or mental knowledge about the respective actor is available.

Utterances An agent action event with the following properties: 1) it is occurring under mutual observation of the communicating agents, 2) without considering social expectation structures, the event would have a very low probability (e.g., it is unlikely that sentences are uttered without the intention to communicate), 3) its expected consequences in terms of physical expectation structures only are of low relevance (think of the generation of sound waves through human voice), and

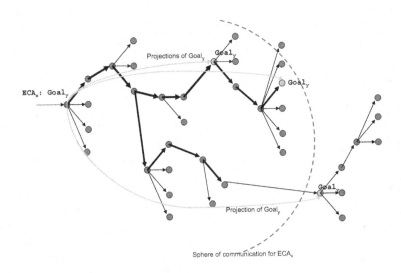

Fig. 6. An EN with projections and a sphere of communication

4) considering social expectation structures, the event needs to be informative, i.e., its probability must be lower 1 and must result in a change of expectations. For utterances using a formal language and reliable message passing, criteria 1) to 3) are clearly met. In our model, each utterance encodes one or more *projections*.

Projections Our replacement to the term "content" used in the context of formal languages like KIF (used to represent the propositional so-called "inner level" of messages described in speech act based ACLs like KQML). A projection is the part of the expectation structures which is selected through an utterance to inform the addressee. Of course, each utterance can also encode multiple projections at the same time. A projection can be considered to be a set of goal states within the EN the uttering agent strives for **rationality**, at least allegedly for the time of the respective *sphere of communication* (see below). Therefore, these goals need not be the true goals of the uttering agent, but at least for some time the agent acts "as if" they were.

The most basic kind of projection is obtained through *demonstrative acting*, where the uttering agent encodes its goals by means of "playing-act". Another possibility is to encode a projections within the traditional speech act form, or as a so-called elementary communication act (ECA) as described in [11]. The latter is more or less a set of pointers at agent-individual goal states of an EN. We consider all kinds of speech acts to be encodable as sets of ECAs together with constellations of given expectation structures (e.g. a command could be encoded as the ECA describing the goal of the command together with additional ECAs to sanction the addressee, and/or social structures which give the commanding agents the required social power to make the command effective). More generally, utterances can encode a projection using a "wishful" expectation network (describing the state the agent appears to desire). These expectation networks need to be matched with the actual EN to identify the states within the actual EN the agent strives for.

If a projection refers to communicative behavior itself (e.g., a question demands a communication), we talk about meta- or higher-order communication (cf. below).

Rational hulls The *rational behavior* an agent is *expected* to perform in order to make a certain uttered projection become reality (using e.g. assertions, sanctions, normative behavior, negotiations, actions to increase trust and his reputation...). The rational hull is defined as the set of social expectations arising from the assumption that the uttering agent tries (at least for some time) to maximize the probability that subsequent events are consistent with its uttered projection (speech act perlocution is a special case of this principle). A social commitment can be seen as one possible means to such maximization: An agent commits himself to perform certain actions to bring about a certain behavior from another agent in order to increase the probability of its goals. Practically, the rational hull of an ECA is computed via a combination of empirically learned, revisable experiences from past agent behavior in a similar context and the application of the rule of rational choice (cf. [11]). Rational hulls are recursive in the sense that each element of a rational hull has its own rational hull and so on, in their sum amounting to the empirical meaning of communication.

Figure 6 shows an EN modeling the future of some communication process. ECA_X is the utterance which encodes $Goal_Y$. This goal itself stands for several (seemingly) desired states of the EN (yellow nodes). Since within the so-called *sphere of communication* of ECA_X (see below) it is expected that the uttering agent rationally strives for these states, certain EN paths leading to these states become more likely (bold edges). Such behavior paths need to be (more or less) rational in terms of their expected utility (e.g. in comparison with competing goal states), and they need to reflect experiences from analogous agent behavior in the past.

Communication processes A set of probabilistically correlated utterances with the following properties: 1) each agent acts in consistence with the rational hulls induced from his utterances (which especially means that he does not contradict itself), and 2) each projection is consistent with 1), i.e. it does not deny that property 1) is met. 2) is somehow an empirical version of mental *understanding* and *trust*: With each communication, an agent acknowledges with his own communicating behavior implicitly that the other agent tries to get accepted his own projections.

Spheres of communication Each utterance (more precisely: each ECA) can have its own spheres of communication which describes the boundary of foreseeability of its consequences (=semantics) in terms of the expected subsequent communication process, i.e. the timely extend of a set of expected communication acts that are consistent and correlated. Every communication process together with the foreseeable expectation structures arising from this process creates thus a set of spheres of communication. Together these spheres form a so-called *social interaction system*. Whereas a communication sphere is similar to the special sort of social system called *interaction system* known from social systems theory [2], and resembles some of the properties of *spheres of commitment* [7], in our model spheres of communications have dynamic, empirically discovered boundaries in the sense that communications which do not fulfill the consistency criteria for communication processes at run-time mark their boundaries and are thus not part of it (e.g., misunderstandings and lies, if they become obvious). The most simple examples for communication spheres are those that rely on normative structures (e.g. protocols), like auctions (cf. [9] for a case study on empirical expectation-oriented modeling of a trading platform) and (agent-supported) forums on the internet, as long as the agents do not break the communication laws of these systems.

A general Mirror-Holon accommodates exactly one communication sphere for its source domain, and one for the targeted domain. Therefore, a single Mirror-Holon is not able to model (communicatively revealed) misunderstandings and two or more sets of communications that are not empirically correlated. In such cases, multiple Mirror-Holons are required to bridge such inconsistencies and incoherencies.

Higher-order expectation structures Social expectations which model multiple, probably inconsistent communication spheres at the same time.

At the moment, our formal model of expectation structures [19] does not allow for an explicit modeling of higher-order expectation structures. But a communication sphere can of course describe processes of higher-order communications (e.g. communications about communications, generated by a Social System Mirror), which can be modeled using an expectation network. Such an expectation network thus models expectations that model expectation structures themselves, therefore some sort of higher-order expectation structures.

Physical expectation structures Optionally, expectation networks can additionally contain domain-dependent expectation structures (i.e., ontological information about the non-symbolic environment). These structures include expectations regarding "physical" agent actions and other events in the agents' environment. Their main characteristic in comparison to communicative events (utterances) is that such events do not consist of projections.

4   Learning and Asynchronous Enactment of Social Structures

4.1   Derivation Loop

Figure 7 depicts the *EMPRAT* algorithm for the derivation of expectation networks (i.e. the semantics of communication sequences) from observed agent messages (please refer to [11] for details). The figure shows its most basic kind—it needs to be adapted depending from the concrete type of Mirror-Holon. If, for example, the system designer

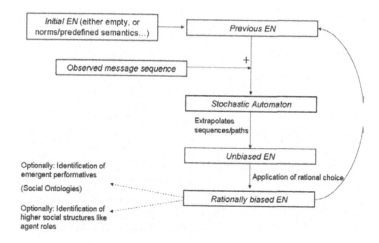

Fig. 7. Learning communication structures rational-empirically

wants to propagate normative social structures to the agents, it would be required to "inject" static expectations (norms) into the derived ENs.

The algorithm starts with the *initial EN* that contains given knowledge about the communication system and predefined communication structures (like communication protocols). Observed agent messages are used as learning examples for the inductive building of a stochastic automaton, which is converted into an expectation network. This "unbiased EN" therefore considers empirical experiences only (besides the initial EN). To speed up the learning process, from this unbiased EN a *rationally-biased* EN is generated by the application of rational choice rules which reflect the agents' decision processes and rational attitudes (limited by the borders of the respective spheres of communications). The process repeats for newly observed messages, using the latest rationally-biased EN as a new initial EN.

The current version of this algorithm does not yet consider higher-order expectation structures (required e.g. for the modeling of *questions*), empirically derived borders of spheres of communications, and misunderstandings. Traditional speech act performatives like assertions as in Figure 1 are also not supported yet, but can often easily be "emulated" using ECAs.

4.2 Execution

The straightforward, yet quite "naive" method to enact an EN is to use *stochastic simulation* [29]. The algorithm can be sketched in pseudo-code as follows:

for $i = 1..n$ {

$\qquad execute(startnode)$

}

with

function $execute(node)$ {

$\qquad$ for each $childnode_j$ in $children(node)$ {

$\qquad\qquad$ if $(1/expect(childnode_j))|i$ { (*)

$\qquad\qquad\qquad emit(childnode_j)$

$\qquad\qquad\qquad execute(childnode_j)$

$\qquad\qquad$ }

$\qquad$ }

}

Here, the whole expectation network is traversed top-down n times, beginning at $startnode$ (please refer to the formal framework of ENs as described e.g. in [19]). The higher n, the higher is the accuracy of the simulation process, i.e., the more closely the probability distribution of the emitted actions resembles the probability distribution represented by the expectation network.

Each call of the function $execute$ traverses the child nodes of a certain node, and recursively calls $execute$ with probability $expect(childnode_j)$ for each child node $childnode_j$ (i.e. calls $execute$ iff i divides the inverse of $expect(childnode_j)$ without a remainder). $expect(childnode_j)$ is the expectability of $childnode_j$ within the EN (i.e. the probability the Mirror-Holons assigns), from the interval $[0, 1]$.

Function $emit$ executes the action associated with the respective node. Depending from the concrete type of Mirror-Holon, the holon could perform this action by itself, or delegate the execution to the agent which originally contributed this action (normatively, or via information only).

Of course, this way of executing an EN has several shortcomings. First of all, repeating the whole execution n times does not necessarily reflect the behavior of the original social system. Seemingly, improvements in this respect would be to call $execute(startnode)$ significantly less than n (or only once), and to replace condition (*) with the non-deterministic result of a random number generator which generates $true$ with probability $expect(childnode_j)$. Furthermore, the difference of emitting communicative actions and "physical" actions is not considered, and no simplification/clearance of the EN (in order to speed up the execution or to make it more reliable) is performed here.

5   Differentiation and Communication of Mirror-Holons

So far, we did not say much about the *boundaries* of Mirror-Holons, i.e., the selection of communication it observes and its sphere of activity within the respective MAS, and the interaction of multiple Mirror-Holons. In general, a single Mirror-Holon could model a complete multiagent system, provided that the trajectories of observed source communications are communication processes in the sense of Section 3, i.e., the Mirror-Holon represents a single sphere of communication . Thus a reason for having more than one Mirror-Holon in a MAS would be the presence of multiple communication spheres. This can occur if 1) some the communications show up inconsistencies regarding understandability (an agent contradicts himself, which can not be modeled within a single sphere of communication) and 2) some of the communications are not correlated statistically. In case 1), to model this inconsistency, we need to introduce a *meta* Mirror-Holon that accommodates higher-order social structures to provide a model which explains these inconsistencies, whereas issue 2) could simply be handled by multiple Mirror-Holons for each identified sphere.

In case a MAS is equipped with at least two Mirror-Holons, these Mirror-Holons typically communication with each other for the following two reasons. First, provided that the interacting Mirror-Holons trust each other, one could supply the other with information about social structures (i.e., meta-communicate about communication processes). This is useful if one Mirror-Holon needs to model a certain source domain, and the other Mirror-Holons emits (e.g., as a Social System Mirror) information about this domain. Then the first mirror can simply query the required social structures from the other Mirror-Holon instead of having to obtain them itself from agent observation. Second, the communicative actions a Mirror-Holon performs in its targeted domain might be observed by another Mirror-Holon. This indirect way of communication is closely related to the concept of meta Mirror-Holons, because observing and modeling the behavior of an actor which represents social structures can be seen as deriving some sort of higher-order expectation structures.

Figure 6 shows a MAS which is equipped with five interacting Mirror-Holons. Mirror-Holon 1 needs to model its targeted domain (Communication set B), which happens to be the source domain of Mirror-Holon 2. As a Social System Mirror, Mirror-Holon 2 can communicate structure information about Communication set B to Mirror-Holon 1, and thus Mirror-Holon 1 does not need to obtain expectation structures for its targeted domain itself (strictly speaking, Mirror-Holon 2 is part of the targeted domain of Mirror-Holon 1, and Mirror-Holon 1 ignores all but the higher-order communication generated by Mirror-Holon 2 within this domain).

The intersection of communication sets B and C shall contain inconsistencies. Therefore, this intersection can not be modeled by a single Mirror-Holon. The source models of Mirror-Holon 3 and 4 shall each represent a consistent subset of this intersection, and put this subset into action in Communication set D. Mirror-Holon 3|4 is a

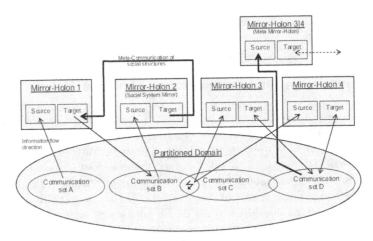

Fig. 8. Interacting Mirror-Holons

meta Mirror-Holon in the sense that it models the behavior of Mirror-Holon 3 and 4 as it appears in communication set D.

6   Conclusion

In this paper, we have introduced Mirror-Holons as means for the autonomy-preserving influencing of multiagent systems at run-time. Because Mirror-Holons are on the one hand based on the only two coordination principles that fully preserves agent autonomy, namely *observation* and non-obstructive *information*, and on the other hand Mirror-Holons can be fully equipped with the ability to act and communicate, they bring together both poles of agent-oriented software development—complete passiveness and the imposition of activity—and allow for a leveled, dynamic weighting of both extremes. General Mirror-Holons are a broad and abstract approach. But, while a lot of work lies ahead, we nevertheless strongly believe that Mirror-Holons have the potential to become useful coordination mechanisms especially *because* of their abstractness. As we have seen, there is a large spectrum of Mirror-Holon subtypes and only a few fixed design constraints which makes it likely that adequately tailored Mirror-Holons are applicable even for ill-defined, underspecified scenarios, where almost no assumptions can be made about agent behavior.

Being an introductional work, this paper leaves much room for further specifications, applications and enhancements. As most important we consider to be the continuation of the implementation and evaluation of basic functional Mirror-Holon types like the AFMH and the SFMH, and the theoretical implications of the general Mirror-Holons, especially regarding the differentiation of multiagent system communications into multiple spheres of communication (respectively their representing Mirror-Holons), as we suspect that this kind of differentiation resembles to some degree the process of *Functional Differentiation* described by Social Systems Theory.

References

1. M. P. Singh. A social semantics for agent communication languages. In Proceedings of the IJCAI Workshop on Agent Communication Languages, 2000.
2. N. Luhmann. Social Systems. Stanford University Press, Palo Alto, CA, 1995.
3. Y. Labrou, T. Finin. Semantics and conversations for an agent communication language. In Proceedings of the Fifteenth International Joint Conference on Artificial Intelligence (IJCAI-97), 1997.
4. M. Schillo and D. Spresny. Organization: The Central Concept of Qualitative and Quantitative Scalability. In this volume.
5. F. Guerin and J. Pitt. Denotational Semantics for Agent Communication Languages. In Proceedings of the 5th International Conference on Autonomous Agents (Agents'01), ACM Press, 2001.
6. P. R. Cohen, H. J. Levesque. Communicative actions for artificial agents. In Proceedings of the First International Conference on Multiagent Systems (ICMAS-95), 1995.
7. M. P. Singh. Multiagent Systems as Spheres of Commitment. In Proceedings of the ICMAS Workshop on Norms, Obligations, and Conventions, 1996
8. K. F. Lorentzen, M. Nickles. Ordnung aus Chaos – Prolegomena zu einer Luhmann'schen Modellierung deentropisierender Strukturbildung in Multiagentensystemen. In T. Kron (Ed.), Luhmann modelliert. Ansätze zur Simulation von Kommunikationssystemen, Leske & Budrich, 2002.
9. W. Brauer, M. Nickles, M. Rovatsos, G. Weiß, K. F. Lorentzen. Expectation-Oriented Analysis and Design. In Proceedings of the Second International Workshop on Agent-Oriented Software Engineering (AOSE-2001), LNCS 2222, Springer, 2001.
10. M. Nickles and G. Weiss. Empirical Semantics of Agent Communication in Open Systems. In Proceedings of the Second International Workshop on Challenges in Open Agent Environments at AAMAS-2003, 2003.
11. M. Nickles, M. Rovatsos, and G. Weiss. Empirical-Rational Semantics of Agent Communication. In Proceedings of the Third International Joint Conference on Autonomous Agents and Multiagent Systems (AAMAS-04), 2004.
12. M. Nickles, M. Rovatsos, G. Weiß. Expectation-Oriented Modeling. In International Journal "Engineering Applications of Artificial Intelligence" (EAAI), Elsevier, 2005.
13. M. Nickles and T. Froehner. Social Reification for the Semantic Web. Research Report FKI-24x-04, AI/Cognition Group, Department of Informatics, Technical University Munich, 2004.
14. T. Froehner, M. Nickles, and G. Weiß. Towards Modeling the Social Layer of Emergent Knowledge Using Open Ontologies. In Proceedings of The ECAI 2004 Workshop on Agent-Mediated Knowledge Management (AMKM-04), 2004.
15. T. Froehner, M. Nickles, and G. Weiß. Open Ontologies—The Need for Modeling Heterogeneous Knowledge. In Proceedings of The 2004 International Conference on Information and Knowledge Engineering (IKE 2004), 2004.
16. M. Rovatsos, G. Weiß, and M. Wolf. An Approach to the Analysis and Design of Multiagent Systems based on Interaction Frames. In Proceedings of the First International Joint Conference on Autonomous Agents and Multiagent Systems (AAMAS-02), 2002.
17. M. Nickles, M. Rovatsos, M. Schmitt, W. Brauer, F. Fischer, T. Malsch, K. Paetow, G. Weiss. The Empirical Semantics Approach to Communication Structure Learning and Usage: Individuals- vs. System-Views. In Nigel Gilbert (Ed.), Journal of Artificial Societies and Social Simulation (JASSS), Issue on Socionics, 2005.
18. M. Nickles, M. Rovatsos, G. Weiß. A Schema for Specifying Computational Autonomy. In Proceedings of the Third International Workshop on Engineering Societies in the Agents World (ESAW). Lecture Notes in Computer Science. Springer, 2003.

19. M. Nickles, M. Rovatsos, W. Brauer, G. Weiss. Communication Systems: A Unified Model of Socially Intelligent Systems. In this issue.
20. M. R. Genesereth, R. E. Fikes. Knowledge Interchange Format, Version 3.0 Reference Manual. Technical Report Logic-92-1, Stanford University, 1992.
21. J. L. Austin. How to do things with words. Clarendon Press, Oxford, 1962.
22. J. R. Searle. A taxonomy of illocutionary acts. In K. Gunderson (Ed.), Language, Mind, and Knowledge (Minnesota studies in the philosophy of science VII), pages 344–369. University of Minnesota Press, 1975.
23. M. Colombetti, M. Verdicchio. An analysis of agent speech acts as institutional actions. In Proceedings of the First International Joint Conference on Autonomous Agents and Multiagent Systems (AAMAS2002), 2002.
24. C. Gerber, J. Siekmann, G. Vierke. Flexible Autonomy in Holonic Multiagent Systems. In AAAI Spring Symposium on Agents with Adjustable Autonomy, 1999.
25. A. Omicini, E. Denti. Formal ReSpecT. Electronic Notes in Theoretical Computer Science 48, Declarative Programming—Selected Papers from AGP'00. Elsevier Science B.V., 2001.
26. R. Dieng, H. J. Mueller (Eds.), Conflicts in Artificial Intelligence. Springer, 2000.
27. A. Koestler. The Ghost in the Machine. Arkana, 1967.
28. F. Heylighen, C. Joslyn. Second Order Cybernetics. In F. Heylighen, C. Joslyn, V. Turchin (Eds.), Principia Cybernetica, 2001.
29. B. D. Ripley. Stochastic Simulation. Wiley, 1987.

Communication Systems: A Unified Model of Socially Intelligent Systems*

Matthias Nickles, Michael Rovatsos, Wilfried Brauer, and Gerhard Weiß

Department of Informatics, Technical University of Munich
85748 Garching bei München, Germany,
{nickles,rovatsos,brauer,weissg}@cs.tum.edu

Abstract. This paper introduces *communication systems* (CS) as a unified model for socially intelligent systems. This model derived from sociological systems theory, combines the empirical analysis of communication in a social system with logical processing of social information to provide a general framework for computational components that exploit communication processes in multiagent systems. We present an elaborate formal model of CS that is based on expectation networks and their processing. To illustrate how the CS layer can be integrated with agent-level expectation-based methods, we discuss the conversion between CS and interaction frames in the InFFrA architecture. A number of CS-based applications that we envision suggest that this model has the potential to add a new perspective to Socionics and to multiagent systems research in general.

1 Introduction

Traditional attempts to model the semantics of agent communication languages (ACLs) are mostly based on describing mental states of communicating agents [2,3,7,27] or on observable (usually commitment-based) social states [6,22,28]. However, both views fail to recognise that communication semantics evolve during operation of a multiagent system (MAS), and that the semantics always depend on the view of an observer who is tracking the communicative processes in the system. Yet this is a crucial aspect of inter-agent communication, especially in the context of open systems in which a pre-determined semantics cannot be assumed, let alone the compliance of agents' behaviour with it.

In [8,12] we have therefore—influenced by sociological systems-theory [9]—introduced both *adaptive-normative* and *empirical expectations* regarding observable *communications* as a universal means for the semantical modelling of interaction structures and sociality in multiagent systems, and in [23,15,16,18,13], we have presented—influenced by socio-systems and socio-cognitive (pragmatist) theories [9,5,11]—formal frameworks for the semantics of communicative action that are *empirical, rational, constructivist* and *consequentialist* in nature and analyzed the implications of our models on social reasoning both from an agent and the systemic perspective.

---

* This work is supported by DFG (German National Science Foundation) under contracts no. Br609/11-2 and MA759/4-2.

K. Fischer, M. Florian, and T. Malsch (Eds.): Socionics, LNAI 3413, pp. 289–313, 2005.

We suggested that recording observations of message exchange among agents in a multiagent system (MAS) *empirically* is the only feasible way to capture the meaning of communication, if no or only the most basic *a priori* assumptions about this meaning can be made. Being empirical about meaning naturally implies that the resulting model depends very much on the observer's perspective, and that the semantics would always be the semantics "assigned" to utterances by that observer, hence this view is inherently *constructivist*. Since, ultimately, no more can be said about the meaning of a message in an open system than that it lies in the set of expected consequences that a message has, we also adopt a *consequentialist* outlook on meaning.

In this paper, we integrate and extend upon these views that were strongly influenced by different sociological views (social systems theory and pragmatism). We present a detailed framework for the formal description of socially intelligent systems based on the universal, systems-theoretical concept of *communication systems*, which subsumes structure-oriented expectation modelling on the one hand, and the modelling of cognitive, goal-oriented social knowledge of active agents on the other.

In the terminology of sociological systems theory, communication systems are systems that consist of interrelated communications which "observe" their environment [9]. For the purposes of this paper, we will use the term "communication system" (CS) to denote computational entities that possess empirical information about observed communication[1] and use this information to influence the behaviour of the underlying system. Their distinct features are (i) that they only use data about communication for building models of social processes, the underlying assumption being that all relevant aspects of social interaction are eventually revealed through communication, and (ii) that, different from a passive observer, they may take action in the system to influence its behaviour; in other words, there is a feedback loop between observation and action, so that a CS becomes an autonomous component in the overall MAS.

Note, however, that CSs need not necessarily be (embedded in) agents. Although their autonomy presumes some agentification, their objectives need not be tied to achieving certain goals in the physical (or pseudo-physical simulation) world as it is the case with "ordinary" agents. Thus, they are best characterised as components used to (trans)form expectations (regardless of how these expectations are employed by agents in their reasoning) and which are autonomous with respect to how they perform this generation and modification of expectations.

Our hypothesis regarding the Socionics endeavour [10] is that its main contribution lies in the construction of appropriate communication systems for complex MAS, or, to take it to the extreme, we might summarise this insight as

$$Socionics = empirical\ communication\ analysis\ +\ rational\ action$$

because the CS viewpoint extends the traditional outlook on MAS taken in the field of distributed artificial intelligence (DAI). Thereby, the "semantics" aspect mentioned above plays a crucial role, because meaning lies in the sum of communicative expectations in a system, and CS capture precisely these expectations and how they evolve.

---

[1] I.e., our CS realises some kind of *second-order observer* in terms of sociological systems theory.

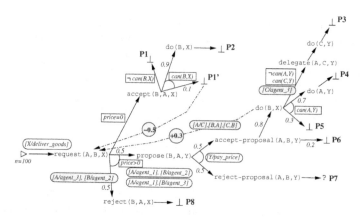

Fig. 1. An expectation network. Nodes are labelled with message templates in typewriter font and the special symbols "▷", "⊥" and "?"; they are connected by (solid) cognitive edges labelled with numerical expectabilities in *italic* font, or (dashed) normative edges with round circles containing a numerical "force" value in **bold** face. Substitution lists/conditions belonging to edges appear in rounded/edged boxes near the edge. If neighbouring edges share a condition this is indicated by a drawn angle between these edges. The path labels **P1** to **P8** do not make part of the notation and are simply used to refer to paths in the text.

The remaining sections are structured as follows: We start by introducing expectation networks in Section 2, which constitute our formal model for describing communicative expectations. Then, we formally define communication systems and their semantics (Section 3). As an example of how CS can be used to model socially intelligent systems, we discuss the conversion between the social reasoning architecture InFFrA and CS in Section 4. Section 5 discusses possible applications of the CS, and section 6 concludes.

2   Expectation Networks

Expectation networks (ENs) [8,12] are the data structures on which communication systems operate.[2] They capture regularities in the flow of communication between agents in a system by connecting message templates (nodes) that stand for utterances with each other via links (edges) which are labelled with (i) weights (ii) a logical condition and (iii) lists of variable substitutions. Roughly speaking, the semantics of such a labelled edge is that "if the variables in the messages have any of the values in the substitution lists, and the logical condition is currently satisfied, then the weight of the edge reflects the frequency with which a message matching the label of the target node follows

---

[2] This view of expectations and sociality follows widely the *Theory of Social Systems* ("systems theory") of the sociologist *Niklas Luhmann* [9] and is described from a computer scientific point of view in [8,1].

utterance of a message matching the label of the source node of the edge." Before presenting a full definition of ENs, we have to introduce some basic notions and notation we use, and to make certain auxiliary definitions and assumptions. The example network in Figure 1 will be used throughout the discussion of ENs to illustrate the purpose of definitions and assumptions.

The formal framework we present in this paper covers one type of EN which is especially suitable for the mapping to so-called *interaction frames* [25] - details on general ENs and other types of ENs can be found in [12].

2.1 Basics

A central assumption that is made in ENs is that observed messages may be categorised as *continuations* of other communications and events, or may be considered as the start of a new interaction that is not related to previous experience. So an edge leading from m to m' is thought to reflect the *transition probability*, i.e. the frequency of communication being "continued" from the observer's point of view. Usually, continuation depends on temporal and sometimes spatial proximity between messages, but it might also be identified through a connection about "subject", or, for example, though the use of the same communication media (m' was shown on TV after m was shown some time earlier on).

Apart from "ordinary" node labels, we use three distinct symbols "▷", "⊥", and "?". "▷" is the label occurring only at the root node of the EN. Whenever a message is considered a "non-continuation" of previous sequences (i.e. the start of a new interaction), it is appended to this "▷"-node. Nodes labelled with "⊥" denote that a communication ended after the label of the predecessor of this node was observed. The label "?", finally, indicates that there exists no expectation regarding future messages at this node. Nodes with such "don't know" semantics are usually messages that occur for the first time— the observer knows nothing about what will happen after them being uttered. To define the syntactic details of EN, we have to introduce formal languages $\mathcal{L}$ and $\mathcal{M}$ used for logical expressions and for message templates, respectively. $\mathcal{L}$ is a simple propositional language consisting of atomic propositions $Statement = \{p, q(X, s), \ldots\}$ potentially containing (implicitly universally quantified) variables (for which we use capitalised letters, e.g. X), of the usual connectives $\vee, \wedge, \Rightarrow$ and $\neg$, the logical constants "true" and "false", and braces () for grouping sub-expressions together (the language is formally given by the grammar in Table 1). We write $\models \varphi$ if φ. A *knowledge base* $KB \in 2^{\mathcal{L}}$ can be any finite set of formulae from $\mathcal{L}$. For simplicity, we will often write $KB \models \varphi$ to express $\models (\wedge_{\varphi' \in KB} \varphi') \Rightarrow \varphi$.

As for $\mathcal{M}$, this is a formal language that defines the message patterns used for labelling nodes in expectation networks. Its syntax is given by the grammar in table 1. Messages observed in the system (we write $\mathcal{M}_c$ for the language of these *concrete* messages) can be either physical messages of the format $do(a, ac)$ where a is the executing agent and ac is a symbol used for a physical action, or a non-physical message *performative*(a, b, c) sent from a to b with content c. (Note that the terminal symbols used in the *Agent* and *PhysicalAction* rules are domain-dependent, and that we take the existence of such symbols for granted.) However, the message labels of type *MsgPattern* used in expectation networks may also contain variables for agents and

$$Var \rightarrow X \mid Y \mid Z \mid \ldots$$
$$AgentVar \rightarrow A_1 \mid A_2 \mid \ldots$$
$$PhysicalActVar \rightarrow X_1 \mid X_2 \mid \ldots$$
$$Expect \in [0; 1]$$
$$Agent \rightarrow agent\_1 \mid \ldots \mid agent\_n$$
$$Head \rightarrow it\_rains \mid loves \mid \ldots$$
$$Performative \rightarrow accept \mid propose \mid reject \mid inform \mid \ldots$$
$$PhysicalAction \rightarrow move\_object \mid pay\_price \mid deliver\_goods \mid \ldots$$
$$Message \rightarrow Performative(Agent, Agent, LogicalExpr)$$
$$\mid do(Agent, Agent, PhysicalAction)$$
$$MsgPattern \rightarrow Performative(AgentTerm, AgentTerm, LogicalExpr)$$
$$\mid do(AgentTerm, AgentTerm, PhysicalActTerm)$$
$$\mid \triangleright \mid \perp \mid ?$$
$$PhysicalActTerm \rightarrow PhysicalActVar \mid PhysicalAction$$
$$AgentTerm \rightarrow AgentVar \mid Agent$$
$$LogicalExpr \rightarrow (LogicalExpr \Rightarrow LogicalExpr) \mid (LogicalExpr \vee LogicalExpr)$$
$$\mid (LogicalExpr \wedge LogicalExpr) \mid \neg LogicalExpr$$
$$\mid Statement$$
$$Statement \rightarrow Head \mid Head(TermList) \mid true \mid false$$
$$TermList \rightarrow TermList, Term \mid Term$$
$$Term \rightarrow Var \mid AgentTerm \mid MsgPattern \mid Graph$$
$$EdgeList \rightarrow (MsgPattern, Expect, MsgPattern, LogicalExpr, SubstList) EdgeList$$
$$\mid \varepsilon$$
$$Graph \rightarrow \langle EdgeList \rangle$$
$$SubstList' \rightarrow SubstList' Subst \mid \varepsilon$$
$$SubstList \rightarrow \langle SubstList' \rangle$$
$$Subst \rightarrow [AgentVar/Agent] \mid [PhysicalActVar/PhysicalAction]$$
$$\mid [Var/Term]$$

Table 1. A grammar for messages, generating the languages $\mathcal{M}$ (the language of message patterns, using *MsgPattern* as starting symbol), $\mathcal{M}_c$ (the language of concrete messages, using *Message* as starting symbol) and the logical language $\mathcal{L}$ (using *LogicalExpr* as starting symbol.

physical actions (though not for performatives). As we will soon show, this is useful to generalise over different observed messages by adding a variable substitution to each node. The content c of a non-physical action, finally, is given by type *LogicalExpr*. It can either be (i) an atomic proposition, a (ii) message pattern or physical action term, (iii) an expectation network, or (iv) a logical formula formed out of these elements. Syntactically, expectation networks (*Graph*) are represented as lists of edges (m, p, n, c, l)

where m and n are message patterns, p is a transition probability from m to n, c is a logical condition, l is a list of variable substitutions. The meaning of these will be clarified once the full definition of expectation networks has been presented.

2.2 Normative and Cognitive Edges

A distinct feature of ENs is that their edges fall into two categories, *cognitive* (also called *adaptive*) and *normative* edges. A cognitive edge e (also called observation edge) denotes a correlation in observed communication sequences. Usually, its expectability $Exp(e) \in [0; 1]$ reflects the probability of $target(e)$ occurring shortly after $source(e)$ in the same communicative context (i.e. in spatial proximity, between the same agents, etc.). Although expectability values need not directly reflect the frequency of a continuation that matches the source and target node labels (in the context of the path leading to the source node), they should somehow correlate with it.

Normative edges, on the other hand, represent knowledge about correlations between messages that does not have its origins in observation.[3] In particular, normative edges may link messages together that do not occur successively, and therefore the EN is not a tree if we include normative edges in the edge set. Therefore, they are not annotated with degrees of expectation, but with a numerical assessment of the "normative force" they exert. This value $Fc(e, n) \in \mathbb{R}$ is thought to increase or decrease the probability of $target(e)$ whenever $source(e)$ occurs *regardless* of any observed correlation between $source(e)$ and $target(e)$. The second argument n used to compute this force is the time that passed since last observing a message that matched $source(e)$. Obviously, its absolute value should decrease with time passing, and it should become zero after some time, i.e.

$$\forall n_1, n_2 \in \mathbb{N}. n_2 > n_1 \Rightarrow |Fc(e, n_2)| < |Fc(e, n_1)| \tag{1}$$
$$\exists n_0 \in \mathbb{N}. \forall n > n_0. Fc(e, n) = 0 \tag{2}$$

Computation of changes in the impact of a normative edge necessitates, of course, keeping track of the time $\tau(v)$ that has passed since a message was observed that matched the label of node v. Note that, usually, the function definition for Fc will be identical for all normative edges in an EN except for initial values $Fc(e, 0)$. Computation of changes in the impact of a normative edge necessitates, of course, keeping track of the time $\tau(v)$ that has passed since a message was observed that matched the label of node v. To illustrate the usefulness of normative links, consider the following paths in the EN of Figure 1:

> **P2** : $\text{request}(A, B, X) \rightarrow \text{accept}(B, A, X) \rightarrow \text{do}(B, X)$
>
> **P1'** : $\text{request}(A, B, X) \rightarrow \text{accept}(B, A, X) \rightarrow \perp$

---

[3] In practice, normative edges can be the product of "very long term" observation of communication. However, we will uphold this clear distinction between cognitive (i.e., adaptive) and normative knowledge here because normative knowledge can probably not be derived in the scope of observation we assume here. Introducing a gradual sense of normativity and cognitivity for edges would be another option that is investigated in [8,12].

These represent two possible runs in a conversation in which A wants B to perform some physical action X. In the first case, B executes the promised action X, in the second he does not. What normative edges would be reasonable to add? Possible suggestions would be

$$e_1 = (\text{do}(B, X), \text{request}(A, B, X)), Fc(e_1, n) > 0$$
$$e_2 = (\bot, \text{request}(A, B, X)), Fc(e_2, n) < 0$$
$$e_3 = (\text{accept}(B, A, X), \text{do}(B, X)), Fc(e_3, n) > 0$$
$$e_4 = (\text{do}(B, X), \text{request}(A, B, X)), Fc(e_4, n) > 0,$$
$$subst(e_4) = \langle [A/C], [B/A], [C/B] \rangle$$

e_1/e_2 would increase/decrease the probability of future requests from the same agent A to B depending on whether the conversation "worked out" for him or not.

Note that e_2 (which is actually present in the EN of Figure 1) will only have negative consequences for the "reputation" of B if he promised to perform X—if he used reject instead (path **P8**), he would not be sanctioned, and this would effectively strengthen the normative character of accept. Edge e_3 induces an increase on the probability of do once an agent has accepted, i.e. it suggests some semantic relationship between accepting to do something and then actually doing it. If an observer is using e_3, this means he is implementing a norm which does not depend on how often actually agents were observed to perform some task that they had previously accepted to take over. Finally, e_4 represents a relationship between messages more complex still: it suggests that if agent B does what A requested of him, this increases the probability of B asking something from A in reverse ($subst(e)$ being the list of substitutions stored with edge e). This example nicely illustrates the different uses of normative edges in particular in their different functions as "expectability manipulators" in prospective and retrospective ways.

2.3   Edge Conditions

As a final ingredient to network edges, we briefly discuss edge conditions. The idea is that this condition should further define the scope of validity to cases in which a formula can be shown to hold using the observer's knowledge base. So, if $\varphi = cond(e)$, then e is only relevant iff $KB \models \varphi$. Although this idea is straightforward, we have to make some additional assumptions regarding these conditions to facilitate the definition of EN semantics.

First of all, the sum of expectabilities of all cognitive out-edges of a node should be one for any state (i.e. set of believed facts) of the knowledge base. In other words, the condition

$$\forall v \sum_{e \in out(v), KB \models cond(e)} Expect(e) = 1 \tag{3}$$

should hold. This can be ensured, for example, by guaranteeing that the following condition holds through appropriate construction rules for the EN. Assume the outgoing links $out(V)$ of every node v are partitioned into sets $O_1, O_2, \ldots O_k$ where the links' expectabilities in each O_i are non-negative and sum to one.[4] Now let all edges in O_i share the same edge condition, i.e. $\forall i \exists \varphi \forall o \in O_i.(cond(o) = \varphi)$ and define $cond(O_i)$ as precisely this shared condition φ. (The O_i sets are precisely those sub-sets of $out(v)$ connected by a drawn angle in Figure 1.)

If we make sure that the outgoing links of every node are partitioned in this way, we can assign mutually exclusive conditions to them, i.e. ensure that

$$\forall i \neq j.cond(O_i) \wedge cond(O_j) \equiv false \quad \text{and} \quad \vee_i \, cond(O_i) \equiv true \qquad (4)$$

This way, it is not only guaranteed that we can derive unambiguous probabilities directly from the *Expect* values, but also that we can do so for *any* knowledge base contents.[5]

2.4   Formal Definition

Having discussed all the prerequisites, we can now define ENs formally:

Definition 1. *An* expectation network *is a structure*

$$EN = (V, C, N, \mathcal{M}, \mathcal{L}, H, n, mesg, \tau, cond, subst, Expect, Fc)$$

where

- $|V| > 1$ *is the set of* nodes,
- $C \subseteq V \times V$ *are the* cognitive *edges of EN,* $N \subseteq V \times V$ *are its* normative *edges,*
- $G = (V, C)$ *is a tree called* expectation tree, $G = (V, C \uplus N)$ *is a graph,* $N \cap C = \emptyset$,
- $\mathcal{M}$ *is a* message pattern language, $\mathcal{L}$ *is a logical language,* $cond : C \uplus N \to \mathcal{L}$,
- $mesg : V \to \mathcal{M}$ *is the* message label *function for nodes with*
  - $mesg(v) = \triangleright$ *exactly for the root node of* (V, C),
  - $\forall v \in V.\forall e, f \in out(v).\neg unify(mesg(target(e)), mesg(target(f)))$ *(target node labels of outgoing links never match)*,
- $H \in \mathbb{N}$ *is a finite* communication horizon,
- $n \in \mathbb{N}$ *is the total number of* non-continuations,
- $Expect : C \to [0; 1], \tau : V \to \mathbb{N}, Fc : N \times \mathbb{N} \to \mathbb{R}$,
- $subst : C \uplus N \to SubstList$ *(with SubstList as in table 1)*.

Through this definition, all elements discussed above are included: networks contain cognitive edges (labelled with expectabilities) and normative edges (labelled with normative force values); *cond* returns their conditions, and *subst* their substitution lists. Nodes are labelled with message templates through the *mesg* mapping, so that "▷" occurs only at the root node, and neighbouring nodes' labels never match (otherwise the expectability condition in equation 3 would be corrupted).

The only two elements of this definition that have not been discussed so far are the horizon constant H, which denotes the scope of maximal message sequence length for

---

[4] Formally, $out(v) = \cup_{1 \le i \le k} O_i$ and $\forall 1 \le i < j \le k.O_i \cap O_j = \emptyset$, and $\forall i \le k.(\forall o \in O_i.Expect(o) \ge 0 \wedge \sum_{o \in O_i} Expect(o) = 1)$.

[5] This comes at the price of having to insert redundant edges in some situations. For example, insertion of a new edge e with $cond(e) = \varphi$ if $out(v) = \emptyset$ necessitates insertion of another edge e' with $cond(e) = \neg \varphi$.

which the EN is relevant, and the total number of "non-continuations" n. Usually, this will be incremented each time a node (1) is appended to the root node, (2) matches one of the children nodes of the root node. Both are necessary for defining the semantics of the EN, which are discussed in detail in the following section.

2.5 Formal Semantics

For an arbitrary set S, let $\Delta(S)$ be the set of all (discrete) probability distributions over S with finite support. We define the semantics $I_{EN}(KB, w)$ in a network EN as a mapping from knowledge base states and current message sequence prefixes to the posterior probability distributions over all possible postfixes (conclusions) of the communication. Formally,

$$I_{EN}(KB, w) = f, \quad f \in \Delta(\mathcal{M}_c^*) \tag{5}$$

where

$$f(w') = \frac{g(w'\bot)}{\sum_{v \in \mathcal{M}_c^*} g(v\bot)} \tag{6}$$

is defined as the normalised value of $g(w'\bot)$, which represents the probability that w will be concluded by message sequence w', for any $w, w' \in \mathcal{M}^*$. We compute the probability for $w'\bot$ to make sure w' is followed by a node with label $\bot$ in the network, because the probability of w' is the probability with which the communication sequence will *end* after $w'_{|w'|}$ (and not that w' will simply be the prefix of some longer sequence). Also note that the sum in the denominator is not, as it may seem, infinite, because f has finite support.

Informally, the probability of w' should be inferred from multiplying all the expectability weights along the cognitive path that matches w' (if any), and increasing/decreasing these values with current force values from normative edges, if such edges end in nodes on this matching path. Before presenting the top-level formula for $g(w')$, we need some auxiliary definitions:

Firstly, we need to determine the node in a network EN that corresponds to a word w, which we denote by $mesg^{-1}$:

$$mesg^{-1}(\varepsilon) = v \quad :\Leftrightarrow \quad mesg(v) = \triangleright$$

$$mesg^{-1}(wm) = \begin{cases} v' & \text{if } \exists (v, v') \in C(KB(w)).\exists \vartheta \in subst(v, v'). \\ & (mesg(v') \cdot subst(w)\vartheta = m \wedge mesg^{-1}(w) = v) \\ \bot & \text{if no such } v' \text{ exists} \end{cases} \tag{7}$$

if $w \in \mathcal{M}_c^*$, $m \in \mathcal{M}_c$. The first case states that the node corresponding to the empty sequence ε is the unique root node of (V, C) labelled with $\triangleright$. According to the second case, we obtain the node v' that corresponds to a sequence wm if we take v' to be the successor of v (the node reached after w) whose label matches m under certain conditions:

– Edge (v, v') has to be a cognitive edge that is available in $EN(KB)$, where the elements of prefix w have already been executed. Since these can be physical actions, we must capture the restriction imposed on possible successors by having executed physical actions. Let $\xrightarrow{m}$ a function that modifies the knowledge base after message m is uttered. For a knowledge base KB, we can define

$$KB(w) = KB' :\Leftrightarrow KB \xrightarrow{w_1} \dots \xrightarrow{w_{|w|}} KB'$$

so that the successors considered in each step for determining $mesg^{-1}(w)$ always take into account the consequences of previous actions.[6] Therefore, (v, v') has to be in the set of cognitive edges $C(KB(w))$ still feasible after w.

– There has to be a substitution $\vartheta \in subst(v, v')$ which, when composed with the substitution $subst(w)$ applied so far to obtain the messages in w_1 to $w_{|w|}$ from the respective nodes in EN, will yield m if applied to $mesg(v')$. This is expressed by $mesg(v') \cdot subst(w)\vartheta = m$. In other words, there is at least one combined (and non-contradictory) variable substitution that will make the node labels along the path $mesg^{-1}(wm)$ yield wm if it is applied to them (concatenating substitutions is performed in a standard fashion). Thereby, the following inductive definition can be used to derive the substitution $subst(w)$ for an entire word w:

$$w = \varepsilon : \qquad\qquad subst(w) = \langle\rangle$$
$$w = w'm : \quad subst(w) = subst(w') \cdot unifier(mesg(mesg^{-1}(wm)), m)$$

where $\cdot$ is a concatenation operator for lists and $unifier(\cdot, \cdot)$ returns the most general unifier for two terms (in a standard fashion). Thus, $subst(w)$ can be obtained by recursively appending the unifying substitution of the message label of each node encountered on the path w to the overall substitution.

With all this, we are able to compute $g(w')$ as follows:

$$g(w') = \begin{cases} |\cup_{i=1}^{H} \mathcal{M}_c^i|^{-1} & \text{if } \exists v \in out(mesg^{-1}(w)).mesg(v) = ? \\ \prod_i \left(\sum_{e \in pred(ww',i)} S(e) \right) & \text{else} \end{cases} \qquad (8)$$

which distinguishes between two cases: if the path to node $mesg^{-1}(w)$ whose labels match w (and which is unique, because the labels of sibling nodes in the EN never unify) ends in a "?" label, the probability of a w' is simply one over the size of all words with length up to the horizon constant H (hence its name). This is because the semantics of "?" nodes is "don't know", so that all possible conclusions to w are uniformly distributed. Note that this case actually only occurs when new paths are generated and it is not known where they will lead, and also that if an outgoing link of a node points to a node with label "?", then this node will have no other outgoing links.

---

[6] Note also that $mesg^{-1}(w)$ can only be determined unambiguously, if for any knowledge base content, a unique cognitive successor can be determined (e.g. by ensuring that equations 3 and 4 hold). This is another reason for the constraint regarding non-unifying out-links of nodes in definition 1.

In the second case, i.e. if there is no "?" label on the path p from $mesg^{-1}(w)$ to $mesg^{-1}(ww')$, then the probability of w' is the product of weights $S(e)$ of all edges e on p. Thereby, $S(e)$ is just a generalised notation for expectability or normative force depending on the typed edge, i.e. $S(e) = Expect(e)$ if $e \in C$ and $S(e) = Fc(e, \tau(source(e)))$ if $e \in N$. The sum of these S-values is computed for all ingoing edges $pred(ww', i)$ of the node that represents the ith element of w', formally defined as

$$\forall w \in \mathcal{M}_c^*.pred(w, i) = \begin{cases} in(mesg^{-1}(w_1 \cdots w_i)) & \text{if } mesg^{-1}(w_1 \cdots w_i) \neq \bot \\ \emptyset \end{cases} \tag{9}$$

Note that summing over edges $pred(w)$ we calculate the sum of the (unique) *cognitive* predecessor of the node corresponding to $w_{|w|}$ and of all ingoing *normative* edges ending in that node. Finally, we compute the product of the probabilities along the w' path to obtain its overall probability. Looking back at the definition of $mesg^{-1}$, if no appropriate successor exists for m, the function returns $\bot$ (and $pred$ returns $\emptyset$, so that the probability $g(w')$ becomes 0 for continuations w' for which there is no path in the network). It is important to understand that condition

$$\text{if } \exists (v, v') \in C(KB(w)).\exists \vartheta \in subst(v, v')$$
$$(mesg(v') \cdot subst(w)\vartheta = m \wedge mesg^{-1}(w) = v)$$

of equation 7 implies that only those continuations w' of a prefix w will have a non-zero probability that are *identical* to the result of substituting a message label by one of the existing substitutions. Using this definition, the generalisation aspect of the EN is quite weak, as it only allows for generating "lists" of concrete cases.

Of course, alternatives to this can be applied, e.g.

$$\dots \exists \vartheta \in SubstList \dots$$

which would allow *any* substitution to be applied to the node labels (and render edge substitution lists useless), or

$$\dots \exists \vartheta \in \left(subst(v, v') \cup \left(SubstList - \bigcup_{e \neq (v, v'), e \in out(v)} subst(e) \right) \right) \dots \tag{10}$$

which would allow any substitution that (i) either pertains to the substitution list of (v, v') or (ii) that makes *not* part of one of the substitution lists of outgoing links of v other than (v, v'). The intuition here is that "unless the substitution in question indicates following a different path, it may be applied". In fact, we will use condition 10 unless stated otherwise, because we assume a maximally general interpretation useful, which can of course be further restricted by semantic constraints in the edge conditions to yield arbitrary criteria for message pattern matching.

This concludes the definition of the semantics of a message (sequence) in a given expectation network. Essentially, all the formalisms introduced above allow for capturing statistical as well as normative knowledge about possible communication behaviour in a system in a compact fashion: each edge is tagged with logical constraints, and each potential path can be interpreted in an adjustably general sense by using appropriate variable substitution lists for the edges. Then, we defined the meaning of a message (sequence) as an estimate of its potential consequences in terms of *concrete* message sequences.

A final remark should be made about the use of performatives in this model. Their use should by no means imply that we expect them to have fixed semantics or induce reliable mentalistic properties on the parties involved. Much more, we employ them as "markers" for paths in the ENs, that can—unlike all other parts of the messages—*not* be replaced by variables. The intuition behind this is that there should be a non-generalisable part of each message that forces the observer to make a distinction. Next, we define communication systems as mathematical structures that operate on ENs.

3   Communication Systems

A communication system describes the evolutionary dynamics of an expectation network. The main purpose of a CS is to capture changes to the *generalised* meaning of communicative action sequences in the course of interaction in a multiagent system, in contrast to expectation networks themselves, which model meaning changes of certain messages in dependence of the message context (i.e., its preceding message sequences within the EN) only. These changes, which can be expressed in terms of expectations about future behaviour, are derived from statistical observation. However, they may be biased by the beliefs and belief transformation functions of the CS, i.e. the CS is an *autonomous observer* that may have its own goals according to which it biases the expectations it computes. In contrast to agents who reason about expectations (such as InFFrA agents, cf. section 4), though, a CS need not necessarily be an active agent who takes action in the MAS itself, as described in Section 1. Describing how communication systems work should involve (at least) clarifying:

- which communicative actions to select for inclusion in an EN,
- where to add them and with which expectability (in particular, when to consider them as "non-continuations" that follow "▷"),
- when to delete existing nodes and edges (e.g. to "forget" obsolete structures), and how to ensure integrity constraints regarding the remaining EN,
- when to spawn insertion/deletion of normative edges and with which normative force/content/condition/substitutions.

A formal framework for specifying the details of the above is given by the following, very general, definition:

Definition 2. *A communication system is a structure*

$$CS = (\mathcal{L}, \mathcal{M}, f, \kappa)$$

where

- *$\mathcal{L}, \mathcal{M}$ are the formal languages used for logical expressions and messages (cf. table 1),*

- $f : \mathcal{EN}(\mathcal{L}, \mathcal{M}) \times \mathcal{M}_c \rightarrow \mathcal{EN}(\mathcal{L}, \mathcal{M})$ is the expectation update function *that transforms any expectation network EN to a new network upon experience of a message* $m \in \mathcal{M}_c$,
- $\kappa : 2^{\mathcal{L}} \times \mathcal{M}_c \rightarrow 2^{\mathcal{L}}$ is a knowledge base update function *that transforms knowledge base contents after a message accordingly,*

and $\mathcal{EN}(\mathcal{L}, \mathcal{M})$ is the set of all possible expectation networks over $\mathcal{L}$ and $\mathcal{M}$.

The intuition is that a communication system can be characterised by how it would update a given knowledge base and an existing expectation network upon newly observed messages $m \in \mathcal{M}_c$. This definition is very general, as it does not prescribe how the EN is modified by the CS. However, some assumptions are reasonable to make (although not mandatory):

- If EN is converted by f via EN' to EN'' if m and m' are observed successively (with τ' and τ'' the respective times since the last observation of a label),

$$\tau''(v) = \begin{cases} 0 & \text{if } (\exists v' \in pred(v).\tau'(v') = 0 \land unify(m', mesg(v)) \\ 0 & \text{if } pred(v) = \{v_0\} \land mesg(v_0) = \triangleright \land unify(m', mesg(v)) \\ \tau'(v) + 1 & \text{else} \end{cases}$$

So, the τ-value is reset to 0 if v is a successor of the root node, or if its predecessor's τ-value was just reset to 0 and the node in question matches the current message m'. Effectively, this means that the duration since the last occurrence of a node is incremented for all those nodes who have not occurred as successors of nodes that occurred in the previous step.

- If KB is the current knowledge base, $\kappa(KB, m) \models KB(m)$ should hold, so that all facts resulting from execution of m are consistent with the result of the κ-function.
- If any message sequence w' has occurred with frequency $\Pr(ww')$ as a continuation of w in the past, and EN_C is the same as EN reduced to cognitive edges, $I_{EN_C}(KB, w)(w') = \Pr(ww')$ should be the case, i.e. any bias toward certain message sequences not based on empirical observation should stem from normative edges. Note that this requirement says nothing about the probabilities of sequences never experienced before which result from applying the criterion in equation 7.

Normative edges left aside, an EN should predict the future of the respective observable communication sequences as accurately as possible. To achieve this, the respective CS is supposed to provide at least the following functionality:

Message Filtering and Syntax Recognition. Depending on its personal goals and the application domain, the observer might not be interested in all observable messages. Since ENs may not provide for *a priori* expectations, the discarding of such "uninteresting" messages can only take place *after* the semantics (i.e., the expected outcome) of the respective messages has already been derived from previous observation. Because discarding messages bears the risk that these messages become interesting afterwards, as a rule of thumb, message filtering should be reduced to a minimum. More particularly, messages should only be filtered out in cases of more or less settled expectations.

Paying attention to every message and filtering uninteresting or obsolete information later by means of structure reweighting and filtering (cf. below) is presumably the more robust approach.

A very important feature of communication languages is their ability to effectively encode the generalised meaning of utterances by means of syntax. Our computationally tractable approach [17] to this phenomenon relies on the assumption that the syntax of messages somehow reflects expectation structures which have already been assembled.

Structure Expansion. Structure expansion is concerned with the growth of an EN in case a message sequence is observed which has no semantics defined by this EN yet. In theory, such an expansion would never be necessary, if we could initially generate a *complete EN* which contains dedicated paths for *all* possible message sequences. In this case, the observer would just have to keep track of the perceived messages and to identify this sequence within the EN to derive its semantics (provided there is no "semantic bias" in form of observer predispositions or norms).

For obvious reasons, such a complete EN cannot be constructed in practice. In contrast, the most general *minimal EN* would yield "?" for every message sequence, thus being of no practical use. As a solution, we could start with the minimal EN and incrementally add a node for each newly observed message. This is still not smart enough, because it does not take advantage of generalisable message sequences, i.e. different sequences that have the same approximate meaning. In general, such a generalisation requires a relation which comprises "similar" sequences. The properties of this relation of course depend on domain- and observer-specific factors. A simple way of generalising is to group messages which can be unified syntactically.

Garbage Collection. Several further methods of EN processing can be conceived of that aid in keeping the computation of (approximate) EN semantics tractable. This can be achieved by continuously modifying expectation structures using certain meta-rules, for example:

1. "fading out" obsolete observations by levelling their edge weights;
2. replacing (approximately) uniform continuation probability edges with "?";
3. removal of "?"s that are not leafs;
4. keeping the EN depth constant through removal of one old node for each new node;
5. removal of very unlikely paths.

4   Integrating the Agent Perspective

In this section, we will explain how the Interaction Frames and Framing Architecture InFFrA [24,25] fits into the communication systems view. Interestingly enough, despite the fact that this architecture was developed independently from the CS framework using interactionist theories (yet also based on the socionic principles discussed in Section 1), it soon proved to be very similar to it. As a result, we have tried to adapt the notation of both CS and InFFrA so as to minimise variations between them. The re-interpretation of framing-based systems as communication systems is useful, because it

- explains how InFFrA is a "special case" of CS, specifically designed for practical, agent-level social learning and decision-making;
- points at strengths and limitations of InFFrA that result directly from making specific design choices in the communication systems framework;
- is an example for agent-level use of CS (recall, though, that embedding CS in agents is just one possibility);
- illustrates how information can be exchanged between InFFrA agents and other system components that follow the communication systems paradigm by using ENs as an interface.

To achieve this re-interpretation, we will use the formal m^2InFFrA model introduced in [24] (in this volume), based upon which we will discuss how CS might be mapped to InFFrA agents and vice versa. A brief overview of m^2InFFrA shall suffice for this purpose. For the full m^2InFFrA notation and definitions, please refer to [24].

4.1 Overview of m^2InFFrA

m^2InFFrA agents are agents that engage in discrete, turn-taking conversations (so-called encounters) between two parties, and maintain a frame repository $\mathcal{F} = \{F_1, \ldots, F_n\}$ in which they record knowledge about past interactions to apply it strategically in future encounters. Any such frame is a structure $F = (T, C, \Theta, h)$ that consists of a trajectory T, lists of conditions/substitutions C/Θ and an occurrence counter vector (we write $T(F)$, $C(F)$, $\Theta(F)$ and $h(F)$ for the respective elements of frame F). The meaning of such a frame is best explained by an example:

$$F = \Big\langle \langle \xrightarrow{5} \texttt{propose}(A, B, X) \xrightarrow{3} \texttt{accept}(B, A, X) \xrightarrow{2} \texttt{do}(A, X) \rangle,$$
$$\langle \{self(A), other(B), can(A, X)\},$$
$$\{agent(A), agent(B), action(X)\}\rangle,$$
$$\langle \langle [A/\texttt{agent\_1}], [B/\texttt{agent\_2}], [X/\texttt{pay\_price}]\rangle,$$
$$\langle [A/\texttt{agent\_1}], [B/\texttt{agent\_3}], [X/\texttt{pay\_price}]\rangle\rangle \Big\rangle$$

This frame states that five encounters started with a message matching $\texttt{propose}(A, B, X)$, three of them continued with $\texttt{accept}(B, A, X)$, and two were concluded by agent A performing physical action X (we use the abbreviated syntax $T_h(F) = \xrightarrow{h_1} p_1 \xrightarrow{h_2} p_2 \cdots \xrightarrow{h_n} p_n$ (where $h_n = h(p_n)$) to combine $T(F)$ and $h(F)$ in one expression). The remaining two observations might be due to encounter termination after the first message or were continued with a message that does not match $\texttt{accept}(B, A, X)$, and one encounter either finished after $\texttt{accept}(B, A, X)$ or continued with something different from $\texttt{do}(A, X)$. Also, the agent stored the two sets of conditions (and respective substitutions) under which this frame occurred (where the ith substitution applies for the ith condition).

m^2InFFrA agents who use such frames are defined as structures

$$a = (\mathcal{L}, \mathcal{M}, \mathcal{E}, n, u, f, \kappa, \sigma)$$

with logical/message pattern languages $\mathcal{L}$, $\mathcal{M}$ (deliberately identical to the languages introduced in Table 1), a set of encounter names $\mathcal{E}$, a count n of all encounters perceived so far, a utility function u, functions f and κ that transform frame repository and knowledge base when an encounter is perceived. Finally, they employ a similarity measure σ for message pattern sequences which they use to derive a probability distribution for potential message sequences given their similarities to those stored in interaction frames in the repository.

Such a probability distribution is called a *framing state* $[a](\mathcal{F}, KB, w) \in \Delta(\mathcal{M}_c^*)$ that maps any frame repository and knowledge base contents $\mathcal{F}$ and KB to a probability distribution over message sequences. For any two message sequences w and w', this distribution assigns a probability that an encounter which started with w will be concluded with w' (e.g. if $[a](\mathcal{F}, KB, w)(w') = 0.3$, then an encounter that started with w will be concluded by w' with a probability of 30%).

4.2   Communication Systems and m^2InFFrA

At first glance, quite some similarities between CS and m^2InFFrA become obvious. Most prominently, these are

1. the use of message patterns to generalise from concrete instances of messages and the recording of past cases in the form of variable substitutions;
2. the conditioning of message sequences with logical constraints to restrict the scope of certain expectations;
3. the evolutionary semantics of messages, updated with new observations;
4. the formalisation of a social reasoning component (CS/agent) as an "expectation transformer" (cf. functions f and κ in both definitions).

However, there are also distinct differences, which shall be made concrete by discussing the possibility of converting expectation networks to frame repositories and vice versa, the central question being whether an m^2InFFrA agent can be built for an arbitrary CS and vice versa.

Converting Frames to Expectation Networks. Up to minor difficulties, this conversion is quite straightforward. We sketch the most important steps while leaving out certain formal details. Any frame can be transformed to a set of so-called "singular" frames with only one condition set and no substitutions. For a frame F, this is achieved by generating the set

$$F_s = \left\{ (T(F)\vartheta, C[i]\vartheta, \langle\rangle, 1) \mid \vartheta = \Theta(F)[i], 1 \leq i \leq |\Theta(F)| \right\}$$

Thus, any frame in F_s covers exactly one of the cases previously represented by the substitutions in $\Theta(F)$ (and its trajectory is variable-free up to variables in logical content expressions). To build an EN incrementally from a repository $\mathcal{F}$ that consists of singular frames only, we proceed as follows.

1. Add a root node v_0 with label "▷" to the new network EN. Let $i = 1$.
2. For each $F \in \mathcal{F}$:
   (a) If $T(F)$ does not end with "?", set $T(F) \leftarrow \triangleright T(F)\perp$, else $T(F) \leftarrow \triangleright T(F)$.
   (b) Set $c = \bigwedge_j c_j$ where $C(F) = \langle \{c_1, \ldots, c_m\} \rangle$.
   (c) Search EN for the longest path p whose node labels match a prefix of $T(F)$. Let v be the last node of p (potentially the root node of EN).
   (d) If $|p| \geq |T(F)| - 1$ (i.e. p matches the trajectory at least up to the last symbol), then:
       – Let c' the condition list of the last edge of p.
       – If p ends in a "?" label, erase its last node and edge.
   (e) Construct a new path p' consisting of nodes for the postfix of $T(F)$ that does not appear on p. Append p' to v. Let v' the first node of p', and e' the edge connecting v with v'.
   (f) Set $cond(f) = c \vee c'$ where f is the *last* edge on the new path p'.
   (g) Update $Expect(e') \leftarrow ((i-1)Expect(e') + 1)/i$ and $Expect(e) \leftarrow ((i-1)Expect(e) + 1)/i$ for other outgoing edges $out(v)$ of v.
   (h) Set $Expect(e) = 1$ for all other new edges on p'.
   (i) Increment i.

The idea behind this conversion is to construct a single path for each distinct frame, where shared prefixes have to be merged. Each singular frame covers a single case that has occurred exactly once, and whose trajectory contains no variables (for which reason it has no substitution). Two cases can occur: either the frame ends in "?" or not. We prepend a ▷ to the trajectory, and append a ⊥ symbol if "?" is not the last symbol (step 2a). Then, we look for the longest prefix of $T(F)$ that is already in the network (step 2c) and append new nodes and edges for the remaining postfix. If (case 2d) the trajectory is already contained but possibly with previous "don't know" ending, we delete the last edge and node (step 2d) and memorise its condition c', so that we can add it in a disjunctive fashion to c in step 2f. Thus, if F itself has "don't know" semantics, two "?" nodes become one, and if it ends with ⊥, the previous "don't know" semantics are not valid anymore. Also, in step 2f the new condition is "moved" to the very last edge of the new path. Expectability update (step 2g) is a matter of straightforward counting.

Thus, we obtain a very simple EN without normative edges and substitution lists, where all conditions (which summarise the frames with identical trajectories) only occur at the very last edge of any path (leading to ⊥ or "?").[7]

Of course, it is not possible to prove that a CS can be constructed using this EN whose continuation estimates will be identical to the agent state of *any* m²InFFrA agent, especially because agents might apply arbitrary similarity measures σ. This is because there is no equivalent notion for this measure in CS (equation 7 is used instead to estimate the probability of new cases). However, if a very simple σ is used, which assigns similarity 1 to identical message patterns and 0 to all other comparisons, the construction of an equivalent CS is straightforward. The CS would simply generate a new singular frame for any encounter, and call the procedure sketched above after each

---

[7] For EN semantics, the edge on which conditions occur on a path do not matter, but, of course, this EN would be very inefficient for computing continuation probabilities because all paths have to be followed to the end before their logical validity can be checked.

newly observed message. Whenever the m²InFFrA agent starts a new encounter, this would be considered a non-continuation in the CS sense. This CS would compute the same probabilities as the original agent if the conditions in frames fulfil the conditions 3 and 4.

Converting Expectation Networks to Frames. In an attempt to convert ENs to frames, we might proceed in a similar manner by trying to generate a frame for every distinct path. This would imply

- substituting sender/receiver variables by new variables so that a turn-taking, two-party trajectory is obtained; this involves adding extra conditions that state which agent may hold which of these two roles in which step;
- joining all edge conditions on the path to obtain frame condition lists; however, conditions in ENs need only hold after the edge on which they appear, so a notion of time has to be introduced;
- generating a list with all possible substitutions occurring on the path to be used as a frame substitution list.

For lack of space, we cannot introduce all of these steps formally. Let us look at an example of a frame generated from path **P6** in Figure 1 called F_6 shown in table 2: Variables A and B have been replaced by I(nitiator) and R(esponder),

$$F_6 = \Big\langle \big\langle \xrightarrow{100} \text{request}(I, R, X) \xrightarrow{50} \text{propose}(R, I, Y) \xrightarrow{25} \text{accept–proposal}(I, R, Y) \big\rangle,$$

$$\langle \{ current(E), message(M, E, 1) \Rightarrow price > 0 \},$$

$$\langle \{ current(E), message(M, E, 1) \Rightarrow price > 0 \},$$

$$\langle \langle [I/A], [R/B], [X/\text{deliver\_goods}], [Y/\text{pay\_price}], [A/\text{agent\_1}], [B/\text{agent\_2}] \rangle,$$

$$\langle [I/A], [R/B], [X/\text{deliver\_goods}], [Y/\text{pay\_price}], [A/\text{agent\_1}], [B/\text{agent\_3}] \rangle \rangle \Big\rangle$$

Table 2. A frame for path **P6**.

and the reverse substitutions have been pre-pended to the substitutions in Θ. Although this is not necessary in this frame, frames for paths **P2** or **P3** would require introduction of these new variables, as they involve messages subsequently sent by the same agent (**P2**) or more than two parties (**P3**). Also, by adding the statements $current(E)$ and $message(M, E, 1)$ as preconditions to $price > 0$, where $current(E)$ means that E is the current encounter, $price > 0$ need only hold after the first message, as in the EN. This "contextualisation" of conditions has to be performed for each original edge condition. Thirdly, we need to generate all feasible substitution list combinations along all edges, as is shown by the substitution lists in F_6 which contain both cases $[A/\text{agent\_1}], [B/\text{agent\_2}]$ and $[A/\text{agent\_1}], [B/\text{agent\_3}]$. However, a problem appears here, which is that we cannot discriminate whether $[A/\text{agent\_1}], [B/\text{agent\_3}]$ is an actual case of **P6**: looking at **P2**, we can see that $[C/\text{agent\_3}]$ contradicts $[B/\text{agent\_3}]$, so it seems logical that $[A/\text{agent\_1}], [B/\text{agent\_3}]$ yields **P6**. But which conclusion of the encounter does $[A/\text{agent\_1}], [B/\text{agent\_2}]$ belong to? We simply cannot tell.

There are several further reasons for which ENs cannot be converted into $m^2\text{InFFrA}$ frames by a generic procedure that will ensure equivalence of semantics:

1. Normative links may link non-subsequent messages statistically with each other. Such links exceed the expressiveness of frame trajectories, and although there may be ways to treat certain normative links by meta-rules in the agent's knowledge base, there is no generic procedure of generating frames with these conditions, because the effects of normative links are *non-local* to frames.

2. Cognitive links may link messages that do not represent continuations occurring *within* encounters. These cannot be included in frame trajectories, because trajectories end whenever encounters end.

3. Even if we know the total number of non-continuations n, no frame counters can be reconstructed for edges with different conditions. For example, in Figure 1, the distribution of outgoing edges of $\text{request}(A, B, X)$ between cases $price = 0$ and $price > 0$ is not available, so that some hypothetical (say 50/50) distribution between would have to be made up.

4. The computation of continuation probabilities in ENs proceeds by "identification with previous cases and exclusion of cases on different paths" as reflected by condition 7. For example, after $\text{request}(\text{agent\_3}, \text{agent\_2}, X)$, the possibility of $\text{propose}(\text{agent\_3}, \text{agent\_2}, X)$ (continuation with **P3–P7**) is ruled out by $[A/\text{agent\_3}], [B/\text{agent\_2}]$ appearing on **P8**. There is no way a similarity measure σ can be conceived that can reflect this solely by comparing $[A/\text{agent\_3}], [B/\text{agent\_2}]$ to the previous cases $[A/\text{agent\_1}], [B/\text{agent\_2}]$ and $[A/\text{agent\_1}], [B/\text{agent\_3}]$ without any non-local information.

All this nicely illustrates what we would expect of a sociological comparison between systems theory and interactionism, namely that the general theory of communication systems obviously subsumes interactionist approaches, since interaction systems are specific kinds of communication systems tied to a number of particular assumptions. These are: (i) co-presence and spatial/temporal proximity of context-generating communication, (ii) ego/alter distinctions, (iii) locality of processing of social knowledge ("blindness" to expectations relevant in other contexts during involvement in a particular encounter), (iv) expectation formation by analogy (rather than possibility) and (v) simplicity in the representation of expectations (to ensure efficient processing with bounded cognitive resources).

The fact that these elements have been made concrete and that distinctions between several socio-theoretical approaches have been mapped to formal computational models constitutes a major advance in Socionics as it not only furthers the understanding of the underlying theories, but is also instructive in the identification of how to apply CS and frame-based agents in different applications. Some of these potential applications will be discussed in the following section.

5   Discussion: Applications and Extensions

The modelling of social structures on the basis of expectation networks and communication systems allows for novel approaches to a variety of DAI themes. We review (i) identification of ontologies for inter-agent communication and—closely related—the finding of verifiable and flexible semantics for agent communication languages; (ii) *mirror holons* as a new model for holonic theories of agency and software engineering methods based on expectation-oriented modelling and analysis of multiagent systems.

5.1   Social Ontologies

In DAI, an ontology is a set of definitions as a means to provide a common ground in the conceptual description of a domain for communication purposes. Ontologies are usually represented as graphical hierarchies or networks of concepts, topics or classes, and either top-down imposed on the agents or generated in a bottom-up fashion by means of ontology negotiation. In a similar way, expectation networks are descriptions of the social world in which the agents exist. But ENs do not only describe social (i.e. communication) structures, but indirectly also the communication-external environment the message content informs about. Thus, communication systems can be used, in principle, for an incremental collection of ontological descriptions from different autonomous sources, resulting in stochastically weighted, possibly conflicting, competitive and revisable propositions about environmental objects. The crucial difference to traditional mechanisms is that such a *social ontology* (realized e.g. as *Open Ontologies* [19,20,21] and *Open Knowledge Bases* [19]) represents dynamic expectations about how a certain domain object will be described as *emergent*, not necessarily consented knowledge in future communication, without making a priory assumptions about the existence of a "commonly agreed truth", or the reliability and trustability of the knowledge sources. This opposes the "imposed ontologies" view somewhat, where the ontology provides a commonly agreed grounding for communication only, and makes this approach appear particularly suitable for open multiagent or P2P systems with a highly dynamic environment, where homogenous perception among agents cannot be assumed. Also, it is appropriate whenever descriptions are influenced by individual preferences and goals such that a consensus cannot be achieved (think, e.g., about "politically" biased resource descriptions in the context of the Semantic Web [14]). In the following, we will sketch two approaches for extracting social ontologies from expectation networks.

Extraction of Speech Act Types. The current version of FIPA-ACL [4] provides an extensible set of speech-act performative types with semantics defined in a mentalistic fashion. In our approach, we can imagine some system component (e.g., a so-called multiagent system *mirror* [17,8]) that provides the agents with a set of performatives *without* any predefined semantics and wait for the semantics of such "blank" performatives to emerge. To become predictable, it is rational for an agent to stick to the meaning (i.e., the consequences) of performatives, at least to a certain extent. This meaning has been previously (more or less arbitrarily) "suggested" for a certain performative by some agent performing demonstrative actions after uttering it.

Of course, a single agent is not able to define a precise and stable public meaning for these performatives, but at least the intentional attitude associated with the respective performative needs to become common ground to facilitate non-nonsensical, non-entropic communication [23]. A particular performative usually appears at multiple nodes within the EN, with different consequences at each position, depending on context (especially on the preceding path), message content and involved sender and receiver. To build up an ontology consisting of performative types, we have to continually identify and combine the occurrences of a certain performative within the current EN to obtain a general meaning for this performative (i.e. a "type" meaning). Afterwards, we can communicate this meaning to all agents using some technical facility within the multiagent system, like a middle agent, a MAS mirror or an "ACL semantics server". Of course, such a facility cannot impose meaning in a normative way as the agents are still free to use or ignore public meaning as they like, but it can help to spread language data like a dictionary or a grammar does for natural languages. The criteria for the identification and extraction of performative meaning from ENs are basically the same as the criteria we proposed in section 3 for the generalisation over message sequences.

Extraction of Domain Descriptions. While a set of emergent speech act types constitutes a social ontology for communication events, classical ontologies provide a description of an application domain. To obtain a social version of this sort of ontology from an EN, two different approaches appear to be reasonable: (1) Inclusion of environment events within the EN and (2) probabilistic weighting of assertions.

The former approach treats "physical" events basically as utterances. Similar to the communicative reflection of agent actions by means of do, a special performative happen(*event*) would allow EN nodes that reflect events occurring in the environment. These events will be put in the EN either by a special CS which is able to perceive the agents' common environment, or by the agents themselves as a communicative reflection of their own perceptions. A subset of *event* is assumed to denote events with consensual semantics (think of physical laws), i.e., the agents are not free to perform any course of action after such an event has occurred, whereas the remainder of *event* consists of event tags with open semantics that has to be derived empirically from communications observation just as for "normal" utterances. If such an event appears the first time, the CS does not know its meaning in terms of its consequences. Its meaning has thus to be derived *a posteriori* from the communicational reflection of how the agents react to its occurrence. In contrast, approach (2), which we proposed for the agent-based competitive rating of web resources [14], exploits the propositional attitude of utterances. The idea is to interpret certain terms within *LogicalExpr* as domain descriptions and to weight these descriptions according to the amount of consent/dissent (using predefined performatives like *Assert* and *Deny*). The weighted propositions are collected within a knowledge base (e.g., KB) and are communicated to the agents in the same way as the emergent speech act types before. Unlike approach (1), ontologies are constructed "by description" not "by doing" in this way. The advantage of approach (1) lies in its seamless integration of "physical" events into the EN, whereas (2) is probably more easy to apply in practice.

5.2   Mirror Holons: Multi-stage Observation and Reflection

In [1,8], we have introduced the *social system mirror* architecture for open MAS. The main component of this architecture is a so-called social system mirror (or "mirror" for short), a middle agent which continually observes communications, empirically derives emergent expectation structures (represented as an expectation network, which might also contain normative structures) from these observations, and "reflects" these structures back to the agents. Its goals are to influence agent behaviour by means of system-wide propagation of social structures and norms to achieve quicker structure evolution and higher coherence of social structures without restricting agent autonomy, and the provision of a representation of a dynamic communication system for the MAS designer. While a mirror only models a single communication system, and, except for the propagation of expectations, is a purely passive observer, the successor architecture *HoloMAS* [17] is able to model multiple communication systems at the same time through multiple *mirror holons* in order to model large, heterogenous systems. In addition, a mirror holon can take action itself by means of the execution of social programs which are generated from emergent expectation structures. "Ordinary agents" (and other mirror holons) can optionally be involved in this execution process as *effectors*, which realise holon commands within their physical or virtual application domain (unless they deny the respective command). In any case they can influence the social programs within a mirror holon through the irritation of expectation structures by means of communication. A mirror holon thus represents and (at least to some extent) replaces the functionality of the ordinary agents that contribute to the emergence of the respective expectation structures, but it does not disregard the autonomy of his adjoint actors. Another difference between mirror holons and traditional agent holons [26] is that a mirror holon does not represent or contain groups of agents, but instead a certain functionality which is identified in form of regularities in the observed communications. This functionality is extracted and continually adopted from dynamic expectation structures regarding criteria like consistency, coherence and stability, corresponding to the criteria sociological systems theory ascribes to social programs [9]. Mirror holons pave the way for applications in which agent autonomy should not (or cannot) be restricted on the one hand, while reliable, time-critical system behaviour is desired. They can also be used as representants for entire communication systems (e.g., virtual organisations) that behave smoothly towards third parties whenever the communication system itself lacks coherence due to, for example, inner conflicts.

Expectation-Oriented Software Development. It has been long recognised that due to new requirements arising from the complex and distributed nature of modern software systems the modularity and flexibility provided by object orientation is often inadequate and that there is a need for encapsulation of robust functionality at the level of software components. Agent-oriented approaches are expected to offer interesting prospectives in this respect, because they introduce interaction and autonomy as the primary abstractions the developer deals with.

However, although interaction among autonomous agents offers great flexibility, it also brings with it contingencies in behaviour. In the most general case, neither peer agents nor designer can "read the mind" of an autonomous agent, let alone change it.

While the usual strategy to cope with this problem is to restrict oneself to closed systems, this means loosing the power of autonomous decentralised control in favour of a top-down imposition of social regulation to ensure predictable behaviour. The EXPAND method (*Expectation-oriented Analysis and Design*) [1] follows a different approach. EXPAND is based on adaptive and normative expectations as a primary modelling abstraction which both system designer and agents use to manage the social level of their activities. This novel abstraction level is made available to them through a special version of the social system mirror very similar to a CASE tool. For the designer, this mirror acts as an interface he uses to propagate his desired expectations regarding agent interaction to the agents and as a means for monitoring runtime agent activity and deviance from expected behaviour. For agents, this mirror represents a valuable "system resource" they can use to reduce contingency about each other's behaviour. EXPAND also describes an evolutionary process for MAS development which consists of multiples cycles: the modelling of the system level, the derivation of appropriate expectation structures, the monitoring of expectation structure evolution and the refinement of expectation structures given the observations made in the system. For a lack of space, we have to refer the interested reader to [1] for details.

In addition, *Expectation-oriented Modelling* (EOM) [12] has been introduced as a more general approach in comparison to EXPAND, but for lack of space, we have to ask the reader to refer to [12] for details.

6   Conclusion

This paper introduced communication systems as a unified model for socially intelligent systems based on recording and transforming communicative expectations. We presented formalisms for describing expectations in terms of expectation networks, the formal semantics of these networks, and a general framework for transforming them with incoming observation. Then, we exemplified the generic character of CS by analysing its relationship to micro-level social reasoning architecture using the InFFrA architecture as an example. Finally, a number of interesting applications of CS were discussed, some of which have already been addressed by our past research, while others are currently being worked on.

While a lot of work still lies ahead, we strongly believe that, by virtue of their general character, CS have the potential of becoming a unified model for speaking about methods and applications relevant to Socionics. Also, we hope that they can contribute to bringing key insights of socionic research to the attention of the mainstream DAI audience, as they put emphasis on certain aspects of MAS that are often neglected in non-socionic approaches.

References

1. W. Brauer, M. Nickles, M. Rovatsos, G. Weiß, and K. F. Lorentzen. Expectation-Oriented Analysis and Design. In *Procs. AOSE-2001*, LNAI 2222, Springer-Verlag, Berlin, 2001.
2. P. R. Cohen and H. J. Levesque. Performatives in a Rationally Based Speech Act Theory. In *Procs. 28th Annual Meeting of the ACL*, 1990.

3. P. R. Cohen and H. J. Levesque. Communicative actions for artificial agents. In *Procs. ICMAS-95*, 1995.

4. FIPA, Foundation for Intelligent Agents, http://www.fipa.org.

5. E. Goffman. *Frame Analysis: An Essay on the Organisation of Experience*. Harper and Row, New York, NY, 1974.

6. F. Guerin and J. Pitt. Denotational Semantics for Agent Communication Languages. In *Procs. Agents'01*, ACM Press, 2001.

7. Y. Labrou and T. Finin. Semantics and conversations for an agent communication language. In *Procs. IJCAI-97*, 1997.

8. K. F. Lorentzen and M. Nickles. Ordnung aus Chaos – Prolegomena zu einer Luhmann'schen Modellierung deentropisierender Strukturbildung in Multiagentensystemen. In T. Kron, editor, *Luhmann modelliert. Ansätze zur Simulation von Kommunikationssystemen*. Leske & Budrich, 2001.

9. N. Luhmann. *Social Systems*. Stanford University Press, Palo Alto, CA, 1995.

10. T. Malsch. Naming the Unnamable: Socionics or the Sociological Turn of/to Distributed Artificial Intelligence. *Autonomous Agents and Multi-Agent Systems*, 4(3):155–186, 2001.

11. G. H. Mead. *Mind, Self, and Society*. University of Chicago Press, Chicago, IL, 1934.

12. M. Nickles, M. Rovatsos, G. Weiß. Expectation-Oriented Modeling. In International Journal "Engineering Applications of Artificial Intelligence" (EAAI), Elsevier, 2005.

13. M. Nickles, M. Rovatsos, M. Schmitt, W. Brauer, F. Fischer, T. Malsch, K. Paetow, G. Weiss. The Empirical Semantics Approach to Communication Structure Learning and Usage: Individuals- vs. System-Views. In Nigel Gilbert (Ed.), Journal of Artificial Societies and Social Simulation (JASSS), Issue on Socionics, 2005.

14. M. Nickles. Multiagent Systems for the Social Competition Among Website Ratings. In *Procs. ACM SIGIR Workshop on Recommender Systems*, 2001.

15. M. Nickles and G. Weiss. Empirical Semantics of Agent Communication in Open Systems. In *Proceedings of the Second International Workshop on Challenges in Open Agent Environments at AAMAS-2003*, 2003.

16. M. Nickles, M. Rovatsos, W. Brauer, G. Weiss. Towards a Unified Model of Sociality in Multiagent Systems. Proceedings of the Fourth ACIS International Conference on Software Engineering, Artificial Intelligence, Networking, and Parallel/Distributed Computing (SNPD'03), 2003.

17. M. Nickles and G. Weiss. Multiagent Systems without Agents - Mirror-Holons for the Compilation and Enactment of Communication Structures. In this volume.

18. M. Nickles, M. Rovatsos, and G. Weiss. Empirical-Rational Semantics of Agent Communication. In *Procs. of the Third International Joint Conference on Autonomous Agents and Multiagent Systems (AAMAS-04)*, New York City, NY, 2004.

19. M. Nickles and T. Froehner. Social Reification for the Semantic Web. Research Report FKI-24x-04, AI/Cognition Group, Department of Informatics, Technical University Munich, 2004. To appear.

20. T. Froehner, M. Nickles, and G. Weiß. Towards Modeling the Social Layer of Emergent Knowledge Using Open Ontologies. In *Procs. of The ECAI 2004 Workshop on Agent-Mediated Knowledge Management (AMKM-04)*, Valencia, Spain, 2004.

21. T. Froehner, M. Nickles, and G. Weiß. Open Ontologies – The Need for Modeling Heterogeneous Knowledge. In *Procs. of The 2004 International Conference on Information and Knowledge Engineering (IKE 2004)*, 2004.

22. J. Pitt and A. Mamdani. A protocol-based semantics for an agent communication language. In *Procs. IJCAI-99*, 1999.

23. M. Rovatsos, M. Nickles, and G. Weiß. Interaction is Meaning: A New Model for Communication in Open Systems. In *Procs. AAMAS'03*, Melbourne, Australia, to appear, 2003.

24. M. Rovatsos and K. Paetow. On the Organisation of Social Experience: Scaling up Social Cognition. In this volume.

25. M. Rovatsos, G. Weiß, and M. Wolf. An Approach to the Analysis and Design of Multiagent Systems based on Interaction Frames. In *Procs. AAMAS'02*, Bologna, Italy, 2002.

26. M. Schillo and D. Spresny. Organization: The Central Concept of Qualitative and Quantitative Scalability. In this volume.

27. M. P. Singh. A semantics for speech acts. *Annals of Mathematics and Artificial Intelligence*, 8(1–2):47–71, 1993.

28. M. P. Singh. A social semantics for agent communication languages. In *Procs. IJCAI Workshop on Agent Communication Languages*, 2000.

Author Index

Lecture Notes in Artificial Intelligence (LNAI)